A GAME
RANGER
REMEMBERS

A GAME RANGER REMEMBERS

BRUCE BRYDEN

JONATHAN BALL PUBLISHERS
JOHANNESBURG & CAPE TOWN

First published in 2005 in trade paperback by
JONATHAN BALL PUBLISHERS
(A Division of Media24 Pty Ltd)
P O Box 6836
Roggebaai
8012
Reprinted six times in 2006 and 2007

The paperback edition published in 2008 by
Jonathan Ball Publishers
(A Division of Media24 Pty Ltd)

Reprinted once in 2010. 2011, 2013

This limited edition published twice in 2015, 2016 and once in 2017

ISBN 978-1-86842-315-6

Edited by Willem Steenkamp
Typesetting and design by Alinea Studio, Cape Town
Cover photograph by courtesy of South African Tourism
Cover design by Triple M Design & Advertising, Johannesburg
Printed and bound by CTP Printers, Cape Town

CONTENTS

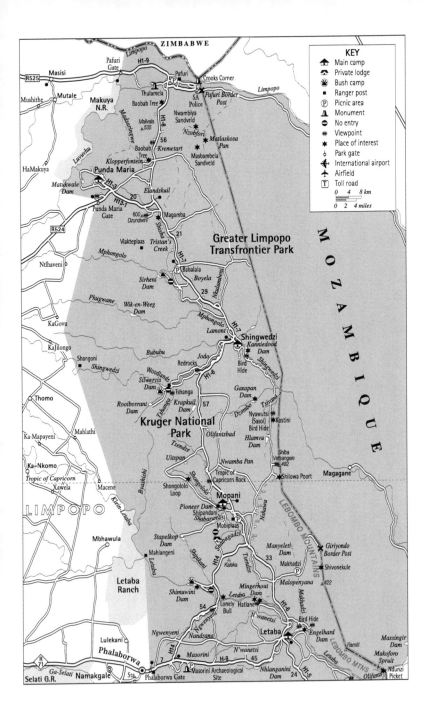

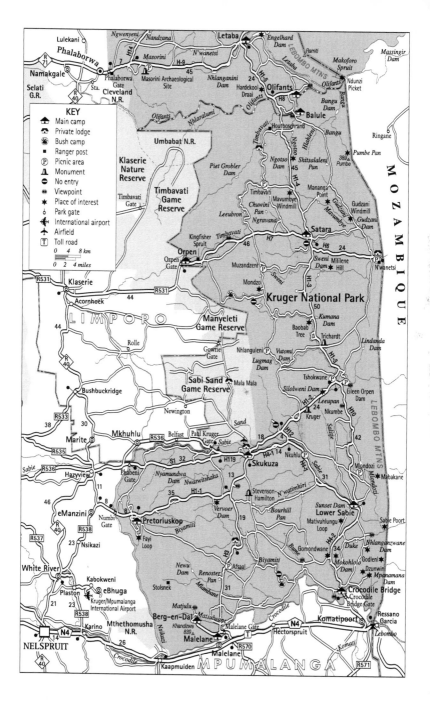

To conservation officers and their wives,
dead or alive: it was great being part of the team.
Thank you.

FOREWORD

I spent 30 of my best years – from 1971 to 2001 – as a nature conservation officer with South African National Parks. Of these, all but three were devoted to the Kruger National Park, that great and justly famous sanctuary for the animals of southern Africa that have been so grievously sinned against by mankind.

The retreat of the game herds and the shrinking of their habitats is a matter beyond pity or regret; in the end, as it is everywhere in the world, it is part of a greater cycle of change that is driven by the struggle for resources (not unmixed, of course, with depredations inspired by sheer greed, and compounded by silly or short-sighted actions), and inevitably the animals have lost, so that they have become prisoners in the land where once they teemed in great numbers almost wherever the eye could see. But game reserves like the Kruger National Park and many others have ensured that although a relatively pristine southern Africa has disappeared, most likely for ever, most of the veld creatures in all their enormous diversity have survived, although there have been a few grievous losses along the way, among them the bloubok, the black-maned Cape lion (although I don't really believe that it was a different species from our common lion) and perhaps the quagga. The quagga might still be dragged back from oblivion by a re-breeding programme that is currently in progress, but generally speaking, the species that have gone are gone forever.

That is primarily why the game reserves exist. It is not the only reason – they are invaluable to scientific research, for example, and can make significant contributions towards social upliftment by way of direct employment, or indirect employment as a result of tourism – but at the end of the day they are first and foremost safe havens for the 'first people' of the bushveld, and open-air classrooms where human beings can renew the ancient interaction between man and animal that has progressively disappeared in an increasingly overpopulated and technologically advanced world. That is why I said that I had 'devoted' almost my entire career to the Kruger National Park. Dedicated game rangers do not, frankly, gain any noteworthy material reward from their arduous, usually under-funded and frequently dangerous work, but when the time comes for them to hang up their well-worn boots they have the satisfaction of knowing that although they might not be remembered by name to future generations, those generations will reap the benefit of their efforts.

When I became Chief Ranger in 1983 the Kruger National Park was on the threshold of an immensely significant period in its history. It was then almost a century old, and it had developed to a state that would have surprised the pioneers like James Stevenson-Hamilton and Harry Wolhuter, who had nursed it into life and guided it through its perilous infancy to the beginning of more enlightened times. When the Park was proclaimed by President Paul Kruger, attitudes toward wild animals were still based on a very literal interpretation of the biblical injunction that God had given Man dominion over the birds of the air and the fishes of the sea. By the time the pioneers bowed out the world was coming to realise that such dominion meant not the conferral of a licence to plunder but the assumption of a great and noble responsibility. Now, at the dawn of the 1980s, the Kruger National Park was about to go through another great – if vastly different – transition period, a time of immense social and political change, protracted civil warfare, widespread population movement and great want. We were lucky enough to be the midwives during that period – I say 'we' because the hands of many men and women contributed to the task. They came from a variety of backgrounds, walks of life and cultures. Some were black, some were white, and between them they worshipped a variety of different deities and spoke half a dozen different languages. A few went bad in the process and betrayed their trust. Most of them did not, and when they retired they handed their successors a going and even flourishing concern.

In those 27 years in the Kruger National Park I served at every level, starting as a humble but rather grandiosely titled 'Post-Graduate Assistant Biologist' and working my way up to Ranger, Chief Ranger and finally to Senior Manager: Conservation Support Services. Every step up the ladder exposed me to new experiences and new insights, all gained the hard way, so that my personal conservation ethic was in a constant state of development and maturation as I did things under my own steam and benefited from the influence and mentoring of various individuals I encountered or worked with. Formal education is a vital part of the modern game ranger's professional repertoire, but book-knowledge is useless without a sound leavening of experience – both personal and the kind that can be gained only by listening to those wiser than yourself.

I wrote this book partly at the urging of various friends and colleagues. I might not have undertaken the task except that so many of my contemporaries and near-contemporaries had promised to do the same but had never actually got around to the task. To me it has always seemed such a terrible waste that those life experiences – an enormously varied and often unique body of knowledge – should be allowed simply to evaporate instead of being shared with people not fortunate enough to have acquired them. So I decided to spend a year writing down some of my memories.

Readers who expect a solemn dissertation on conservation in southern Africa and my scientific contribution to it will be disappointed, as will those who approach the whole subject of game conservation in more or less the same spirit as a devout church-goer attending early-morning mass. There are enough books like that around. What I have ended up with is a collection of stories, spiced with a few philosophical reflections (but only a few, I promise), that will give my readers a taste of the bushveld conservationist's lifestyle, as it is lived at the ground level by that elite band of men and women who actually guard our game at the cost of much sweat and, not infrequently, quite a bit of blood. If it is a bit too informal and irreverent for some refined tastes, I regret it, but not very much.

It is a mixed bag because my experiences were so many and

varied. Most of them are concerned with the things I encountered while doing research on lions or performing my duties as a game ranger, but there is also much else: adventures and misadventures (a good number of the latter!), stories devoted to most of the dangerous animals and my experiences with them – humorous, sad or frightening – and a good sprinkling of others on some related subjects. I hope that you, the reader, will enjoy them as I did (although, in all honesty, only in retrospect in some cases).

Every so often you will read about the effect of my mentors, both black and white, on my personal and professional development as I moved up through the ranks, and the deep respect that developed between us. Here I think particularly of the 'mapoisas', the field rangers. Few of them had had any formal schooling at all, in fact most were completely illiterate, but they had grown up in the bush and they could 'read' it as easily as a university graduate absorbs the essence of a complicated thesis. These men were my teachers – and at times my guardian angels as well.

It might be that what I have written above sounds a bit solemn and pompous, as if game rangers are dedicated missionaries with space for little else in their lives. Well, of course they are dedicated, or they would not put up with the conditions of their service, and of course they are missionaries when it comes to conservation. But they also enjoy life whenever they can, like all other South Africans, and sometimes in unique ways. In my opinion there are only two great certainties in a game ranger's career. The first is that you will never be well off. The second – and best by far – is that you will do things that most other people only get to dream about. Consider the following, an ever-shining moment in my memory, all the sweeter for having a bitter end.

Well into my career the KwaZulu-Natal department of conservation asked us to help out with the most welcome of all problems – one that had arisen as a result of a successful project. The young elephants nurtured by the KZN elephant conservation programme were growing up and the population was expanding, so they asked if we could teach some of their staff the right way of culling them. Of course the request was approved, and in due course the KZN rangers arrived at Letaba, where I was to put them through the training drills. We all stayed in the rest camp, which to my mind has the finest camping ground in the world. That is a large statement, but I stand by it. There are great ablution blocks and lovely trees, and a multitude of animals, large and small, on your very doorstep. There are always bushbuck right in the camp and elephants just outside it, and every night you can exchange words with the hyaenas begging next to the fence. It is a rare occasion when you aren't woken in the morning by the grumpy 'one pound, two shilling' call of a ground hornbill. And that's just the start of it, because it just keeps getting better as the day progresses. And of course you are bound to hear the haunting call of a fish eagle, without which no camp in Africa would be complete.

It was not all work and no play. The KZN men had been warned to bring their fishing rods, and one day, after a rather abortive start to the elephant culling, I called a break and took them to the Olifants trail camp. Just below the camp, the Olifants River tumbles through a series of rhyolite gorges and into a series of potholes. The nutrient and oxygen-rich water in the potholes, together with the barrier created by the falls, provide a unique habitat for just about every fish and aquatic predator found in the Olifants River. The potholes were the best spot for bream and tiger fish that I had ever encountered, and for extra excitement there were crocodiles of monstrous size, often up to five metres long or more. Three or four kilometres downstream, where the river is slowed by a series of rocky shelves before it joins the Letaba to flow into Mozambique, the monsters were slightly less monstrous, hardly ever reaching more than a comparatively puny three or four metres, but there were lots of them, so that at one stage this last stretch of South African water was home to the highest concentration of crocodiles found anywhere in Africa.

In any case, because it was Thursday the trails camp was vacant that night. We got our heads down, and next morning early we were on the rocks with our rods. The tigers we hooked did their bit in grand fashion, and in the best tradition of happy endings lived to tell the tale, because of course we put them straight back into the river again. About 10 o'clock we left for Letaba again to carry on with the culling. That task completed, we headed back to the rest camp for our last night together. We sat around the fire and told good stories while nibbling on prime rump steak, dressed in a cream and garlic sauce and sliced up on a chopping-block, all of it washed down with a cold beer or three. It was a sublime moment, and Graham Wiltshire, then warden of Ndumu, summed it up when he said: 'Who can beat this for lifestyle? Catch tiger fish in the morning, shoot elephants in the afternoon and end up with beer and steaks.' None of us knew it, but Graham had only a short time left on earth; a few weeks later he came to a tragic end in an aircraft accident. I do not believe, however, that any of us who were there that night will ever forget his words. He had said all that needed saying.

That memory has helped to shape this book. So relax, imagine you're sitting somewhere in the Kruger National Park a little after nightfall, and enjoy the stories. Everybody knows that the best ones are told around a campfire, when your world is bounded by the flickering edges of the fire's light and you sit on a rickety folding chair, wriggling toes that are sore from a day's walking, your well-worn jersey keeping the cold away from your sweated-out body, a can of ice-cold beer sending frissons down your face as you roll it against your forehead. That's when the good tales come creeping out, while the night creatures sing their unforgettable accompaniment from somewhere out in the great darkness that falls so swiftly over Africa when each day's sun has set.

1
HOW IT ALL BEGAN

When I commenced sifting through my many memories in preparation for writing this book, I actually had to stop and ask myself when and where my love for and interest in nature started. Even now I am not sure I really know, but what I do know is that genetics is a scary thing. To a great degree you are what you make of yourself, but what you do make of yourself also depends on the genetic ingredients at hand. You might be able to change the recipe, but you can't make biltong if you don't have meat. And then, of course, there is the influence that other people have on your development.

One personal factor that made a very early appearance, it seems, was a phobia about roofs and walls around me. Even as a toddler I preferred to use the orchard to relieve myself, rather than the more orthodox facility; and I have to confess that this urge is as strong now as it was then. Since my family was living in Johannesburg when I was born in 1948, this might eventually have resulted in a problem, but fortunately my father made a packet on the stock market just two years later and decided to try his hand at farming, so we moved to Erfenis, one of the family farms near Edenville in the Free State. All of a sudden an acre of toilet turned into 3 000 morgen of stamping grounds, an infinite amount of space to move around in and explore.

The best thing about the farm was that I had a great-grandfather who lived about four kilometres away and seemed to enjoy my company. The result of all this was that most mornings I would gallop through my compulsory plateful of oats, then propel my three-year-old body across the veld to his house, where I would eat a second breakfast consisting of thick slices of home-made bread, spread with real farm butter and garnished with springbok biltong, all served in an enamel dish. The result of this double dose of morning nourishment was that I had more than enough energy to play with all the black boys on the farm; it was a fruitful association because I learnt many facts about farm life from them.

But my great-grandfather, whom we called Oupa Mê because of his flocks of sheep, had the single most important effect in shaping my interests. He taught me to ride a horse, shoot accurately with a rifle and appreciate the natural things around me, which last probably laid the foundation of my conservator's soul. But he taught me a great deal more as well. I never realised it, but during our time together he put me through a years-long learning process, each lesson of which was carefully timed to aid in my maturing process. I could not have had a better childhood mentor. Oupa Mê was a remarkable man who had led an interesting life, starting with the time when, as a young commando soldier in the Anglo-Boer War, he had been shot through the neck, chained to a plough and left to die. Naturally, being Oupa Mê, he not only escaped death but did so in a remarkable way, when a young farm-girl found him in extremis, freed him and nursed him back to health. If this incident had been a work of fiction they would have fallen in love, married and lived happily ever after. Since it was real life, they did not, but they maintained discreet contact until he died, much to my great-grandmother's displeasure, although the 'relationship' was innocent enough, in all conscience – to the best of my knowledge it amounted to no more than an exchange of letters on their birthdays. This led directly to my first responsible job. Every year, starting a week before Oupa's birthday on 8 July, I was responsible for sorting out the post before the old lady could get to it, and intercepting the one from his nurse of so long ago. I shouldered this responsibility before I had learnt to read, and acquitted myself of my important task by showing Oupa each letter in the post-bag on the way home from town. Later, when I had learnt my letters, it was naturally much easier, but by then the letter interception was only one of my manly duties.

Some people might regard it as a little reckless to set a boy on to monitoring the mail before he was able even to read the addresses on the envelopes, but Oupa's mentoring started very early in my life. One of the first things I remember being taught was the difference between a Cape sparrow and a house sparrow; he hated house sparrows, which were introduced from England, and taught me to hate them too. I suspect that this was not unconnected with his having been wounded and left to die by those other interlopers from England, although he claimed it stemmed from the fact that the house sparrow was an exotic and would destroy one of our own bird species. Whatever his full motivation, they were wise words in an era in which hardly anybody regarded exotic species as a threat. Such were Oupa's feelings towards the invaders that he paid me a bounty of one penny per bird to kill as many of them as I could. Ultimately that spelt the end for the house sparrow species on the family farms. As far as hunting other birds was concerned, Oupa's policy was simple and specific: the only ones I was allowed to shoot were species that either competed with the poultry for their food or competed with us by eating our fruit. There was no question of shooting something simply for the sake of shooting it.

Another thing I learned on the farm besides marksmanship and practical conservation was horsemanship, and my training started early on, at the time when I was barely able to steer a tricycle. I started off riding bareback, Oupa's philosophy being that if you could ride bareback there was no horse that you couldn't ride saddled. Eventually I graduated to a saddle, but I was never allowed to wear shoes when riding. This stemmed from another of Oupa's maxims: toes did not get hooked in stirrups, so you would never get dragged if you came off. It was a valid point because even the best horseman is likely to lose his seat at one time or another, and being dragged by a frenzied horse because your boot is jammed in a stirrup is tantamount to a death sentence. Many years later one of the last true cowboys and rodeo riders in the USA, John Gardner, told me that an old-time cowboy didn't carry a handgun to defend himself against bandits, but to shoot his horse if he ended up being dragged.

My horse was a yellow mare named Mary, the last of the line of the old man's war-horses. She was small but gutsy, and I liked to think that she adored me just as much as I adored her. No one else rode her, not even the grooms who looked after her once I went to live with my grandparents in Johannesburg to go to school, but during school holidays we spent a great deal of time together. Strangely enough, I probably walked more than I rode, because Mary was stabled at the old man's house, so before I could climb into the saddle I had to 'beat the feet' for four kilometres to visit Oupa. When I was older Mary was my hunting steed as well as my friend. If Oupa wanted a springbok or a blesbok he would send me out with his .22-calibre Mauser rifle; Mary would carry me into the middle of the herd, and I would pick my animal and kill it with a brain shot. She was so well trained that when I aimed the Mauser she stopped breathing till I had fired; I do believe that if I had ever lifted the Mauser and then refrained from firing she would have suffocated rather than breathe before the shot cracked out. Wonderful hunting horse though she was, though, Mary couldn't be persuaded to allow the dead springbok or blesbok to be tied to the back of the saddle. I tried it only once, but she showed such severe signs of stress, rolling her eyes and hyperventilating, that I got rid of the buck as quickly as possible. Instead I would bleed the buck, leave it in the veld and ride home to have someone come out with a vehicle to fetch it.

Observing Oupa's springbok provided me with some of my earliest lessons about the behaviour of game. One of the things I learned was that when springbok are under pressure they tend to 'pronk', bounding into the air up to six times in succession – yet, although it was nothing for a pronk to take the buck a couple of feet off the ground, they never used their agility to jump over fences. I have never seen springbok clear fences; they prefer to crawl through under the lowest strand of wire. I also received my introduction to problem animals, a recurring headache in my later professional career, in the shape of two springbok rams that regularly broke out of the game camp and then proceeded to make a nuisance of themselves. The rams were also the unwitting authors of the greatest moment of anguish I had suffered up to then, but which I was to experience again and again in later life.

The school holidays were on and, as usual, I was on the farm when the rams pulled off another escape and Oupa instructed me to chase them back into the game camp or, failing that, to kill them. Happily I climbed into the saddle and Mary and I set off on the latest of our many expeditions. It was not long before we caught up with the miscreants and started chasing them back to the game camp. Then disaster struck – swiftly and unexpectedly, as it usually does. Mary stood in an unseen hole at full gallop and broke her left front leg. I heard the awful sound of the bone snapping and then she was down, pinning my left leg under her.

I checked myself quickly and realised that I had suffered no serious injuries. But I knew there was no hope for Mary. I unslung the little Mauser and shot her in the back of the head as she lay screaming in pain, then dragged myself out from under her and walked back to the house. Oupa met me on the verandah, saw the state I was in and, of course, immediately asked what had happened. Somehow I choked out the story, so devastated that I was almost unable to speak.

In death my beloved little Mary taught me two lasting and very painful lessons that were to stand me in good stead in the future. Firstly, how hard it is to lose an animal friend that you loved dearly. Secondly, how traumatic it can be to put down an animal, even if doing so was an act of mercy.

Dead animals were usually dumped in a gravel groove for the vultures, but horses – and Mary in particular – occupied a very special place in Oupa Mê's heart, and so she was buried where she fell.

A problem animal of a different kind in my younger years was a large and ferocious Afrikaner bull that seemed to have a personal dislike for me. What made him even more sinister in my eyes was that he was yellow instead of red, like all the other Afrikaner cattle I knew about (I didn't know yet that in fact yellow Afrikaners are not uncommon). My daily journeys to Oupa's house frequently turned into impromptu long-distance treks to avoid the attentions of this demon of my early years. If he was in one of the camps on the route between our houses, I would have to make a detour, because if this monster in bovine clothing spotted me, no matter how far away I might be, he would run at me. 'Charge' is perhaps slightly too strong to describe that terrifying approach, but even as a four-year-old I knew it wasn't because he wanted me to rub his forehead. This unpleasant behaviour taught me another veld lesson, though: that animals can instil fear in human beings, and also that it was quite possible to actively hate a particular animal.

The passing of time didn't mellow this chap, and for four years he routinely terrorised me whenever he had the opportunity. I wasn't the only one to be the target of his spleen; he was so aggressive that even some of the adult cattle herders refused to work near him. He got away with this antisocial behaviour for a long time, because he had one great virtue – he fathered a long string of first-class calves. Still, all good things come to an end. Eventually hardly any of the herders were willing to come near him, so that the other cattle in his herd had to be moved along with a vehicle. By this time Oupa had had enough of his trouble-some maker of good calves, and he chose the annual game-culling as the right time to take appropriate steps. There were about 600 springbok and blesbok on the farm, and during my first winter there, I had learned yet another important lesson from Oupa Mê, about carrying capacity and the need to reduce the size of the game population at regular intervals to avoid destruction of the habitat.

The annual culling coincided with the main domestic slaugh-ter of the year and always took place in winter, which meant that I was invariably present because of the mid-year holidays. It was not until just after my eighth birthday, however, that Oupa let me take a full part in the culling operation, under his strict tutelage, of course. The proceedings would open with the slaughtering of a pig and an ox, and after that Oupa Mê and I would shoot up to 60 or 70 blesbok and springbok, all on the same day; some of the animals would be given away and the rest would be turned into a year's supply of biltong and sausage. Oupa was, it seemed, happy with the way I had handled myself during my first tenta-tive essays at culling.

Needless to say Oupa was perfectly aware of my long-stand-ing dispute with the yellow bull – or perhaps I should say the yel-low bull's dispute with me – and so I was delighted when he asked me whether I would like to take on the task of readying my old enemy for the attentions of the ladies' sausage machine. Of course I accepted the offer – pay-back time at last! 'When do we go?' I asked immediately, assuming we would go out in the truck to shoot the bull. But, as always, Oupa Mê saw the task as a way-station on my personal learning curve. 'You go on foot, alone, tomorrow morning,' he said, 'and remember to take a knife to cut his throat after you've shot him.' The Joseph Rogers I usually carried in my pocket obviously would not be up to this challenge, so the old man armed me with a butcher's knife from the kitchen, together with a handful of cartridges. I had been hoping they would be the long, sleek ones for the 7x57 mm Mauser, but they were .22 Long Rifles which he took out of a cardboard Eley box. I still believe that these were the best .22 cartridges ever made, but of course I'm prejudiced because those little red, yellow and black Eley boxes with the running rabbit on them are such a vivid part of my childhood memories.

Next morning early I set off to hunt the yellow bull with my .22 Mauser rifle. As usual he came for me as soon as I hove into sight, but this time I was one up on him. I kept the fence between us and took careful aim from a dead rest on one of the fence-posts while he stood snorting and pawing the ground. Then I fired and he dropped like a stone, and I climbed through the fence and slit his throat. As the blood gushed out, the tragedy of the situation struck me and I cried as only an eight-year-old boy can. I wept until I had no tears left, then pulled myself together and went to collect the farmhands and the truck to bring the yellow bull's massive carcass back to the farmyard. I did not know it then, but I had just passed another examination in the rough-and-ready curriculum Oupa Mê had prepared for me. I realised that next day, though, when we went out to shoot the springbok and blesbok. To my surprise and delight, Oupa Mê handed me what he called his 'Maanlicht' before we set out on the hunt, a Mannlicher-Schoenauer rifle firing the renowned 6.5x5 mm Mauser cartridge. Magic rifle! It was a huge step up from the .22 Mauser, and I felt as if I had been elevated to another plane of existence.

It was Oupa Mê's custom to have the culled animals gutted and then laid out under the trees in descending order of magnitude, those with the least amount of damaged meat being at the top end of the scale; the two best buck, one of each species, went to the minister of the local parish, and the ones further down the line to lesser lights such as the bank manager and the magistrate, and finally to family and friends.

That culling stays in my memory for another reason, albeit one far less dramatic than the other things I experienced. The dramatis personae consisted firstly of the pig that was to be slaughtered and secondly of one Rhagane Mogonedi, friend and soulmate of my maternal grandfather, who was generally known as Oupa Kuku because of his love for fighting cocks. Oupa Kuku and Rhagane Mogonedi were nearer to being brothers than anything else. They had grown up and grown to maturity together, and a mark of their mutual respect and appreciation was to be found in the fact that every evening they sat down over a glass of Chateau brandy for a bit of what would now be called 'private time'. In those days, of course, hard liquor was supposed to be barred to blacks, but Oupa Kuku did not give a damn about such stupidity, particularly when it came to his brother under the skin.

I mention all this because it has a bearing on what happened. Oupa Mê didn't believe in wasting bullets on a pig, so with his usual sagacity he would teach each year's sacrificial pig to assist in its own demise. He would put it in a separate pen, where it received only the best provender, and then train it to come and literally beg for its food, thus presenting its forehead in a handy position for it to be despatched with one hard and well-aimed blow from a hammer when the time came.

Oupa Mê usually dealt with the pig himself, but that particular year Rhagane talked his way into the job of executioner. Rhagane despatched the pig in a style worthy of Oupa Mê himself, and he was so proud of this accomplishment that that night he demonstrated the right technique on his brother Losilu, with whom he had been biting at a bottle of Chateau brandy. Losilu dropped in his tracks in a manner remarkably similar to the pig, and a horrified and panic-stricken Rhagane rushed over to the house to babble out the bad news. Oupa Kuku, who was a doctor, hurried over to the recumbent Losilu. A rapid examination showed that Losilu was certainly dead to the world but had not expired in the clinical sense, so Oupa Kuku poured a bucket of water over him, which brought Losilu around with the beginnings of an enormous bruise on his forehead that at its full extent made him look like a latter-day unicorn. The only conclusion to be reached from this farcical episode was that the pig's skull had obviously been softer than Losilu's.

I might add that when Rhagane died in 1971 we buried him in a tailor-made suit and a new pair of Swiss Bally shoes, with a bottle of brandy on his chest so that he could wet his whistle now and then on his journey to wherever he was headed. We failed him in only one respect: it was Richelieu brandy because nobody could lay hands on a bottle of his preferred lifelong tipple, Chateau.

*

I got into the Kruger National Park, if not by the back door, then certainly through a side-entrance. The men in my family had almost always been either doctors or engineers, and in fact my father had been studying medicine when, as he put it, Adolf Hitler stole his stethoscope by igniting World War II. The stethoscope was replaced by the joystick of a Royal Air Force bomber, and by the time dear Adolf did himself in it was too late for Dad to resume his medical activities. When I was born, therefore, it seemed clear that I would step into my father's shoes, or at least become a veterinarian, but my years of tutelage at the hands of Oupa Mê had set my feet on a different path altogether. So in due course I was ready to face the world as a jobless honours graduate in wildlife management.

The side-entrance creaked open for me as a result of an over-population problem in the Park. Between 1965 and 1969 the number of wildebeest and zebra increased so dramatically, especially in the southern and central districts, that certain areas became overgrazed. The Park management launched a culling programme that had the desired effect, but then found that the numbers of both species continued to decline after it was wound down. It was suspected that lions were probably a major cause of the continuing decline, and several research programmes were initiated to identify the problem. One of these programmes involved research on lions and wildebeest, as there were doubts as to what effect these two species were having on each other and the Park's ecosystem as a whole. I heard about the programme, applied and, probably more through damn-fool luck than anything else, was appointed as a post-graduate assistant biologist on the lion research programme, which would lead to my master's degree.

Thus it came about that on 2 January 1971 I set off for the Park's headquarters at Skukuza in a very excited frame of mind, accompanied by my parents. My mother, I remember, was keen on testing my allegedly vast knowledge of the veld and was continually asking questions like: 'What tree is that?' My vast knowledge being anything but, I soon developed a stock answer, 'a wild tomato tree', which she accepted without question – after all, no son would lie to his own mother! – until the penny finally dropped.

My field assistant for the duration of my lion research was a Swazi by the name of Philemon Chauke. He was a singular character. Rake-thin and ugly as sin, he sported a set of teeth such as orthodontists dream about and had the habit of falling into a strange stammer that emerged as an exclamation that sounded like 'mambrr' when he was in doubt about something. Mostly he was known simply as 'Chauke', although among the black staff he was also called 'Mambrr' in commemoration of his stammer.

Chauke aka Mambrr was a real pleasure to work with. He was energetic, a great humorist and, like most people who had grown up in the Park, possessed a vast fund of stories, peppered with strange sayings that made sense only to him (if you did something that was not quite acceptable to him he would say: 'Where do you come from, man . . . Kuruman?' Why he cherished such disdain for that little town on the edge of the Kalahari Desert, and in fact whether he had ever been there, was a secret known only to himself). Somewhere along the line, Chauke also cultivated his own name for me, 'Britsumpie,' when discussing our comings and goings with the other blacks. This was in no way derogatory, but I didn't understand at first what it meant, until I managed to associate the word 'Britsumpie' with anyone whose home language was English (at that stage the majority of Park staff were Afrikaans-speaking and English was rarely heard). For a long time I thought 'Britsumpie' was a kind of food that Chauke regarded as more or less exclusive to English-speakers, something like Yorkshire pudding, until the penny dropped and I realised that it was actually 'British Empire' and marked Chauke's respect for anything British, including the Queen. It is quite possible that Chauke was, in fact, the last out-and-out British imperialist in southern Africa.

Chauke and I shared some memorable and occasionally very frightening adventures. Fortunately for him – and for me – this early bushveld mentor of mine possessed a great survival instinct and, when the circumstances required it, a turn of speed which would have put an Olympic sprinter to shame, as I was to discover.

My study programme had two aims: firstly to determine the effect of lion predation on the major prey species, which included buffalo, zebra, wildebeest and impala, and secondly to determine the effect on the rarer prey species, such as roan and sable antelope, tsessebe and eland. I was also to collect and collate information on mortality, reproduction, territoriality and movements, with a view to determining the factors limiting the growth and spatial distribution of the lion population. Yet another aim was to conduct a general study of lion predation, and tests were to be carried out on various chemical agents for immobilising lions, as well as the radio collars that would be used for tracking their movements.

The project was to be completed in two years and had to cover the whole Park – a tall order in anyone's book. I grabbed the opportunity with both hands, undismayed by the prospect of two years' very hard grind. Apart from the fact that this was the sort of thing I wanted to do, the survey was my foot in the Kruger National Park's door. I was determined to become a game ranger, and at my age this was the only way into the system. So I went at it hammer and tongs, and it worked. But that comes later.

The study was divided into four sections to cover the important prey populations of the Park, and also to investigate seasonal differences in lion predation. Another postgraduate student, Butch Smuts, was already working on the population dynamics of zebra when I started my research and he later took over the lion research when I was transferred to the Ranger Section. The first and second parts of the study were conducted in the Satara area of the central district. This area contains large herds of migratory and semi-resident wildebeest and zebra, numerous giraffe, buffalo and impala, forming a complex prey community. (Satara, incidentally, is one of those place names that sounds authentically African, like Wenela, Caprivi and Ohohpoho, but is actually just the reverse. It seems that the surveyor who had measured up the state lands for farms in the way back when had had an Asian assistant, and when he ran short of inspiration when it came to naming the seventeenth farm – this happened frequently in the earlies and gave rise to some strange place-names – he called it 'Satara', the Hindi word for 'seventeen'.) The third part took place on the plains north of Shingwedzi, broadly classified as 'mopane shrub savannah', which is part of the favoured roan antelope habitat and also supports zebra, buffalo and tsessebe, while the fourth part covered the south-eastern Lebombo Flats between Lower Sabie and Crocodile Bridge, the home of herds of buffalo and large numbers of impala and zebra. My equipment consisted of an old blue Land Rover (promptly christened 'Betsie') which was fitted out with a collapsible directional antenna and a 20-channel receiver for amplifying the signals from the radio collars and converting them to audible sound-levels. This might not sound very elaborate in view of the technological advances since then, but it broke new ground at the time, and the radio telemetry equipment built and supplied by the Council for Scientific and Industrial Research was the first of its kind in the country.

Procedures for conducting the survey were relatively straightforward, although naturally not always simple actually to apply to our subjects. Once a suitable pride had been selected for study, the area would be baited with a wildebeest or something similar, which would be laid out in an area likely to be visited by the lions; the carcass would be tied to a tree in a certain way, not only to prevent the lions from dragging it away but to make sure they couldn't eat it too easily. This was because the latest the bait could be laid out was dusk, and it was essential to keep the lions at or near the carcass until daybreak, so that there was enough light for darting – two were selected out of every pride, just to cater for unforeseen contingencies – and easy relocation of the darted individuals.

The drugs were fired from either a shotgun or a crossbow. Irrespective of the method of delivery, the result was always the same: the lion would emit an angry snarl, spin around in indignant surprise to inspect the dart and then conk out as the dope took effect. Once the lion was down we fitted it with the radio collar – two layers of rubberised three-ply nylon mesh fitted with a transmitter pack and a battery pack. The collars were of the one-size-fits-all type; each would then be individually fitted to the recumbent lion, so that it was just too small to be pulled over its head, but loose enough to present no hindrance to feeding. Once the collars had been fitted and the transmitters tested, the lions would be injected with a stimulant, and we would then stay with them till they were back on their feet, to make sure that hyaenas, vultures and even other lions did not take advantage of their immobilised state and kill or injure them. A serious limiting fact was that the collars' batteries had an effective field life of only 94 to 128 days, so that for the sake of continuity they had to be changed approximately every 80 days. This was a distinct disadvantage, because capturing the lions unsettled them, so that for about a week after re-darting they would be difficult to observe in their natural state.

Several methods were used for marking lions to assist in observing their long-term movements. Certain individuals, both males and females, were fitted with coloured collars; reports by tourists and rangers alike were collected and collated to track their movements throughout the study period. It worked well, and the collars proved very durable, so that in some cases they were worn for more than two years but remained in perfect condition. Some lions were also hot-branded with a nine-inch number on the left hind leg, and yet others ear-tagged, but this last method did not work well. The tags could easily be lost or torn out, and, given the small size of a lion's ear, proved too inconspicuous, particularly in areas with dense bush cover.

During 1972 the number of lions in the Park was calculated from the month-end reports sent in by the rangers, giving the size of each pride as well as the sexes of the adult individuals and the approximate ages of the sub-adults. These data were then plotted on to grid maps, with coloured pins representing different prides of different sizes, and the maps superimposed on each other to give a distribution pattern. These data were also correlated to known activity zones of the marked animals in each major area of the Park. From this the approximate range and size of each pride could be calculated. From the results obtained the number of lions in the Park was estimated as being 1 000-plus.

To locate the marked lions on a daily basis was, of course, a somewhat hit-and-miss process. We would drive into the area where they were expected to be, park on the nearest high ground and switch on our electronic 'ears'. If nothing was picked up the aerial was disconnected and folded away, and we would carry on to the next likely location. If a weak signal was picked up, we would follow it until we sighted the lions; in our case I would drive while Chauke would be spotting from the higher vantage-point in the back of the Land Rover. As soon as a marked lion was spotted, the field assistant would crouch while the vehicle was reversed into such a position that the lions couldn't see him. This done, the assistant would join the driver in the cab – experience had taught us that if lions spotted a vehicle with people visible in the back they showed signs of nervousness and might even move away altogether, but that they did not associate people with vehicles, so that with all humans concealed in the cab they could be approached and observed under conditions that were as natural as possible.

Our working day started early. Every morning, as soon after sunrise as possible, we would set out to locate the lions by means of the radio signals. If our luck was in and the lions had made a kill during the night or early morning, they would usually still be feeding on the carcass or lying up near by, provided that the kill hadn't been so small or young that they had polished it off. Lions are capable of eating entire small animals and the young of the larger animals at one sitting, so to speak, leaving their alfresco table so bare that not even the vultures can find the remains. In the kind of study I was doing this eating capacity makes for an inherent error that is difficult to eliminate and probably becomes a very significant factor during and immediately after calving and lambing. Fortunately, though, the lions usually remained on or near most kills until the following evening, and from the external appearance of the lions' paunches it was easy to see whether they had recently fed or not. If it appeared that they had eaten during

14

the night and no kill could be found in the vicinity, we would try to follow their spoor back to their resting place of the previous day. At all times we would keep a sharp lookout for the presence of vultures, a good though not infallible telltale sign of a kill – they were particularly active in the southern and central districts of the Park, and on occasion there would be up to 150 or more picking at the remains of a pride's latest meal.

The main findings of the study as regards predation were that a pride as a unit killed an animal of about 200 kg once every four days, meaning that one lion had to make 13 kills of that size annually to obtain the 2 498 kg of meat it needed to survive. This basic figure extrapolated into something fairly awesome. If about 1 000 lions (the minimum estimated figure) ate only one species a year the total killed would come to 10 560 impala, or 2 520 wildebeest, or 2 160 zebra, or 780 buffalo.

I learnt a lot about lions during those two arduous years, much of it running contrary to conventional wisdom. Various authors of the time maintained, for example, that a lion killed its prey by breaking its neck, but in not one of the kills I examined could it be said with any certainty that the neck had been broken and caused its death. In my experience smaller prey were either knocked down by a single blow of the forepaw or caught with both forepaws and then bitten in the neck or throat region. In large animals the final charge usually brought the lion alongside the prey or slightly behind it; almost invariably the lion then leapt on to the back of the animal and grasped it with its forepaws in the shoulder and neck region. From this point onwards, one of two things happened. In some cases the animal lost its balance and fell, the lion falling with it. The lion then immediately went for a bite-hold on the neck or muzzle, although the throat seemed to be bitten into about 75 per cent of the time, and held on until the prey stopped struggling, others in the pride often obtaining their own bite-holds on the downed prey in the meantime. In other cases the lion would let itself slide off the animal, retaining its hold on the neck and pulling the prey down almost on top of it. Once the prey animal was down, the lion would bite it in the throat again and hold it down until it stopped moving. My conclusion was that suffocation was therefore the main cause of death in lion kills.

15

The greatest lesson I learnt was not so much about lions *per se* as about the virtue – in fact the utter necessity – of patience as part of a ranger's professional tools. On average the lions were only active for about four hours a day; until you have observed them for an extended period you have no idea how lazy they are and how much time you have to spend doing absolutely nothing; by comparison the notoriously sluggish puff-adder appears almost hyperactive.

The first of the three prides of lions that I selected for research resided close to the Satara rest camp. It consisted of three adult males, two of which I fitted with radio collars, and four females with seven cubs between them. The cubs, three males and four females, were only about five weeks old when I started the study, and for most of 1971 up to my departure from the programme in May 1972 I observed them nearly every day. In the process I became very good friends with one of the adult males, which I called Number Four because that was his radio-collar frequency. Not handshaking pals, of course, but we understood each other.

One morning early I found the pride at Mavumbye Windmill, where they were lying up for the day under some umbrella thorn trees, and as usual I settled down to wait patiently for them to do something. In due course the something happened, in the shape of a 'daggaboy' (an old buffalo bull) who came out of the bush to have a drink. At that stage the cubs were still less than a year old, but they had obviously decided that it was time to field-test the hunting skills they had been practising on each other and the rest of the pride. Again and again they stalked and rushed at him, sometimes coming so close that they would elicit a snort and horn-hook. The buffalo did not take it too seriously, however, although daggaboys are notoriously cranky of temper, and carried on drinking, although he must have known that there were other lions in the area.

After a while the cubs tired of their game and headed back to the shade; then, totally unexpectedly, Number Four got up again and walked straight towards the buffalo with that characteristic tilted forepaw action of lions. He stopped about 20 metres away from the old fellow, who appeared to ignore his presence. The stalemate held for a few seconds and then Number Four charged.

There was no time for the buffalo to get away and he hit it slightly from behind, just ahead of the shoulder, and both went down. In an instant he abandoned his original grip, clamped his jaws over the buffalo's muzzle and sank the claws of one forepaw into the buffalo's throat. Needless to say, the buffalo just about swept the floor with him, but Number Four held on tenaciously. This struggle went on with gradually diminishing intensity as both buffalo and lion grew tired, and eventually both were on the ground, lying head to head, with Number Four's jaws still firmly around his ferocious victim's muzzle. This stand-off lasted for 45 minutes, and then the buffalo gave up the ghost. When Number Four realised that he had won, he slowly stood up and laboriously limped to the shade, where he lay down to nurse what was obviously a broken front left leg. The rest of the pride, which had not stirred during Number Four's solo struggle, now left the shade and started feeding.

Now comes the strange bit. According to conventional wisdom the pride should have abandoned Number Four now that he was incapacitated. But it did not. For the next three months Number Four struggled after the pride as it moved around, unable to take part in a kill or even keep up. Yet the other lions allowed him to share in their bounty till he was able to take a full role in the pride's activities again. Why? I will never believe in anthropomorphism, but that day I had the distinct impression that Number Four had been giving the cubs a lesson, and it is worth noting that they did not make their first known successful kill till the age of 17 months, when they managed to bring down a 10-month-old zebra. Right or wrong? Well, take your pick. In this case I can only report what I saw and felt.

There was a lot more to the lion research programme than mere observation and periodical battery-changing. When you deal with lions you are always within reach of sudden, shockingly violent death or injury, no matter what you are busy with or what precautions you have taken. As a result, Chauke and I had some memorable, not to say near-fatal, experiences during our time on the lion research programme. Near Satara, for example, we nearly got the chop from a lion that was allegedly out cold after taking one of my darts in the backside, while on another occasion we had to fight off another lion who caught us unarmed on the back of my bakkie and was quite clearly determined to do away with both of us (see 'Close-up Conversations with Lions'). Our association ended in October 1972, as I had finished my part of the project and was appointed relief ranger at Crocodile Bridge, while Chauke stayed on the lion project as assistant to Butch Smuts. Now I had my foot firmly in the door, and when I received a permanent ranger's appointment in January 1973 I threw my weight firmly against that door and kept it there until 30 May 2001. I wish I could say that the inimitable Chauke and I went on to many further adventures, but it was not to be. A couple of years after we parted company he died tragically in a car accident between Tshokwane and Satara. But the little man with the big heart, the strange sayings and the unfailing help and companionship will always occupy an honoured corner in my memories.

2

LAST SIGHT OF THE OLD AFRICA . . .
AND PROBLEMS WITH THE NEW

As a conservationist I am a friend of all veld creatures, but the ones that I love and admire above all others are elephants, the cleverest, most mobile and, above all, most invincible of all the big animals, and so I was very fortunate to become intimately involved with them almost as soon as my career at the Kruger National Park started. It was a mind-altering experience, and I do not mean in the drug-taking sense of the phrase. Firstly it gave me an early lesson in just how easily practical problems can shred fine schemes that are cooked up in air-conditioned offices, far from where they are to be implemented. Secondly it gave me a rare experience of the old Africa that the generations after me will never have the good fortune to witness – an experience both sad and sweet.

First of all, the folly. By the very early 1970s Mozambique was becoming increasingly unstable as the long insurgency ground towards its end and Portugal grew ever more exhausted in both resources and spirit. Naturally this lent impetus to movement westwards over the border, and the South African authorities decided to erect a people-proof fence on the eastern boundary of the Kruger National Park, stretching all the way from the Crocodile River in the south to the Limpopo River in the north. This barrier would consist of a normal, more or less elephant-proof fence, but because it was a well-proven fact that ordinary fences don't stop people, the so-called experts came up with an added refinement. Thus was born Operation Trampoline, which involved planting a sisal fence between two firebreaks a few hundred metres apart along the entire boundary. This would make the border people-proof as well. Oh, yeah . . .

The Kruger rangers were scheduled to play a vital role in

Operation Trampoline by monitoring the movements of both animals and people through areas where sisal couldn't be planted, for example in riverbeds. One of these was Shilowa Poort, about 30 kilometres north-east of Mopani, where the Nshawu River enters the Park; I mention Shilowa Poort specifically because it is a landmark in my memories, as I'll relate later.

The sisal fence idea was a popular conception in those days – the South African government tried the same thing along a stretch of the border between South West Africa and Zimbabwe around this time. It didn't work there, since a sisal fence will not defeat a determined human being, and in the case of Kruger it was not only an ecological failure but a planner's disaster. This was because the alleged experts had failed to take into consideration the fact that if you plant something in the veld, the chances are that one or other animal is going to eat it. So the fencers would plant a stretch of sisal, and every passing elephant, kudu and porcupine would promptly make a hearty meal of the young plants. The best summing-up of this farcical situation that I heard came from a certain Mr Bastos, one of our foremen. Mr Bastos, although somewhat deficient in English, was a tireless worker who laboured mightily to get the sisal plants in the ground, but eventually the bushveld freeloaders broke his spirit, and during one of the regular midday radio calls to his supervisor he said simply: 'Mr Carl, me put-put, elephant take-take. Me go home now!' Which, I suppose, is a suitable epitaph for the sisal fence's tombstone.

Operation Trampoline overlapped to some extent with an extensive and altogether more sensible water provision programme that had been initiated by the Parks Board from the late 1960s onwards, part of which involved bringing in various contractors to drill boreholes that would then be fitted with windmills to pump up water for the game. The programme was aimed at compensating for the ever-increasing amount of water being drawn from the rivers before they reached the Park, and also stabilising the water supply to ensure the survival of wildlife even in times of severe drought.

It was a worthwhile but tedious business. All the wells sunk had to be tested for their delivery capacity. This involved pumping water out non-stop for 12 hours, with the delivery being measured every hour. It was a soul-destroying way of passing the time. You soon got tired of reading, apart from the fact that you invariably ran out of reading material, and other diversions were few. My personal antidote for the boredom was to explore the immediate countryside on foot in between taking the measurements, which was not only suitably diverting but educational as well, because it enabled me to acquire first-hand knowledge of all sorts of nooks and crannies.

One fringe benefit of the programme was that a well could be drilled near Shilowa Poort, where there was no permanent surface water; this well would supply both the mapoisas stationed there and the fence construction teams operating in the vicinity. When it had been dug I was assigned to measure its flow, and one day found me on top of Shilowa Hill during a between-test ramble. There was still water in the poort, but not much, and I knew that there was also quite a bit in the pools to the north, in the Nshawu Spruit on the Mozambican side, because I had been there a few days earlier. I had been helping Corporal Sandros Matsimbe to move some pipes and a Lister engine to his house at Makandizulu on the Shingwedzi River; Sandros planned to pump water out of the river to irrigate his fields in winter, his aim being to plant cash crops. The trip to Makandizulu had provided evidence that a fair amount of elephant lived in the area, and Sandros had explained that their numbers increased in early winter, around May, after which they would move back to the Kruger National Park when the water supplies were exhausted.

From my vantage point on top of the hill I could see at least four or five elephant herds, about 30 animals in total, all on Mozambican soil. The test measurements ended that night, but the sightings had sparked my interest, and I returned to my vantage point early the next morning. There were now even more elephants visible, and when I climbed up the following morning the number had swelled to 100 or so. I returned in the early afternoon, and now it looked as if something was up, because the elephants showed signs of restlessness at a time of day when they normally would still have been resting. When I had climbed the hill on the fourth day they had all disappeared, leaving only a massive spoor-path that headed straight into Kruger. I followed this beaten track all the way to the Tsende River, where the groups dispersed. It was an emotional moment for me: I realised that I had been a participant in what would probably be one of the last large-scale elephant migrations in southern Africa, because from now on the fence – the elephant-proof one, not the failed sisal experiment – would put an end to this ancient pattern of movement.

I would be the first to say that the game-proof fence was a necessity rather than a luxury, but its baneful side-effects must also be clearly understood. One of these was that we soon had to start culling, particularly in areas where these formerly migrant elephants spent the dry winter months in the Park before moving back to Mozambique, to reduce the possibility of their damaging this intrusive man-made barrier to their accustomed wanderings.

There were other routes along which elephant used to migrate once upon a time; one of these, near Matlakosa Pan, was so clear you could actually drive along it, and as time passed I watched with no small sense of sadness as the bush grew over this now-disused trail. When I left Kruger in 2001 there was still a single trail, about 50 metres or so east of and alongside the fence, that appeared to stretch from the Olifants to the Limpopo rivers. How long will this last, if it is still there? We can only hope that some time in the future the Trans-Frontier Conservation Area initiative will restore the elephants' freedom to roam around a homeland that mankind has seen fit to divide into two countries called 'South Africa' and 'Mozambique'.

*

The Trans-Frontier Conservation Area is a wonderful idea, but we should not harbour any illusions about the fact that it will bring some problems in its wake alongside all the good things it will achieve. Elephants and human beings both use up profligate amounts of space and water, and wherever the two species have to live cheek by jowl they will contend for these ever-scarcer resources. Usually it is the elephants that have to give way to the invasiveness of the human species, but fortunately national parks and other nature reserves provide them with secure areas where they can roam free. On the other hand, if the protected areas aren't very well fenced, animals tend to move out of the parks and into areas occupied by humans, which invariably leads to trouble. It has also become very clear that the higher a given protected area's elephant population, the more its members are inclined to venture further afield. This is very evident along the Crocodile River, the Kruger National Park's southern boundary, as well as along the Sabie River, west of Skukuza. This problem will also manifest itself eventually – if it hasn't done so already – along the Limpopo, Shingwedzi and Olifants rivers on the Mozambican part of the Trans-Frontier Conservation Area, not to mention the many small reserves that have acquired elephants.

One can understand why. In the bush the issue is very simple: eat or die. So if an elephant finds itself, on some very dry winter or early summer day, staring across an all-but-empty river at fields of lush vegetation, things are going to go one way. The fact that the 'vegetation' is a farmer's carefully tended crop is not relevant, any more than the fact that the river might be dry because of poor catchment management upstream. What is relevant is that the elephant's extremely capacious belly is empty and there is food right at hand. If a less than adequate fence is all that separates belly from food, or even no fence at all, the result is as inevitable as sunrise. It is, in fact, the mirror image of the subsistence poaching problem. Essentially there is not that much difference between an elephant eyeing a farmer's crop and a hungry man eyeing an elephant that has wandered – or broken – out of a protected area. All of us, man or beast, have to eat, and eat we will, one way or another. And once an elephant has learnt how easy it is pay a nocturnal visit to a farm outside the protected area, or even to somebody's garden inside it, you have a problem. Hell hath no fury like a farmer or smallholder who wakes up to find that an elephant has visited him for a bit of quiet nocturnal 'grocery shopping' before stealing discreetly away before sun-up. And yes, elephants might be the largest inhabitants of the animal kingdom, but if they feel like it they can be amazingly quiet and almost invisible, particularly at night.

In Kruger we started contending with this problem from an early stage onwards. The area along the Crocodile River is prime farming land that produces tons of sugar, citrus fruit and bananas, among other eatables, and in the early 1970s several farmers started experimenting with cultivating vegetables. It was entirely logical: labour was cheap and plentiful, prices were good and this was one of the few areas in the country where a winter vegetable crop could be grown without having to resort to using plastic tunnels. As with the sisal fence, however, everybody overlooked the fact that wild animals are no respecters of private property.

One of these experiments involved growing butternuts. Personally, I feel nothing for the butternut. I have never eaten one and probably never will: it looks too much like a paw-paw, which I don't eat because it looks too much like a pumpkin, which I don't like. Eccentric? Quite possibly. But the fact was that all of a sudden I was allied to these wretched vegetables in a fell struggle against my primary responsibility, namely the Kruger elephants. The outbreak of the 'butternut war' was heralded early one morning by an irate female voice which informed me in a torrent of Afrikaans that one of my elephants was running amok among her cannas, and would I kindly get my arse in gear? I pointed out that I didn't have any jurisdiction to act outside the Park, but added that I would come and have a look anyway, and that she should contact the provincial conservation officer for the area and tell him I would meet him on her farm.

Sergeant James Chauke and I arrived on the farm to be met by an extremely agitated 'tannie', still in her blue dressing-gown, spiky hair-curlers and pompommed slippers, puffing at a cigarette. I introduced myself and set off on a hasty investigation. Three things were immediately obvious. Firstly, the tannie had not lied: her unwanted visitor had most certainly been an elephant and not some other animal. Secondly, this elephant didn't eat cannas, but was not averse to demolishing them. Thirdly, the canna-demolisher was long gone. The tannie told me that the provincial nature conservation officer was unavailable and would not be joining us, but that was no longer important, as it was clear that the elephant was already on his way back home.

I was considering various ways of pacifying the tannie without involving myself or the Park in any murky waters when the situation suddenly escalated. The first sign of this was a blue Datsun bakkie heading in our direction at great speed, bucking and bouncing over the contour walls. With a slight sinking feeling in my stomach I watched as it halted in a growl of tyres on gravel, the driver's door flew open and an extremely large and very angry farmer levered himself out of the Japanese-sized cab. In good country fashion I stuck out my hand and prepared to introduce myself, but the farmer was in no mood to observe the social niceties. Ignoring both my greeting and my hand, he shouted: 'Get into the bakkie!' James summed up the situation in a flash and realised that this was a case of 'go with the flow', so he grabbed my .375 Magnum rifle and leapt on to the back of the bakkie. Next moment I was occupying what little space was left in the Datsun's cab and we were off on another hair-raising trip over the contour walls. Several filling-loosening minutes later the farmer pulled up next to a large cultivated field, about five hectares in size, and shouted: 'Now, you find a whole butternut!'

I looked at the ghastly sight before me and concluded that I might be able to if I really tried, but it would take some doing. The terror of the tannie's cannas had flattened the entire field, which, I gathered, had been due to be harvested that very day. He had been so thorough, so the farmer informed me in tones that they probably heard at Skukuza, that it wasn't even worth the expense of sending in a labour team to look for survivors. I kept a straight face – it wasn't funny at all, except in a rather horrible way that appealed to my little inner devil, and in any case a facetious remark might have resulted in my being dismembered on the spot – and did the only thing I could do to make him feel better about the situation, namely, to promise him that I would track down the elephant and destroy it without delay. This would do nothing to compensate him for what would obviously be a substantial financial loss, but he was obviously an eye-for-an-eye man and this cheered him up a little.

I asked James to follow the spoor back to the Park while I went back to Crocodile Bridge to fetch my spare rifle for him, after which we would meet up again on the road north of the Crocodile River. Some time later we linked up as scheduled and got going on the elephant's spoor. There was something about the spoor that baffled me, but I couldn't really put a finger on it, and in any case there were so many other elephants in the area that we really had to concentrate on what we were doing in case we ended up following the wrong one. After about three hours we found him near the Panamana Dam, about nine kilometres from the scene of his little butternut orgy, peacefully resting under a fever tree in a clearing. Behind him lay an enormous mound of dung . . . and then it hit me. 'It's the wrong elephant!' I said. 'There aren't any pieces of butternut in it.' James concurred. By necessity a game ranger soon becomes a student of dung in its many shapes, sizes and aromas, particularly elephant dung. Now, quite a large percentage of the 150 to 200 kilos of fresh food an elephant eats daily goes straight through its digestive system without being broken down; for example, if they eat a large amount of oranges or marulas you will be sure to find at least some whole fruit in the dung a couple of hours later. Now I knew what had been worrying me while we were tracking the supposed butternut malefactor: it wasn't something I had seen, but something I had not seen – to wit, bits of butternut in the dung-heaps we had passed. Another valuable bushveld lesson learnt!

So we were back to Square One. There was nothing to do but go back to the butternut field and start again. Rather grumpily we did just that . . . and a couple of hours later found ourselves at the Panamana Dam again – our noses pointing at the same elephant! This time there could be no mistake. We had found the culprit, even if his dung had not provided the customary evidence. So I shot him and called in the support team to skin him, chop out his tusks and remove some of the choicer cuts of meat – very little is wasted in nature, and we in Kruger followed the same rule. While one team was doing the necessary I set another on to the unpleasant task of opening up the elephant's intestines to see if I could solve the mystery. This noisome labour was fruitless, or perhaps I should say 'vegetableless'; not a single piece of butternut was to be found. Yet James and I were certain that we had the culprit. The only conclusion I could reach was that, like me, the elephant simply didn't eat pumpkin of any kind, but must have enjoyed squashing them, a pastime for which his enormous feet were, of course, ideal. I hasten to add that I might dislike butternuts, but not that much.

*

Butternuts might not have been at the top of the average elephant's favourite menu, but they all enjoyed citrus fruit, of which, unfortunately, a great quantity was cultivated along the Crocodile River, and on occasions this led to incidents that never should have happened. I remember being telephoned at Skukuza one February evening by Ted Whitfield, the ranger at the Malelane station, who came straight to the point in his very characteristic way. Did I have anything on the go next day? That was one of the great things about being a ranger – you never knew where you would be or what you would be doing from one day to the next. Naturally Ted's inquiry was an irresistible lure, so I set aside what I had planned to do and was at his office with Sergeant John Mnisi long before daylight. Ted had an unpleasant story to tell. The previous afternoon the local provincial nature conservation officer and some 'friends', one of them armed with a .450/400-calibre rifle, had wounded at least one elephant in a cane-field on Riverside Farm, near the Malelane Gate. Now, we had a firm agreement with the provincial conservation officials that whenever they went out to shoot elephants they would take a Kruger representative with them. Obviously they had ignored the agreement, so now we had to sort out the problem after the elephant or elephants had had a head start of 12 hours.

In those backward days we didn't have portable radios to stay in contact with each other, but we all knew the area, so Ted, Sergeant Reis Manique and I concentrated on the spoor while John Mnisi set out to circle around the burning block we were in (patches of veld were periodically burnt to clear old bush and encourage new growth). When he found a sign from us in the road – a fresh twig left in plain sight, and possibly also the time, scratched out in the dust – he would know that we had moved into another block, and would then circle around until he found another sign. This would make it easy for him to see where we were heading.

We set out, soon sweating like fountains: being February, it was as hot as the hinges of hell. The Lowveld is always hot during the day, to be sure, but in summer it excels itself and temperatures of 40 degrees Celsius are not uncommon; at such times the ground is too hot to touch, and you can feel its heat oozing up through the soles of your boots. And just to make things worse the humidity was sky-high because a thunderstorm was building up. After a very considerable while we realised that the elephants were heading for the Sabie River, which is about 70 kilometres from where they were shot at. We were somewhat surprised at the distance, but an elephant's average walking speed is six and a half kilometres an hour, so a distance of 70 kilometres is not at all difficult to conceive.

After about 10 hours and 50 kilometres on the spoor the storm finally broke, and that, of course, was that. I felt very sorry for the wounded elephant or elephants that would now have to suffer unnecessarily, thanks to the bumbling of people who should have known better, but at the same time I was grateful. It had been a long haul, and Ted and I were close to the end of our tether. We were only about 15 kilometres out of Skukuza when the storm caught us, but John and I still had to go all the way back to Malelane to fetch our own bakkie at Ted's office, so we hit the road, hot, tired, fed-up and probably dehydrated as well. Today's Afsaal picnic spot didn't exist then, or we would have been able to stop off for a quick beer or two. So what with one thing and another we were pretty far gone by the time we got back to Malelane.

The arrival was not the end of my suffering. Ted invited me into his lounge and hauled out a couple of cans of Castle beer – and Long Toms, at that! The problem was that he had no lager, only milk stout. I'm not a milk stout fan, but this was an emergency and I forced the contents of the Long Tom down my throat; I don't think it improved my general mien very much because Ted insisted that I finish off the second one as well to speed me on my way. The second one was swallowed with even greater difficulty than the first, and it went straight to my head instead of to my stomach, so that I began to feel distinctly wobbly almost immediately. So wobbly, in fact, that soon after we left Malelane I pulled over and asked John to drive me home, on the grounds that because he had only been walking for part of the day he could not be nearly as – ahem – tired as I was.

Because the incident happened nearest to Ted's section, he promised to take up the matter with the provincial nature conservation officer. There turned out to be two officers involved, with many friends, one of whom apparently had a .450/400 double rifle that he had wanted to test on elephants. I was not particularly surprised because I had had unpleasant dealings with these two before. Shortly after I arrived at Crocodile Bridge I found them, also accompanied by friends, illegally catching tiger fish in the Komati River. To make it worse they were wearing their uniforms, no doubt as alibis for what they were doing there, which according to them was carrying out an official fish survey. This attempt at flim-flam had not worked with me. The locality where they were fishing was in the Park and under my jurisdiction, and they knew very well that they had to have permission from our management to carry out a survey there. Since I would have been informed of any such thing, they did not have a leg to stand on, and I had sent them packing forthwith.

That was not the end of my dealings with them. That same year Piet van Wyk, who was then Kruger's head of research, arranged for a team to remove a number of cycads from Mananga Point, the aim of the exercise being to safeguard these ancient, highly 'poachable' and thus endangered plants inside the Park. It was a worthwhile project, but I was less than thrilled when I heard that departmental protocol demanded that the two so-called conservation officers accompany us. The Mananga Point locality later gained a certain notoriety as the scene of the aircraft crash that killed President Samora Machel of Mozambique and his entire entourage, but I remember it for another reason, not unconnected with the enormous Alsatian dog one of the provincial conservation officers brought with him.

It was rough work because cycads are not user-friendly plants; they have hard, spiny leaves and grow in the worst possible places, which is probably part of the reason why they survived when their contemporaries of millions of years ago, the dinosaurs, bit the primeval dust. Removing the cycads involved levering them out of the ground with crowbars, picks, shovels, and whatever other tools were available, and then carrying them down the mountain. While all this hard graft was going on the dog was wandering around, and there were so many snares on that hill that he got caught at least four times. Perhaps this made him a little snappish, so to speak, because all of a sudden he bit me without any provocation while I was working on a plant growing right on the edge of a cliff. This could have had nasty consequences, because if I had lost my balance, as I nearly did, I would have rolled down a steep incline and probably suffered some bad injuries, if not worse. For the sake of departmental amity I held my tongue and reined in my temper, but his owner thought it had all been very funny, and made sure that he and the dog were always hovering just close enough to distract me from what I was doing. I put up with this for a while, but then I'd had enough, so I warned him that if the dog came near me again I would shoot it. And I meant it, too. One obviously doesn't go armed when digging up cycads, but I had my rifle in my bakkie. Piet picked up on this lack of good spirit and hastily calmed things down, or that Alsatian would have been transformed into a dead duck if he had so much as curled his lip at me again.

*

About six months later we finally achieved closure on the shooting at Riverside Farm that had taken Ted Whitfield and me on such a long and futile ramble. The manager of Lisbon Estates, a fruit farm about 20 kilometres west of Skukuza, called to complain that elephants were raiding his orchards every night, and could I please do something about it? Our patrols confirmed his complaints and we took the next step, which was to identify the culprits by sending out tracking teams to follow them on their raids. The teams came back with a puzzling thing to report: the elephants waded through the Sabie River to get to the farm – which was no great revelation, since to an elephant the shortest distance between two points is definitely a straight line, because not much is capable of standing in its way – but how they got home was a mystery, because although the elephants entered the river on their way back, they didn't emerge on the other side. Now, this was plainly impossible, so I went to look for myself, only to find that the trackers were perfectly correct. I ordered a series of spoor sweeps in ever-larger semi-circles, starting where the elephants were expected to leave the river. The sweeps took us a couple of days and yielded nothing, although the nightly raids on the fruit farm continued.

At the same time another and totally separate problem arose: every night elephants were demolishing the trees in Skukuza, the headquarters of the Park, and on its adjacent golf course. There was no mystery about this problem, and in short order we shot all three Skukuza raiders. When we opened them up we were astounded to discover that we had solved the fruit farm's problems as well: they all had undigested oranges in their stomachs. Obviously these were the fruit raiders that we had been looking for in the Lisbon Estates vicinity, 20 kilometres away from Skukuza! No wonder we hadn't been able to find them. After some detective work we discovered the explanation. The elephants would cross the Sabie, raid the fruit orchards and then re-enter the river, but instead of crossing it they would stay in the water and walk a long way downstream before emerging and cutting away inland to sort out the trees in and around Skukuza.

The body of one of the elephants yielded another discovery. There appeared to be a bullet wound on one shoulder, and when the veterinary technician appeared to inspect the meat I asked him if he would look into it for me. Next morning he gave me a large, rather corroded bullet that he had found in the wound. I checked the available technical literature study and concluded that in all likelihood the bullet was a 400-grain .409-calibre solid fired from a rifle chambered for the .450/400 cartridge. This had once been a very popular cartridge for heavy game, but by the 1970s it had become fairly rare in the field because British ammunition-makers had been reducing their range of heavy rounds for some time, and so I had no doubt that it was the very elephant Ted and I had followed almost all the way to Skukuza that day. The poor animal had been suffering for six months!

As can be imagined, those two 'conservation officers' weren't the most popular boys in the class as far as I was concerned. But in all fairness I must add that in later years both ended up in the Kruger National Park and did sterling work in their field. Why the change-around? Well, remember the old North of England saying that 'there's nowt as queer as folk'. Or perhaps they just hated working for the then Transvaal provincial conservation department, generally referred to as 'the flora and fauna', which was almost universally loathed by the locals and did very little to improve the ill-feeling. I expect that's enough to sour anybody's attitude to his work.

3

MASTER OF LIFE AND DEATH

In my years at the Kruger National Park I killed more animals in the line of duty, particularly large and dangerous game, than even the keenest hunter could dream of doing in his lifetime. That's part of the game ranger's life. By the nature of his work he is master of life and death over the veld-beasts, large and small, that he is sworn to protect. Master of life because he spends most of his waking hours labouring to nurture them. Master of death because sometimes he has to kill them, or stand by and let them die, for any of a variety of reasons.

By and large, game rangers are not sentimental people when it comes to this part of their work, and the reason is that they are locked into the bushveld's inexorable cycle of life and death. The one is as natural as the other. Without life, there cannot be death. Without death, there cannot be life. Humans used to have a clear understanding of that in times past, when there were no wonder medicines or intricate operations. Mostly they have forgotten it now as they become increasingly divorced from the harsh realities of their environment. But in the bush the old truth still holds sway. So a ranger will love all the denizens of his patch of bushveld and go to great lengths to look after them, and at times feel great regret or great anger if they die needlessly or fall to a poacher's rifle, but if he must kill one of them he will not lose his night's sleep about it, because he knows he is a natural part of that ageless and never-ending cycle of renewal.

One of my early elephant kills – which brought with it a conundrum that took eight years to resolve – occurred just after I had moved to the Mooiplaas station in 1973, my personal assistant being mapoisa Amos Chongo, a remarkable man, the first of a long line of field rangers whom I grew to respect and love in my

33

years in the Kruger National Park. Our association was a long and happy one, and I never ceased to marvel at what he had achieved from an incredibly inauspicious beginning.

Born and bred in southern Mozambique, Amos was physically unremarkable, being definitely on the small side, but he was strongly built and full of guts, as he soon showed when he was taken on as a labourer at the Crocodile Bridge station late in 1972, just before I met him for the first time. When he entered the Park's service he was about as devoid of either education or worldly possessions as it is possible to be. He was totally illiterate, so poor that he had never owned a pair of shoes in his life, could speak nothing but Tsonga and had never known a state of life far removed from deprivation and hunger. His paltry conditions of service – R10.60 a month, regular rations, a uniform and a place to sleep – must have represented riches beyond the wildest dreams of avarice. That was Amos Chongo when I first met him, literally on the day he joined the Park service. I could not have guessed at the courage and intelligence this little man carried inside him, or that he would become so much a part of my family that he named his children after my wife Helena and myself, and later after our children, and would often reply 'Amos Bryden' when people asked him what he was called. To us he was just plain 'Amosse' through all the years of our association.

Our long friendship was forged in a hair-raising adventure with a buffalo in which Amos showed his true mettle. He did not stay a labourer for long, but walked into the next mapoisa vacancy. That was all he needed. Within three years he could read, write and drive a vehicle, and had been promoted to corporal. It makes one wonder what he could have achieved if he had had the benefit of a settled childhood. Sadly, Africa has many people like Amos Chongo, who will never come near to realising the potential that inhabits them. But all that was still to come the day he and I were delivering rations to the picket at Shilowa and happened to see an elephant bull enter the Park through the poort from Mozambique. This wasn't an unusual occurrence, because at the time there was no boundary fence and animals, particularly elephants, moved freely to and from Mozambican and South African territory according to the availability of surface water, of which there was always plenty in the Kruger National Park because of our water-provision policy. The bull passed less than 20 metres from where we were standing, and to our surprise we noticed that he seemed to have a severe case of acne on his right side: a series of lumps, each about the size of an orange, scattered over his body from behind his ears to his tail. We were totally baffled as to their cause, but the strange-looking condition appeared not to worry him, so we left him to go about his business.

A few days later I tasked Amos and his colleague Julius Mbombe to check the windmills to the north and west of the Mooiplaas ranger's post, along what is now the tarmac road between Letaba and Shingwedzi. They set off on their bicycles, but not too long afterwards reappeared at my house with Julius half-carrying a much-battered Amos, who was covered in cuts, scratches and incipient bruises. We happened to have a visitor in the shape of Dr Glynn Browne, an old varsity friend of mine, so I invited him to see to Amos's variety of wounds while Julius told us what had happened. They had been pedalling along, Julius said, when they were jumped by a hitherto unseen elephant, the very same 'acne' sufferer that we had observed crossing over from Mozambique. The elephant knocked Amos off his bicycle and then proceeded to roll both him and it along the road, so Julius did the logical thing and fired two shots at the elephant's left or bumpless flank, both of which he was sure had been hits. This was enough to give the elephant second thoughts about his activities and he fled, leaving a battered Amos and an even more battered bicycle lying in the road. Amos's bicycle being a total wreck, Julius loaded him on to the crossbar of his own and brought him and his rifle home; when we examined the barrel of Amos's rifle we found it plugged with gravel from the road, an indication of how harshly he had been treated during his involuntary conversation with the elephant.

It was clear that the elephant would have to die. It was obviously a menace to all human beings, and in any case I always saw the follow-up and destruction of wounded animals as a priority, not only to ease their suffering but also because they would pose a severe threat to the field staff, whose task was quite arduous and dangerous enough as it was. In this case there was another reason. Perhaps the pimpled elephant's condition was worrying him after all, in which case it would be wise for us to find out what had caused the bumps to arise on his body. Julius, Glynn with his medical bag and I got ready to set off after him. I was glad to have Julius available because he was a brilliant tracker – I used to say that he could follow the spoor of a cricket across an all-weather tennis court, and it was only a slight exaggeration – and at the last minute we got another recruit when I looked in at the mapoisas' sleeping quarters to see how Amos was doing. Glynn had bandaged and plastered him so thoroughly that he looked more like a resurrected mummy than a Kruger mapoisa, but he insisted on coming with us, even if only for the ride. Naturally I said yes, not only because he was entitled through his suffering but also because even a wrecked Amos was better than no Amos at all.

When we arrived at the scene of the incident there was no sign either of the perpetrator or of Amos's mangled bicycle. I left Glynn and Amos at the truck with Julius's rifle, gave my spare rifle to Julius and picked up the elephant's spoor. An hour's slog later we were back at the truck, not because we had lost the spoor but because that was where it had taken us. From this point on the character of the spoor changed drastically, with distinct gouges and scratches on the ground and lower vegetation. What had obviously happened, we decided, was that the elephant had returned to the scene for a second go at whatever was left, which in this case, fortunately, was only the bicycle. Sure enough, as soon as we started following the distinct spoor we began to find bits of bicycle scattered about and then, just a few hundred metres along, the rest of the corpse, so to speak, in very poor condition indeed. 'Mpinga' (mad), Julius said with an admirable economy of words, and I found it hard to argue with that assessment. It also made me wonder, as the hours passed and we began to catch up on our prey, how he would react when we got close in. Would he bolt or charge on sight? This was no idle speculation – I was certain that we would find him, even if it took us until the next day. He had to stop some time, even if he were wounded, something I was beginning to doubt in spite of Julius's certainty.

To cut a long story short, we eventually found the elephant under an apple-leaf tree, sheltering from the midday sun as if nothing had happened, the 'acne' clearly visible on his right side. I fired a bullet into his brain that put him down on his left side, then sent Julius back to fetch Glynn and Amos. Glynn, who had originally planned to study veterinary science after we gained our B.Sc. degrees at the University of the Witwatersrand but then switched to medicine, was particularly keen to determine the cause of the bumps, although Amos was content with a sort of grim satisfaction that his attacker had been laid low, part of the satisfaction deriving from the pitiful condition of his bicycle, his most important possession. Glynn's first cut into one of the lumps released a great quantity of pus but revealed nothing else, and the others were equally short on evidence. It was impossible to carry out a full autopsy, so we decided that we would have to be satisfied with the presumption that the bumps had been the cause of the elephant's aggressive behaviour.

It was only eight years later, when Mozambique had been plunged into a long and destructive civil war, we began finding more elephants in the same condition and realised that the bumps were actually bullet wounds resulting from poachers spraying the big animals with automatic fire from AK-47 assault rifles. The AK-47 is efficient at killing people, but to make it controllable during automatic fire it has a relatively low-intensity cartridge with a light bullet that should never be used on any sort of larger game animal; so those poor elephants were war casualties in every sense of the word.

Another question we could not answer at the time, or later, was whether Julius had been correct in claiming that he had scored two hits. Julius said he had fired at the elephant from the left, and there was no way in which we could turn the massive carcass on to its bumpy side to check. But one way or another he certainly saved Amos's life.

*

We were to see many more casualties of war in the next few years, not only from AK-47 bullets but also from landmines, especially the ones laid around Crook's Corner, in the triangular piece of land between the Limpopo and Luvuvhu rivers in Kruger's Pafuri region. Crook's Corner is at the intersection of the borders of three countries – South Africa, Mozambique and Zimbabwe – and earned its name in the wild old days around the turn of the nineteenth century. Actual borderlines were even vaguer in the earlies than they are now, and frontiersmen only paid heed to them if there was some advantage to be gained. Thus certain of the early residents found Crook's Corner a very convenient place to live, since the border beacon had a way of mysteriously moving from one location to another, depending on which country's police were looking for the person concerned.

In the late 1960s and 1970s Crook's Corner acquired a new notoriety when the area on the Rhodesian/Zimbabwean side was heavily mined, not only by the Rhodesian security forces but also by the ZANU and ZAPU armed wings they were fighting. After 1974 the situation got even worse when literally thousands of mines were laid on the Mozambican side by the Frelimo government and its Renamo opponents (although none in South African soil, fortunately). Several types of mines were used. Some were anti-tank mines, capable of blowing up a 50-ton battle tank. Others were the anti-personnel type, which were smaller and weaker but just as deadly to either a human being or an elephant. The more benign anti-personnel mine – if that's the right phrase to describe such a vicious device – was buried in the ground and went off if stepped on. The more evil of the two was what we called the 'jumping jack', which propelled itself into the air when triggered and exploded at a height of about a metre.

Mines are savage and indiscriminate things. They will blow up anything that sets them off, and the worst thing about them is that they can lie undetected in the ground for years and still be capable of detonating. In the South African Army in those days there were detailed procedures for laying, charting and removing minefields, but that sort of conventional-warfare nicety was not observed in the insurgent struggles. Mines were laid completely indiscriminately, usually without any attempt at charting them, and they would still be lying there with lethal patience long after those who had planted them were dead or gone from the area. Since the return of peace there have been various hugely expensive de-mining operations, but they can never totally succeed because the task is simply too enormous, and even now the distant thud of an exploding mine still occasionally disturbs the hot, quiet stillness of the veld. It is a sound with which we and our children will have to live for many years yet.

An anti-tank mine will certainly kill any animal, even an elephant. An anti-personnel mine is crueller because it mutilates a large animal but can't kill it, leaving it to suffer. An elephant, for example, would most likely lose a foot or lower leg if it detonated an anti-personnel mine, and a badly mutilated front leg is a death sentence: for all practical purposes the elephant is immobilised, because one leg can't bear the weight of its massive head, trunk and forequarters when it wants to move. So the elephant will die of hunger and thirst because it will be unable to forage for the large amounts of food it needs every day, or find water to drink – that is, if it doesn't die first as a result of blood loss or sepsis. It might be able to move around to some extent if the injury were to a hind leg, but the end-result will be the same; the agony just lasts longer.

How many elephant and other large game animals were killed or mutilated by mines during my time at the Kruger National Park is known only to God. Certainly we had to destroy quite a number of elephants in the northern areas after they had fallen foul of the mines laid so heedlessly in Zimbabwe and Mozambique. It was a terrible business; my blood boiled every time I heard about or came across one of these landmine victims. Try as I might to forget them, I retain a fund of sickening memories about elephants and landmines that I dislike discussing even today. But I shall summon back just one of them, so sad and terrible that I have total detailed recall of it, even after 20 years, to show what we had to contend with.

One morning I was on my way from Punda Maria to Pafuri by way of the Klopperfontein route, and near Klopperfontein itself I sighted an elephant bull, or what was left of him, standing under a fig tree. He was nothing but skin and bones and was so weak that he was actually leaning against the tree for support; I don't think he was capable of standing unaided. Naturally I decided to have a closer look, so I circled round downwind of him, and walked straight into a stench so unbearable that I threw up on the spot. Admittedly I might have borne it with more composure in earlier days, but I was undergoing post-cancer chemotherapy at the time, which meant that nausea was never very far away. But it is a moot point, because the smell of corruption was so over-powering that it was difficult to understand how the elephant could still be alive.

In any case, I pulled myself together and closed the distance between us. Apart from the smell, there was no doubt that some-thing was very wrong with him: his temples were sunk in and his bones could be seen poking at his loose-hanging skin. At first I couldn't identify any visible wounds because he was covered in black mud he had obviously picked up at the Klopperfontein dam, but then I got close enough to see that his eyes, which should have been brown and shiny, were the dull red of old blood. I was sure now that he was blind, and I walked directly towards him without any attempt at concealment. About 10 metres away I stopped and spoke softly to him. His only reaction was to flap his ears feebly; he didn't even move his trunk, an ele-phant's all-purpose tool and weapon. So with a heart full of sadness I lifted my rifle, jacked a cartridge into the chamber and gave him the only thing I had that could help him out of his agony: a swift and painless death.

Only then was I able to see what ailed him. The pus-filled wounds covering his chest, lower jaw, front legs and trunk, the chips gouged out of the lower aspects of his tusks, told the story: somewhere – probably in Zimbabwe, 50 kilometres away – he had tripped a jumping jack mine, planted and forgotten as if it were a cabbage seed. It made me feel ashamed of belonging to the human species.

*

Not all such occasions were pure tragedy, I am glad to say. Sometimes they were a mixture of high drama and low comedy, as in the incident that I remember as 'the case of the exploding elephant', which occurred when I was still settling into my dream job in the early 1970s. At that time today's Lower Sabie section was still part of the Crocodile Bridge section. This required regu-lar routine visits to Lower Sabie, and on one of these calls during 1973 the mapoisas stationed near the camp reported that an elephant bull had fallen into the habit of ambushing them near the picket when they went out and returned from their patrols. The mapoisas could, of course, have stood their ground, as they had often done before, but this might have necessitated their killing the elephant in self-defence.

This rather frightening game of hide and seek began to take on distinctly lethal overtones when the elephant got more ambitious. First he took to harassing the camp staff, who lived about 500 metres from the rest camp; the kitchen staff were in a particularly uncomfortable situation, because they started early and left late, which meant that they had to undertake the perilous trip in the dark. Then he extended his unwelcome attentions to tourists' cars in what was one of the busiest areas in the Park. This sealed his fate, because he was quite clearly a disaster waiting to happen. Just why this particular elephant got into the people-harassing game was a mystery to all concerned, not least the mapoisas, who had spent a lot of time in his near vicinity to facilitate identifying him. One is tempted say: 'Well, elephants are only human.'

The final straw came after yet another harassing incident. The Chief Ranger had now had enough, and at the regular morning radio session he instructed me to do away with Mr Nuisance forthwith. One of the farmers whose land bordered on the Park, a man called Douw, was in my office when the Chief Ranger pronounced the death sentence, and he immediately asked if he could go along. I was happy with this, because Douw was one of the very few Kruger-friendly farmers along the Crocodile River at that time, a situation that, I am glad to say, improved virtually 100 per cent in ensuing years, so I said: 'Yes. Go and fetch your camping gear – I'll supply the tent.' Douw wasted absolutely no time in complying, and an hour later we were on our way, the Land Cruiser loaded with our gear and that of the labour crew who would skin the elephant and chop out the tusks (which would later be sold to augment the Park funds) and remove meat for distribution among the camp staff.

At Lower Sabie we were reinforced by the ranger, Lynn van Rooyen, and my companion in a later adventure, Sergeant John Mnisi, a good man to have on board because he was very experienced and always an asset to any task team. We set off after the wayward elephant without delay and closed in on him without difficulty, but then something unsettled him; instead of acting in his usual bumptious manner he set off at top speed, heading northwards towards the Sabie River. Hoping to head him off on the plains, we ran to the trucks, crossed the river as fast as possible and turned right into a firebreak that ran eastwards, parallel to the river. This worked to an extent – we were just in time to see him cross the road, still heading north into the very open plains that lay before him. He and four other bulls who had joined him went steadily in single file, obviously not in a hurry, but an elephant's stride is considerably longer than a man's, so that we would have to move fast if we wanted to catch up with them on foot.

Swiftly we made our plans. Moving as a group, we would run up behind them, after which I would move out to one side and shoot the offending bull; in other circumstances Lynn would have joined me in the flanking movement, but there was very little cover in the vicinity and it would be hard enough for one person to get close, never mind two. We steamed along until we were in position and then I started my flanking movement. At this point things went slightly awry, as they often do at inconvenient moments: while looking back to pinpoint John's and Lynn's exact position, I tripped over a log, went derrière-over-teakettle and landed on my head with my backside in the air – all this in clear sight of my colleagues, which did nothing for my pride. The only consolation was that they couldn't laugh out loud for fear of alarming the elephants, which must have frustrated them.

I picked myself up and checked for collateral damage, as military pundits would put it. Luckily it was not catastrophic. I had fallen with my rifle slung over my shoulder and resting against my back, and had tried to turn in mid-air so that the muzzle would not hit the ground first and possibly acquire a plug of soil which would have disastrous consequences when I fired. I had succeeded in keeping the muzzle clear, all right, but in the process some protruding part of the rifle had taken a chunk out of my neck. This was hardly a life-threatening wound, but I knew for certain that it would elicit sly comments from Lynn and John a little later.

As I continued with my flanking movement I noticed that the elephants had now bunched up into a loose group, and of course the one I wanted was on the far side at the back. This left me with a problem because there was a moderate south-east wind blowing, and if I tried to move around the other side where I could get a clear shot the group would get wind of me and put their skates on. This meant that I had only one option, which was to get ahead of the group and wait for them to come to me. It seemed feasible enough because they appeared to be heading in a specific direction, not just wandering around, so I increased my pace, overtook them as planned and crouched down behind a little sickle bush to wait for the right moment. Now everything was in place. Except that 'my' elephant had changed position and was now in the middle of the group! In the circumstances, the only thing I could do was to let the elephants pass around me so that I could get the clear shot I needed. So I crouched behind the little bush, feeling the familiar tightening in my chest as the adrenalin started pumping, and let them come.

Two elephants passed to my left and down-wind, and a third immediately to my right, up-wind and a scant 12 metres away, which is uncomfortably close for this sort of work. But now my target was in clear view at last, and I dropped him in his tracks with one shot from my .375-calibre Magnum rifle. The two elephants on my left hadn't scented me, and when I fired they headed north at speed. The one on the right got a noseful, but to my relief didn't try to get to grips with me. Instead he and the fifth elephant did a smart about-turn and headed straight for Lynn and John, who gave way at top speed, so focused on beating feet to get out of the elephants' way that afterwards neither could remember hearing me fire my second 'insurance shot' into the dead elephant. The 'insurance shot', for those who have never hunted dangerous game, is something you learn about early in your career, whether you're a ranger or a hunter. Its aim is simply to make sure that whatever you have shot has definitely expired, particularly when it comes to dealing with dangerous game; expending an extra cartridge is a lot better and less expensive than coping with a large dead animal which isn't.

Now it was my turn to chuckle, and when Lynn and John

returned after having managed to part company with their recent friends there was much good-natured repartee about my fall as well as their hasty departure. An outsider listening to us might well have feared that a fight and possibly a shooting were about to break out, but friendly insults and robust humour were characteristic of the way we operated. When the rest of the party came up Douw wanted to know where I had shot the elephant, so I showed him the bullet's point of entry and explained to him where the brain was situated, as well as the ways used to visualise the location of the rugby ball-sized organ's location inside the head, which is enormous by comparison; many a hunter has come unstuck by not doing his homework in this regard. While I was pontificating to Douw on the basis of my scanty experience, Lynn was examining the dead tusker for evidence of something that would explain his anti-social behaviour, but couldn't find anything obvious except that the right hind leg looked swollen and felt puffy.

By this time John Mnisi had called me to one side, like the gentleman that he was, to give me a courteous bawling-out for taking chances, among other things pointing out that, quite apart from anything else, I was his responsibility and if I had been hurt he would have been in trouble. I responded by expressing contrition. Now, subordinates do not usually tear a strip off higher-ranking persons, and in that day and age this was particularly the case with black subordinates and white superiors, but things were different in the Kruger National Park's game ranger corps. We respected a man for his deeds and knowledge, regardless of whether he was black or white. John was correct in saying that he was there to look after Lynn and myself, because he had been a ranger for longer than either of us had spent on this earth (I was 24 at this time) and had forgotten more about the job than we had learnt so far. I knew it and he knew it, and so his entitlement to lecture me was not in dispute. It was not the last time a veteran mapoisa would give me the benefit of his bush wisdom, and this transmission of knowledge made me a better ranger and, quite probably, allowed me to survive to the point where I can sit and write these words.

I found out about my unheard insurance shot when Lynn and

44

Douw reactivated the long-running debate among hunters and rangers about the superiority of the .458 Winchester cartridge – which was then replacing many of the older and increasingly hard-to-get British heavy calibre sizes – over the old but bold .375 Magnum round that I favoured. When they found the entrance hole of my insurance shot on the mid-dorsal line at the back of the head they were quick to point out that it had not gone through the skull, and resurrected the old argument that a bullet from a .375 Magnum couldn't penetrate in a straight line, and certainly not as deep as one fired from a .458. I was unmoved. Not only was the argument untrue, I said, but they had forgotten to consider that my first bullet had travelled though about two metres of bone and softer tissue before coming to a halt. Disregarding their chirping, I went back to where I had knelt to shoot my insurance shot, picked up the empty cartridge-case and showed it to them, explaining its presence. At which Lynn exposed his flank in classic fashion by blurting out: 'Nonsense, we only heard one shot.' John wisely said nothing, but Douw disconcerted Lynn by confirming that he had heard the second shot. This left Lynn rather shamefaced, particularly when I said something to the effect that it was amazing how a person's hearing could be affected by the wind rushing past his ears. It was a moment of sweet triumph that pretty much wiped out my humiliating somersault of a little earlier.

After Lynn and John had left, Douw and I pitched our tent and started a fire. The mapoisas and labour crew were already grilling choice bits they had sliced off the elephant and flavoured by rubbing in coarse salt. The meat smelt good; we didn't yet know that the elephant had a massive septic wound, although that probably wouldn't have affected their (or our) appetites anyway. It's as they say: meat is meat, and a man must eat. And besides, elephant meat is very palatable if you can get over the fact that it is, after all, elephant, although it is very coarsely grained and tends to be on the sweet side. On this occasion we were not planning to dine off our late quarry, however. Douw's wife, Charlotte, was a woman of ingenuity, and in spite of our hasty departure she had managed to pack us a fine spread consisting of enormous pieces of rump steak, potatoes, onions and a bean salad, to which Douw had added a plenitude of liquid refreshment.

Alas! The renowned Murphy's African branch office took a hand that evening and sent us a typical Lowveld thunderstorm that forced us to seek refuge in our tent before we had managed to cook the steaks and vegetables. The mapoisas and support crew had no such problems – they had worked on skinning the elephant and chopping out the tusks until it became too dark, then ate and went straight to bed, thus missing the ill-effects of the thunderstorm. Douw and I sat up talking till the early hours, reinforced by a certain quantity of the liquid rations, before taking our empty bellies to bed. In consequence he was not as well as he might have been when we got up a few hours later, turning down an offer of coffee and also, with some vehemence, an ice-cold beer. I was not particularly surprised, having been there myself on occasion. What neither he nor I knew was that his day was not going to get better any time soon.

The mapoisas and staff made breakfast and resumed the chopping-out and skinning, with Douw as a very interested spectator in spite of his rather enfeebled state; born and bred on a farm, slaughtering of large animals was not a novelty for him, but he had never seen an elephant go under the knife. So he was right in there with them, green gills or no, and completely unaware of an impending disaster. The genesis of the disaster dated back to the first phase of skinning during the early part of the slaughtering the previous evening, when one of the skinners had accidentally cut through the elephant's body wall, exposing part of the large intestine. The intestine was full of vegetable material which, since the elephant had now been dead for more than 12 hours, had generated so much gas that a piece of the intestine had actually forced itself out through the cut, and I swear I could see it expanding under my very eyes. Quite clearly something was going to let go in the not-so-distant future, and if I had been a decent fellow I would have advised Douw to reconsider his positioning, but my little internal devil simply wouldn't allow me to say anything that might damage such a ripe opportunity. So Douw kept on giving rapt attention to the slaughtering and the intestinal balloon kept swelling. It had reached awesome proportions before he finally realised what was happening, but by then it was far too late. Before he could even turn to sprint away the enormously distended gut burst, bathing him and some of the support crew in an unspeakably foul shower of body fluids and half-digested plant material. In an instant a fine, upstanding young farmer was transformed into what looked like a particularly repellent alien being, albeit one fluent in choice Afrikaans epithets. When one considers that his general physical condition was not too good anyway, he was now in a truly parlous state, so we unceremoniously loaded him and his fellow stinkers on to the back of our truck to be taken to a suitable water-source where they could cleanse their bodies, if not necessarily their minds or vocabularies.

It wasn't until the skinning was nearly done that we discovered the most probable cause of the elephant's behaviour: a massive infection just below his anus, the pus from which had flowed down in between the muscle and the skin – although, strangely enough, it had not affected his gait at all. So there was some satisfaction in knowing that he had not died simply because of a clash with human intruders; I had performed an act of mercy that had released him from the prospect of a long period of pain and starvation, followed inevitably by a lingering death-agony.

On a happier note, I should mention that Douw, being the good chap that he was, bore me no ill-will for my silence, and when we parted company at Crocodile Bridge presented me with the two prime steaks we had not got around to braaiing the night before. I was far gone in hunger by this stage, and within an hour the first one was history.

*

I have less pleasant memories about the case of what I have filed in my memory banks as 'the Bakers Man and the Elephant'. Essentially it is the story of how a Marie biscuit led to the needless death of an elephant. It started one Saturday morning when Johan, the medical practitioner at Skukuza, telephoned and asked me to come and see him immediately. He wouldn't explain why, but it sounded quite serious, and in any case Johan didn't belong to Kruger's resident corps of practical jokers. I headed for his rooms at a rate of knots and was met by a group of irate tourists who, I judged from the wall-to-wall sandals and short socks (correctly, as it turned out) were either German or Dutch. Johan rescued me from the angry mob and took me into his examination room, where a woman was lying on the examination table with a drip in her arm. She was covered in scratches and cuts, and in such a state of shock that she couldn't utter a coherent sentence. As if that was not bad enough, Johan informed me that she also had a broken leg.

I was not quite sure where I fitted into this scenario, although there was obviously some connection or Johan wouldn't have summoned me, so while he was attending to the woman's less serious injuries before taking her off to the hospital I starting asking the other tourists some questions. It turned out that they had been having tea at the Tshokwane picnic spot, about 40 kilometres north of Skukuza, when an elephant had come walking down the road, passed the picnic spot and then stopped to have a look around. The tourists – who, like so many of their fellows, could not grasp that wild animals are just that and not cuddly Disney-fied creations – decided that they wanted to make closer acquaintance with the elephant. All this, mind you, under the supervision of their guide. Some guide! Where was the Field Guides' Association of Africa then?

The tourists were so forward, and the guide so useless, that some of them actually climbed on to the embankment between the parking area and the tarmacked road, so that they were virtually next to the elephant. The lady currently reclining on Johan's examination table had gone even further in the rashness stakes by offering the elephant a Marie biscuit. The elephant either did not like this traditional South African tea-time staple or objected to the lady's presence, because it reacted in typical fashion by shaking its head and emitting a loud snort. An elephant's snort is an impressive affair, and the tourist lady got such a fright that she leapt back and toppled off the embankment, to her detriment.

I did the necessary and in due course the lady was carted off to hospital, but I felt a distinct lack of sympathy for either the injured party or the somewhat apprehensive guide. There are very good reasons why tourists visiting the Park are warned to keep their distance from the animals. Kruger is not a zoo, or perhaps one could say that it is a zoo in reverse. In a very real sense the countryside belongs to the animals, and the game is played by their rules, not the tourists'. They are certainly not performers, like many of the animals in European zoos. In this case I could understand the lack of caution caused by the tourists' ignorance (although the tourist lady really should have known better), but I found it difficult to understand how the tour guide could have allowed such rashness. This was not the end of the story. There followed a whole series of other incidents featuring this particular elephant, which seemed to have developed a taste for tourist foods but not tourists themselves, and constantly pestered people visiting the picnic spot. Inevitably the moment came when the Park management decided that enough was enough and tasked me to 'sort out the problem', as the customary phrase had it.

Sorting out the problem was nothing new. Any ranger running a section in which there was a rest camp was continually engaged in untangling hassles, most of which involved dealing with support staff troubles, aiding tourists who had got lost or resolving the consequences of other people's mistakes. These problems were a time-wasting pain in the backside, but that was what we were being paid for. In this case, sorting out the problem involved shooting the elephant, and parts of how I accomplished this were as farcical as the original incident with the short-socks lady and the Marie biscuit. An added ingredient was that I decided to make use of a new rifle. The rangers had been having severe problems with the penetration capability of the .458 Winchester cartridge, so much so that I had given up on it and bought a rifle chambered for the well-proven .375 Magnum, a cartridge I had always favoured.

On this occasion I was not carrying my trusty .375 Magnum, however. Dr Lucas Potgieter, the well-known firearms expert, had sent me a custom-made rifle firing a new American cartridge called the .458 Watts, which was supposed to be a great improvement on the standard .458 Winchester round. The Potgieter rifle, built on an example of the famed old P-14 action, had performed exceptionally well during my preliminary testing, and this was an ideal opportunity to try it out in the field.

I set off for Tshokwane with my old mentor, Sergeant John Mnisi, to find the problem elephant, who had pulled off his latest stunt that very morning by holding a group of tourists hostage in the men's ablution block. When we arrived there he had already left, thanks to the resident staff beating on dustbins and anything else that would produce some noise, but he hadn't gone far, and we found him resting under a shade-tree a few hundred metres away, near a rondavel originally built for the game capture officials. John and I considered the matter and decided to approach him from the north-west because there was a slight south-east wind that would alert him to our presence. By this time, I should add, we had acquired a considerable entourage, as was often the case when one worked near places where support personnel were stationed. In principle I was always in favour of taking along a few hangers-on who had been properly briefed on the do's and don'ts and were under the control of a mapoisa to keep them at a suitable distance from the action. My reasoning was that this sort of exposure benefited the staff by providing them with hands-on knowledge and experience.

Visitors – particularly overseas ones – to a park like Kruger were almost invariably under the impression that all the staff they met, and particularly the blacks, were bush-wise. This was and is far from the truth, since they came from all over the place and, except for the rangers, did not spend their time out in the veld. As I saw it, therefore, my mission was to educate as many members of the non-ranger staff as possible on the basics of why and how we did certain things. I might add that in my opinion conservation as a cause would be streets ahead of where it is now if this approach were to be universally applied. But be that as it may. There were John and I, he armed with my .375 Magnum and myself with Dr Potgieter's loaned .458 Watts, sneaking along on the last leg of our journey, which involved wading through the steeply banked Vutomi Spruit. We managed to reach level ground again without the elephant hearing us, so close to him – no more than about seven metres – that the only shot I could take was through the condyle of the jaw. This is not a good option, but we had no alternative and in any case it would be a searching test for the .458 Watts cartridge, so I lined up my sights and fired. The elephant didn't drop but took off like a rocket, running broadside on and presenting a far easier shot. I had already reloaded, of course, and tracked him with my foresight until he ran in behind a knob-thorn tree; when his head cleared the tree I would fire.

Moments later the elephant's head emerged. I took careful aim and squeezed the trigger. To my consternation nothing happened. No click, no bang – nothing! The elephant, on the other hand, was not consternated, if there is such a word. He swung around and came straight at us with his ears flat back against his head and his trunk coiled over his chest. There is a common misconception that an elephant charges with his ears flapping and his trunk up in the air, but that is usually just a mock charge, a bit of psychological warfare, as one might say. It is when he clears for action like this one that he means business. There wasn't enough time to grab the .375 from John, so I did the only thing I could, which was to eject the unfired cartridge, load a fresh one into the chamber and squeeze off again. This time it worked. The rifle bellowed and the elephant went down, so close that he fell between myself and John, who had the .375 up and ready to shoot. I gave the elephant the customary insurance shot and then endured the expected rebuke from John for not firing sooner, although just for once I was innocent – he wasn't aware of the misfire and hadn't seen me eject the dud round because he had been concentrating so hard on moving into firing position when I cycled the bolt.

Needless to say, we held a short but thorough debrief, which might so easily have been a post mortem, with the offending cartridge as the chief witness. The cartridge's primer exhibited only a shallow dent, showing that the firing-pin had not struck it with the force required to initiate the ignition process. From this I deduced that the trigger had not properly connected with the sear in the loading process; if there had been a full contact the round would have gone off prematurely and the rifle probably would have exploded, with ghastly consequences for both of us. All in all it was a most sobering experience, the good aspect of which was that it was an antidote to the masters-of-the-universe feeling of omnipotence that healthy young men tend to suffer from, and that has brought a premature end to the career of many a bushvelder. Say that my third shot had also misfired – John might have been able to drop the elephant, but he was too close and moving too fast for there to be any certainty about this. It was also a powerful reminder that at the end of the day any firearm, no matter how well made (and Lucas Potgieter did not make rubbish), is only a machine that might malfunction quite unexpectedly at some time when you need it badly. For example, the Potgieter rifle had worked perfectly during my test firing, or I would definitely not have taken it into the field. Then it failed to perform when the chips were down, nearly resulting in the deaths of both of us. The lesson here is that a bushvelder should exercise good sense and veldcraft whenever possible, rather than simply rely on technology. It is true that John and I had not had an alternative in this case, but that does not invalidate the principle.

Another interesting bit of technical information came to light, thanks to our entourage of camp-followers. When they arrived to look at the carcass they proudly informed me that they had heard the bullet from my first shot whistling off into the sky (obviously tumbling end-over-end, which would have caused the characteristic sound). This proved to me that even a hairy-chested .458 Watts couldn't shoot through the condyle of a bull elephant's jaw.

I expect some people would be very doubtful about the morality of killing an elephant 'simply because he hassled some tourists', but it is not as simple as that. Firstly, other people than tourists live in the Kruger National Park, and they deserve protection as well. Secondly, the elephant's activities were getting worse, and sooner or later there would have been a fatality or serious injury. Thirdly, he had developed a pattern of harassment (as opposed to, say, an elephant who sits on the bonnet of a car because the driver has been hooting at him, and then ambles away to sin no more). Fourthly, tourists are not seen as a nuisance by Park staff. Quite apart from the fact that conservationists like to share their love of the bush with others, the money that tourists spend are the life-blood of the Kruger National Park, and without them it would not be able to survive in its present form. This is a fact as uncompromising and real as the harsh but logical laws of survival that all wild animals practise; put another way, a dearth of tourists is as life-threatening to the Park as a lack of rain-water is to the animals. If one looks at it from that angle alone there can be no doubt about the correctness of killing the Tshokwane elephant. Take all four points together and you have a compelling argument that brooks no dissent.

*

On one occasion I felt very bitter about catering to the tourists' needs, but in mitigation I must add that it was on one of the most unforgettably painful days of my career, when the presence of visitors made it impossible for me to confer the gift of swift and painless surcease from suffering.

A technical college nature conservation diploma course that had been introduced in the early seventies required aspirant rangers to do a year's practical training with an accredited organisation. Kruger had been given the first two, Johnny Clarke and Ben de Klerk, and at the time of my story Johnny was serving as relief ranger at Tshokwane. It was holiday time and the Park was full of tourists who were feeding us with daily reports about an elephant with a broken leg in the Tshokwane area. It was clear that we would have to destroy it, because for an elephant a broken leg meant a lingering death. Johnny was ready to shoot the elephant, and normally would simply have been told to 'sort it out', but naturally this was completely new to him and we couldn't afford to take a chance, given the number of tourists around. On the other hand, we couldn't just let the poor animal suffer. Consequently my next-door neighbour at Skukuza, who also happened to be the Chief Ranger, Dirk Ackerman, called me over to our joint backyard fence one Saturday morning and told me to take care of the matter. Helena packed up some lunch, and off we went to link up with Johnny at Tshokwane.

Any idea I might have had of quietly dealing with the elephant out of public view was dispelled by the sight that met our eyes at Tshokwane. Literally hundreds of people were watching the poor creature struggling to get to the water's edge at the Shilolweni Dam, but making very slow progress because its right front foot was obviously very seriously hurt. In other circumstances I would have shot the elephant there and then, but doing so in front of hundreds of tourists simply wasn't on. So I stood there helplessly, suffering along with the elephant as it slowly and painfully dragged itself towards the water. It was an experience so traumatic that I can't describe it eloquently enough – it is something you have to see and feel for yourself to truly understand the extent of my pain. Eventually the elephant reached the dam and stumbled in. The coolness must have eased its pain, because it stayed in the water for the rest of the day, while I sat under a tree out of sight of the tourists, torturing myself by watching its obvious agony. Then, at last, it grew late and the tourists left to get back to their camps before closing time. When the last one had gone I waited for the elephant to leave the water, and then belatedly exercised my power of life and death.

The post-mortem revealed that the elephant's leg was not broken, as everyone had supposed. What had happened was that a piece of wood had penetrated the foot, causing a massive abscess that was as mortal an injury as a broken leg. General Park policy was to let nature take its course in the case of natural injuries, and in any case it is impossible to treat such injuries successfully. Theoretically we could have darted the elephant and cleaned out the wound, but a single treatment would not have been enough. All medical interventions need some form of follow-up, and to find a single animal in an area of two million hectares would have been an almost impossible task. There was also the fact that there were far too many elephants in the Park anyway, so that it would have been folly to try and save one from what would most likely be death from natural causes.

A weight lifted off my shoulders when my bullet penetrated the elephant's brain and it collapsed, dead instantly. But the memory of one of the most traumatic days in my life will always remain with me, and anger, too. I had spent almost an entire day helplessly watching the greatest animal on earth suffering terrible pain, knowing that I could release it from its suffering merely by crooking my index finger; knowing, too, that this could not happen until there was no one around to witness my act of mercy. There just didn't seem to be any fairness about it.

As a footnote: Johnny and Ben proved satisfactory during their year in Kruger and went on to achieve their ambition of becoming game rangers, but both died in tragic circumstances within a few years. Johnny was killed by lightning in the Loteni Game Reserve in the Drakensberg, while Ben was found dead at a waterhole in the Vaalbos National Park, where he was the warden at the time – probably the result of undetected injuries suffered in a fall from a helicopter some time before.

*

Finally, there was the time I didn't have to exercise my power. One July holiday the Shingwedzi camp was crammed with tourists, and every last one of them (or so it seemed) called in at some stage to report seeing a sick elephant at the Kanniedood Dam in the Shingwedzi River. None of the reports gave any indication of what ailed the elephant, other than that it was 'sick'. Poachers were active in the Shingwedzi area at the time, and naturally my first thought was that it might have a gunshot wound, so I went to have a look. If I could detect any physical damage to the elephant that could be attributed to a poaching-related incident I would probably destroy it, depending on my judgment about the seriousness of the wound. If I couldn't, Park policy was clear about letting it die by itself.

I found the elephant, a young bull, near the dam wall, up to his belly in the water. He was so thin that his temples were hollow and his skin seemed to be three sizes too large for him. I couldn't see any bullet wounds on the exposed parts of his body, but he was quite obviously not at all well, since an elephant of his age should be well-rounded out. I told the expectant hordes that I did not believe the problem was a bullet wound, but that I wasn't going to take any further action because of Park policy. This elicited suggestions such as 'get in the helicopter and fetch a vet and treat it'. I explained why such a course of action was not practical, although I don't think my explanations really satisfied the customers.

The elephant then solved the immediate problem by vanishing during the night. Our patrols found no vulture activity, from which it could be deduced that in spite of its ravaged appearance the elephant obviously hadn't been sick enough to die there. However, most of the time things are not that simple in the African bush, and two days later another tourist flagged me down and reported seeing a strange object in the dam. I was going in that direction anyway, so I followed the tourist, who was only too pleased to show me what he had seen. His report was spot on: there was a large, dark object right in the middle of the dam. It was obviously an animal, but which species I couldn't say. It certainly wasn't a dead hippo, which often expose a foot above the water, apart from the fact that the pink belly skin is a sure giveaway. I told the tourist that I would come back later and have another look, which I did, but by then the object had gone, leaving me with a puzzle I had no answer for.

That afternoon yet another tourist reported that the mysterious object had reappeared, but in another part of the dam. This added another layer to the puzzle, because the river was not currently flowing into the dam and therefore the water was not in movement. This time, however, I was able to identify the mysterious floater as the sick elephant of the previous day – the skin was now visible above the water, and there was no mistaking its texture. I noticed several crocodiles worrying the carcass in search of eatables, though they had not yet been able to get through the formidable skin. At some time during the night the floating carcass beached itself on the southern bank, very close to the dam wall where the elephant had first been seen, and it goes without saying that it was a fascinating attraction for the hardier types among the tourists who could endure the smell of at least four tons of rotting meat situated not more than five metres from the road. I was not unhappy about the beaching, since it would make it easier to recover the tusks, and in the meantime it had all become such a sensation that next morning tourists were queuing at the gates long before opening time in order to get the best vantage point for watching the crocodiles' assault on the elephant's belly.

When the tourists finally got there they were surprised to find that the carcass had moved during the night and was now near the bird hide, a good 700 metres from where it had beached. This happened several times more in the next couple of days, and I can only suppose that these posthumous wanderings resulted from a combination of wind and crocodile activity. And then, quite suddenly, it was gone for good, tusks and all – probably because the crocodiles had finally found their way in, so that the gases keeping the enormous corpse afloat could escape and let it sink.

It was a lesson in bushveld ecology that I suspect not many of the spectators absorbed along with the spectacle. Nothing is wasted in the bush; a rotting elephant carcass might be offensive to our over-civilised eyes and noses, but it has a purpose to serve in the cycle of survival. That is why a game ranger is not unsettled by his role as master of life and death. When he lifts his rifle and kills a great suffering beast, he becomes as much a part of the cycle as those crocodiles tearing at the dead elephant's thick grey skin in the Kanniedood Dam.

4
ADVENTURES WITH
WINGS AND WHEELS

In Harry Wolhuter's day a Kruger game ranger had just two means of patrolling his vast domain and its unruly citizens – a horse or his two flat feet. These methods of locomotion had certain disadvantages: it took a long time to get anywhere, the ranger was exposed to all the dangers of the bush and he was only aware of what was going on in his immediate vicinity, so that game estimates were often not very accurate. And horses, although a bit better than walking, of course, were not always that much safer – Wolhuter's famous knife-fight took place after the lion concerned had snatched him right out of his saddle.

By the time I arrived at Kruger things had improved considerably. We still spent a lot of time beating our feet, but horses had long since given way to the ubiquitous bakkie or light utility truck (which is probably South Africa's national vehicle in the same way as the king protea is the national flower), and the era of the light aircraft and helicopter was firmly established. I was personally responsible for yet another innovation, but more about that later.

Aircraft, with their bird's-eye view of the surrounding countryside, have been an indispensable tool in Kruger's never-ending surveys of the game population since 1964, when the first helicopter census of buffalo and elephant took place. It worked so well that it immediately became a regular feature, and from 1968 helicopters were also inspanned for elephant and buffalo culling, not to mention a variety of other tasks. In 1972 the Parks Board bought a fixed-wing aircraft and a Bell G47 helicopter. A Bell Jet Ranger helicopter was acquired in 1974 to assist with the building of the eastern boundary fence, and in 1975 the Bell G47 was replaced by another Jet Ranger. These machines did more than their fair share for Kruger, and in the process they were worked hard.

Apart from about 120 flying hours during the census the helicopters flew about 300 hours a year during the culling operations, and many more on such tasks as helping with game captures, tracking animals – particularly elephants and wild dogs – that had been fitted with radio-collars, ferry flights and flood rescues. Not much of it was your average Point-A-to-Point-B flying. When visiting representatives of the Bell company witnessed our flying operations they didn't hesitate to admit that they hadn't realised their Jet Rangers could be used the way we were using them, which was definitely not what they had been manufactured for. But we hadn't known that, and so we did the seemingly impossible, because that's what the job required. I suppose it's like the common bumble-bee, which theoretically can't fly because it doesn't have enough wing-surface, but buzzes around quite happily all the same because it doesn't know that it can't fly.

To explain why our visitors found our methods slightly hair-raising, I had better explain what we did and how we did it. The number of buffalo and elephant to be culled in a year was determined after the annual aerial census in August and September, when visibility was at its best, because many of the trees were leafless at that time of year. This particular census is of primary importance to the game management programme, and over the years we evolved a very effective system that gave the accurate results required. In essence we would follow the watersheds on either side of each river's drainage system from start to finish, continually watching and counting. This sounds simple, but if you convert the hours and speed flown into kilometres during any census you come up with a figure that approximates to a flight halfway around the world in an area of two million hectares. That's something to write home about.

During the taking of the census we also pinpointed the areas for future culling operations. Then would come the culling itself, which would take place while the weather was still cool so that the carcasses were as fresh as possible when they arrived at the Skukuza processing plant. The actual culling process was divided into several phases. In the first phase the pilot and at least the section ranger would go out on a reconnaissance flight to find a suitable group. This done, they would summon the recovery teams, wait until the latter were in position and then begin with the culling.

The pilot would split the designated herd into a large and a small group, the aim being for the small group to contain the number of animals that were to be culled that day. This wasn't an easy operation at the best of times, and sometimes it was downright difficult and more than a little dangerous. Elephant herds split up easily and family groups within a herd tended to stay together, which facilitated our task because it was policy to cull such groups in their entirety. Buffalo, on the other hand, were not all that easy to cull, and they also tended to split up in all-comers groups when fleeing from the chopper.

Buffalo were killed with darts containing scoline, which initially affects the peripheral nervous system and shortly after goes on to shut down the breathing system, at which the animal concerned goes into a coma and dies; it also has the advantage of rapidly breaking down into harmless components, so that the animal's flesh is safe for human consumption. For one or other reason buffalo are very susceptible to scoline and die fast after being darted, although in later years we revised our procedures so that when a buffalo went down the manager of the ground team went in as soon as possible and gave it a bullet in the brain, just to make absolutely certain that it was dead and not suffering.

Having encouraged the target animals to hive off into the small group, the pilot would then have the frequently difficult task of taking up a position from which the ranger could fire the darts, while at the same time keeping the group in tight formation to make recovery easier. The pilot would make an upwind approach and give the ranger the opportunity to fire two darts. When the ranger signalled that he was finished the pilot would pull up, circle the herd and come back again. By this time the ranger had had time to reload, and he would fire two more darts. This would go on until the entire group was down; if things had gone according to plan, which they normally did, one would end up with 30 or 40 buffalo lying in an area no larger than a tennis court. What impressed the Americans was that if the terrain permitted this was all done at a height of less than 10 metres above the ground.

At first we used scoline darts on elephants as well, but research revealed that they were less susceptible and therefore suffered more stress, so we switched to shooting them with the standard R1 rifle, using a special cartridge containing a solid brass bullet which was designed by my fellow ranger Ted Whitfield, gunsmith-cum-instrument maker Fritz Rohr and myself. It was harder to cull an elephant than a buffalo, because only a brain shot will put it down almost instantaneously. Most people don't know where an elephant's brain is situated and even fewer can hit it regularly, even when the animal is stationary; so the difficulty of putting one down with a brain shot while it is fleeing from the chopper at anything up to 40 kilometres an hour can be imagined.

Culling, especially elephant culling, was traumatic for any ranger, and the best way to limit the stress factor on both the shooters and the animals was to do it as clinically and rapidly as possible. That was one reason why we used the self-loading R1 service rifle. Although its 7.62 mm cartridge (the equivalent of the well-known .308 Winchester sporting round) was theoretically a little light for large game, it was quite adequate for the purpose in the hands of a good marksman, and only the best shots were detailed for elephant culling. We all knew, for example, that WDM 'Karamojo' Bell, one of the last great elephant hunters of the pre-World War I days, killed most of his 1 000-plus elephant with brain shots from rifles firing light cartridges like the 7 mm Mauser and 6.5 mm Mannlicher-Schoenauer, which today would normally hardly be used on anything larger than, say, a kudu. Bell managed this because he was a superb shot and had made a careful study of elephant skulls to determine where the brain was located.

Using a semi-automatic rifle like the R1 speeded up the process because the shooter did not have to move his head or change his grip to work the bolt. This meant he could keep his eye on his target or targets all the time, so that aimed shots could be fired at shorter intervals. That was the theory, and unlike some fine-sounding theories it worked in practice: the first time the R1 was used for culling it took just one minute and twenty-one seconds to kill 19 elephants, or just over four seconds for each kill. Talking of records, as far as I know, Hugo van Niekerk and I still hold the one for the fastest time ever recorded during a buffalo culling operation. This was in 1982, when no more than six minutes and 26 seconds elapsed between the moment we left the recovery teams and the downing of the last of 36 buffalo.

*

In spite of this down-in-the-weeds flying we never had any serious helicopter accidents during my time in Kruger, which can be attributed mainly to the fact that we had really good pilots who knew when to push the envelope but nevertheless always bore in mind the old saw that 'there are old pilots and bold pilots, but no old, bold pilots'. Although some good luck never failed to come in handy, of course. This is not to say that we didn't have some close shaves, and it was my misfortune to have first-hand experience of three of them. Still, they taught me the truth of that other old saw in aviation circles, namely that any landing you walk away from is a good landing.

My first brush with disaster took place in 1973, while we were culling buffalo at the Mokohlolo Dam. At that stage we were still using the Bell G47, commonly referred to by us as the 'windmill' chopper because the tail boom looked like a horizontal windmill tower with a tiny propeller at the end. As usual we were flying virtually at zero feet and hit a tree with such force that the radio aerial on the nose was completely destroyed. It need hardly be said that this incident cheated us all out of ten years' age, but the Bell suffered no other serious damage, and we carried on with the culling.

The second experience, during the winter of 1974, was a good deal worse. Captain Claude Berteaux, who was Kruger's first full-time helicopter pilot, and I were on our way to cull elephant along the Olifants River in that same G47; the plan called for us to meet the rest of the team at the mobile workshop facility near Hardekool Draai on the river, where we would finalise the plans, collect the darts and dart gun and get the operation going. When we came in to land neither of us spotted the team's radio aerial, a quarter-inch copper cable, strung across the road between two trees. Next thing the cable cracked the canopy and got tangled up in the rotors and control rods. The helicopter went into a list of about 90 degrees (on my side, of course, so that I could see the ground rushing up at us), then partly righted itself and hit the ground so hard that the landing struts were damaged. Credit for the fact that we walked away from *that* 'good landing' – albeit with rubbery knees and pounding hearts – can be laid at Claude's door: how he managed to get us more or less right-side-up for the landing I'll never understand. Good landing or no, though, that was it as far as culling was concerned for the time being, and we had to down tools until we got our panel-beaten chopper back, several weeks and hundreds of thousands of rands later.

The third of my 'good landings' took place in the 1980s, while Piet Otto and I were culling buffalo south of Shingwedzi at the Ganspan Dam in one of the Jet Rangers, a technical member of the state veterinary services serving as ballast in the front left seat while I crouched by the side-door with my dart gun. All of a sudden I heard a tremendous bang from somewhere above me, and milliseconds later the Jet Ranger swerved to one side and then dropped two or three metres. This might not sound a very dramatic descent, but if you consider that at the time we were only about five or six metres above the ground it becomes rather more significant. I had no idea of what had happened, of course, and Piet's remarks on the intercom weren't much help, although they would have given Mother Theresa a coronary. The veterinary technician turned to look at me, all eyes and teeth, too petrified to utter a word, even a swear-word (I discovered later that he had thought I had fired a shot inside the chopper). I probably didn't look much more composed myself at that moment. The chopper was now acting quite normal again, so Piet opted to carry on. Then, scarcely a couple of minutes later, the same thing happened. The technician's eyes went from saucer to dinner-plate size while Piet fired off some more coronary-inducing expressions and gave it as his considered opinion that we should call it a day and head back to Shingwedzi. I had no argument with that, and Piet started climbing to a more normal attitude, but damned if we didn't have a third bang and swerve before he had made much upward progress, and this time we missed going into the ground by a matter of feet, not even metres.

As I said earlier, we had exceptional quality pilots in Kruger, but Piet was the best of them, at game-capture and every other aspect. If he hadn't been, he wouldn't have been able to get some power back and claw us out of danger, especially since we were surrounded by high trees. Having dragged ourselves back from the brink of disaster for the third time, we headed for Shingwedzi, a short but pretty tense journey. But the bang-swerve stayed away now, and we made the third of my 'good landings', after which we proceeded to get pleasantly plastered on Oros mixed with cane spirit and Castle beer. This sounds pretty ghastly, and was, but then our recent experience had been even ghastlier. And the cause of the bang-swerve incidents? It didn't take long for the mechanics to discover that they had resulted from a faulty pressure valve in the Jet Ranger's turbine. Not that I was too interested in the cause of our terrifying little excursion. What counted was the fact that I had walked away from it.

*

It took a reasonably strong stomach to fly at grassroots level in a chopper that had to contend with unsettling up-draughts. I was not personally prone to air-sickness, but I suppose you could describe me as a sympathetic puker – if a fellow passenger gets the heaves I tend to get them as well . . . and sometimes they (and I) did. At this point I should explain that ideally a helicopter crew for a census flight would consist of the pilot, a senior staff member each from the management and research sections and an extra observer. The extra man would normally be a section ranger, but if one wasn't available I would take whoever was available: I liked to get as many staffers as possible involved because this would mean that the maximum number of people, and especially those who worked with tourists, would be able to explain coherently what we did, and why.

On this occasion the section ranger wasn't available, and I invited a traffic policeman stationed at Satara, Chris (I'll omit his surname for reasons that will become obvious a little further on) to take his place. Chris was only too delighted, and assured me that he had never been airsick or even seasick in his entire life; but he really should have added that this was because he had never flown or gone to sea. Having learnt caution by this stage in my life, I told him to bring along a few plastic bags just in case. Then I got tied up in other things and didn't notice that he'd omitted to take this excellent and painfully learnt bit of advice. This was doubly unfortunate because our pilot that day, Danie Terblanche, was first-class at his job but was notorious for the fact that he had flown more observers into green-gills condition than any of his colleagues, and was particularly fatal to his passengers' digestive equilibrium when flying straight and level.

We took off just after seven in the morning and flew up the Olifants/Satara power line to the Olifants River, which is a straight and level flight of less than 10 minutes. When we reached the river I looked back to check on how Chris was doing, and saw that he was already looking a little the worse for wear. But he was not a quitter and gave me a thumbs-up to let me know that all was well. Unfortunately it wasn't, and the first few turns we made, gradual though they were, awakened the beast in his belly. I saw the cold sweat on his forehead and his pale, bulging cheeks, and knew that Chris was nearing the *moment critique*, so I pulled my collar closed and braced myself for the inevitable ghastly consequences. But nothing happened, and when I looked back again a couple of minutes later I noticed a marginal improvement in his condition – he was still wan and sweaty, but at least his cheeks had returned to normal. A couple of minutes later I did another check, saw that Chris's cheeks were bulging again and hurriedly told Danie to land. By the time we settled on the ground Chris's cheeks were back to their old dimensions, and he managed to climb down without spraying us with his breakfast. Then, as he walked away, he made a fatal mistake: he turned around to look at us. I suppose the mere sight of the helicopter finally snapped the last restraints, and he fired away with such enthusiasm that, aided by the down-draft of the rotors, he managed to achieve the difficult feat of puking on the back of his own neck.

We gave Chris 10 minutes to pull himself together and took off again. Almost immediately he went back into the sweat-and-bulging-cheeks routine. It was obvious that things weren't going to get any better, so I told Danie to drop Chris off at the nearby old Gorge Camp, telling him we'd pick him up again in about two hours' time. Chris was considerably less than happy about spending two hours alone in the bush, which was definitely not his style, but time was too tight and he was too weak to plead for any other course of action. We completed the morning's work with a substitute I had summoned by radio and then went back to fetch Chris. His time on the ground had done nothing for him, and when we landed at the Gudzane windmill to refuel, he had another bout of shouting at the ground. The rest of us sat down to a hearty breakfast of hamburgers and Coke, neither of which appealed to Chris in his enfeebled state. It was also clear that the eager volunteerism of earlier had left him along with all the other things. Chris himself put this very succinctly, I thought, with the remark: 'I prefer to do copping.' The sad state of our resident car-chaser proved too much of a temptation for Ian Whyte, our party's photographer and tallyman. Greasy hamburger in hand, he went up to Chris and remarked: 'Chris, I know why you're so sick. It's because your stomach is full of vomit.' This broke the camel's back all over again and Chris damped the dust once more to a chorus of unfeeling onion-scented laughter. I wouldn't be surprised if his stomach still turns when he lays eyes on a helicopter.

*

In the mid-1970s, with the oil crisis resulting from the Middle East wars hitting South Africa in general and the National Parks Board in particular, it was decided that large sums of money could be saved if the rangers were to use motorbikes instead of trucks whenever the job allowed this. I must admit that I was one of the main instigators behind this idea, being a long-time motorbike lover. But we soon discovered that motorcyclists, like the horsemen of an earlier era, were sometimes at a distinct disadvantage; at times all of us had close encounters, usually involving unexpected meetings with dangerous animals that were distinctly less intimidated by the bikes than would have been the case with, say, a Land Cruiser. It was also easier to come off your bike than to roll your bakkie, and at least two people ended up with broken legs after parting company with their iron steeds.

Although we had a lot of fun and got into places and situations that you wouldn't normally get into, we also got loads of work done, and so there was considerable regret when the motorbikes were phased out in 1980 because they had turned out to be more expensive to run than we anticipated initially. The motorcycle era didn't die, however, it just went to ground, and that same year Honda tried to revitalise the project by donating a new 500XL to the Conservation Management Section for testing under bush conditions. There was some competition as to who should get the bike, and my background as the original initiator of the project, not to mention my status as regional ranger of the north, won the day. Naturally I decreed that I would personally put the big Honda through its bushveld trials, and I didn't let the grass grow under my feet. Thus the reason why I was burning up the road in the direction of the Kostini police base south of the Shingwedzi River one day, heading straight into one of the more humiliating episodes in my life.

That year the major spruits along the way to Kostini all still had flowing water, even though it was midwinter and they should have been dry, and so while crossing the Dzombo Drift the bike and I fell foul – literally – of the slippery algal slime and went over. I picked the bike up and started to push it through the drift, but the slime got at us once more and we went down again. So it went until, by dint of much struggling and the occasional naughty word I managed to wrestle the Honda and myself to dry land. No doubt it all must have looked pretty funny, but by now I was soaking wet, hurt not in body but in pride – which is just as painful – and suffering from a serious sense of humour failure. How fortunate that no one had been present to witness my struggle in the spruit! Never one to dwell on things, I got astride and resumed my journey to Kostini . . . but not for long. At the next big spruit I came to, the Tsivana, the same bloody thing happened. That was it! I always carried a length of rope on my motorbike so that if I got a lift in a passing truck I'd be able to secure it in the back, and I tied one end to the Honda, grabbed the other end and pulled it through the drift instead of pushing it. Then came the final act. Thanks to my pre-occupation with the consequences of riding over algal slime, I hadn't noticed that a car full of tourists had been following me for some time, and that the occupants, lavishly equipped with video cameras, had filmed not only my undignified crossing of the Tsivana but also my earlier fiasco in the Dzombo Spruit. Well, that's show business. My only consolation was that at least the tourists in the car who had gone to the expense and effort of visiting Kruger couldn't complain about not getting their money's worth.

Another motorbike incident that I remember very vividly features one of those typical Kruger incidents that are quite funny in retrospect but might have been a bad business if the gods of the bushveld had been in a sour mood at the time. It happened one morning when I was on my way to visit Paul Zway, the ranger at Shangoni. As usual, I was cruising along at a leisurely pace so that I could enjoy the air and smells of the veld, which you can do much better on a motorcycle than when you're behind the wheel of a truck. It was an enjoyable but uneventful journey until I reached the southern approach of Tsange Drift in the Shingwedzi River. The road on either side had a right-angle bend, followed by a steep downhill section that effectively blocked the view until you were virtually at the water's edge, so as I got closer I slowed down even more and concentrated hard on what I was doing, because I had no intention of repeating my algal slime stunts at the Dzombo and Tsivana Spruits. I was concentrating so hard, in fact, that when I rounded the corner to go into the final downhill stretch I found myself literally surrounded by a pride of lions that obviously hadn't heard my slow, quiet approach. It was, to put it mildly, a ticklish situation, since I couldn't stop, turn around or reverse, and a startled lion tends to turn quickly into an aggressive lion. So I took the only option left: I hit the juice and roared through the pride as fast as I could, and to hell with the algal slime. The lions got such a fright that they quite forgot that cats of all sizes hate getting wet, and hurled themselves into the water on both sides of the causeway. It would not be correct to say that I crossed the spruit without touching the water, but I certainly reached the other side in record time, after which I could let my heartbeat return to normal and enjoy the humour of the situation. How the distinctly soggy lions I left in my wake felt about it I have no idea.

Another time I was travelling south along the Mphongolo River between Babalala and Shingwedzi, one of my favourite roads in the Park because in late winter you often saw large concentrations of elephants there as they came to drink at the last remaining natural waterholes. I was cruising along as usual when I saw what looked like a sizeable stick lying in the road, then realised when I was almost on top of it that it couldn't be a stick but must be a snake. I couldn't stop because I was so close now that if I did I would probably end up on top of it, so I threw the Honda into a flat 180-degree turn with the throttle wide open just to speed things up a bit more. In the process I saw a large snake's head flash past me, which inspired me to pour on even more throttle. The bike slewed around in a great cloud of dust and I really stepped on the gas as soon as the front wheel was pointing down the road. I put a respectable distance between us and then stopped, shaking like a leaf, to get myself in hand before cautiously heading back to the scene of my recent conversation with the snake. To my utter surprise there was no sign of the encounter – no tracks in the road, nothing. This shook me up again until I realised that I had been so enthusiastic about saying goodbye to the snake that I had turned a full circle and was now approaching the spot *from* the south. Fortunately the snake, having expressed its displeasure with that initial swipe at me, must have been as keen to find healthier climes as myself. Long live petrol power! An encounter like this gives a man a new perspective on global warming.

My trusty motorbike featured in another funny-in-retrospect incident that was also so unlikely we would sneer if we saw it in an adventure film. I was due to attend an early-morning meeting at Letaba and decided to go there the day before and spend the night instead of dragging myself out of bed at an unholy hour on the actual day. For some reason that now escapes me I decided to go by motorbike instead of my truck, and thanks to unscheduled delays it was almost dark enough to switch on the headlight by the time I crossed the Letaba River. Not quite dark enough, though – dusk is the worst time to travel in Kruger because it's very difficult to tell the difference between animals and trees or shrubs in the gloaming, but before a certain point, lights are not much help either. As a result of this betwixt-and-between situation I managed somehow to miss seeing an enormous bull elephant standing broadside in the road just ahead of me until he was literally only a few metres away. As with the lions, my options were extremely limited. Since I was doing 60 km/h on a dirt road, there was no question of being able to stop in time. Swerving to left or right was obviously out of the question as well. So I flattened myself over the petrol tank, revved up and shot through the gap between his raised trunk and his forelegs. I don't think the elephant became aware of my presence until after I had virtually scraped the hairs off his chest, and by that time I was a fast-receding cloud of dust.

And in conclusion, a motorbike story that just begs to be told, the hero(?) in this case being my erstwhile colleague Ludwig, whose career in the Park later came to a bad end when he became a rhino poacher. I'm not saying this incident had anything to do with his descent into wrongdoing, but it was certainly a classic teeth-grinder at the time. His customary cigarette jammed between his teeth, Ludwig was crossing the narrow one-way causeway over the Olifants River on his bike when a small traffic jam suddenly formed (yes, they have them in Kruger: it's just that the causes tend to be radically different). Ludwig did the only thing possible in the circumstances: stopped and put out one foot to balance himself. Unfortunately he had stopped too close to the edge and what his foot met was not solid concrete but thin air. Next moment he and his bike parted company; by some fluke the bike remained *in situ*, but Ludwig made a one-point landing in the river, which promptly swept him under the bridge. He emerged on the other side, the now-sodden cigarette still clamped between his teeth, and scrambled back on to the causeway. Needless to say, Ludwig was not a happy chap as he stood there with plentiful quantities of river water running off him, and just to make his day a tourist pulled up next to him and said: 'I've seen nothing the entire day, but you've just made up for it. Thanks.' Grrr!

In wilder moments one can't help wondering what a motor-bike rally of the Paris-Dakar type would be like if the route ran through the Kruger National Park. I think it would be likely that, first, some very good and possibly even sensational TV footage would result, and, second, that all the surviving contestants would go on strike unless the organisers changed the route.

5

THE MAGNIFICENT SEVEN

I don't think it would be an exaggeration to say that even South Africans, who tend to be slightly blasé about these things, felt a surge of national pride when wildlife artist Paul Bosman's series of paintings depicting 'The Magnificent Seven' – not the cowboy film of that name, but the group of famous tuskers in the Kruger National Park – were made public in the early 1980s. Pictures of game animals are as common as sand on a beach in this country, but 'The Magnificent Seven' were something else again, and their fame soon spread far beyond the borders of South Africa, so that in the course of time Bosman's paintings were to be seen around the world, whether as individual prints or collected in the handsome coffee-table book on which he collaborated with Dr Anthony Hall-Martin, one of the Park's resident scientists and a world-renowned authority on elephants.

All of which was, of course, a source of great pleasure to me. It was good for the Park, which was and is very dependent on a strong and steady flow of tourists, and it pleased me because elephants have always been my favourite animals; when you have worked with these magnificent, highly intelligent creatures for as many hours as I have, there is no way to avoid developing a deep affection for them. And much as I do not believe in anthropomorphism, I have no hesitation in saying that they were unique in appearance and personality.

The project was started by Bosman and Anthony Hall-Martin in the early 1980s to identify, paint and publicise the big tuskers in the Kruger National Park, and I am pretty sure that the success of their efforts exceeded their wildest expectations. And rightly so. They were truly magnificent animals, and I'm proud to be able to claim a solid acquaintance with most of them.

The genesis of Bosman's paintings can be traced back to the first days of the Sabie Game Reserve in 1902. It is hard to believe today, but there was not a single elephant in the Sabie Reserve when Stevenson-Hamilton became the first resident warden just over a century ago. But because Sabie had retained its basic ecological dynamics there were soon signs of recovery under his regime of protection and loving care. By 1905 the spoor of a few elephant were spotted near the confluence of the Letaba and Olifants Rivers, and after that began a steady increase. Harry Wolhuter, another of the pioneer rangers, believed that he saw the first elephants in the Park while patrolling along the Olifants River, and later described it in his memoirs. Unfortunately he does not give the date, but it must have been in those very early years after the re-proclamation in 1902: 'One early morning, as I rode towards the Olifants, I saw what I at first took to be two huge rocks away out in the sandy bed of the river. It struck me as strange that I had not previously noted these rocks, as I had passed that very spot many times; and then, as I watched, one of the rocks moved distinctly, and it dawned on me that of course in reality they were elephants! I obtained a good view of them before they disappeared from view in the bush; and I think that these were the first elephants seen in the Game Reserve.'

As the elephant population of the Park grew it was noted that big tuskers – of which there had long been a dearth because they were always the hunters' prime target – had started reappearing. This led to a natural desire to find out how many good-sized tuskers were in the Park and which were the greatest of them all. During the 1980 annual elephant and buffalo helicopter census, therefore, the teams recorded with the greatest accuracy possible the number of bull elephants carrying at least one tusk estimated at 45 kilos or over, and where they were located.

To our surprise we found we had 41 bulls in this class, mostly located in the Park's northern region where I was the regional ranger, of which a minimum of eight had at least one tusk with an estimated weight of over 60 kilos. Anthony Hall-Martin then wrote a magazine article about some of these big fellows, and Paul Bosman was so inspired by it that he contacted Anthony about the chances of painting Mafunyane, the most elusive of them. Anthony liked the idea, and the project began to grow. The upshot was that Paul painted not only Mafunyane but six other tuskers: Shingwedzi, João, Dzombo, Nshawu, Ndlulamithi and Kambaku. They then collaborated on the book whose title turned the tuskers into living legends.

The most famous of the Magnificent Seven was Mafunyane, whose name, literally translated, means 'wanting lots of little things', or, more prosaically, 'bad tempered'. Mafunyane didn't like people, probably with good reason: he had a hole the size of a man's fist in the top of his head, and one theory was that it had been caused by a bullet fired into his skull by someone sitting in a tree. This was quite a common technique, particularly among subsistence poachers, in the days before Africa was flooded with modern military weapons, and the average bush hunter would have no more than an antiquated muzzle-loader firing a large bullet of soft lead, which was not all that much more advanced than the 'Brown Bess' muskets used at Waterloo. The only way to kill an elephant on the spot is to shoot him in the brain, but lead bullets aren't good at penetrating bone and the black powder used in the old muzzle-loaders didn't generate all that much energy. So the idea was to get as close as possible and try to avoid the heaviest bone mass. Another theory was that Mafunyane's wound resulted from a tusk-thrust during a fight with another bull in his younger days, an equally plausible explanation. Whatever the case, Mafunyane was a grumpy old fellow and did not encourage social calls on him at his favourite haunt, the remote area north and east of the Shangoni ranger's station on Kruger's western boundary, near where the Shingwedzi River enters the Park.

When Paul and Anthony first obtained permission to track down Mafunyane I was tasked to accompany them. A helicopter dropped us off as near as possible to where he and his 'askari' (a young bull who could be termed his esquire, if one wants to be a little fanciful) hung out, but it still took us quite a while to track them down to a grassy clearing where they were loafing among the shrub mopane. Our encounter turned out to be short but hair-raising. Mafunyane and his askari picked up our scent from the light breeze and reacted immediately. The askari fled without further ado, but Mafunyane turned and came at us. It was only a short rush – about four metres – but caution is always advisable in such a situation, and I was about to tell Anthony and Paul to run when Mafunyane turned away and vanished into the bush. The encounter could have ended badly, either for us or for Mafunyane, but all I felt was admiration for his tusks: beautifully matched and only slightly tapered, they were so long that he had to hold his head higher than normal to keep them from digging into the ground when he walked or ran. Here was the ultimate touch of the old Africa, when Mafunyane would have been only one of many great tuskers!

Magnificent though he was, Mafunyane was not as huge physically as the instant legends had it, although most of the handful of people who had had the opportunity of seeing him – usually from the air – believed that he stood at least an awesome four metres (12 feet or so) at the shoulder and carried tusks in the 90 kilogram (about 200 pounds) class. After every sighting there would be heated arguments about this, but usually I did not join in, because I had no intention of adding fuel to the flames without being able to furnish hard evidence. I reckoned I had a fairly accurate idea about the size of both his body and his tusks because I was actually stationed at Shingwedzi during the final phases of the fervent publicity generated by the release of Bosman's paintings, and had been able to observe him at close range on several occasions. Subsequently my estimates turned out to be pretty much spot-on.

The next time I saw Mafunyane was when I took Professor Fritz Eloff, then chairman of the National Parks Board, to see and photograph our wonderful old media star. A light aircraft went out to locate Mafunyane and his askari, then radioed back some directions so that Professor Eloff and I could follow in a helicopter, accompanied by Ranger Piet van Staden and photographer Anthony Bannister. We landed about a kilometre from the elephants and set off on our approach, while Piet and Anthony waited for me to bring Professor Eloff back so that they go could go in. We found Mafunyane without difficulty and, under cover of a conveniently placed Dopperkiaat (otherwise known as a round-leaved teak tree), got to within about 12 metres of him. That was about as near as I thought we should go, and I signalled that we should stop so that Prof Eloff could take his photographs. I was under the impression that he had been taking photographs all along our approach; I had been concentrating so hard on the task at hand that I had not registered the fact that I had not heard the clicking of the camera's shutter. He hadn't, and by great misfortune contrived to drop the camera's lens cap as he made ready. It clattered down on the stones at his feet and alerted Mafunyane, who gave us one quick look and vanished into the thick bush, heading south.

Prof Eloff was dreadfully disappointed, of course, and eagerly agreed when I suggested that we try to catch up with Mafunyane again. My offer was more an attempt to soothe Prof Eloff's disappointment than anything else, because I frankly did not believe that we would get another sighting of Mafunyane, who appeared to be on the way to the Shingwedzi River area, where there was a heavy population of bull elephants. Still, it would make Prof Eloff feel better, and we would end up back on the road, where we could be picked up. Mafunyane had left a good clear spoor which I had no difficulty in following until it mingled with the footprints of several other elephants just before reaching a patch of small pebbles in an open area. I thought this was pretty much the end of our quest, but when I examined the pebble patch I could make out Mafunyane's spoor quite clearly, so I told Prof Eloff to wait at the northern edge while I went ahead to look for firm confirmation that I was indeed on his heels again. I had nearly crossed the open area when, to my great astonishment, I saw Mafunyane not 30 metres away, standing under a tree facing away from me, completely at ease with the world. Immediately I signalled to Prof Eloff to come closer. He saw my urgent signal, and in a moment of absentmindedness responded, very audibly: 'What do you see?' That was it. Mafunyane burnt rubber getting out of there, taking with him Prof Eloff's last hope of a photograph.

It was clear to us that Mafunyane was nearing the end of his long life. There was nothing we could do about that, of course, but we were worried about losing those truly wonderful tusks of his, which we were determined should be a permanent memorial to him for the benefit of future generations. There were at least two possible scenarios in this regard. Because Mafunyane liked to keep to himself, well off the beaten track, it was entirely possible for poachers to slip in, kill him and carry off the tusks – it should be remembered that the emergence of the Magnificent Seven coincided with the high point of the elephant poaching 'war' in the northern region. Alternatively, he might die of natural causes without our realising it immediately, and have his' armament snatched by whoever found him first.

It was therefore decided that Mafunyane must be darted and fitted with a radio collar so that we could track him constantly, and for good measure casts would be made of his tusks while he was in dreamland. This was a tall order. Firstly, given the fact that he was a media celebrity verging on a national treasure, thanks to all the hoopla following publication of the 'Magnificent Seven' paintings series and all the articles in magazines and newspapers (it got even worse later when the book was published), we could not risk shooting a dosage of capture cocktail into him that might prove lethal – not only was he a fairly old gentleman, but the mixing of such cocktails was then still very much a mixture of art and science; and in any case there was already the built-in risk that he would injure himself when he collapsed. Secondly, casting an immobilised elephant's tusks in the field was a very new technique that would need to have the snags thoroughly ironed out beforehand because there would not be a second chance any time soon, if ever.

We decided that the best approach would be to experiment on a guinea-pig, in this case an elephant bull of similar size, the day before we tackled Mafunyane himself. I was entrusted with finding the right guinea-elephant (so to speak) and darting him, so off we went in the helicopter and soon spotted one that I liked just south of Shingwedzi. I let him have a dart with a Mafunyane-sized dose of drugs, and down he went. The Park Warden, Dr Tol Pienaar, was not too impressed by my choice when he arrived soon after: the elephant was far too small, he said. I demurred, holding that I had put considerable thought into the question of Mafunyane's actual rather than rumoured size, and was convinced that I was right. Dr Pienaar finally accepted this and next morning we left Shingwedzi to tackle the star of the show. It was definitely the most exciting thing to happen in Kruger for some time, and people came from near and far to be part of it – from my vantage-point in the helicopter it looked more like a circus procession than a serious elephant-darting operation.

The early stages went well: we found Mafunyane without problems, I darted him and he went down without hurting himself. The entourage immediately descended like a pack of flies to have a close-up look at this legendary veld-beast, and to their surprise (although not to mine) found that he wasn't nearly as big as legend had it. In fact, he was relatively small for a bull elephant of his age – only 3.27 metres at the shoulder, which was significantly smaller than the allegedly under-sized practice animal I had selected the day before. My three-year-old son Robert was one of the spectators, and his trenchant remark of 'Daddy, this is little Lefunyane. Where's his daddy?' pretty much summed up the general disappointment. Dr Pienaar's comment was more to the point. He eyed the recumbent Mafunyane, came over to me and said simply: 'You were right.'

There was no argument about the magnificence of Mafunyane's tusks, though; they lived up to everything that had been said about them, even if their owner was, relatively speaking, a bit of a short-arse. Each of them was 2.51 metres long – taller than the average circus giant – and weighted a massive 55 kilos; truly a marvel of the bushveld. Before getting down to business we took the opportunity of having a close look at the famous hole in the top of Mafunyane's head. It was an impressive thing, literally large enough for me to fit my fist into, and extended all the way into his nasal passages, so that he was actually breathing through it. I wondered whether he was able to drink in the way favoured by elephants, namely sucking the water into their trunks and then blowing it into their mouths. I couldn't make out whether Mafunyane could do this, given the alternative breathing arrangement. If he couldn't, how did he manage to drink? It was a total mystery, but there was no time for further investigation.

Fitting the collar, measuring Mafunyane, drawing blood for analysis and making the casts of his tusks all proceeded smoothly, and when we were done the veterinarian, Dr Vossie de Vos, injected the antidote into one of the prominent blood vessels in Mafunyane's ear to wake him up. Soon Mafunyane was wide awake, but to our concern made no attempt to get to his feet. We tried every method of provoking him into action, but all we got was a couple of feeble heaves, followed by a slump to the ground. The problem wasn't laziness or a sudden love of human company. Simply put, Mafunyane's greatest asset had turned on him. Because of his relatively small body and very large tusks, he was unable to swing his head and forelegs enough to enable him to lift his body off the ground. We tried helping him by hand, but that didn't work (if you have ever tried this, one of the first things you learn is that reclining elephants are not only first class for inducing a hernia but also have no handles to hold on to). Hours later Mafunyane was still down, and the general mood of both the capture team and the spectators had become distinctly glum. Was the Magnificent Seven about to become the Magnificent Six? Obviously some drastic remedy was needed, so the mechanical workshop manager was radioed and instructed to bring a front-end loader from Shingwedzi as soon as he could.

When the front-end loader arrived we tied a thick log to the loader-bucket to prevent possible injury to Mafunyane and then tried to lift him to his feet with it. It didn't work, so we tried another approach. We covered Mafunyane's head with a large green tarpaulin to protect his eyes and then had the front-end loader push a substantial wall of soil up against and under him. This, it was hoped, would lift him to the point where he would be able to swing his head and forelegs enough to rise under his own steam. To everyone's vast relief the second approach worked, and after much engine-roaring and soil-shovelling by the front-end loader Mafunyane finally got somewhat shakily to his feet and looked around him for a second or two, to loud applause from the spectators.

The applause didn't last long. The famously grumpy Mafunyane was now in a state of fearsome irritation towards both men and machines. First he attacked the green tarpaulin used to cover his eyes, ripping it to pieces with his feet and trunk. Then he went for the front-end loader, butting it backwards with his great head, even though it was in gear. Then he hooked his tusks under the bucket and lifted the whole massive vehicle up so that its front wheels were about half a metre from the ground. Fielies, the driver, very wisely bailed out and headed for cover, and I couldn't blame him: at that moment Mafunyane certainly didn't look like a smallish elephant at all. In fact, he looked positively gigantic! By now our formerly appreciative audience had vanished. Some of the spectators were hiding behind convenient trees, while others had got into their vehicles and put some distance between themselves and Mafunyane. The only vehicle still within convenient reach of Mafunyane was a brand-new bakkie the Park had just acquired, which stood a mere 20 metres or so from where he was arguing with the front-end loader and was clearly going to become the next focus of his wrath.

I was the only one not to have taken cover, because I was the person in charge of the area and therefore responsible for protecting both people and property, and all this left me pretty much between a rock and a hard place. Just say Mafunyane's bad temper did not abate and I had to shoot him before he destroyed the new bakkie or myself, or both? That would definitely be the worst day of my life, and probably in the Park's as well. I thrust the thought aside and attended to my first priority, which was to draw his attention away from the bakkie. I ran in between them and fired off not a bullet but a volley of bad language. Perhaps the sheer desperation radiating from me had an effect, because Mafunyane changed direction. This saved the bakkie from destruction but brought a new problem, because he was now heading directly towards a large ant-heap behind which Prof Eloff was hiding, not to mention some mopane shrubs in the rear of the ant-heap that harboured another population of refuge-seekers.

This danger was warded off when the pilot, Hugo van Niekerk, having managed to get his chopper off the ground, dived down and induced Mafunyane to change direction yet again . . . straight towards a tree behind which Mike Rochat, the helicopter engineer, was hiding. Mike immediately came to the not unnatural conclusion that Mafunyane had it in for him personally and fled precipitately, unfortunately in the same direction as his perceived pursuer. A panting Mike was losing ground fast when an amused Hugo noticed his predicament, managed to persuade Mafunyane to change direction once again and landed briefly to pick up his very relieved engineer. This time, to everyone's relief, there was nothing in Mafunyane's path and he kept going till the bush closed behind him and he was seen no more. We headed home laden with photographs, measurements, blood samples, tusk casts and a multitude of 'I was there' stories, and it was a very long time before tales of the Mafunyane adventure, gaining new embellishments with each re-telling, ceased to be the main topic of conversation in Kruger.

Sadly, it was Mafunyane's last hurrah, because he died only a couple of months later. But we saved his beautiful tusks, and today they are on display in the Elephant Hall in the Letaba rest camp. There the youngsters can marvel at them, and old-timers like myself can spend a couple of pleasant moments speculating about what might have been if Mafunyane had grown to the size of Shawu, at a shoulder-height of 3.4 metres the largest of the Magnificent Seven. It is not impossible that he would have had the largest tusks the world has ever seen. But I'm not complaining. Mafunyane was quite magnificent enough, and I am grateful that I was there to have some personal dealings with him, hair-raising though they were.

*

Mafunyane's colleague Shingwedzi was named after the rest camp and river, and he was known for his placid nature. I can attest from personal experience to the fact that, unlike the irascible Mafunyane, he was basically a peaceable character, in spite of his great size and strength – and make no mistake about it, there is no animal on earth that can stand up to a healthy bull elephant if he decides to take executive action.

I got to find out about Shingwedzi's mild manners when I was returning to the rest camp one night with the roads foreman in the north, Oom Daan Marais, known variously as Oom Daan, in deference to the fact that he had been around the block more than a few times, and 'Baas Nineteen' because he was lacking one finger. Oom Daan could not be broken of the habit of driving too fast, and that night he paid the price when he rounded a corner at his usual intemperate pace and rammed his Isuzu bakkie square into the backside of a hitherto unseen elephant.

The elephant promptly sat down on the bonnet, instantly turning the front end of the Isuzu into a disaster area, although Oom Daan escaped without any injury except to his nerves. Now, if the elephant concerned had been Mafunyane Oom Daan's condition, not to say that of the bakkie, might have worsened considerably in the next few minutes; but Shingwedzi – for it was none other – merely lifted his enormous bottom off the remains of the Isuzu and fled into the night. I say 'remains' advisedly, because the size of the bakkie's repair bill was a seven days' wonder when it arrived.

Shingwedzi never strayed far from his haunts, and one morning in January 1981 I found him dead not more than 100 metres away from the camp whose name he had made famous. I concluded that he must have died instantly from either a stroke or a heart attack, because brain-shot elephants' legs collapse under them and they end up in a kneeling position, still upright. That is how I found Shingwedzi, his tusks embedded in the sand of the river's bed and holding him as upright in death as he had been in life. I was deeply touched by the sight of his great corpse, lifeless now after so many years and so many perils and adventures, but glad that his death had been so quick and painless. A couple of days later we were able to remove his tusks, which weighed in at 58 kilos and 47.2 kilos.

Dzombo was yet another one of the Magnificent Seven I was familiar with, his favourite place of residence being the Dzombo Spruit, south of Shingwedzi. Seldom seen by tourists, although a familiar sight to field staff, Dzombo was the only one of the seven actually to fall prey to poachers, who killed him in October 1983. Thanks to a freakish coincidence we managed to save his tusks, though. Ampie Espag, then the ranger at Mooiplaas, was on his way to service the windmills at Dzombo when the tusker was killed. Neither Ampie nor his staff heard the shots or saw the poachers, but when they arrived at the windmills they found Dzombo lying dead not more than 200 metres away. He was obviously freshly dead, and his tusks – later found to weigh 55.5 kilos and 56.8 kilos respectively – were still intact, although chop-

Oupa Mê and Bruce, May 1956. My great-grandfather taught me to ride a horse, shoot accurately with a rifle and appreciate the natural things around me.

A programme to study the effect of lion predation on major prey species as well as the rarer prey species such as roan, sable, tsessebe and eland provided me with a foot in the door at the Kruger National Park. First the chosen lions had to be darted:

Top: Preparing darts before a capture operation with fellow researcher Butch Smuts.

Bottom: Preparing to dart a lion from the safety of my old Land Rover, Betsie. *(Photos by Jimmy Soullier)*

The radio telemetry equipment we used in our lion research was built and supplied by the CSIR and was the first of its kind in the country.

Top: A radio collar – two layers of rubberised three-ply nylon mesh fitted with a transmitter and a battery pack.

Bottom: The first radio-collared lion ever. *(Photos by Jimmy Soullier)*

Top: The darts had to be removed before we could proceed with the fitting of the radio collars. When this was done we would inject a stimulant to wake them faster. We had to stay with the lions until they were back on their feet.

Bottom left: The king of beasts wakes up with a capture drug-induced hangover.

Bottom right: Drugged, and still not out of it. Note the darts. *(Photos by Jimmy Soullier)*

My old blue Land Rover, 'Betsie', was fitted out with a collapsible, directional antenna and a 20-channel receiver for amplifying the signals from the radio collars.

Top: Butch Smuts and myself treating a lion before fitting a collar, with our assistants, mapoisas Chauke 'Mambrr' and Philemon Nkuna, looking on.

Bottom: Testing transmission before the lion recovers completely. *(Photos by Jimmy Soullier)*

Top: Langhaaktand – the final hours. He died of wounds possibly caused by poachers' bullets. Note his sunken temples and skin that is too big for his frame.

Below: Langhaaktand's tusks at Shingwedzi rangers' quarters. These are the third and fourth largest tusks ever recorded.

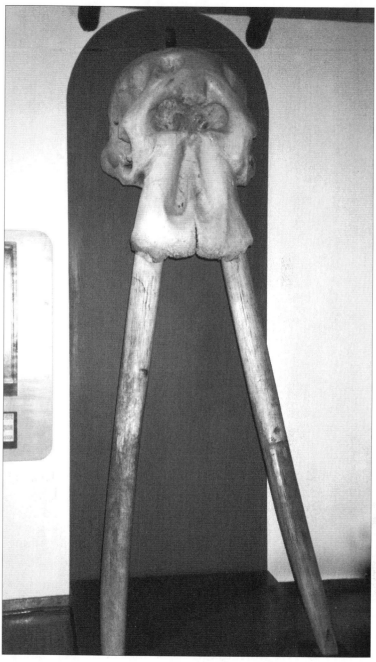

Mafunyane's tusks in the Letaba Elephant Hall. His tusks were so long that he was unable to stand on his own after being immobilised, so we had to help him to his feet with a front-end loader.

Top: One of the Magnificent Seven, Mandleve (Tsonga for ear), identified by the cut in his ear.

Bottom: No one special, but still a magnificent animal. During the 1980 census we recorded 41 bull elephants carrying at least one tusk estimated at 45 kilos or over, at least eight of which had one tusk with an estimated weight of over 60 kilos.

Above: Rangers pose with a white rhino that was shot by poachers and later died of its wounds.

Bottom: A poacher's trademark: the horns are on their way to the Middle East or China to be used as medicine, dagger handles or as an aphrodisiac.

Top left: Back after an extended anti-poaching patrol with Piet van Staden.

Top right: Junias Nyalungu and me, celebrating Junias's reward for turning state witness in a rhino poaching case.

Above: Poachers at work – with the obligatory AK-47 rifle.

Right: A five-star anti-poaching camp.

Top: Hell on earth: a snare around an elephant's foot.

Bottom: An elephant carcass with tusks chopped the mark of a poacher.

A large set of tusks lost by the poachers – and a lesson for my son in conservation. The author (holding the tusks) is 1,86m tall; this would make the larger of the tusks about 2m long.

marks showed that Dzombo's killers had been busy removing them when they were spooked off the kill. Ampie concluded that the poachers had either heard the sound of his approaching vehicle or seen his labourers climbing on to one of the windmills, and had then fled back empty-handed to Mozambique.

The Shawu I knew was named after the Nshawu Valley, along the Nshawu Spruit, which originates in Mozambique and passes through the Lebombo Mountains at Shilowa. When I was stationed at Mooiplaas during the first part of 1974 I found a huge pair of tusks, which I believed were Shawu's, near the Nshawu picnic spot along the Shabarumbi Spruit, and so I was rather surprised when in 1980/81 Anthony Hall-Martin identified an elephant we knew as Lang Haaktand ('Long Hook-Tooth' in Afrikaans) as the Shawu of 'Big Seven' fame. I had no photographic or other evidence to the contrary, however, and Lang Haaktand metamorphosed into the famous Shawu.

During one of our regular encounters I noticed that Shawu's condition was deteriorating. I contacted Anthony, and next day we set out by helicopter to seek him out. We failed, even though, strangely, we could pick up a signal from his radio collar, but next day a cloud of vultures pointed the way to his body. Now we knew why we had not been able to find him: we had been looking for a live elephant, and he had already died. The cause of his death was a number of infected wounds which could have been caused by bullets. We chopped out his tusks and took them back. They were truly awesome. One was 3.17 metres long and weighed 52.5 kilos, and the other was 3.06 metres and weighed 50.8 kilos; as far as I know they rank third and forth on the list of the longest elephant tusks ever recorded.

Kambaku (Tsonga for a solitary elephant bull) was the only one of the Magnificent Seven that didn't live around Shingwedzi. The largest of the large, with an almost matched pair of tusks that later weighed in at an astonishing 63.6 and 64 kilos, he frequented the southern Lebombo plains between the Crocodile and the Sabie rivers, from where he made periodical forays into the cultivated areas. Kambaku's life of crime ultimately cost him his life. A trigger-happy individual wounded him in the leg while he was out on one of his raids; it was impossible to treat his wound, and, knowing what lay in store for him, we reluctantly decided to put him down. When we performed an autopsy on his enormous body we found several healed wounds from bullets he had collected during his wanderings in the cane-fields.

The only member of the Magnificent Seven that I had no personal acquaintance with was the bull called Ndlulamithi, whose remains were found about 20 kilometres west of Shingwedzi in July 1985, the tusks weighing in at an impressive 64.6 and 57,2 kilos. Was he the one and only Ndlulamithi of Magnificent Seven fame? I am not absolutely sure. The name 'Ndlulamithi' is often bestowed on very large elephants by the people of the Lowveld, so there could have been any number of animals by that name in different places at different times.

*

João, the Portuguese equivalent of 'John', was the last of the Magnificent Seven, and I have special memories of him. He took his name from a place where he was frequently spotted, the João Windmill close to Shingwedzi, which commemorated João Albasini, a pioneer Lowveld hunter and trader. One memory concerning João reaches back to the day he gave me a graphic demonstration of just how awesomely strong a large elephant really is. I was on a helicopter reconnaissance flight while preparing for a culling operation, and spotted João standing bolt upright, fast asleep, with his very considerable tusks and enormous head supported by the fork of a sjambok pod tree. His slumber was so deep that he was totally unaware of our approach until we were virtually overhead. Then he woke up with such a start that he uprooted the entire five-metre-high tree in an effort to swing his head around to see where we were. It was a salutary demonstration of sheer physical power, and it was just as well that João, like many of the really big guys, was generally good natured – although when he was feeling his oats, for example during musth, he was not averse to occasionally 'revving' a tourist car or two.

Keeping tabs on João by technological means was not easy as he wore out no fewer than four radio transmitters, one after the other. Why the rate of wear and tear on his transmitter was so high was just one of those bushveld mysteries. The radio collars, incidentally, were also believed to deter poachers, but I didn't see why this should be so, and João provided proof that I was right when I darted him to change one of his much-abused collars and found he had four bullet wounds. Fortunately we managed to catch them in time, and thanks to treatment with long-acting drugs João survived. He faded into obscurity, like an old actor whose name disappears from the cinema billboards when his looks vanish. His public career began to decline in the latter part of 1984 when he snapped off both his tusks, probably in a fight with another bull. After that we didn't keep any real track of him, since he was no longer in any particular danger from poachers; he was last seen in 1986, the sole survivor of the storied band of tuskers which touched the hearts and imaginations of millions of people around the world.

So there you have the Magnificent Seven, as varied in their appearance, personalities and ultimate ends as any similar-sized group of human beings. They might be gone but they will never be forgotten, and certainly not by my generation of Kruger rangers. They were not the last of the big tuskers in the Kruger National Park; several others have come and gone since their time, and yet others will appear, because the Magnificent Seven may have turned to dust, but their genes survive. All we have to do to ensure that the children of the Magnificent Seven continue to make the nation proud is to see that they are allowed to grow old, safe from those who, for the sake of a paltry sum of money, would turn them into nothing more than a heap of gigantic bones lying forgotten somewhere in the veld.

6

CLOSE-UP CONVERSATIONS
WITH LIONS

Lions seem to inspire most people with equal parts of admiration and fear; admiration because they are such magnificent animals, and fear because they have such a reputation for fierceness and aggression. It's not an entirely accurate picture. Being basically lazy animals, like all cats, they aren't as consistently dangerous or aggressive as most city people seem to believe, or as hooked on human flesh as one would think from watching certain movies. Yes, they'll eat people if they're hungry enough, or can't find or catch game, but it's nothing personal, you might say – to a lion a human is just another food source, no different from a buck it catches, some smaller predator's fresh-killed prey that it has hijacked or even some fairly gamey carrion it has found in the veld. How a lion reacts to humans all depends on the circumstances, and that is when it helps to know which situations to avoid and how to handle the ones that can't be avoided. A good dose of old-fashioned luck doesn't do any harm either.

My earliest close-up conversation with a lion took place in 1971, in the company of the redoubtable mapoisa Philemon Chauke, at the very start of my career in the Kruger National Park. It evolved out of a routine task, changing the batteries of one of the lions' radio collars, but in the bush routine tasks sometimes transform themselves into something else altogether, and this was one of those occasions.

At first all went well; I darted the lion several times in the shoulder and he hit the ground, filled to the gills with Ketamine. Just to be doubly careful we approached him in the vehicle instead of on foot, and when we were alongside I threw a rifle bag at him to make extra sure he was in dreamland. The lion did not so much as twitch, and we got out to change the batteries in the collar – painfully, in my case, as I was very gammy in one leg from a rugby injury incurred the previous Saturday. I bent over to undo the collar, and all of a sudden the allegedly comatose lion woke up and gave me a healthy belt with his fore-paw which sent me flying into a patch of *Acacia borleae* scrub, better known as sticky thorn. A sticky thorn bush is an unpleasant customer at the best of times, since it has many stems armed with straight white thorns up to 45 millimetres long, but there was no time to be sorry for myself, because the lion was plainly keen on making a closer acquaintance.

I streaked towards the Land Rover with the lion in hot pursuit, both thorns and gammy leg forgotten. As I neared the vehicle I felt a touch on my shoulder that gave me no cause for comfort in the circumstances, but it wasn't the lion, which, unbeknown to me, had passed out again. The touch I had felt was Chauke, who had passed me and was using my shoulder as the launching pad for a gravity-defying leap to relative safety on top of the Land Rover. Rather shakily we went back and changed the batteries as required, then sat and waited for the lion to recover. I passed the time treating my wounds, which were considerable (if non-lethal) for such a swift interlude: the sticky thorn had torn up my arms and legs, and the lion's claws had left me with a sizeable gash in my side and a couple of cracked ribs. The gash was easy to treat, although I still bear the scar, but the ribs gave me hell for a couple of weeks. No doubt it all provided fresh material for Chauke's extensive fund of veld tales.

On another occasion we were catching lions when an irate male climbed on to the back of the Land Rover to get at us. Chauke's first reaction was to try to kick the lion off the vehicle, which didn't have much effect, probably because he only weighed about 50 kg and wasn't even wearing boots, just a pair of soft velskoene. However, he retained enough presence of mind to pass me a spade that we always carried in the back, and so while Chauke was distracting the intruder with his size 6 vellies I had an opportunity that – thankfully, in retrospect – seldom occurs in a lifetime, namely to knock an angry lion senseless with a shovel.

*

In my years in Kruger I saw a distinct modification in the behaviour of the Park's lion population. When I first started working there they had tended to be wary of humans, like most lions elsewhere in Africa. Then from the mid-1970s onwards their attitude began to change for the worse when the political instability in Mozambique resulted in thousands of people seeking refuge in South Africa by hook or by crook. Many of the refugees passed through the Kruger National Park, which shares a 300-kilometre boundary fence with Mozambique and about 50 kilometres' worth with Zimbabwe; some made it, some died of hunger and thirst, and some – one can only guess at the number – were killed by wild animals.

Whether they made it or not, however, the constant movement of people on foot brought about a change in lion behaviour. The lions became so accustomed to humans that in certain areas the prides were not only unafraid of human voices but became actually attracted to them. This was bad news, given the fact that in the right (or wrong) circumstances lions can be ferociously aggressive in any case, whether they are wary of humans or not. Just how aggressive I learnt one frenzied Saturday morning when I was still a young ranger living in the 'Ramkamp' single quarters at Skukuza, long before the exodus from Mozambique had made them overly familiar with humans. I was lying on my bed in the minimum of clothing, wrapped in pleasant anticipation of a day's rugby and other forms of recreation, when one of the mapoisas, Corporal Japie Mangane, burst in without ceremony. The Chief Ranger, Don Lowe, wanted to see me right away, he said.

Instantly I was up and pumping adrenalin, which is what you did when you were a 23-year-old new boy and the formidable 'Kushumu' (meaning big and strong, the mapoisas' name for him) crooked a finger at you. In Oom Don's vocabulary 'right away' meant you were supposed to be there already – dressed, armed and ready for anything. I didn't even put on my shoes, just set off at a flat run towards Oom Don's house. Scant minutes later I burst into his presence, Mangane-style. Oom Don informed me that lions had found their way into the enclosure surrounding the sewerage pump station next to the rest camp, where the Volkskas Guest House stands today. The how and the why was a mystery, then and later – they might have climbed over the fence after some prey animals or perhaps they had wanted to get to the river to drink water – but that was not Oom Don's immediate concern, which was that the place was crammed with tourists who needed protecting.

Oom Don gave me the gist of this almost in less time than it takes to write it, then sent me on my way with the usual detailed instructions Kruger rangers used to receive: 'Sort it out!', which he kindly amplified by telling me to dart them and then get them back in the veld to sober up. I grabbed my basic working tools from my room – dart gun, some darts loaded with immobilising drugs and my rifle – and Japie and I set off for the pump station. It was only about 100 metres down the road from the Ramkamp, but we went the long way around through the rest camp itself, my reasoning being that if I started working on the lions from that direction and they jumped the fence, which was only about a metre high, they would head for the village, the river or the veld, rather than the rest camp.

What I saw when we arrived at the pump station frankly terrified me. An entire pride of 12 lions of all sizes was trapped inside the pump station's flimsy enclosure and growing angrier by the second. What made this bad situation even worse was that not 10 metres beyond the enclosure was a large and constantly growing crowd of fascinated tourists, getting ever closer to the wire as reinforcements pushed forward from the back. And just to add a little more fuel to my despair, ever-increasing numbers of staff members and their friends were coming up to their side of the enclosure to watch the fun.

Fun? It was the precursor to a bloody massacre, and I mean 'bloody'. The lions were furious, launching one charge after another, only to be thrown back against the wire; I could see blood running down their faces where it had cut them. It was quite clearly only a matter of time before one of them broke through the fence. What would happen then literally did not bear thinking about by anyone who knew what an incredible amount of death and destruction just one lion could cause in a matter of seconds, never mind 12 all at once. The amazing thing was that no one, neither the camp staff (at least some of whom really should have known better) nor the tourists, seemed to have any conception of the deadly danger facing them. One idiot had not only left the safety of the group, such as it was, but was actually walking towards the fence with a baby held out in front of him, saying: 'Look at the lions, my boy, look at the lions.' I found it hard to believe that anyone could be so rash.

I did a swift – very swift – re-think. Although Oom Don had told me to dart the lions, things had obviously gone far beyond that. If only one lion escaped while I was darting, there would be blood and guts all over the place. In addition, the immobilising drugs did not take instantaneous effect, and if a lion is frightened or angry enough, an instant is all it needs to wreak mayhem. So the only thing I could do was to kill the whole pride. My first move was to get some distance between the lions and the onlookers and obtain a clearer field of fire, so I sent Japie to get the camp staff and their friends out of the way by saying that I was going to shoot the lions and that if they stayed there they had a good chance of being hit by a ricocheting bullet. At the same time I called on the tourists to move back because of the danger.

Our efforts were not all that successful. Some of the camp staff and hangers-on did move, but the rest stayed put. As for the tourists . . . no one took any notice of me! In all fairness, I did not exactly present an authoritative appearance – a bare-footed 23-year-old kid in a T-shirt and gym shorts. In desperation I took some executive action by firing a shot that was carefully angled away from the remaining staff so that the bullet would land in the river, and then the onlookers started getting the message at last, in no uncertain terms. By now the noise-level was horrific, a jumble of blood-curdling growls from the lions, the screams of fleeing staff members and friends, and confused shouting and more screams from the tourists. Amid all this distraction I somehow managed to shoot straight and killed all 12 lions as fast as I could aim and fire.

Oom Don arrived just after I had finished off the last one, a forbidding presence but also a comforting one, because I knew that he understood how I felt and what I had done. His only comment was: 'What would have happened if you'd wounded one?' I had no answer to that, and didn't even try to find one; there are some situations in which the dividing line between complete success and utter disaster is gossamer-thin, with absolutely no grey areas.

Two years later, at the annual rangers' party at Skukuza, Oom Don brought a bottle of brandy to our table, crushed the top, then sat down and said, 'We're going to finish this bottle before we go home tonight.' To be honest, I didn't really have a clue what he meant by this gesture then, but I think I found out later, on a rainy day at White River years later, when we carried Oom Don, alias Kushumu, to his eternal rest.

*

Lions are an irreplaceable part of the Kruger National Park's attractions, of course, but they often break out, and the almost inevitable consequence is a huge nuisance to all concerned, particularly if domestic livestock on the other side of the fence get turned into an alfresco meal. Sometimes it goes even further than that: in the 1980s some of these travelling gentlemen came across a burglar fleeing with his takings from the village of Marloth Park, on the edge of Kruger, and promptly ate him. This was a bit tough on the burglar, but in all honesty nobody had much sympathy for him, given the fact that Marloth Park instantly gained an enviable notoriety as an unhealthy place for people of that ilk.

The problem with such a break-out is always that there is no way of herding the lions back to the Park, and so inevitably they have to be killed; in one 18-month period early in my career, starting at the beginning of 1973, at least 26 lions were shot south of the Crocodile River. The breakers-out posed a particular problem to the provincial conservation officials, whose responsibility they became as soon as they crossed the Park boundary. Like all conservation officials these poor guys were under-funded and understaffed, and they often called on us for help, which, naturally, we were always willing to provide.

On one occasion three lionesses broke out and more or less took up residence at the Malelane Gate Lodge on the southern side of the Crocodile River. They didn't make a particular nuisance of themselves, but were a definite potential safety threat to the guests at the hotel. The area was unfenced, and having them wandering around the lawns of the lodge, the nearby Leopard Creek

Golf Estate and the farm Riverside was definitely not a positive factor as regards the well-being of the guests, not to mention the year-round inhabitants.

My great friend Tom Yssel, the ranger at Malelane at the time, and the provincial conservation officers from what was then the Eastern Transvaal Province (now Mpumalanga) tried repeatedly but unsuccessfully to track down the lionesses. At length the provincial officials were so desperate to see some positive action being taken before something terrible happened that they issued Tom and myself with a permit to shoot the lionesses on sight if the opportunity arose. Tom was the more likely of us to react to an alarm-call because his house was just three kilometres from where the lionesses were regularly spotted, but I had a large staff component in the area and often spent time with him, and, as fate would have it, I was visiting at his house when the Malelane Gate Lodge's manager telephoned after dark one evening to say that the intruders had taken over his front lawn again.

Tom and I went off with our spotlights and rifles, but by the time we got to the lodge the lionesses had passed out of sight. Neither of us felt like beating the darkened bushes of the hotel gardens, so we took advantage of our location to go and have a beer in the pub. We had not got more than half the beer down our throats, however, when a guest turned up with the news that the lions were taking their ease next to the hotel's access road. Regretfully we abandoned our beer and went to the indicated spot, where we found two of the lionesses and killed them. This done, we loaded up the carcasses and brought them back to the hotel, which virtually ceased to function for a while because everybody wanted to see, touch and smell the animals.

The Malelane Gate Lodge lioness saga was to have a rather nasty postscript a while later, when one of the managers at Riverside Farm allowed his son-in-law to shoot a kudu at a spot which, so Tom's mapoisas determined, was not on the farm's land but inside our boundary. We preferred charges against the son-in-law for hunting inside the Kruger Park and refused to withdraw them, even after heavy pressure was exerted on the Park, in the form of a threat to prosecute Tom and me for illegally hunting lions on Riverside Farm property. Being the local ranger, Tom was held primarily responsible. In due course he was called to appear before a team from the Park management and, to all intents and purposes, tried and found guilty on the illegal hunting charge. Now a clearer picture began to emerge. Obviously a mutually satisfactory deal had been negotiated at some level above our heads: the Park would withdraw the changes against the kudu poacher, and Riverside Farm would drop the lion hunting charge. Then everybody would be happy – except of course, the two pawns in the game, who had been let down so badly by their own side.

Tom knew that he was about to be drawn and quartered when the team asked him if he had anything to say in mitigation, but he and I still had one shot in our locker, in the shape of myself. To their surprise he said yes, he would like to call me to give evidence (I was standing by in my office just down the corridor for just such an eventuality). The team was baffled: apart from attesting to Tom's worth, what could I contribute? Well, more than a little, and when I appeared I gave them an ever bigger surprise than Tom had. First I pointed out that the access road where we shot the lionesses was on our side of the boundary, so we had done nothing illegal. Then I handed around the provincial conservation department's permit to shoot the lionesses. That fairly knocked the wind out of the kangaroo court's sails; the sick looks on the faces around the table showed that the trumped-up charge against us was as dead as the two lionesses. For a while Tom and I weren't too popular with either the Riverside Farm management or those of our own who had been ready to sell us down the river. We didn't spend too much time worrying about it, though; we had Africa's greatest game park to run, and for that you needed more than the ability to make back-stabbing deals.

*

My cousins Terry and Phillippa Watson have the unenviable distinction of twice coming up against the new-model Kruger lions. The Watsons and their two sons love Kruger, and used to come and visit us from time to time for a round of sightseeing, braaiing and family tennis matches (the Brydens always lost, as far as I can recall). The Watsons' first encounter with the hard-arse modern lions occurred one afternoon while we were getting ready for a Sunday lunchtime braai at the gauging weir in the Sabie River, between Skukuza and the Kruger Gate. We had built a nice fire under an enormous sycamore fig tree about 20 metres from the river's edge, and now the steaks were sizzling over the coals while Helena and Phillippa were breaking out a bottle of first-class JC le Roux sparkling wine.

The food was almost ready and everybody was waiting in hungry anticipation – even my son Robert, who would normally be off angling by himself on such an occasion – when Helena detected movement about 40 metres away. At first she thought it was a group of impala, but then she looked again and saw a pride of nine lions walking along the sandy bed of a small spruit that entered the river near where we were. At that moment the lions became aware of us, and one lioness immediately sank down almost to ground level, her tail twitching from side to side in a classic sign of aggressive intent. When Phillippa saw all this she didn't hesitate for a moment before snatching up her children and legging it for the safety of my Toyota, where she insisted on eating lunch. You can call it an overreaction, if you like – the rest of us saw the close encounters only as a great experience – but Phillippa's reaction was exactly the same as that of any female with young in the Park's game population: save the children, then save yourself. The reaction of a rather more sensible person, I think, than that fool of 'look at the lions, son' fame.

A couple of years later we took the Watsons to a braai at this very same spot – no lions this time, only an elephant bull that didn't want to leave the area, so we joined him – after which I left to do some other things at Letaba, where the Watsons were to join me a day or two later. By the time we linked up again I had had a further lion encounter (what was it about these cousins of mine?). I was hosting the KwaZulu-Natal rangers I mentioned in the Foreword, and after work on the Monday headed for the river to do a bit of catch-and-release angling at the same pool where Robert had hooked the biggest catch of his life with a ball of chicken liver (see 'The Hippo: Killer and Comedian'). We had hardly unloaded the truck when I saw a pride of lions about 300 metres away in the open area between us and the river's bank.

Normally this would mean that both we and they had enough personal space for peaceful coexistence, but not this time: the pride came straight for us at a fast trot. We did the normal shouting and waving that usually sufficed to make lions change direction, but they just kept on coming; it was as if the noise we were making actually egged them on, rather than deterred them. Then I realised that this was probably a pride that lived in the area and was known to have killed several people. Presumably it was our turn today: the pride's actions could be interpreted in only one way – they meant business, which, in turn, meant that we had to make dust.

We piled into the vehicle as quickly as we could and moved off. This improved our safety rating substantially but did not let us off the hook. Since we were still in the river bed, we still had to climb the bank to get away, and to do so we would have to drive directly past the rapidly approaching lions, not such a good idea because some of my colleagues were sitting on the back of the truck. We only had to cover about 70 metres to reach the relative safety of the upper plain, but that is a long distance when you have a pride of lions chasing you. Still, there was nothing for it. I put my foot to the floor (relatively speaking, given the difference between driving on a dirt road and tarmac) and off we went. The lions took note of this and altered course to intersect with us. Fortunately we were going just a bit too fast for them to head us off, and after a short but exciting ride we made it to safety with the lions remaining in a bitter-end hot pursuit that left no doubt in anyone's mind that we had been designated the main course on that day's menu.

A day or two later the Watsons arrived in Letaba as scheduled, and that afternoon I took them out to have sundowners at a particularly charming spot at the Engelhardt Dam. This spot was often used by the staff members themselves and had a well-defined path leading to it, the entrance being protected from unauthorised access by a steel cable hooked between two poles. We spent an enjoyable hour drinking our sundowners and generally chewing the fat, then loaded up to return to the rest camp. The Watsons' boys pleaded to be allowed to stand up in the back of the Toyota for the return trip, and I indulged them, since it was well after closing time and no tourist would see them. We had scarcely gone 40 metres, though, when we drove into a pride of lions. It was quite possibly the same ones that had chased the KZN rangers and myself earlier that week, and its members certainly made it clear that their intentions were exactly the same. This being the case, there was only one thing to do, and that was to put my foot down.

In a couple of moments we reached the barrier; obviously I couldn't stop to release the cable, so I drove around it with the lions still dogging our heels. One lioness was so determined to catch up with us that she took a short cut and ran straight into the cable with enough force to rip it loose from its supporting poles. All this we saw through the back window of the cab, and, as soon as we had convincingly outdistanced the pride, Phillippa insisted that we stop so that the boys could climb inside with us. Unlike their mother, they were exhilarated by the chase, and that night some remarkably tall tales were told at the supper table. Or perhaps I should say 'one tall tale'. The Watson boys could not get over their adventure and kept describing and re-describing it, and every time it was re-told the lions got bigger, the pride's numbers expanded and the distance between us and them got shorter. Their 'what I did this holiday' essays on returning to school must have been a revelation to the teacher who read them.

*

I prefer to write about things I have actually experienced, but there is an exception to every rule, and in this case it concerns another frightening but rather more amusing encounter with lions that took place at the Mokohlolo Dam, very early in my career. Chemical capture techniques were still in their infancy at the beginning of the 1970s, and during the winter of 1971 the Kruger management invited Jan Oelofse of Natal Parks, who had worked out an efficient technique for mass captures that involved the use of plastic sheeting, to come up and show us how he did it. Jan was happy to do so, and in due course arrived at Mokohlolo with a large entourage of staff, among them several Zulus, whom he had trained in the capture procedures.

The first run involved capturing zebras. We built bomas and

set up the nets, and our helicopter then stampeded the zebras into them. Unfortunately a few wildebeest were trapped in the capture boma as well, and thanks to their panic-stricken efforts to get out we soon had zebra bleeding from horn wounds wherever we looked. There was nothing for it but to shoot the wildebeest and the more severely injured zebra, then drag their carcasses out of the boma and deposit them some distance away. This was like Christmas to the labour staff, who had the insatiable meat-hunger typical of all Africans, white or black. They helped themselves freely to the meat, some of which they grilled on sharpened sticks at their cooking fires for that night's meal after hanging the rest in the branches of just about every tree in their camp.

The surrounding area has always been known for its large lion and leopard population, and at bedtime our people advised Jan's Zulu staffers to follow their example and spend the night in the tents, because they knew very well that the meat hanging in the trees was bound to attract predators. The Zulus scorned this advice: they would sleep next to the fires, they said, as they were accustomed to doing in Natal. In part this was due to sheer ignorance – they had no knowledge of lions' habits because there were none in any of the Natal parks at that time – and in part to the fact that they considered themselves a cut above the Shangane tribe from which the Kruger staffers originated.

Sure enough, the din created by the day's activities and the smell of raw meat and stomach contents attracted the attention of a group of lions, so that night they strolled casually into the camp to help themselves to the meat hanging from the trees. Lions being anything but silent feeders, one of the Zulus woke up, apprised himself of what was happening and let out a piercing scream which not only woke up his comrades but led to a stampede by the fireside sleepers to reach the safety of the nearby transporter trucks. The lions ignored all the hubbub and simply carried on eating till their bellies were full, after which they strolled away as calmly as they had strolled in, leaving the Shanganes undisturbed in the tents and the Zulus huddled inside one of the transporter trucks in an understandably unsettled frame of mind.

Next morning the Zulus were distinctly subdued; the Shanganes, on the other hand, looked distinctly pleased with themselves at their temporary colleagues' comeuppance, and that night rubbed a little more salt in the wounds by sitting around the fires, cheerfully consuming the meat that the lions had not been able to get at, after the Zulus had retired to their transporter.

I like this story because, unlike some others, it has a useful moral to it. In the bush, pride goeth before a fall, and if you're lucky you will only be cast down and not dragged away and eaten.

The funny thing was that the rangers knew nothing about any of these nocturnal goings-on because our camp was located some distance away from the labourers'. This was just as well, seeing that it had been a sociable evening for everyone, although less so for myself on account of the fact that I had been stung on the hand by a scorpion and was hurting a trifle. Apropos of nothing in particular, for years afterwards the spot where the scorpion's sting went used to tingle whenever I held a cold beer in that hand. Whether this was because the cold somehow activated some residual poison, I can't say. But either way it was altogether a less frightening keepsake of that trip than the memories Jan's Zulus took back home with them.

Decades later I returned to this very spot for some weekend family camping – lions and leopards apart, the Mokohlolo Dam is famed for the number of game species that come to drink there – and damned if I didn't have another lion encounter of the less pleasant kind. We had two guests with us, my old friend Rudi Sippel, Kruger's head of maintenance, and his wife Loretta. Rudi, who was about to retire after 30 years of service, had never spent a single night in the veld in all his time in the Park, and I decided that it would be bordering on sacrilegious for him to depart without having put things to rights. Rudi and Loretta agreed with this reasoning, not knowing what they were letting themselves in for (I didn't know either, of course). Our plan to spend a Friday-to-Sunday long weekend in the veld was delayed at the last minute when Rudi had to resolve a late-breaking labour dispute among the maintenance staff, but by Saturday morning we were bowling down the Lower Sabie road with my caravan hitched on to my Toyota and Rudi following in his own truck. Here Rudi got an early initiation into the unique, if sometimes frightening, delights tourists enjoyed. As was usual at that time of year the road was packed with cars, which at the time of our arrival were heavily engaged in getting out of the way of a herd of elephants moving in our direction with their usual lordly unconcern for the occasions of lesser mortals.

I didn't take much notice of all this – the elephants weren't in an aggressive mood – and kept moving forward through the crush, which no doubt seemed an insanely foolhardy action to my fellow motorists. At one stage we passed a stationary car facing in the direction from which we had come, occupied by a wide-eyed driver and an obviously terrified family; the driver threw some remark at us as we passed, and Robert, who was sitting in the rear seat of the Toyota, pulled himself up and said, 'Dad, did you see what that guy said? He said: "Are you f . . . mad?"' Robert was already in high school, but this was the first time we'd ever heard him swear, and Helena nearly fell out of the Toyota in sheer astonishment. Mentally I tipped my hat to him: he'd virtually grown up in culling and hunting camps in the company of tough bushvelders who didn't mince their words, so it must have taken considerable strength of character to rein in his vocabulary in our presence for so many years.

I don't know if Rudi took the right lesson to heart – namely that the Park belongs to the animals rather than the humans in it – but he got another opportunity that night, and this time the message came through loud and clear. At the campsite we got the caravan rigged for the ladies and for Robert, Rudi and myself we pitched a tent alongside, one of those flimsy three-by-three nylon jobs with just enough space inside for our three stretchers. The basic housekeeping done, we went off to enjoy ourselves. We came back well before sundown, by which time lions were roaring all around us at ever closer range. We were all tired, and after supper the three menfolk left the caravan to the ladies and retired to the tent. It was a bit of a squash, as I've said: Rudi's and Robert's stretchers were along the sides, while I lay across the entrance, which was only covered by a mosquito net zipped to the main tent structure because as usual I liked as much fresh air as possible.

But we weren't fated to have a restful night. The lions we had heard earlier must have planned a reunion of some sort at our campsite, and the fact that we had set up there first didn't worry them at all. They roared, squabbled, growled, knocked over chairs and rubbed up against the tent and, from what Helena and Loretta told us later, the caravan as well. At one stage a lion actually lay up against the tent, so that the wall bulged inwards. This was a bit much, so I gave the bulge a hefty kick, at which the lion growled but moved away.

It was a pretty rough initiation into the delights of outdoor life in Kruger, and Rudi was understandably terrified (so were Robert and I, but we weren't going to let on to Rudi). Eventually he said, 'I've had enough. I'm going to get into the truck.'

'Rudi,' I asked, 'how are you going to get there?' It was a provocative but reasonable question. Rudi's truck was parked about 10 metres from the tent. That qualifies as a long and dangerous trek when you have a bunch of lions in between. Rudi acknowledged the good sense of it, although not in words which are really printable in a decent book, and went back to his stretcher while the lions carried on making the night hideous.

By dawn the visitors had left to go and sleep off their partying. I ventured out, did a quick check and declared the campsite lion-free. A somewhat baggy-eyed Rudi emerged from the tent and went straight to the cool box on the back of his truck, where he filled a beer glass with schnapps and did a bottoms-up. Rudi being a German and all, this fearsome Teutonic pick-me-up had the desired effect.

*

Is the Kruger lions' attitude towards humans likely to change? That's anybody's guess, but I would say certainly not in the short term. In the past few years the refugees from Mozambique have dwindled, but they are still coming and they have been augmented by others from Zimbabwe, whose gradual implosion has left many thousands of its people with a stark choice between starvation and running the Kruger National Park's gauntlet. When the flow stops it might be different, but to judge from the Mozambican experience Zimbabwe is going to be on its uppers for a long time, even after it eventually reaches the turn-around point.

That's bad news for everyone concerned – including the lions. The animals might be the first-class citizens in the Kruger National Park, but humans are in control of it. So it is quite possible that at least some lions are going to be destroyed because they have picked up bad habits deriving from the consequences of decisions taken far beyond its boundaries.

7

POACHING AND
COUNTER-POACHING

There is not one game ranger in Africa who hasn't had to struggle with poaching. If he denies this, either he and his field staff can't spot the problem or, which is much worse, his field staff don't want to. Africa will always be hungry because of its ever-increasing population, and protected game areas will always be a tempting source of food for the empty stomachs outside the boundaries. The growth of the human population also stimulates the desire for land, and that is when nature conservation goes out through the back door. The 17-year-old 'veterans' of a war that ended almost 30 years ago in Zimbabwe are proving that for us.

This is not a new phenomenon by any means. One of the causes of the French Revolution was the rural inhabitants' irritation at not being allowed to hunt, and it is not surprising that one of the first privileges the nobles had to abandon was this one. In all revolutions, one of the first things that the people have done was to jump over or tear down fences protecting game and then hunt them down in the pursuit of what they see as social justice.

Apart from the fact that Africans in general struggle to accept conservation measures developed by the Western world, there are just too many empty stomachs and too few people with sufficient knowledge of how to produce enough food to balance the equation. Subsistence farming can only feed a limited number of people on a continent plagued by drought, disease and other afflictions, and inevitably this leads to a 'help yourself' philosophy. The nature of this 'help' can be anything from a cash-in-transit robbery to (in the context of this book) setting a few snares or launching a full-scale onslaught on an area where game is protected, be it a farm or a reserve. The fact that in the last case there is usually nothing left afterwards is not a consideration, because a person who is hungry today cannot afford to think too deeply about tomorrow. This is true not only in Africa but in all other poor, overpopulated parts of the world. It is just as true that where there is something to poach there are unscrupulous people whose motivation is not feeding themselves but exploiting the overwhelming need of the deprived for their own gain . . . and, let it be said, mainly at little risk to themselves unless they become too greedy. Essentially they create a demand that would not exist but for their own cupidity.

Thus there are two distinct kinds of poaching. The most basic and least harmful form is subsistence poaching. The subsistence poacher's aim is to keep himself and his family alive, and he practises a utilitarian form of hunting that has not changed since the time of Palaeolithic man: he takes what he needs and leaves the rest. I could almost live with this, because in its pure form it is sustainable, but times have changed, and living off the land in this age-old way simply can't work anymore; there are just too many mouths to feed.

A related sub-category is what might be called 'sport poaching'. Unlike subsistence poachers, sport poachers have always tended to be of the rather better-off type. People like these hunt for meat or trophies or both, rather than out of sheer necessity, and the main difference between them and the average law-abiding hunter is that they pursue their activities in areas where game is protected, or out of season in legitimate hunting areas. They are a contemptible bunch, because they are not driven by hunger or even greed, and they cannot claim not to know what they are doing. All they are after is easy meat and the best trophies, and if either or both are to be found in a game park where they have been carefully nurtured, that's just too bad.

The commercial poacher is something else altogether. For him, poaching is not a question of either sport or survival but a way of making money by stealing from others. Whether he hauls the fish out of a trout farm's tanks or shoots protected elephants for their ivory, he is nothing but a common thief, with a thief's callous disregard for the rights and property of others.

*

The commercial poaching scenario can be depicted by visualising two equilateral triangles of risk and profit, positioned on top of each other to form a six-pointed star with an apex at the top and bottom. These two triangles have to function together, or there will be no gain for anyone. At the base of the risk triangle with the apex at the top of the star we have the field poacher who actually goes out to do the illegal hunting, at the risk of ending up in jail (which frequently happens) or, at worst, being shot dead in a skirmish with the rangers. Assuming he is not caught, he then takes the additional risk of transporting his goods to a dealer, who pays him next to nothing. The dealer then moves the illicit goods to another middle-man, who moves them to yet another way-station – the risk diminishing at each stage as the illicit goods move up the risk triangle – until they finally reach the end-user, who might be (in the case of rhino horn, for example) half-way around the world from where the poacher killed the animal. The profit triangle works exactly the opposite way, increasing all the way through to its apex at the bottom of the star. The hunter/collector level ventures everything for almost no reward, while the end-user – 'final seller' might be a better term – at the base of the triangle reaps the profits at little to no risk. The other four points of the triangles on the sides are spin-offs, and this is where the middle-men fit in.

The bottom line to this equation is that the entire process is based on illegally killing wild animals out in the veld, even if this eventually leads to their extinction. Stopping this malign process in its tracks is the task of game rangers everywhere. Sometimes they succeed and sometimes not, but they are the first – and usually only – line of defence against the two-legged predators

A successful method is not always the most obvious one. For example, I would fight to conserve merino sheep if there were ever a danger to their existence. Defending the existence of a hybrid domestic animal bred by man might sound like a strange course of action for a conservationist, but let me explain why. Farmers who raise merinos often keep some springbok as well, because they are nostalgic or like the novelty, or for any of several other reasons. But if they can't afford to farm with merinos they certainly would not be able to afford to keep some game either, so exit the springbok. But if merinos are there to gladden the pocket and springbok to gladden the heart, man and beast alike score from the deal.

Rhino have pretty much been wiped off the face of Africa north of the Zambezi, and are tottering at extinction level between the Limpopo and Zambezi rivers. This dreadful situation is not going to get any better in the foreseeable future, since most of the few remaining rhino are on private land which is being redistributed by the Zimbabwean government. But it is a futile gift, as the recipients will soon begin to realise. Something that the Zimbabwean government has not taken into account is that the conservation areas are located where they are because the natural or available water supply is inadequate for cultivation or the soil is not suitable for growing crops. It will not be long before the relocated subsistence farmers start discovering this bitter truth. But by that time the game will be gone.

Good intentions can pose almost as great a danger as commercial poaching or government 'gifts' of unsuitable land to the landless. For example, in certain areas of southern Africa elephant are close to becoming a pest because of overpopulation that results in the destruction of vast areas of veld. But by international convention we are not allowed to cull them, so they keep reproducing and thus destroying the very environment that feeds them. It is surely a great irony that the very people who are striving to save elephants are also signing the environment's death-warrant in the areas where elephants are protected. I agree totally with Anthony Hall-Martin that the CITES ban on the selling of elephant products will not feed one single hungry African, while animal welfare organisations such as the Humane Society of America, although their intentions are totally sincere, will not prevent the ultimate downfall of the African elephant. Conservation in Africa cannot succeed unless it becomes a profitable business for the governments involved. The only solution would be to stop the politics and to get on with the work of conservation, which also involves culling when necessary.

That is the philosophical side of the poaching question. Actually dealing with it on the ground is a considerably more hands-on affair, as I discovered fairly early in my career at the

Kruger National Park, when I helped to bag (in the non-hunting sense) a posse of Mozambican poachers.

Mozambique has been a major factor in the Kruger National Park's problems with poaching for several decades. Sport poaching by Mozambicans dwindled to a great extent after the mid-1970s, but subsistence poaching – and commercial poaching by subsistence poachers – escalated from that same time-frame onwards as decades of war and economic mismanagement progressively impoverished the population. This is unlikely to change until Mozambique manages to drag itself out of the morass it created for itself between the 1970s and the mid-1990s.

My first encounter with poachers from Mozambique took place at Pumbe Pan, north of the Nwanetsi ranger's post and just west of the boundary fence, in my very early days at Kruger, when I was still engaged in the lion research programme. This Pumbe Pan is actually a typical bit of Africa-baffling, since the real Pumbe Pan is just over the border in Mozambique. The Kruger version of Pumbe Pan, incidentally, is one of the few places in southern Africa where one finds the killifish (*Nothobranchius* species) – a strange, beautiful little creature that lives in temporary rain pools, where the adult females lay the eggs, which survive the dry periods and then hatch when it rains again. 'Our' Pumbe was not particularly impressive to look at – a typical Lebombo rhyolite pan, probably no larger than a tennis court at maximum size – but it was a popular drinking place for game and thus was an equally popular venue for poachers, so that when there was a new moon on a weekend in late winter it was usual for people with spotlights and rifles to arrive from all over southern Mozambique to organise some easy meat.

I became acquainted with the goings-on at Pumbe when Jan de Kok, the district ranger at Satara, asked me to help him with a counter-poaching operation there because he felt it would give me some good experience. I was only too willing, of course, and so it came about that one evening Jan, Corporal Joe Rangane and I lay in wait at Pumbe. Sure enough, that night the poachers came into the Park and blatantly positioned themselves on the western side of the pan so that the game coming to drink wouldn't smell them because of the prevailing south-east wind, and couldn't flee east due to the ten-strand game fence. This trap worked both ways, however, because we came up from behind and took them to Skukuza in irons. Jan went even further, collecting their Land Rovers at the village near by and having them driven to Skukuza as well. This put a bit of crimp in the poaching at Pumbe, cost the poachers a few months' freedom and provided me, as Jan had foreseen, with some hands-on experience of the conservationist's greatest enemy.

In 1973 I had another and rather more hazardous encounter with non-subsistence poachers while I was stationed at Crocodile Bridge and Louis Olivier at Tshokwane. At this time the poaching was getting out of hand on the eastern boundary, just north of the Sabie River, with weekend forays from Mozambique by large parties of armed people. The Chief Ranger instructed Louis and me to do something about the situation, so we rounded up Sergeants Judas Ndlovu and James Chauke, Corporals July Makuvele and Amione Muzimba and a couple of other mapoisas, and headed for Mabakane, where we expected the poachers to come in. .

We had no real plan, except that we knew these fellows came in every Saturday, so we made sure we arrived at Mabakane long before dark and took up position around a little ravine where their spoor was occasionally found. Then we waited in the cold darkness, wrapped in our greatcoats. We could expect very little moonlight, which poachers prefer, but on the other hand there were large tracts of burnt veld, which were sure to be attractive because such areas were always heavily used by various species, especially zebra and wildebeest. The down-side was that the burnt patches would provide little or no cover to us; but there was nothing we could do about that.

In due course the poachers arrived, a very confident bunch who made no attempt at stealth but boldly parked their trucks next to the boundary fence and climbed over it into the Park. There were quite a few of them, including a few helpers carrying grain bags containing the car batteries that powered the shooters' spotlights. The poachers walked down the path directly at us, shining their lights around, looking for eyes to shoot at. It goes without saying that we didn't oblige; we kept our heads and all other parts of our bodies well down, and they didn't spot us, even though their spotlights' beams washed over us.

Louis and his men were concealed on one side of the path and I was on the other with my group, and when he gave the agreed-on signal we all got up, targeted them with our torches and told them to drop everything. They did: we had totally surprised them. They offered no resistance when we started handcuffing them, with the exception of one rash fool who belatedly went for a handgun but then swiftly changed his mind when Louis immediately took his front teeth out with his rifle-butt. This scuffle was the signal for general chaos, with the ones we hadn't handcuffed yet trying to escape in all directions while we tried to stop them without taking our attention away from the others. Short but fierce struggles followed – fortunately without any shooting – and although some of the unwelcome visitors managed to escape, we ended up with quite a good bag and were very pleased with ourselves.

Louis taught me a handy trick that I was later to employ to good effect on a number of occasions. If there are only a few of you and you have a large number of unwilling customers who have to be restrained and moved, don't fasten the handcuffs in the normal way. Instead, cross-fasten them, left hand to left hand and right hand to right hand, and as an added precaution against mass escape you make one or two of the captives walk backwards with his cuffed arms crossed over his chest. Thus encumbered, our captives were marched down the mountain, a journey that was frequently uncomfortable for them, and occasionally for us, because it was pitch-dark and not always easy to keep our footing. We arrived at the Skukuza police station just before sunrise, all of us slightly the worse for wear. A slight problem arose at this stage because we had lost half the handcuff keys in the initial scuffle, but Louis and I did not let this worry us over-much. We left them safely lodged in the tender care of the Skukuza station commander and went off for a quick shower to get rid of the dirt, sweat and blood we had acquired in the course of our little excursion. Then we went back to the police station, where the station commander had a nasty surprise for us: we would have to release our prisoners and take them back to Mozambique. To say that we reacted badly to these tidings would be an understatement. Having failed to budge the station commander, we pulled the Chief Ranger, Don Lowe, out of church and complained bitterly.

Oom Don went into instant rage mode and returned to the police station with us, but the station commander would not be moved and Oom Don's blood pressure reached gasket-popping level. The upshot of the ensuing fuss was that eventually a magistrate arrived from White River, took our statements and told us to appear in his court at nine o'clock next day. We considered this a satisfactory arrangement, our ill-temper subsided and Louis and I went off to lunch with the Park's instrument maker, Oom Gert van Rooyen, a virtuoso of the early crossbows used for darting animals, and his wife, Tant Sannie. All four of the Van Rooyen sons happened to be home, and we had a really convivial meal. Our confrontation with the Skukuza station commander hadn't spoilt my appetite, which was pretty powerful by now, and Louis was in much the same condition, so we did some heavy damage to the Van Rooyen food stocks before indulging in a much-needed nap. Later we had a few beers at the restaurant, frankly basking a little in the attention people paid us – talk of our mega-bust was on everyone's lips – and then got our heads down in preparation for the court hearing.

Next morning early we and the mapoisas left for White River with all the money we could gather, the intention being to give our testimony and then celebrate big time when justice had taken its course. That it would do so we didn't doubt for a moment. We had hordes of witnesses, rifles, lights, car keys, the lot; if ever there were certain convictions and some heavy sentences coming, this was it. We gave our evidence and, in a distinctly sanguinary mood, sat in the courtroom and watched the case against the poachers march remorselessly towards its inevitable conclusion. We did notice that on several occasions the magistrate was called out of the court by an orderly, but we took no special heed, although we'd never seen this happen before.

Then, around noon – disaster, unexpected and devastating. The magistrate abruptly adjourned the hearing and summoned us to his chambers, where he informed us that the charges were being withdrawn and that we had no further duties except to take the soon-to-be-former prisoners and their equipment back to Mozambican soil. Once we had recovered from our total shock, Louis and I refused point-blank to do any such thing. The magistrate said that we had no discretion in the matter: the poachers and their kit were to be released. To soften the blow he offered to buy us a beer and explain the situation to us.

Still half-stunned by this incredible reversal of fortune, we gave the mapoisas one of the trucks and what money we could spare and told them what the situation was. As flabbergasted as we were, they loaded up the poachers and left for the scene of the crime while we adjourned to the Glue Pot Bar. There the prosecutor joined us and told us why the prisoners had been released. It all came down to one word: politics. Our prisoners had included three senior Mozambican police officers, the head of security at the Maputo power station, the head of security at the Maputo oil refinery and oil storage depot and one or two others of similar ilk. So in the interests of international amity they not only got off scot-free after being trapped red-handed – not to mention after committing several other offences such as illegally crossing the border, threatening our lives with a dangerous weapon (Louis's toothless friend) and attempting to escape from custody – but got their rifles and spotlights back.

I don't think you can get over that kind of thing in one lifetime. If they had been ordinary Mozambicans with empty bellies they would all have gone to jail for a long time; so let nobody tell me there isn't one law for the rich (or influential, in this case) and one for the poor.

Two years later I was involved in another confrontation with Mozambicans, just after a couple of the most tiring days I have ever spent. On a certain Tuesday morning Dirk Ackerman and I set out to net tiger fish at Hatlane in the Letaba River, the aim of the exercise being to determine if they could, in fact, migrate upstream from the Engelhardt Dam, because none could be found in the pools of the fish ladder at the dam wall. In the process a silver barbel spiked Dirk in his Achilles tendon, the worst possible position for such an injury because there is very little blood flow in the area and there is no way to rest the wound except by staying off your feet. This turned out not to be an option, because a little later we saw smoke to the north and west of us, hurriedly exchanged our nets for fire-fighting equipment and headed for the blaze.

The conditions were ideal for a fire to get out of hand – it was hot and dry, with a hot north-west wind blowing – and the fire did just that. It took us until the afternoon of the third day to beat it out. At this stage two of our colleagues, Hans Meyer and Rhein Ernst, tracked us down to where we were catching a breather along the Letaba River and plied us with food, ice, water and beer, all of which went down extremely well. I was about to reach for my second beer when Rhein said, 'Lynn needs help. His fire is out of control.' I might have groaned aloud; I certainly did inside. Lynn, one of the two Van Rooyen ranger sons with whom we had had lunch the day before our disastrous bust-that-wasn't, was stationed at Shangoni, almost 160 kilometres away, and Dirk and I were absolutely exhausted. But the unwritten code was unambiguous, so we packed our kit and, feeling distinctly used up, set out on the long drive.

When we arrived at Shangoni, however, we saw no signs of a serious fire, so we went to Lynn's house to find out what was going on. There we knocked and knocked but couldn't raise Lynn. Unable to get inside because the door was locked, we ended up throwing pieces of firewood onto the roof to get him awake. That didn't work either, but I finally got his attention – and that of his self-loading shotgun – when I squeezed in through a kitchen window. At this point Lynn came marching down the passage, chambering a round while mumbling something unintelligible. I did some fast talking to identify myself and he opened the door to the rest of the house. His crisis was over, he said, and he was dead on his feet, so he would show us where to find the makings of coffee, and then he was going back to bed. Dirk and I were in about the same condition as Lynn, but we drank some coffee to kick us awake and then left for Mooiplaas to spend the last bit of the night at my house; we were so far gone in exhaustion that I was actually hallucinating – the road to Mooiplaas was mostly quite flat, but I kept hitting the brakes because it felt as if I were driving downhill. We arrived at Mooiplaas in the early hours of the morning, hit the blankets – or rather the sheets because it was very hot – and passed out cold.

Next morning, a Saturday, we finally arrived back at Letaba, where we were warmly welcomed by our wives – remember, we'd said goodbye to them on the Tuesday morning when we left for a project that was supposed to take only one day – and I leapt into the shower. I had scarcely finished towelling off when Dirk rolled up to report that word had been received that some Mozambican poachers were coming in through the Olifants River Gorge that night. Kissing goodbye to all thoughts of a leisurely weekend, we hastily re-packed our kit, collected our mapoisas and headed for the eastern boundary. We left the vehicle at the Ndunzi Picket camp, on the rim of the Ndunzi Gorge, and climbed down the mountain from there with all the necessary equipment, including a good supply of food, cold drinks, ice and beer from the restaurant that the camp manager had hastily packed into Willow cold boxes (Colemans were not available yet).

It's rough country around there, and we had to battle to get down the cliff and then through the Makoforo Spruit, but by late afternoon we had settled into an observation point on a high sandbank beneath the cliffs, shaded (and camouflaged) by a great fig tree. Although the spot was not quite ideal – we were immediately assailed by man-eating sand fleas that had obviously not tasted blood for some while – our field of observation was good, and before too long we sighted two poachers downstream, about a kilometre away, in a boat that looked more like a bath-tub with a small outboard engine attached. It was obvious that they were testing the engine and their spotlights while waiting for night to fall. So we sat tight. At last light they started their little engine and chugged upstream in our direction. We bided our time, our only fear being that they would find something to shoot before they had passed our position, but there were no crocodiles or hippos to be seen: quite probably our somewhat noisy journey to the sandbank had motivated all the usual residents to seek some peace and quiet further up-stream.

The intruders were almost inside our carefully laid trap when they somehow became aware of us and promptly turned the boat to head back downstream. I shouted at them in Portuguese, ordering them to stop, and Dirk told the mapoisas to shine the lights on them. This should have been enough but wasn't, so I shot away the boat's bow with my R1 service rifle. They were now in distinct danger of going down unless something concrete was done, but these two clearly knew about boats, because they moved to the stern to get the bow out of the water and then gunned the engine.

By now everyone was shouting at them to stop, and to make sure they got the message I fired a couple of shots into the water, only inches away from the boat. These shots across the bow were the last straw; they turned around again, headed for our sand-bank and beached the remains of their paltry vessel. This done, it was 'explain, please' time, and the explanation they had certainly was a sad one that rang true to us.

Mozambique was going downhill fast at this time, and, as is the usually the case, the availability of even the most common-place commodities had just about dried up. The would-be poach-ers, both stevedores in Maputo harbour, were not only in deep financial trouble but the child of one of them needed asthma medication, which was not obtainable in Mozambique at normal trade prices any more. So they had organised the boat and a 7x57 mm Mauser rifle, they said sadly, their intention being to shoot hippos and crocodiles in the Olifants River and sell their flesh in order to pay for the kid's medicine.

As I say, their story evoked some sympathy, but on the other hand we could not simply overlook what they had been doing. Yet what real benefit would there be in arresting and jailing them? Dirk and I discussed the matter and decided to use our initiative, so we stripped them naked, confiscated the rifle and the boat's engine and then pushed them and their boat back into the river to find their way home. We didn't talk about it afterwards, because what we had done was certainly not what 'the Book' demanded of us. But it still seems fair to me. They had not actually done any harm, and they had been driven by the most desperate need. So we had made sure that they couldn't do any harm, given them a good fright and seen to it that a sick child would not be deprived of its father in the middle of a civil war.

*

113

I might have created the impression that everything that came out of Mozambique was a threat to the Kruger National Park. This is not so, however, and here I think of a Portuguese named Martinez, whom I met during the first year of my stay at Mooiplaas during 1973. Martinez was a big shot in the Lourenço Marques/ Maputo business world, and a real conservationist who owned a large part of what is now the trans-frontier conservation area, which he protected with a field staff of rangers who were just as good as ours. I often visited him when he was staying at his cottage near the Park boundary, and we became good friends.

One day soon after Mozambique's independence Corporal Sandros Matsimbe came into my office and handed me a letter from Martinez asking that I meet him at a certain spot on the boundary at a given time. I went there, and what I saw made me deeply uneasy: his rangers with their Browning B5 semi-automatic shotguns were in a defensive position around his Land Cruiser. Our discussion was brief and did nothing to ease my mind either. The gist of it was that Martinez feared for his life and the lives of his family. Would I be prepared to take him to safety if this became necessary at a future date? I replied that this would be against the law, but if the need arose I would be willing to escort him to the South African security forces base in Phalaborwa. Martinez was satisfied with this assurance, and we agreed to exchange news on a weekly basis via our respective field staffs.

I never saw him again. Martinez's fears had been justified, because less than a fortnight later I received a handwritten note from one of his field staff, saying that he and his entire family had been killed on the runway of Maputo Airport when they were about to take off for the game ranch in their private aircraft.

It is bitterly ironical that what had been Martinez's wonderful game ranch was to become the springboard for the elephant poaching war we waged between the Shingwedzi and Letaba Rivers between 1981 and 1983. Some people might think it is going a little far to use the word 'war' to describe the long, hard struggle that was waged against poachers along the eastern boundary of the Kruger National Park from 1981 to 1983, but that is really what it was, albeit a low-intensity one. Most of the protagonists on both sides were trained soldiers, every encounter had the potential to turn into a fatal shoot-out and the lives of an entire population were at stake. Granted, the lives in peril belonged to elephants rather than human beings, but genocide remains genocide. This time the good guys came out on top, but only after desperate effort, much physical hardship, intricate planning, betrayal and, most important of all, a devotion to duty that often went far beyond what 'the book' expected.

The 'war' started during May 1981, when a number of elephant carcasses were found in the Mala Mala/Shintomaneni region north of the Letaba River, close to Kruger's eastern boundary, all shot and with the tusks chopped out. This was not really a huge surprise, because there was a civil war going on in Mozambique and it is a known fact that poaching has a tendency to increase in such times. At that time the South African Police were tasked with protecting the boundary between the Park and Mozambique, and had established two bases in the area between the Shingwedzi and Letaba Rivers which were staffed by a total of about 80 men.

The police had also undertaken to handle the poaching problem, and their commanding officers assured us that they were up to the task. The scoreboard showed a different picture, however, as did the spoor follow-ups we launched after finding fresh carcasses of tuskless elephants. In one particular incident, four poachers and two donkeys loaded with ivory walked through a police ambush in broad daylight without being apprehended. The SAP's excuse was that the ambush party's light machine-gun had jammed, but this did not explain why the ambushers did not make use of the three R1 self-loading service rifles they had between them – formidable weapons against human beings, particularly at close range.

In any event, that first year cost us 180 elephants, and those were only the ones we knew about. This was too much for me to live with, so I approached my two immediate seniors, reported in full on what was happening on the eastern boundary and asked them to back me in negotiations with the officer in charge of the SAP Counter-Insurgency Unit about taking over the anti-poaching actions on the boundary. They agreed and I approached the officer concerned. He proved to be very co-operative and not only

115

gave me the go-ahead but offered the SAP's on-going assistance and logistical support, which was to be a great help. We formally assumed the anti-poaching responsibility in February 1982, and immediately went on the offensive (and also a steep learning curve).

On 3 March we launched our first solo operation along the Makhadzi Spruit, where the poaching was the most severe, saturating the area with rangers and applying maximum pressure. Just seven days later the first three poachers were apprehended in their camp at Shivonekule, which means 'to see far' in Tsonga; indications were that they had been using it sporadically for a long time. In truth the bagging of the poachers resulted more from luck than anything else. The rangers had heard a shot, followed it up, found a spoor and then lost it again, and in their wanderings had more or less stumbled on the camp in the poachers' absence. They had then staked out the camp and grabbed the poachers when the latter returned.

Our early successes persuaded the poachers that we meant business, and soon they shifted their focus further north. Later operations proved that we couldn't rely on luck or our ability to follow a spoor. Time and time again our rangers would hear shots, follow them up and find they were too late: the poachers had already chopped out the dead elephants' tusks – which took only a few minutes – and set off back to Mozambique as fast as their legs could carry them.

We soon understood the need to do our homework, make careful preparations and, most important of all, maintain a very low profile. The most vital factor, however, was never to lose either the desire to catch the people who were stealing our elephants or the determination to carry on when things got tough. We managed to hang on to both. Part of the dogged sense of purpose stemmed from the physical, financial and mental loss the Park – and therefore we – had suffered, and also (perhaps the greatest single motivator) the sense of losing our personal space. A ranger's section or region is his personal stamping ground, to protect and preserve, and he feels intensely possessive about it and every living thing in it. From personal experience I know exactly how deep and strong this possessiveness is, and I retain a vivid recollection of the time

I had an outsider's view of it. This was the day I had to inform Flip Nel, the ranger at Pafuri when the poaching was at its height, that I had found a carcass on his section, lying in the Shilahlandonga Spruit, not 30 metres from the boundary fence. Although I knew how he felt I couldn't believe his reaction. The utter disbelief, the facial expression, the things he said: this couldn't be the Flip Nel I knew so well. Fortunately we were on motorbikes when I took him to the spot, so I didn't have to share the emotional stress that gripped him, and which I knew so well from my own experience in similar circumstances.

We needed every scrap of that motivation. The poachers were no pushovers. They were tough, fit and hard, mainly ex-soldiers, either former Mozambican government troops or South African insurgents living in exile over the border. They were bush-wise because mostly they had grown up living off the land, and they and their families were hungry and poor. In a nutshell, they were both equipped and motivated to stay alive. So we had to be, too, and moreover we also had to be better at their game than they were. I take off my hat to the rangers involved in those early operations. Most of us were over thirty, and some were in their mid-forties, but this didn't stop anyone from pitching in and mounting a maximum effort, constantly adapting techniques as our knowledge of the poachers' modus operandi expanded.

One of the early casualties was the rangers' long-established social life-style, which changed dramatically because all of a sudden we were spending long periods away from home, and not only those of us in the poacher-hit areas but also rangers from other parts of the Park who had to be drafted in because we were so thin on the ground north of the Letaba.

There were painful setbacks. I was running what appeared to be an efficient operation in other people's regions and sections, but on Christmas Day 1981 I was shattered when the first elephant was shot in my region, not more than 500 metres from the police base at Kostini. The second one was shot on Easter Saturday 1982, only five metres from the tourist road along the Shingwedzi River. The blacks have a saying which translates as 'my blood shivered', and that was exactly how it felt when I laid eyes on those huge mutilated corpses

We kept on learning new tricks of the trade – and discovering things about ourselves. At one stage we were foiled time and again because as soon as we moved into an area that was being actively hunted the poachers would stop and move elsewhere. There was obviously something fishy going on, but what was it? And meanwhile the frequency of our failures kept growing. Eventually we found the answer, and the final clue to the puzzle turned out to be something so obviously visible as to be virtually invisible – little shreds of cloth tied to the boundary fence, which I had seen on various occasions but ignored because I had assumed they had been left there by the fence-repair team.

The first clue was a deserted poachers' camp that Piet van Staden and I came across along the Nzobfori Spruit, near the eastern boundary. There we found the remains of the type of ration packs issued to our mapoisas, including Boxer tobacco packets and matches, and the same brand of torch batteries that we gave our staff – none of which were available in Mozambique. This could only mean that some mapoisas were in cahoots with the poachers, and a day or two later our suspicions were confirmed by intelligence sources working independently during the saturation operations. At that time many of the mapoisas on the eastern boundary were Mozambicans with family ties across the border, and it turned out that they were not only informing their relatives and friends of our activities by way of the shreds of cloth tied to the wire but actually crossing the border to spread the news of where we would be operating.

Thus armed, we changed our tactics. We did not do the obvious thing by cracking down on the mapoisas; instead we used them against themselves. After we had completed the overall planning for an operation I would summon all the rangers and mapoisas to brief them on procedures, tactics, time and place. This done, I would inform them that I was going on leave, nominate the ranger in charge during my absence and load my car with fishing rods and other supposedly necessary items in full view of anyone who cared to look. Helena would then drive me to an agreed rendezvous where I would meet up with the rest of the party of 'anglers.' As soon as we had gathered we would hide the fishing gear, haul out our backpacks and R1 rifles, and head for a suitable spot to establish an observation point. For the next week or two we would be out of sight of the mapoisas and, more importantly, out of mind.

For a while our success rate climbed meteorically, but this couldn't and didn't last for long, because the lack of information going out to the poachers didn't stop them from operating. They knew that we were very thin on the ground and just kept on coming – in fact, they probably intensified their activities. But so did we. Once again we changed our style of operations, going in with smaller groups and for longer periods. It was a classic cat-and-mouse game. We couldn't move around very much, because every time they found out that we were in an area they would move out, so we had to hide our activities very carefully and exercise plenty of patience.

Each of us had our own techniques, but generally speaking the first step would be for the section ranger to identify areas where the risk was high or poacher activity had been detected. He would then go in – alone, most of the time, without the knowledge of his field staff – to reconnoitre, trying to work out which routes were being used and how often, and identify the poachers by their footprints. The next step would be to cache food and water in the area, after which a two-man team would take position at an observation point.

The secret at this stage was to move around as little as possible and, if movement was absolutely necessary, to try not to leave any spoor. I went barefoot most of the time, and it paid off, although this was only possible on the plains of the northern mopani veld, which is not known for its thorn trees (unlike the Lebombo Mountains, where duwweltjies, or devil's thorn, make it hard even to walk in boots). This precaution was particularly important because merely encountering the spoor of two or more people, especially if they were wearing boots, would be enough to make a poaching party flee the area. A single set of barefoot prints was far less likely to be regarded as a threat.

Every now and then I would circle back on my own spoor to see if anyone was following me; I don't think this ever happened, but more than once I found proof that my stratagem worked when I saw that a group of poachers had crossed my spoor, examined it and then obviously ignored it and went on. Why should they worry about a single barefoot person? Clearly it could not be the rangers – perhaps it was just some other poacher. I often followed poachers' spoor even when it was several days old, just to keep my skills sharp and to see what they were up to and where they went. Every time they crossed or found a booted patrol spoor they would show alarm, while finding my spoor elucidated no reaction. The funny thing was that all the poachers we followed or found wore boots or shoes. To quote singer Johnny Clegg, 'The days of mapashanes and bare feet are long gone.'

We spent many long hours confined in the cramped lookout and observation posts, and every ranger found his own way of passing the time in a way that also let him stay alert. Ted Whitfield made wooden objects, Johan van Graan did leather work and I read. On one long day I read James Michener's *The Covenant* from cover to cover. That should tell you something. My longest solo observation post stint was a 17-day stretch I spent at a waterhole, and I learnt a lot during that time – about myself, but also about the creatures with which we share this earth and the natural phenomena that regulate our existence. Ants, birds, animals, even clouds. All of these creatures ran like clockwork, while the clouds, as clouds will, went their own way.

During that long period of solitude I discovered a few things about animals' powers of observation, too, and their adaptability to new circumstances. I had thought I was well hidden, but tsessebe could spot me from at least 500 metres away, and spent hours each day making sure I was not hostile. The white-headed vultures who came in every afternoon between twelve and one o'clock to drink never acknowledged my presence, but the francolin did: they would stop about 50 metres away and take a good look at me before moving on. The elephant bulls that visited the waterhole were very wary on the first few days, but after that I could have been Lot's wife for all they cared. The plentiful zebra and wildebeest likewise didn't mind my presence at all. My observations led me to change my mind about kudu: I concluded they were rather stupid, which is contrary to what everyone who has hunted them has to say, because they didn't seem to notice me at all.

Getting lost in the bush was part of the war. Some of my readers might be surprised that veteran rangers like my colleagues and myself managed to lose themselves at times, but occasionally it happens to everyone who works in the wide open spaces of Africa, Europe, Asia or America, or journeys through the largest 'continent' of all, the seven seas. 'Getting lost' is possibly not the most accurate term to use. The legendary American mountain man Davy Crockett was once asked if he ever had been lost and replied: 'No, but I have at times been confused for a week or two.' That pretty much sums it up. When that happens you have to get your wits together so that you can work things out and point yourself towards your destination. There are exceptions to this, of course, and most field people will admit that overcast days are a bitch, while cloudy nights are real nightmares, and if you're walking with your eyes on the ground to follow a spoor you are likely to become confused sooner or later.

Nearly every person has a natural tendency to pass obstacles on the same side, and inevitably it causes one to veer off to one side or the other. This is why you read or hear so often of people who are lost ending up back where they started. Staying on course isn't difficult if you have a distinctive landmark, even a distant one, to act as a marker, but in the almost trackless bushveld plains, especially on days where the sun isn't visible, even the experts are liable to fall into Davy Crockett's 'confusion'. During the time of the elephant-poaching war we had more than enough opportunity to get lost – and a few times we did, always for the reasons I have just described.

During one three-week operation my colleagues Flip Nel and Piet van Staden and I, each of us accompanied by a partner from the South African Police, manned different observation points north of the Shingwedzi River. On the late afternoon of the sixteenth day my partner and I apprehended three poachers and called out the policemen from the Kostini base to collect them. This they did, and were thoughtful enough to bring along two cases of cold beer and some scrumptious-looking rump steaks as a reward. At my request they took us and our meagre kit to where Flip and Piet were camped so that we could celebrate our success. At first they were furious that I'd blown their cover; so I had, but it was pretty academic, since the group we had been after were now out of harm's way. So we made short work of the steaks and most of the beer, and worked out a new operational plan. We still had four days left on our deployment schedule, so we decided to stay together and work the very thickly bushed area to the north of us along the Nkulumbeni and Nzobfori Spruits, also known as the Masbambela Sandveld; during the planning phase of the operation we had found signs of poacher activity there as well, and thanks to the arrests we now had time to extend our activities.

The next day was cloudy, with a light drizzle, and we were tempted to stay put and relax while we finished digesting the treats of the previous day. After due consideration, however, we reluctantly started packing up; we had no tents for shelter and so were going to get as wet doing nothing as walking. This didn't take long, since we had very little with us, and before long we moved out in a loose formation that allowed us to keep one another in sight most of the time. In the lead were Flip and Piet, who were confident about their knowledge of the area. Every so often we would stop for a smoke-break and chat, then move off again.

As time passed I began to get a distinct impression that we were moving in a circle, which is not really a problem if you are doing it on purpose, but something else again if you are supposed to be going somewhere specific. The feeling got stronger and stronger, and by mid-morning I was so convinced that about it that I raised the matter with Piet and Flip at the next smoke break. They pooh-poohed the idea; they were pretty confident that they knew where they were, they said. I remained unconvinced – the surroundings looked very familiar to me – so I went for a little walk-around while the others sat and smoked, and soon I found what I was looking for: the dottle that Flip had cleaned out of his pipe about four hours earlier. I called Flip over to show him. He was stunned, but soon recovered his confidence and maintained that he knew how to get us back to the camp. Three hours later we crossed our own spoor again, very near to where we had found the pipe-dottle. I pointed it out to Flip for the second time, and he conceded that he was lost. Piet was no help, because by now he was thoroughly confused. We set off again in the supposed direction of the camp, trailed by three very apprehensive policemen. A couple of hours later we were back at Flip's pipe-dottle once more.

My personal feeling was that we were less than 30 minutes from our old camp, and that if we crossed the firebreak road at more or less the right place the camp would be only a few hundred metres further on. We set off once more, crossed the road and walked boldly down an elephant path, too tired by now to worry about stealth or subterfuge, and found ourselves on the threshold of the old camp. We killed the last few beers and had a good chuckle or two about our fiasco, but, as always, there was a good object lesson to be found in our day's worth of sweaty and fruitless wanderings: even an old hand can be caught out by the bush.

Piet and I had a similar experience in the Masbambela Sandveld on a later occasion, when one of the counter-poaching groups heard shots shortly after dark one evening. We decided to react very early next morning, and so at two o'clock Piet and I were taken by truck to a spot about ten kilometres from where we calculated that the shots had been fired, in the vicinity of a camp known to have been used by poachers in the past. Our plan was to walk along the road until we got close to where we thought the shots had been heard, wait for light and then move in on the poachers. Either way we would be picked up at a prearranged spot on the eastern boundary around noon.

Walking in Kruger at night is always a nerve-racking business, especially when the road you are using is lined with thick bush, but we finally reached our jumping-off point and settled down in foetal positions against a mopane tree to wait out the bitterly cold pre-dawn hours (yes, Kruger can get very cold indeed at times). While we were sitting like this, teeth chattering and bodies shaking, the strangest sensation came over me: it felt as if my body was dying. At first I thought it was just the cold, but it wasn't – I had been in this situation often enough to be sure of that. It felt as if my body, starting with my feet, was gradually being immersed in lukewarm water. I sat as if turned to stone as the warmth crept up higher and higher, completely at a loss as to what to do. Then the warmth reached my chest and I fell over. When I got myself upright again it had gone and didn't come back. What it was I still don't know – it certainly couldn't have been ordinary hypothermia or it wouldn't have vanished so suddenly. All I can say is that I was glad it was gone, and I hope it never happens to me again.

Several interminable and uncomfortable hours passed, and just to make matters worse, a dense mist made its appearance long before first light, so that when dawn finally arrived it didn't help us much, because visibility was zero. We did the only thing possible, which was to sit and freeze some more until the mist had lifted a little. When it got to the stage where we could see a few metres ahead we moved off eastwards. By our calculations we would reach the Nzobfori Spruit after about 15 minutes; we would cross it and then move along it until we reached the old poachers' camp. We didn't find the Nzobfori Spruit, however. What we did come across, after about 30 minutes, was a road that shouldn't have been there.

To say that we were baffled would be an understatement. The fact was that we had totally lost our sense of direction, so we sat down while the mist clung about us, as thick as ever, and tried to work out where we were. The only road we could have intercepted was, as far as we knew, about three hours' walk east of where we had started. This road couldn't be running parallel to the boundary because that was simply too far from where we started off for us to have reached it in the elapsed time. The only other possibility was that it was the road that intersected the boundary road at an angle from the southwest. Fair enough – but where was north, or any other compass point, for that matter? We came to the conclusion that we must have been walking southwards instead of towards the east, as we had intended. If this assumption was correct, it meant that east was left of the road, and so was the location on the boundary where we were to be picked up. Having settled the matter of our location (or so we hoped) we sat down to wait for the mist to lift a little more; there was no point in going back into the bush because we could see nothing.

The mist eventually thinned out to the point where we had some visibility, and we set off in high gear; we had about 18 kilometres to go and only slightly more than three hours to do it. We made it, possibly because at one stage we ran several kilometres to catch up with someone I spotted ahead of us who could only be a poacher or illegal immigrant, but turned out to be a ground hornbill going about its lawful occasions. That pretty much set the tone for the whole farcical episode. We took it in our stride:

you win some, you lose some. If you work in Kruger and you don't have a sense of humour, you shouldn't be a ranger.

There were, of course, lighter moments of a more pleasant kind, even if only in retrospect in some cases. For example, the party for a veteran ranger, Dirk Swart, who was universally known as Snorre (Moustaches), near the end of our first year of operations. Snorre and his equally veteran colleague, Ampie Espag, were manning an observation post at Shilowa, which was a known entry point for poachers and also one of the historic passes through the Lebombos. The reason for the party was that it was both Snorre's birthday and my wedding anniversary – and here we were in the veld, acutely aware of the fact that the spousal atmosphere at our various homes was, understandably enough, far from cordial as a result of our absence. I was doing the logistics run, which involved taking fresh supplies to the observation posts and dropping them at predetermined places to be picked up (this was actually just a blind – the idea was that if poachers were in the area they would see me pass and be lulled into a false sense of security about the other groups all over the area), and I made sure to bring a couple of treats along.

The mosquitoes had been feasting on the two old-timers, and they were a sorry sight when I arrived at Shilowa. Snorre, who at the best of times had droopy eyelids (which we unkindly referred to as his reserve tanks), couldn't see at all, because he had been bitten so many times on his face that his eyes had swollen completely closed. He was so blind that Ampie had had to lead him foot by foot down the mountain. Ampie was marginally better off, but not by much: he could still see, but his hands were so swollen that he couldn't flex them. I wished Dirk a happy birthday and gave him a bottle of brandy, a bottle of Diet Coke and a cool box full of ice, and then told them both to go home. But these two remarkable old-timers were having none of that. They thanked me for the provisions and told me to move on, refusing point-blank to return home. These were special people, all right. How many of today's rangers would do something like that? Not many. Some don't even know the boundaries of their sections, let alone what it is like to live for weeks on what you had hidden in holes in the ground months before, or make do with what you can carry on your back.

In the early days – the 'saturation operations days', as we later called them – we used Shipandani as our kick-off base. At this stage we were still working with our mapoisas and the South African Police, and we looked on our activities as military operations . . . which they were. It was war out there; everybody knew it, and took their work seriously. This is not to say that the things that worried our ranks were always what one might anticipate. One morning I teamed up with a Captain Swart of the SAP to give a briefing, which ended in the customary way with Captain Swart asking: 'Any questions?' 'Yes, Captain,' piped up Johnny, a constable from Durban, 'What about the f. . .ing ants?' This was how these fellows were. The fact that they had to live like animals for up to two weeks at a stretch with no support was part of the deal and was accepted as such . . . but the bloody ants, they were something else!

Religion affects people in different ways, but one of the things almost everyone does is pray before going into battle. I can't fault this practice if you are that way inclined, but many of those who have dedicated their lives to the protection and study of natural phenomena have other approaches and ideas on the situation. That same morning one of the SAP officers, who also happened to be a trainee preacher, asked if he could close the briefing with a prayer before we left for our various posts. This prompted one of the rangers to say, in a voice that was much more than a whisper: 'Can't this guy do anything alone?' This rather crass remark sounded out of place at the time, but not once we were among the rocks and ants in the Lebombos. You were never alone there. You might not have had a buddy to hold your hand or tuck you in at night, but there was this huge piece of Africa that you were looking after. Why? Because it was a friend that needed your help. And apart from that, you enjoyed every second of it. At least I did.

Would I go back tomorrow? No! There are enough youngsters who feel the same way we did to do what we did, and they can do so with our support. We taught them how to do it; all that is necessary is to get the politicians to go back to the places where they can do the least damage, and then stay there. This doesn't include only the party politicians – it applies equally strongly to the ultra-green people in their sneakers and short white socks. The sooner we get back to realistic conservation practices, the better for us all.

*

By 1983 we had achieved much success in reducing the poaching, but we had not yet dealt with the mapoisas who were passing information about our operations to their friends and relatives on the other side of the fence. Something had obviously to be done about it, and I tackled the matter in the middle of 1983, when I was promoted to Chief Ranger and moved to Skukuza. The Manager: Nature Conservation and I visited all the sections in the Park and explained to the field staff what was going to happen and why; then we dismissed between 40 and 45 of the 54 mapoisas in the north and transferred the rest to other sections. It was a very traumatic experience for me because so many of them were good friends, but I was at peace with myself about it: I had not forgotten the sight and smell of herds of rotting elephants with just their tusks removed, or the hardships we had endured to claw the situation back to where we were now.

The dismissal of the mapoisas meant that for a while the eastern boundary would be virtually unpatrolled. As a temporary solution it was suggested that trained army personnel be deployed in the affected area. The South African Defence Force readily accepted this scheme, but problems arose during the implementation, because the allocated troops refused to be transferred to Kruger. Instead we decided to provide black rangers with basic infantry training, and in 1982/83 a total of 78 were trained. In 1983/84 another 30 mapoisas were dismissed and replaced, and at the same time it became policy not to employ any Mozambican citizens as rangers. The responsibility for training the new mapoisas was undertaken by myself and Arrie Schreiber, a former SADF infantry major and then the ranger at Kingfisherspruit near Orpen, with Douw Swanepoel, a former sergeant and tracking instructor in the SADF, to help us in his particular field of expertise.

The new scheme worked very well. We stopped the poaching along the eastern boundary and then kept up the pressure on the poachers when they moved westwards – a stupid move on their part, in truth, because now we could follow them to their homes and arrest them legally. Once this penny dropped the poaching faded out almost completely, so that by the end of 1983 it was virtually at a standstill, down from 180 elephants a year to one or two.

All of us were later targeted by the present management system and retrenched in 2001 because 'ex-soldiers appointed for their terrorist fighting and tracking skills and a lack of conservation qualifications have had to make way for a new generation of qualified conservationists'. Granted, men like these were appointed for other skills, which were desperately needed at the time, but subsequently all the ex-soldiers obtained at least the nature conservation diploma. South African conservationists should raise their hats to these rangers for what they did to further the cause, but instead they were simply shown the door, as were many of the other dedicated and qualified people – both black and white – in the interests of 'transformation', an imprecise term at best. But nothing can dim our achievements; the figures speak too eloquently for themselves.

The treachery of some mapoisas should not be allowed to sully or obscure the role of many others who performed so well in the battle against the poachers. Before the betrayal on the eastern boundary they were the mainstay of our efforts, and among them were many brilliant and dedicated men who were prepared to – and often did – give all they had to preserve our wildlife. It would be impossible to mention them all by name, but men like James Chauke, July Makuvele, Helfas Nkuna, Reis Manhique and Simeon Mulhovo come immediately to mind, because they were the ones who taught me the business; they are the legends in my life. But there were many others who played as important a part.

The ones who betrayed their trust also deserve to be named. One was Amione Muzimba, who as a very junior field ranger was with Louis Olivier and myself at Mabakane in 1972 when we caught all those high-ranking Mozambicans and had to let them go again. He not only sold out to the poachers but denounced his fellow mapoisa Wilson Dinda to the Frelimo government for helping us with the elephant counter-poaching campaign, as a result of which Wilson spent six months at the Xai Xai security forces base, cooped up in a corrugated-iron box two metres high and two wide, with a beating every day to loosen his tongue.

Wilson didn't die or talk, and after six months the Frelimo torturers gave up and let him go. Eventually Wilson arrived back at the Park after a lone 400-kilometre walk. Tough is not the word for this small man, no more than five feet six inches with his boots on. He had more guts than just about anyone else I have ever met, and he was also a real conservationist, the epitome of a veld person in my eyes, who taught me much of what I know. Amione was transferred to Malelane to get him away from Wilson who, I am sure, would have killed him if he had had the opportunity. Here Amione organised a poaching syndicate, and he is probably still in jail for his efforts.

Another bad penny was Corporal Sandros Matsimbi from Mooiplaas, who helped the poaching groups north of the Shingwedzi. Matsimbi came to a terrible end when he died of thirst in the forbidding Nwambiya Sandveld, although one of his partners in crime, the main coordinator of the poaching assistance group, escaped retribution and ended up as chief ranger at a private game reserve in the Lowveld. A sadder case was that of another Mooiplaas mapoisa, a superlative tracker named Julius Mbombe, who also turned poacher and, like Matsimbi, died in the veld.

*

The saturation operations at the height of the elephant poaching bred a quick-reaction reflex in all of us that frequently made all the difference between success and failure, but sometimes led to farcical situations that would eventually turn into treasured fireside tales, once the circumstances in which they had occurred had acquired a little distance. What one might call 'the case of the Shingwedzi shots' is typical of this genre. The main player was myself, and the occasion was one peaceful Sunday morning. A weekend off was a rare treasure in those hard-pressed times. For two days we would be away from privation, danger and hard slogging through the bush; we would steep ourselves in simple pleasures like playing tennis with family and friends or watching rugby on television, although the reception at Shingwedzi tended to make it look as if the game was being played in the depths of a blizzard.

On this particular Sunday morning I was peacefully cleaning the swimming pool when I heard a shot to the north of the house, followed shortly after by a second. 'Here we go again,' I thought, my adrenalin kicking in. I paused only to grab my rifle and a small rucksack of extras that was always kept ready for just this sort of occasion before heading north in my bakkie. It was not really a good idea to set off by myself on such a mission, but the shots had sounded so close that I didn't want to waste any time getting on the poachers' trail. I crossed the Shingwedzi River causeway and turned right at the Nwamayiwane firebreak, following it for a couple of hundred metres before parking the bakkie and setting out on foot. The poachers had obviously had to walk from east to west into the Park and thus would have to reverse direction to get back to Mozambique, so I set off northwards in the hope of finding a spoor I could follow.

I covered about three kilometres, then turned westwards for about another three kilometres, then headed southwards and finally eastwards. By the time I had completed the last leg of the search square I had covered an area of at least nine square kilometres . . . and found absolutely no trace of the poachers. So I tried Plan B — a 360-degree circle search, heading west initially and then curving around. Eventually I was more or less back where I started, having found nothing, not even fresh elephant spoor. Although fairly tired after all this, I set off on another full circle search, heading eastwards at first. Still nothing: obviously I had misjudged the distance and direction from where the shots had come.

I gave up in disgust and headed back to the bakkie. By this time it was very hot and I was very thirsty, so on the way home I swung by the rest camp to buy a couple of beers. At the camp's main complex I ran into the manager, Oom Pieter Coetzee. Always interested in what was going on, he asked where I had been, so I explained to him about the shots and what had followed. His reply wasn't exactly what I had expected: 'I also heard the shots,' he said, 'but they weren't shots.' I made no bones about the fact that I wasn't in the mood to discuss shots that were not shots, but Oom Pieter insisted on taking me to the camp's linen room, behind which stood a steel trailer he used for removing rubbish from the camp – a contraption with four large hinged lids about two metres long on each side. He lifted the nearest lid and then let go of it. It slammed down with a loud bang. Then he did the same with another lid. Same thing: bang! I felt like a fool, and a sweaty, leg-weary one at that, because there could be no doubt that I had spent my morning chasing the sounds emitted by Oom Pieter's rubbish-trailer lids. My only consolation, a mighty small one, was that at least I had got the direction right.

I remember another embarrassing false start, although this time there was definitely an element of bad luck involved. It started when Heinie Sleigh, who was in charge of maintaining the eastern boundary fence, burst into my office early one morning, saying that he had just a heard a volley of shots north of the camp followed by a scream from an elephant. Heinie wasn't one to exaggerate, so I grabbed the usual and headed off. No more than 500 metres north of the Shingwedzi I picked the spoor of four people heading westwards, and, given the shots that Heinie had heard, I was pretty certain that they were poachers and not illegal immigrants. That was enough for me. I gave very careful chase, stopping to listen every few paces – apart from the danger of walking into an ambush set by a group of armed poachers, there was also a distinct possibility that I would find myself in an encounter with a wounded elephant.

I remember feeling very confident about my chances of intercepting and arresting the poachers, but in fact my worst nightmares were about to be realised. The bad-luck sequence started when I picked up the distant sound of an aircraft from the south. There were no flights scheduled to land at Shingwedzi that day, so I hoped fervently that it was heading further north, because if it came close to Shingwedzi the poachers would be scared off. No such luck. The aircraft came straight on till it was overhead, circled twice and landed about a kilometre away. I ground my teeth, because it was a dead certainty that by now the poachers were making all speed for the Mozambique border. I pushed on nevertheless, and not ten minutes later found a dead elephant with its tusks partly chopped out; quite obviously the poachers had taken fright at the arrival of the aircraft and decamped. I ran back to the truck, where I found Heinie – who had arrived in the meantime – almost as livid with rage as I was.

I knew that Mozambican poachers often used a certain route to enter and leave the Park; with luck, they would use it today as well on their way out, giving me a chance to cut them off. Heinie and I got into the bakkie and we set off for the most appropriate jumping-off place. He had brought along a litre of soda water, and I drank it all – not without difficulty, since the bakkie was leaping from one bump to another – to wet my whistle as copiously as possible in preparation for what promised to be a long, hard road ahead. In due course Heinie dropped me off at the spot we had selected and I set off after the poachers again. I could have lain up at a suitable spot and waited for the poachers to walk into the trap, but I decided to head down the route itself, the more danger-ous but potentially also the more fruitful option. So off I went, my heart full of determination, my hands full of rifle and my stomach full of Heinie's soda water. And found absolutely nothing. What-ever route the poachers were using, it was certainly not this one. I don't know when they reached their destination, but I got back to Shingwedzi late that afternoon, much the worse for wear after my hot and arduous veld walk and with nothing to show for it but a bad mood.

I retain painful memories of another Shingwedzi fiasco. One morning I was following the spoor of four people along the Dzombo Spruit, this time south of Shingwedzi. The spoor was only a few hours old and there was an even chance that it had been made by poachers – very relaxed ones, it appeared, to judge by the wet patch I found that showed one member of the group had stopped to urinate, turning around to chat to his companions while thus occupied. It was clear that they didn't know I was hot on their heels. I was alone, as usual, but that wasn't a problem because I knew I was ready for anything. Anyone who has been in this kind of situation knows that feeling of invincibility. It is really very stupid to feel that way, of course, but that's what happens. I pressed on; they were walking in single file, leaving an easy spoor to follow, and I calculated that I was probably gaining on them. Then the warning bells in my head went off, ringing the message 'watch it, Bruce!' Long experience had taught me to heed those bells, and my senses went into turbo-boost.

Up to then I had been looking for people, at the height and in

132

the shapes and places where people would be, but now I shifted priorities and modified the scan-pattern that you acquire only after years of working in the bush. It was then that I saw what had set off the bells: not five metres from me, partly shaded by a lala palm tree, a buffalo bull lay fast asleep. There I was in an instant sticky situation. Buffalo bulls fear nothing on this earth, and their first reaction in what they perceive to be a conflict situation is to attack – and I was definitely inside this one's attack zone. I had one option, and one option only: to retreat very slowly and very quietly, because I would be in serious trouble if he woke up while I was still there. The only way I would be able to walk away from a situation like that would be to drop him in his tracks with a bullet, but I was armed with an R1 assault rifle, and it just wasn't enough gun to stop an aggressive buffalo bull at close quarters.

So I started moving, very slowly and very quietly, as the situation demanded. The first steps went well. Then I felt myself sliding down into an aardvark hole that I had not seen or had forgotten about because of the press of other matters. In no time I was up to my armpits in that damned hole . . . and at this stage the buffalo woke up and leapt to his feet! This was a real loser-loses-all bushveld scenario. But to my astonishment and relief the buffalo let out a snort, inspected the parts of me protruding from the aardvark hole – to wit, a head and an arm – and took off at speed. With him went all desire on my part to resume tracking my suspected poachers; a wise man knows when to pack it in.

*

It would be naïve to assume that there can be guarantees that the current lull in serious poaching of large game in the Kruger National Park will more or less automatically continue throughout the first decade of the new millennium. Nor must it be assumed that elephants are the only large game that might be targeted. Rhino are in equal potential peril, and I venture to predict that they will be the poachers' next point of focus. The current administrators should also bear in mind that the danger might come from within the rangers' ranks as well as from without, as it did during the struggle along the eastern boundary. Rhino horns have been a very valuable commodity for many years, and in the past more than one ranger has been subverted by the money that illegal dealers pay for them.

The subject of conservation staff who turned on the animals with whose well-being they were entrusted is a painful one for me, because on a number of occasions during my 27 years in the Park I had to deal with rangers who had deviated from the straight and narrow path of duty. Even now it is a part of my life that I am reluctant to talk about, but this book is not meant to be only about the good parts of my career in South Africa's greatest game park.

Other than my dealings with the many field rangers in the north who worked against us, my most traumatic experience with a ranger who had gone bad took place when we discovered that somebody I had considered a trusted colleague had taken to poaching the animals he was supposed to look after. We were boyhood friends who had played rugby as youngsters and tennis in our maturity, downed many a beer after our play, teamed up to capture game and watched our children play together. And he threw our friendship and everything else away by declaring war on the animals in his care. How many he destroyed to line his pockets will always remain a mystery but we know for certain that over a period of several years he and an accomplice shot at least 27 rhino, two elephant, one lion and a hyaena. We caught him in the end. He was found not guilty on some of the charges, but enough remained for the doors of Pretoria Central Prison to slam shut on him for 12 years, leaving a trail of hurt behind. Hurt among those who remembered the good times before he went bad, the huge hurt to his children, the hurt in his colleagues' hearts when they thought about his treachery.

My former friend's accomplice, an experienced maiposa, drove the nails into his coffin by turning state witness. Rhino carcasses are not easily detected, especially if they are dragged into a thick patch of bush, say, or hidden in a spruit, because among other things the hyaenas and other scavengers soon make off with the bones. But the accomplice's rich knowledge of the bushveld had not disappeared like his integrity, and his recall of their exploits was amazing as he led us from one killing scene to another, some of them separated by hundreds of kilometres and anything up to five years in terms of time. Nor did he crumble under the defence counsel's cross-examination when the case finally came to court. His co-operation bought him another chance, but the rot had set in, and it wasn't too long before he was caught in nearby Hazyview while selling poached impala meat. When last I heard about him he was cultivating vegetables in a prison garden, a very long way in all respects from the wide bushveld he had once roamed as a guardian of our children's heritage.

Corporal Sam Nkuna is another poacher I remember with pain. He had been a prison warder at Barberton before becoming a mapoisa stationed at Crocodile Bridge. Sam was a first-class field ranger, but temptation overcame him and he took to hunting the Park's rhino; we will never know how many he shot before finally being arrested.

The end of the road for Sam Nkuna started when our pilot Piet Otto flew a scientist as part of a radio tracking operation on wild dogs in the Crocodile Bridge Section. They had barely got going when Piet spotted a fresh rhino carcass with its horns chopped off, just north of the Mokohlolo Dam. Piet immediately radioed Skukuza, and soon afterwards the other pilot flew Tom Yssel, Sergeant Simeon Mulhovo and myself to the scene. We landed close by and Simeon and I immediately started looking for clues. Simeon found the first when he spotted a new-looking axe with a red handle, clearly Parks Board issue, lying near the carcass. More clues were turned up in rapid succession: spoor left by issue boots, and a few cartridge-cases that had obviously been fired from an issue R1 rifle. It was a deeply upsetting moment for me, because there could be no doubt that the culprits were Kruger staff. The whole affair became even more upsetting when we cast around some more and found the spoor of a second rhino that had fled the scene, everything indicating that it had also been hit.

We wound up our quick look-around and set off after the poachers, only to be foiled by classic anti-tracking procedures, so instead we back-tracked along their incoming spoor. That brought us to their bicycles, hidden in a culvert under the tarmac road between Crocodile Bridge and Lower Sabie. By this time we had a bakkie on the scene, so we loaded up the bicycles and headed for Crocodile Bridge, where we hid them in the veld near the house. When Sam Nkuna and his accomplice returned from their supposed patrol I had the other mapoisas bring them to where we were waiting in the garden of the ranger's house (the section ranger, Kobus Kruger, was on leave). I asked Nkuna where he had been that day, and he told me that they had patrolled along the Crocodile River. Asked where their bicycles were, he said they had been left under a sausage tree at the hippo pools. I arrested and handcuffed Nkuna and his accomplice and then took them to the hippo pools, where I asked the guard on duty if he had seen the two that morning. 'Yes,' he replied. 'I saw them early this morning when I came to work. They had a new axe with a red handle tied to the carrier of one of the bikes.' Needless to say, there were no bike tracks anywhere near the sausage tree. Nkuna's response was to insist that we were visiting the wrong tree. I went along with this blatant lie and tried to find the right one. When this proved impossible, Nkuna tried to convince me that the bikes had been stolen, and even invited me to check whether his rifle had been fired recently. I didn't take him up on his offer because I knew that he was bright enough to have cleaned the rifle after shooting the rhino or rhinos, thus destroying any tell-tale residues.

After completing the initial interrogation we went back to the carcass to look for more cartridge-cases, using the possible direction of the wind and the position of the rhinos as indicators. Sure enough, we found a few, and next day I flew to Johannesburg with both rifles and cartridge-cases so that the police forensic experts could examine them. In due course the SAP forensics laboratory sent back positive results, but for only one of the rifles. Baffled but determined, we went back to search the scene for a third time. This time we found another batch of cartridge-cases and sent them off; the SAP forensics people reported that they had been able to match this latest batch to the other rifle. Both poachers' guilt was now proven beyond doubt. I wasn't there to see Nkuna and his accomplice convicted, my annual leave having clashed with the trial date. But before I left the prosecutor assured me: 'Don't worry, you have a good case,' and so it was. Both were found guilty and sent to join Nkuna's former charges at Barberton Prison.

During the eighties Nic Steele (formerly of Natal Parks Board) started the internationally funded Rhino and Elephant Security Group with the aim of advising the rest of Africa on how to protect their rhino and elephant. Initially I was vice-chairman, but when Nic lost his battle against cancer I took over the post, ably assisted by Ian Thompson (formerly of KwaZulu-Natal Parks) as permanent co-ordinator.

Various theories had been put forward as to why rhino populations all over the world have declined dramatically, apart from providing knife handles in Yemen and hoarding for investment purposes. Although the World Wildlife Fund investigated the matter, they came up with a 'don't know' answer, probably because they sent a blond Englishman, six foot six inches tall, to China to investigate the trade. This was probably as sensible as providing a bull with strap-on mammary glands. It did become clear, however, that although rhino horn is renowned (rightly or wrongly) as an aphrodisiac, it has some actual medicinal value. Tests on rhino horn, which is nothing more than a close cousin to hair, have revealed that keratin, the senior protein in the equation, has the potential to lower fever.

Clive Walker, one of the greats in the private conservation sector and also a member of the Rhino and Elephant Security Group, did a bit of homework of his own in the field of rhino-horn trading. He discovered that there were about a million registered traditional healers in China and that each could legally keep a rhino horn stock of 10 kilos. This meant that there were up to 10 million kilos of legal rhino horn in China. No wonder rhinos are under threat!

Is rhino horn truly an aphrodisiac? That I can't say. I did once raise the subject on an unsolicited basis when I was delivering the keynote address at an international wildlife law-enforcement conference in Reno, Nevada. I didn't know if rhino horn was in fact an effective aphrodisiac, I informed the audience, but what I could say with authority was that it tasted terrible. I expected that this sally would evoke at least a modicum of amusement from the audience, but was disconcerted to find that they took it quite seriously.

I had a better response from the rich Miami widows, the old dears with their white socks and tackies who control the 'green people's fund' in the USA. None of them seemed to have heard my earlier attempt at a witty remark, and one asked me about the best way to use rhino horn as an aphrodisiac. My little internal devil awoke and I answered: 'Strap it on.' There was a shocked silence, then hell broke loose: laughter, applause and everything else that goes to make a person from the bush feel that he has got his message across.

8

LIONS ON MY LAWN AND
ELEPHANTS IN MY LETTUCE BED

When I first set up house with Helena I knew that being a house-holder in the Kruger National Park was a little different from what it would be in, say, Johannesburg or Cape Town, one of the differences being that unexpected visitors to your doorstep tended to be rather more formidable than you would expect in the bright-lights part of the continent. And, of course, the conse-quences of such a visit (or perhaps a better word would be 'visi-tation') could be anything from funny to frightening to tragic. But I didn't realise the scale of that difference.

I found out soon enough, though, not long after Helena and I had left our temporary accommodation at Shipandani in April 1974 and moved into the house at the Mooiplaas ranger station, which was still so new that it did not even have a garden fence yet. A friend of mine from varsity days and his elderly stepfather-in-law paid us a weekend visit during this fenceless period, and on their first night, while Stepdad was visiting the toilet, a pride of lions chased a herd of zebra past the house and right through the garden, in the process catching and killing one of them to the accompaniment of the usual sound effects. Now, Stepdad wasn't very easy in his mind about being in the wilds anyway, and the lions' hearty zebra supper was simply too much for him. He locked himself into the toilet and smoked up an entire packet of cigarettes before the night was over, then called on his stepson-in-law to bring him another packet, which was also finished by the time dawn broke. I think one could say that the aged gent had got a well-nigh terminal fright, since the average medium-to-heavy smoker will take quite a lot of chances if he is in danger of run-ning out. And it wasn't even an outside toilet . . .

I got to know all about elephant visits when I was stationed at

Shingwedzi, where we stayed from March 1980 to July 1983. There were always elephant bulls in the area around the camp – the most prominent of these was, of course, Shingwedzi himself, founder-member of the Magnificent Seven, but he was not the only one by any means – and interactions between staff and the resident pachyderm visitors were inevitable. Having an elephant visit your garden is an occasion fraught with possibilities. Generally speaking it is not good for the nerves, and usually it is very unhealthy for whatever you have growing there. On the other hand, it can be quite funny (usually in retrospect) if things don't go the wrong way.

One winter my brother-in-law, Manie, his wife Ina and their children paid us a visit, which we all enjoyed, especially our children, who didn't often have playmates. One night we were sitting and yarning around the kitchen table, while the children were playing in the living room with our terrier, Eggs; in accordance with Kruger's laid-back way of living, the outside doors of both the rooms were open, although the screen doors were closed. At one stage we heard a noise that sounded like something scratching against the kitchen's screen door. Then it went away, came back and faded away again.

I suppose I should have smelt a rat by this stage, but your guard tends to go down when you're having a good time, which we were, and so it wasn't until we heard branches breaking very close by a couple of minutes later that I realised that at least one elephant was in my garden. Then the sounds came even closer: quite evidently it was now pulling snacks for itself off a baobab tree only 10 metres from the kitchen door. I went to the door and shouted, and the elephant moved off – permanently, so we thought, because we heard nothing more from the garden – and we went back to our conversation. A while later Ina needed something from the guest rondavel, which stood in a corner of the front garden about 20 metres from the house, and she took the shortest route there, which was by way of the washroom at the side of the house. She didn't bother to take a torch because she had been there for a couple of days and knew that the house was fenced in. This was definitely a mistake, as she discovered when she was about half-way to the rondavel and came within a hair's-breadth of walking slap into a huge, dark object standing directly in front of her.

It was, of course, none other than our baobab snacker of a little earlier, virtually invisible in the gloom, as elephants tend to be, but not so invisible that Ina didn't realise instantly what she had literally run into. She let go with a truly blood-curdling scream, which was immediately answered and drowned out by the elephant's squeal of distress, covered the rest of the distance to the rondavel at breakneck speed and slammed all the doors and windows shut. At the same time there was a sound like a giant guitar being strummed, followed by the unmistakeable crashes of an elephant in full flight. Without wanting to seem callous, I could only conclude that it was a toss-up as to which of the two got a greater fright. I don't know how the elephant soothed its shattered nerves, but a glass of wine did the trick for Ina after we had fetched her from the rondavel (from which, understandably enough, she refused to budge without an escort).

Dawn broke to reveal a scene of devastation. As we reconstructed its movements, the elephant had started by totally destroying a fig tree (we hadn't even heard *that* little demolition job taking place), spent some time in the front garden, which was when he rubbed up against the kitchen's screen door, helped himself to small branches and strips of bark from the baobab, and then went around the house to the vegetable garden. Here he ate some of my much-prized lettuce crop, flattening the rest in the process (which really got up my nose, because fresh fruit and vegetables were hard to come by at a place such as Shingwedzi, which was about 160 kilometres from the nearest greengrocer) before breaking down the fence surrounding the swimming pool, where he either cleared his throat or blew his nose into the water – the evidence was unmistakeable in the form of large blobs of mucus floating around.

Having shot his wad, so to speak, he washed down his stolen meal with a long drink from the pool and returned to the front garden by the same route as he had arrived at the pool area. The lawn was nice and soft, having been watered just the day before, and so he left a trail of footprints between five and ten centimetres deep. It was on his return around the western side of the house that he met up with Ina, got the fright of his life when she let rip and fled right through the wash-line and some vineyard support wires (there was the origin of the giant guitar). Not a bad evening's work; at least from the elephant's point of view; I daresay that if Winston Churchill had been present he would most likely have coined a new phrase to the effect that 'never in the field of nature conservation has one elephant done so much damage to a ranger's garden in so short a time'. I can't honestly say that it had been all take, take, take, however, since the elephant had kindly scattered generous donations of dung all over the place in addition to his souvenirs in the pool.

It took us a while to get things back in shape. The fig tree was a goner, of course, along with the lettuce-beds, but we could repair the fences and some of the other damage, and we managed to get rid of the footprints on the lawn by filling them with soil and waiting for several weeks for the grass to recover. We also prepared a reception committee for the elephant in case he felt like availing himself of our hospitality again, which he did several times. Since the metre-and-a-bit fence around the house was no match for an elephant strength-wise, we decided to electrify it, which would be much cheaper than trying to fortify it anyway, and we did this as soon as I could organise an energiser ('organise', for non-South Africans, means the gentle art of acquiring some necessity by means other than paying for it or stealing it. By force of budgetary circumstances Kruger National Park rangers were expert organisers).

It did not take us long to get the fence ready for action. As it happened we put the final touches to it just before lunch one day, so I sent my workforce off for their meal while I carried out a discreet test, using an insulated screwdriver. The fence generated an impressive spark, so I switched off the system . . . only to be gripped once more by that little devil of mine. Like one gripped by an evil trance, I hung a pair of pliers in a strategic spot and switched on the power again, then waited for my faithful followers to return from lunch so that we could have the official testing. When they were all assembled in an expectant half-circle I made as if to activate the fence, 'noticed' the pliers and asked someone to remove them. Like the great and good man that he was, Amos was the first to step forward, and what happened then exceeded my little devil's wildest expectations. As Amos grabbed the pliers there was a loud crack and his arm shot into the air, followed by a yell from the rest of him. When he hit the ground again he stood looking around with an expression of total disbelief on his face. By now his colleagues were falling about laughing. Amos bore us no ill-will, once he had recovered his wits; on the contrary, he made it plain that he was particularly impressed by the fence's potency.

Unlike Amos, the lettuce elephant, as we called him, didn't immediately fall victim to our new defences. Elephants seem to be able to sense when a fence has been electrified, and when this happens they are likely to use all kinds of stratagems to bypass it. There have been cases where adult elephants have pushed a couple of younger ones into an electrified fence to take the heat and flatten it so that they can simply walk through, which is a very good idea except if you are one of the young elephants. The lettuce elephant was no exception. Morning spoor inspections showed that he had been back, but had not had the courage to try the fence yet. But one evening about a week or so later, I heard an elephant breaking branches just outside the front garden. I went out through the back door armed with a five-shot self-loading shotgun, loaded with 'bangers', which are nothing more than fire-crackers adapted for firing out of a shotgun, and sneaked around the house to find the lettuce elephant stretching over the fence to get to a coral tree inside the garden. I waited; it was only a matter of time before he touched the electric fence with his legs. Sure enough, within a couple of seconds there was a crack and a flash as he made contact with the live wire, and immediately I fired a banger into the air above me. The elephant instantly lost his appetite and fled down the hill, followed by the rest of my crackers. That was the last we saw of him, and the other elephants in the vicinity soon found out why. So our restored garden stayed restored, and no jumbo got to toot his nose in the swimming pool again. Not bad for a few strands of wire and a couple of pieces of 'organised' kit. But that's the bush for you: you live by your wits or you go under.

*

In mid-1983 I was transferred to Skukuza, the Park's nerve-centre, and we moved into a house which was one of a few situated next to the rest camp and the nature conservation offices instead of in Skukuza village itself. The house was surrounded by a garden of a size and magnificence the average urbanite can only dream about; it was about 30 by 80 metres in extent, filled with many huge trees, including some sycamore figs, a couple of Natal mahogany trees, marulas, wild mangos and a nice-sized baobab, not to mention about 16 large cycads and a couple of big palms. Between the trees grew a profusion of shade-loving plant species such as ferns and the colourful impatiens. I need hardly say that all this attracted all sorts of birds, and on a nice Sunday morning we could see as many as 70 different species there. The length of the garden ran basically east to west, with the front of the house facing the eastern part of the fence, where there were two gates: a small pedestrian gate more or less in line with the front door and a main gate to the left. The northern length of the fence we shared with the house next door (this, incidentally, was the house that we lived in during our first stint in Skukuza).

It so happened that the confluence of my fence, my neighbour's fence and the rest camp fence created a cul de sac in front of my house that was a perfect trap for lions to catch impala in, which they did at regular intervals. The southern length of the fence ran along the access road to the nature conservation offices, our neighbours on the other side of the road being the local police. Behind the house ran the western fence, which also featured a pedestrian gate. An extremely convenient situation for both Helena and myself, because when we left our house just before seven every morning, we exited our garden through this gate and then had about a minute to walk across the parking area of the offices to reach our places of work. Our move to Skukuza didn't mean the end of my one-on-ones with Kruger's inhabitants of the tooth-and-claw variety by any means – in fact, that very garden in which we were to spend so many happy hours with our family and friends was the direct cause of some tense incidents as well, since birds were not our only unexpected visitors.

Skukuza had quite a substantial human population by Park standards, but the bottom line was that Kruger belonged to its animal population, and within certain limits they did what came naturally to them. Thus all its houses were fenced in, and there was a standing instruction that all garden gates had to be closed between sunset and sunrise. I stuck rigidly to this very sensible rule, because dangerous animals are inclined to become even more dangerous when they feel trapped. But sometimes, of course, this was not enough. Leopards, for example, were frequent visitors to the garden because climbing over the fence was no problem at all to them. Lions dropped in less frequently, but they were often in the neighbourhood. If there were no impala to hand they would crawl into the stormwater drain that ran along the eastern fence, a favourite sleeping-place for warthogs, and drag one out for supper. As a result it wasn't unusual for us to be woken up by the squeals of terrified pigs being extracted from the drain, followed by the lions' grunting and growling as they squabbled over the remains – all this at such close range that if we switched on the light at the front gate we could see them going about their business.

As I say, I was strict about the standing procedure, but people are fallible creatures and now and then one of our gates would be left open by accident. Next morning we would often find spoor telling us that during the night one or more lions had quietly prowled around the garden, found nothing interesting and then left as silently as they had arrived. Hyaenas were a different story. If there was nothing worth eating, they would always manage to find something to chew up, regardless of its nutritional value – unpalatable but munchable objects like hose-pipes, plastic pots or bags, bicycle tyres and even vehicle tyres not excluded. Sometimes, though, the nocturnal visits by lions were a good deal less discreet. One of them involved Dr Roy Bengis, a government veterinarian in Skukuza, with whom I had been fast friends since our university days in the 1960s during the height of the 'flower power' era (no, we weren't flower children, in spite of our love of nature – we just enjoyed the music and the more liberated lifestyle in which we could indulge ourselves in our spare time). Our friendship endured after university, and with both of us in Kruger we had a firm custom of enjoying a beer and chat every Monday evening. When we couldn't get together, we'd have our Monday beers in what we

called 'alone togetherness', which was sometimes more meaningful than the physical version.

On Monday afternoon, 26 February 2000, I was at Roy's house as
usual for a couple of beers and a chinwag about things of mutual
interest like fly-fishing, clay-pigeon shooting and just straightforward shooting at beer cans for fun. I went home just after six in the
usual sanguine mood our togetherness sessions induced, not
knowing that our next meeting was going to be a damned sight
sooner and more eventful than I expected. I got home and, as usual,
made sure I closed the main gate behind me, but although it was
still light I didn't realise that some impala remained in the garden,
out of sight behind the house; the first time I realised they were
there was when Helena saw them moving past one of the windows
while we were watching that year's Oscar awards ceremony on TV.
As before, I decided to leave them be for the night. But we had
barely got our eyes back on the Oscar awards when we heard the
unmistakable sound of something being killed, then the equally
unmistakeable sounds of lions vying for choice bits of the carcass,
overlaid by the sounds of yet another kill in progress.

We went to the front door and switched on the outside lights.
There, under a large sycamore fig tree about halfway between the
house and the front fence, was a lioness standing over a dead
impala, and a lion off to the right, half-hidden behind our baobab
tree. Whether there were more lions in the garden we didn't
know, of course, but it was quite possible. How had they got in? I
had personally closed the front gate, I could see that the small
pedestrian gate was also closed, and we had not heard the audible crash of the spring-loaded back gate slamming shut. I decided
not to worry about it. The lions were doing no harm (except to the
impala, of course), and fooling around at night with lions that are
not only eating but might feel trapped if disturbed was right up
there with leaping in front of moving locomotives as a life-threatening pastime. So we settled for peeking through a small gap in
the partly drawn bedroom curtains to watch the lioness tearing at
her impala's carcass, and then went to bed.

We had calculated that the lions would finish their meal and
then leave, but when I got up at half-past five next morning they
were still on the front lawn, the lion and lioness I had seen during

the night plus another lion. There was no way I was going to stroll past them to open any of the gates as a gentle hint for them to hit the road, so I called to Martha, the domestic aid, to tell her to stay put in her room behind the house with her boy-friend Robbie and son Colin. Then I got Roy on his cellphone and asked him to climb into his Land Cruiser and open the gates from the outside. Soon afterwards Roy and his wife Birgit pulled up at the front gate, where they found the three lions still in occupation. I stood just outside the front door with my .44 Magnum revolver in one hand and my cellphone in the other while Roy chased the lions away so that he and Birgit could open both the main gate and the small pedestrian gate. Roy then drove slowly along the southern side of the fence, shouting at them and banging his hand on the Land Cruiser's door. They got the message and went out through the front gate, first the male, then a female and then another female.

Roy had now arrived back at the pedestrian gate, and I started crossing the lawn to go and thank him. I had travelled only about five metres, however, when yet another full-grown male lion popped out of the shrubbery on my right and launched himself into a charge. Immediately I went into a crouch and prepared to shoot – it's my experience that if you crouch when a lion charges it usually hesitates for a moment, which buys you time to take better aim and also gives you a steadier platform for the shot. My finger was on the trigger and tightening when the lion stopped within spitting distance and also crouched, growling and flicking his tail. Then, to my relief, he began to back off until he was at the shrubbery again. He was obviously feeling frustrated, however, and when he reached the shrubbery he treated us to a bravura display of ill-temper, dashing around the garden and throwing out a series of ferocious growls.

I took advantage of all these histrionics to dash back to the house while he galloped up and down the driveway, so worked up that he didn't notice that the gates were now wide open. If I slammed the front door behind me with a little more force than was absolutely necessary, you can put it down to the fact that a lion in such a state of agitation is awesome to see and just as awesome to hear. While the lion was performing in the driveway Roy returned to the back gate and raised a fresh din, but just as he was getting into full cry the lion finally discovered that the main gate was open and escaped. Roy and I did a quick sweep of the garden, where we found the remains of a total of four impala but no more lions, so I thanked him and he went off home, having had an exciting start to his day. When he had gone I took Martha, Robbie, Colin and William, the gardener, on a quick educational tour of the garden, showing them where the carcasses were and where I had seen the various lions. When they had been suitably enlightened I told William to gather up the few remaining bones, stomach contents and the attendant lion droppings and then dump everything in the veld in front of the house. Then I hurried off for a quick shower: it was now 6.45 am and I had to be at the office for the seven o'clock radio session.

The radio session over, I went back to my house to reconstruct the lions' activities. I soon found the place where they had climbed over the fence, which was a fairly formidable barrier (by human standards, anyway) consisting of about 1.3 metres of diamond mesh, topped by another two strands of barbed wire: I could see tufts of hair stuck on the barbs, and on the garden side about two square metres of vegetation had been flattened by the impact of the lions coming down to earth again. I found it strange that they climbed over at a spot where very dense scrub grew right up to the fence, so that they would not have been able to see what was on the other side. The front fence was partly protected by the open stormwater ditch, but even so the gates were easier to cross and the ground on the other side was clear. Whatever the reason, that was where they had decided to get over the fence, and then, as lions will, they had showed no interest in getting out again or indulging in any other meaningful activity once they had filled their bellies with the four impala.

Having satisfied myself about the crossing-place, I walked around to the front pedestrian gate, where I was greeted by a lion's unmistakeable growl, followed by what was unmistakably a human scream. Moments later a lioness charged me from the right. All I could do was to fend her off with the gate, close it and then run like hell for the back gate so that I could get into the house and fetch my rifle: dealing with the lioness took priority over everything, including the source of the screams. Breathing down my neck as I ran was Martha's son Colin, who had suddenly appeared from somewhere and was as hell-bent on getting away as I was. It was a short but terrifying journey to the back gate. Part of the way along the lioness, which had been shadowing me on the other side of the wire, lunged at me but was thrown back by the fence. When we reached the back gate I instructed Colin to wait in what I reckoned was a safe place, to keep watch in case the lioness left the garden before I came back, and then went through. There Martha met me with the news that the lioness's latest victim was William the gardener, who was already at the back door. He was alive but in a gory state, with bites and claw-marks on one upper arm and shoulder, his chest and one thigh.

I was still gauging the extent of the wounds, which were serious but did not appear life-threatening, when Colin ran up to report that the lioness had left via the main gate. This simplified matters considerably, and I took William to the doctor without any further delay. The doctor agreed with my rough-and-ready diagnosis, gave William the necessary immediate primary treatment and shipped him off to hospital. There he stayed for seven weeks, longer than would have been the case, except that his elbow developed an infection – not unusual in the case of a lion-inflicted wound. The garden stank of lion for about three days before a rainstorm washed the smell away, and whenever I scented it I thought again about our recent encounter. It had certainly provided more frightening moments than anyone needs at breakfast time, and the most frightening of them all was that at one stage there had been seven of us walking around within five metres of where the lioness had been hiding under some tall ferns. Why hadn't she charged then? She could have killed most or all of us. I had no answer. But it proved to me once again that the only predictable thing about wild animals is their total unpredictability.

While on the subject of my garden, I should mention that lions and leopards weren't the only large and lethal visitors we had to be braced for. There was the amorous young rhinoceros bull, for example – an unusual case, since rhinos had frequently visited my various camps in the veld, but only the one ever came calling on us at Skukuza. His appearance had less to do with the attractions of my garden and more with over-active gonads and an under-active brain (rhinos aren't the brightest bulbs in the bush-veld chandelier; one of my favourite self-coined sayings was that 'a rhino will do something, and then decide ten minutes later what he's going to do', and I was never proved wrong).

This rhino normally hung out around Renosterkoppies, about 15 kilometres from Skukuza, but one day in the year 2000 our game capture team caught him and put him in the bomas near Skukuza, preparatory to shipping him off to another park. The bull didn't take kindly to captivity and wouldn't eat, so rather than run the risk of having him starve to death it was decided to take him back to Renosterkoppies and let him loose again. This was duly done, but instead of settling down in his old stamping-grounds he wasted no time in heading right back to Skukuza again, for reasons best known to himself; the only likely explanation we could offer for this dogged ingratitude was that he had unfinished business to transact with a fellow occupant of the Skukuza boma, a rhino cow who happened to be in oestrus.

The bull made it to Skukuza all right, but there he got a bit confused about the location of the boma, so after taking a few minutes off to chase a motorist he wandered up to my front gate with the obvious intention of paying a call. This was not a good idea from my point of view, seeing that even a large garden tends to be too small for a rhino, but, fortunately for both my garden and myself, his attention was distracted when he spotted one of the clerks at the Nature Conservation office, a chap called Martin, who was unsuspectingly returning to his place of work from the post office. The rhino decided it would be a much better idea to change direction and chase Martin, which he did. Martin correctly divined the rhino's intentions, put on a burst of speed that he had not realised he was capable of, and outran him. By this time a con-siderable number of spectators had gathered, and it was all too much for the rhino's nerves, so he let Martin go and vanished into the bush without satisfying either his passion for his lady love or his desire to gallop Martin's guts out. This was just as well for all concerned, not least the rhino himself.

Another and even larger unwanted visitor was drawn by the two large lemon trees in our garden. We used their fruit for all sorts of things, including the preparation of that traditional anti-malarial potion, gin and tonic, but they produced much more than we could possibly use, so we used to give bags full of their fruit away to anyone who wanted them, and wink an eye at the depredations of passers-by, baboons and monkeys – there was enough for everybody. Things got a bit much, however, when a certain bull elephant decided to help himself as well. Elephants are notoriously fond of citrus fruit, so much so that visitors to Mana Pools in the Zambezi Valley are actually prohibited from taking oranges with them because if the elephants there smell the fruit they will come to get them, usually with disastrous consequences.

My problems with the lemons started during a dry spell in the early 1990s, when elephant herds and also individual lone bulls moved to the area around the Skukuza staff village in search of food and water. Inevitably this resulted in nightly foraging raids that equally inevitably inflicted serious damage to fences and vegetation. In my personal case the elephant in question, a large bull with quite sizeable tusks, formed the habit of breaking through my fence virtually every night to help himself to my lemons. After a while this became a bit too much, so I applied myself to chasing him away. I was a trifle handicapped in my choice of modus operandi because my house was very close to the rest camp, which meant that I couldn't make effective use of one of my proven successful tactics, a volley of curses uttered at top volume, in case I offended the paying customers. So I went over to an equally well-proven Plan B: a bucket that I kept filled with cricket ball-sized stones, with which I would give him a good pelting every time he broke through the fence.

This worked every time, but my nightly victories were invariably soured by the fact that next morning nearly every ball of elephant dung in the village would contain at least one lemon. One might say I was winning the battles but losing the war. Eventually we won the war as well, however, when the damage to Skukuza's fences became so expensive that it was decided to remove the main culprits from the area. The erring elephants were captured and translocated to other game reserves. This solved the immediate problem, and when the drought broke there was enough food and water in their home areas to keep the elephants on their own doorsteps (until the next drought, anyway), so that we could go back to lions-on-the-lawn time again.

The miscreant who had made so free with my lemons was among the removees, but never saw his home area again because he died after suffering an intestinal injury while being captured. I regretted his death because I held no grudge against him – as a hearty eater myself, how can I look with disfavour on another keen trencherman?

9

DAGGABOYS AND LESSER BUFFALOES

Let no one tell you that animals have no discernible character, because they certainly have. Some species are fierce, some are docile, some are venturesome and others just the reverse. Some are downright difficult, the prime example being buffalo. They have plenty of character, all of it unfriendly. They take no guff from anyone or anything, are usually ready for a punch-up and are very unpleasant customers to follow up on when they have been wounded and the bush is moderately thick. The late Robert Ruark once described how a buffalo looked at him 'like I owed him money', and that pretty much sums them up; it is particularly applicable to the most bloody-minded of the breed, the ones universally known as 'daggaboys'.

The reader might well be more than slightly baffled by the term 'daggaboys' in a chapter of buffalo tales, seeing that there is little discernible connection between the bushveld's ferocious wild cattle and what would appear to denote a young man smoking cannabis. But there is a reason. Most of the permanent bushveld dwellings erected in the earlies consisted of wooden frames packed with walls of stiff mud which was produced by filling a hole in the ground with pulverised antheaps and water, then beating it into the right texture with hands, feet and whatever else would do the job. The result was known for some reason as 'dagga', and it was surprisingly durable; it is sometimes still used today and is still known as 'dagga' building, although the name now indicates the method rather than the original ingredients. But, as I say, it was very messy, with the 'daggaboys', as the mixers were called, invariably ending up plastered from head to toe. The name became attached to solitary old buffalo bulls because they like to wallow in shallow pools to cool off and end up plastered with mud. Thus 'daggaboys'. Some hypersensitive people might regard the name as derogatory, but no one else does, and in Kruger, as is the case elsewhere, 'daggaboy' has become a generic term that belongs to everyone in general and no one in particular; and since the daggaboys in Kruger personify the character of its buffalo, I thought it was only right to include the name in the chapter heading.

Officially the buffalo's scientific classification name is *Syncerus caffer*, but until comparatively recently it was *Bos caffer*, which always struck me as very apt in the South African context. *'Bos'* has bovine connotations in Latin, but *'bos'* also means 'bush' or 'bushveld' in Afrikaans, and if you add on an extra 's' it pretty much sums up your average old daggaboy's attitude in most situations. He likes to take control, and if he is thwarted it becomes hell-on-four-feet time. And that's when he's in a *good* mood. Wound him just enough to anger him, or make a nuisance of yourself, and it becomes clear why the scoreboard of buffalo victims, ranging from innocent water-carriers to professional hunters, is such an impressive one. I mention all this because if one wounded buffalo – whether it is a daggaboy or not – is a menace to humanity, there are hardly words to describe the lethality of a situation in which a whole slew of them are packed into one small area, generating an almost palpable cloud of ill-will. This happened to me once, and I'll never forget it . . . nor will a certain nature conservation official who was not used to the rough-and-ready nature of our daily lives.

I was stationed at Skukuza when a herd of about 40 buffalo broke out of the Park through the Sabie River and squatted on a lovely piece of riverine forest with adjacent bush adjoining the Lisbon Estate farms that did not really belong to anyone. This meant that the animals became fair game for anyone who owned a rifle, from the local chemist with his Daisy air rifle to top government officials venturing forth from their air-conditioned offices, and by the time the local provincial nature conservation department got to hear about it there were wounded buffalo everywhere in an area of only 200 morgen or so. One of the nature conservation officials was promptly sent out to assess the situation. He went in on foot, and hadn't gone more than 200 metres when the first wounded bull took exception to his presence and tossed him into a tree; it was his extreme good fortune that, apart from suffering a massive fright, he sustained no injury because the bull's horn had hooked into his belt rather than his body.

The official managed to hang on instead of falling out of the tree again, which was just as well, because the buffalo wasn't done with him yet, and made several attempts to bite him (that's what I said, *bite*) while he clung to his precarious perch. In the meantime his assistant took advantage of the buffalo's concentration on galloping the guts out of his superior and wisely got out of there at a rate of knots, after which he put in an agonised call for help from us. I was told to go and investigate, which I did at top speed. By the time I got there the daggaboy had got bored and wandered off, allowing the treed official to climb down and make himself as scarce as his assistant . . . for all I know he left not just the area but the country as well, because I never laid eyes on him again.

The immediate problem having solved itself, I tackled the next one in line in what was clearly a real hair-raising situation in more ways than one. Quite apart from constituting a menace to the life and limb of anyone in the vicinity, the buffalo were like so many time-bombs waiting to go off because they are major carriers of not one but two dreaded animal diseases. One of them is foot-and-mouth, an outbreak of which has enormous economic implications for the whole agricultural industry because it attacks all livestock. The other is corridor disease, which is deadly to domestic cattle. Consultation with the provincial and national authorities, as well as the Department of Veterinary Services, confirmed the conclusion I had already reached in my own mind, that the situation left us with no option except the most drastic one of killing them all: quite apart from the fact that a large number had been wounded and were suffering, they simply could not be allowed to mingle with domestic stock.

In Wolhuter's day it would have been a formidable, not to say very dangerous, undertaking, but times had changed; I called in one of the park helicopters and shot them one by one, wounded and unwounded alike, until not one was left alive. It was an unsavoury task that went very much against my conservationist's grain, but choices are sometimes very stark in the bushveld, and you dare not shy away from them. The good news is that at least there were some winners in the matter, in the form of the local population, because after the buffalo had been shot they were butchered and the meat was handed out to all and sundry after being cooked on site (animal health restrictions prohibited the movement of 'infected' meat). So at least a lot of hungry bellies were filled.

And the beautiful no-man's land where all this happened? Well, after all these years it's still no-man's land, thanks to a combination of politics and greed that have slowed the laggard wheels of bureaucracy even further. But it's not beautiful any longer. The forest and bush have given way to a cardboard-and-plastic shanty town, populated by refugees from the rest of Africa.

*

Daggaboys get away with murder (sometimes literally) for the same reason that a dog is able to lick unmentionable parts of its body – because they can, being big, strong and appallingly bloody-minded. They also tend to have distinct personalities and quirks, and one of the latter that I saw time and again was their habit of taking up residence near places frequented by human beings, such as pickets and river pump stations. Why? Only the dagga-boys know, and they aren't telling.

I first came across this strange predilection as a new boy on the block in 1972, when the Skukuza pump station nearly always had a daggaboy in its vicinity. At one stage after I had moved to Skukuza in the 1980s there was even a resident buffalo cow making a nuisance of herself; she was so obnoxious that one is tempted to call her a 'daggagirl'. The main victim in this equation was, of course, the pump attendant, who had to run an actual or potential gauntlet every day when he went to check the siphon pits and pumps. In addition to this there was the foot traffic between the rest camp and the staff village along a short-cut running past the pump station. The management's view was that animals were rarely to blame, since most problems were people-induced, and our solution was to limit pedestrian use of the road past the pump station to the absolute minimum.

As usual when people are involved, this proved only partly successful. Workers would use the road in spite of all the ukases handed down by management, someone would get bumped or chased, new warnings and prohibitions would go out and be rigorously obeyed for a few days, then things would slacken off again until someone else had an encounter. Surprisingly enough these encounters didn't result in many serious injuries, but one afternoon a domestic worker who had taken the short cut was fatally gored by the 'daggagirl' cow. That was it. Louis Olivier, who was then resident ranger at Skukuza, was given the usual detailed orders – 'do something about it' – and invited me to assist him in disposing of the problem. Louis's was a sensible precaution. The pump station is on the eastern bank of the Nwaswitshaka Spruit, where it flows into the Sabie River, and there are houses on both banks and large reed-beds in both rivers. In conditions like these the margin of error is very small, and two guns make more sense than one.

Finding the culprit wasn't difficult – when we arrived at the pump station the 'daggagirl' was grazing calmly in the reeds on the west bank, only about 80 metres away from the pump station. Swiftly we hatched a plan. A direct approach was out: two bushbuck were grazing on the short grass between the reeds and the fence of the first house on the west bank, and if we scared the famously wide-awake bushbuck they would warn the buffalo. Our best option, therefore, would be to act naturally, on the assumption that the bushbuck regularly frequented the area and would not be alarmed by the arrival of visitors at the house. So we would walk along to the house like ordinary visitors, go into its garden and shoot the cow over the back fence. Which is exactly what we did, although not without a certain element of farce creeping in when Louis accidentally touched a live wire on the house's electrified fence and spent a few seconds vibrating like a tuning fork, rifle and all. This afforded much innocent amusement to our accompanying mapoisas and myself (the mapoisas managed to control themselves but I literally rolled in the dust). I can record that for some reason Louis didn't show any signs of being amused. But he went on to shoot the daggagirl rather than me, so perhaps he was just hiding his mirth rather well.

The pump station at Shingwedzi, although much more ex-posed than Skukuza's, also had its share of daggaboy troubles. One incident I remember well happened years after Louis's fight with the electrified fence, by which time I was Chief Ranger. One of my duties was to make periodical visits to the various stations and talk things over with the rangers, and on this particular day I was on the way to Shingwedzi to meet with Flip Nel, the resi-dent ranger, and his colleague Piet van Staden. When I was with-in a couple of kilometres of Flip's house, however, they radioed to ask where I was and asked me to meet them at the entrance-gate to the rest camp instead. It was clear that something was up, and when I got to the gate Flip and Piet told me that a group of illegal immigrants on their way from Mozambique had just been spotted heading north near the pump station.

I hadn't seen them, I said, although I had spotted three dagga-boys in the river, which Flip and Piet noted but took no great cognisance of, seeing that there were usually a few of the old sore-heads hanging around in the vicinity, and we cooked up a quick plan which was so simple as to be almost non-existent. Flip and I would head off the immigrants, while Piet would be the rear-guard. The fact that we were all unarmed did not, for some reason that I now forget, worry us much.

Flip and I drove over the causeway to the northern bank of the Shingwedzi, proceeded to where we thought the illegals were and then set out on foot. But we had walked no more than 100 metres or so when one of the daggaboys I had seen earlier waded out of the river about 50 metres to our left, a second one close on his heels. When they spotted us they did what daggaboys like to do in a situation like this – they came straight at us with obvious malicious intent. A moment later the third daggaboy climbed out of the river as well, paused briefly to assess the situation and then followed his friends' example. It was obviously time to find some-thing to hide in or on top of, so I turned and took off with all the afterburners going. I didn't get more than three paces, however, before I ran into a log hidden in the vegetation and was up-ended so violently that my tin of Zam Buk lip ointment fell out of the tickey pocket of my pants, my pocket-knife shot out of my hip pocket and I never did find my pen. It just goes to show how inspirational a charging daggaboy can be when a man has to get up a good turn of speed in a hurry.

The good news, however, was that while I was still lying there, trying to collect my scattered wits and pump some air back into my lungs, I heard the welcome sound of thundering buffalo hoofs fading away as their owners made for the bush. With the excitement over, I picked myself up and looked around for Flip. At first I couldn't see him and feared the worst. Then he emerged from behind a tree, understandably slightly shaken by it all. In retrospect I don't think that these three old daggaboys really wanted to flatten Flip and myself. They were probably just unimpressed by the fact that they were boxed in between Piet and the illegal immigrants on one side and Flip and myself on the other. Whatever the case, they certainly managed to leave two middle-aged rangers with significantly elevated heart rates. On the other hand, both Flip and I were grateful at having come out of it unscathed, except perhaps for bruised egos and, at least in my case, an equally bruised body.

That's the sort of encounter that convinces me that the '*Bos*' of *Bos caffer* might as well have that extra 's' added on to it. There was absolutely no doubt about who was running the show in that little incident. And the illegal immigrants? Oh, yes . . . while the daggaboys were explaining matters territorial to us, Piet managed to grab the whole lot.

*

A daggaboy (and, indeed, any other buffalo) might be tough but is not invulnerable. He will always come off second-best in the face of a cool head, a little know-how and a good rifle. He is also vulnerable to that mean and callous poacher's weapon, the fence-wire snare. I detest snares and those who set them in the same way as I detest landmines and mine-layers. Both are completely indiscriminate, and the people who set them are completely unconcerned about what activates them.

A buffalo and a snare were responsible for, although not directly involved in, one of the greatest frights I received in my time in Kruger and also the most embarrassing incident of my career. To put this in context I have to explain that in my time about 600 000 tourists visited the Kruger National Park annually, so obviously they often saw sick and injured animals before the field staff did. Sometimes this was a nuisance, with the same animal being reported over and over, and on occasion the reports were incorrect, but on the whole it was a valuable help to the over-stretched ranger staff to have several hundred thousand interested eyes out and about.

One of these spottings concerned a buffalo bull with a wire snare around its neck at the Nwatimhiri Bridge, about 13 kilometres west of Lower Sabie on the road to Skukuza. I went out with my old side-kicks Sergeant James Chauke and Corporal July Makuvele to investigate; general park policy, as I've mentioned elsewhere, was to let nature take its course in the case of sick or injured animals unless the cause was man-made or the animal concerned merited a quick and merciful death. But there was nothing natural about a snare, so the animal had to be found, its condition assessed and the most humane option exercised.

James Chauke dropped off July, another mapoisa and myself west of the Nwatimhiri Bridge and went on ahead to wait for us at Lower Sabie while we set off after the buffalo to do what was necessary. This took a bit of time, because we followed up on at least two sets of the wrong spoor before we found the buffalo we were looking for. When we did, we saw that the report had been accurate: the snare had cut through the skin, causing a festering circular wound around his neck. There was clearly no hope of recovery, so I killed him without further ado, my heart full of anger towards the people who had set the snare with such blithe unconcern for the consequences. By now it was midday and very hot, and we were all pretty tired and dirty as we started our trek back to Lower Sabie (not so tired, though, that July and the other mapoisa didn't first hack off a hunk of buffalo rump steak each and stuff the meat into their rucksacks).

The road between Lower Sabie and Skukuza follows the river, but this reach of the Sabie River has lovely vegetation, and – ever mindful of the park's bread and butter – we left the road to avoid being seen by any passing tourists. It was no hardship in any case, because the vegetation provided plenty of shade and we could slake our thirst with fresh, cool water from the river whenever we

160

felt like it. After a bit July asked if we could stop at a pool and fish for barbel. I had no objection to this, seeing that we were in no particular hurry and it was time for a lunch break anyway, not that we had any lunch. July, who had obviously come prepared, promptly dug into his 'joysak' and came out with two hand-lines, one of which he gave to me. I should explain at this point that for many years park policy was to allow staff members to make personal use of certain renewable resources like sedges, mopane worms and fish, which was an extra benefit for them without resulting in any noteworthy impact on the environment. In earlier years an unlimited amount of fish could be caught, but because of increasing numbers and the difficulty of exercising proper control a new system was introduced that designated certain sites for staff members, required a permit and limited the size of the catch.

In any case, the three of us baited up with a strip of buffalo meat each and in no time at all we had four large barbels on the bank, each of which I pithed as it was pulled out (this involves pushing a wire or even a suitable grass stem into the fish's brain, and if properly done it leaves the fish alive but brain-dead). This might sound a little excessive, since we could just as well have killed the fish then and there, but the Kruger Park is not Johannesburg. We still had a few hours' walk ahead of us before we reached Lower Sabie and then another 30 minutes' drive to Crocodile Bridge, which was quite enough time for a dead barbel to rot to the point of inedibility. Pithing them kept them alive – barbel have accessory breathing organs and can live for extended periods out of water – but docile and beyond pain.

We prepared the barbel for easy carrying by piercing their lips and inserting hooked sticks through them, and I looked around for a place to wash off my hands, which were pretty smelly by now. I didn't fancy the spot where we had been fishing because it was being patrolled by at least one large crocodile, but about 20 metres from the main body of water was an isolated pool holding reasonably clean water (much cleaner than my hands, at any rate). I noted that the pool, which was about four metres across, had plenty of impala spoor leading to and from it, so obviously they thought it was safe. I walked over, leaned my rifle against a tree and bent down to palm up some water. As I did so the placid surface in front of me erupted. Instinctively I threw myself back, or perhaps I simply fell – it all happened so fast that afterwards I couldn't remember – and as I sprawled on the sand I saw a very large crocodile bursting out of the little pool with blinding speed, fortunately in the opposite direction. I can only assume that it had been lying in ambush for an unwary impala and that my sudden appearance at the water's edge had panicked it into flight.

Any doubts I might have had about why crocodiles catch so many people every year vanished right there and then; there is nothing like a near-death experience to concentrate your mind on the essentials. Certainly my mind was so concentrated right then that I turned my back on the little pool and washed my hands and face at our fishing spot, patrolling croc or no patrolling croc. Then I attended to a final pressing need before starting the return journey. Whether or not my encounter with the croc had anything to do with it I don't know, but suddenly my bladder was telling me in no uncertain terms that it needed to be emptied – right away! I stepped away from the mapoisas, as bush etiquette demands, and let go . . . at which stage I heard the hiss of air-brakes and a tourist bus pulled up not more than three metres away from me. How it was that we didn't see or hear the bus was a mystery (although in my case it was probably shock), but clearly we – and particularly I – had inadvertently wandered closer to the tourist road than we had realised.

About the only positive thing about this blush-making moment was that I was facing *away* from the bus, although only a blind man could have been unaware of what I was doing. I can't even begin to guess what the people in the bus thought when they saw three very dirty armed men emerge from the bush with four large fish and a couple of blood-soaked rucksacks, brazenly unconcerned to the point of openly piddling by the roadside. If it had been 20 years later they would probably have resigned themselves immediately to being hijacked and robbed. Whatever the case, some interesting theories and speculations must have flown back and forth over the cold beers in the rest camp that evening.

*

I had not been in the Kruger National Park for more than a few years when links were formed with the South African Defence Force that were still in place when I retired in 2001, although forms had changed over the decades. Kruger's eastern boundary is also, of course, the international border with Mozambique, and when the SADF started taking over the border protection function from the South African Police after 1974 it was only a matter of time before the military arrived in our stamping grounds.

We feared the worst, and we were right. At that time virtually the only combat troops the SADF had were a handful of full-time units manned by national servicemen with a sprinkling of professional soldiers leading them, and a large second layer of part-time units, some trained for conventional warfare and the others for internal security. The part-time units were not often used for routine tasks, so that what we would get in Kruger would be national service units, rotated in and out at fairly frequent intervals.

We calculated that this would cause trouble, and we were right. Officers and men would arrive with some strange (to us) ideas and have to pick up the tricks of the trade the hard way. Then, just when they were becoming really useful, their tours would be over and we would have to start again with the next lot. The struggle went on for quite some time until the penny finally dropped at Defence Headquarters – although not without a long struggle on our side – and the SADF established an infantry battalion that was locally recruited and permanently stationed in the park. This provided the necessary continuity of institutional knowledge and worked well.

My first run-in with non-orientated outside troops was in 1975, when border protection of any kind was pretty rudimentary in any case. Military intelligence received word that the Mozambicans, who were then still in the first flowering of revolutionary fervour, planned to carry out an armed incursion into Kruger through Shilowa Poort. The aim of such an incursion eluded me at the time and eludes me still, but there it was, and something had to be done about it. The 'something' consisted mainly of deploying a battery of artillery minus its guns in the Shilowa area. Deploying artillerymen on what was obviously an infantry task was not an ideal situation, but they were all that the Army had immediately available.

In due course the troops arrived, somewhat unhappy, as gunners tend to be when torn away from their beloved artillery pieces and turned into foot-soldiers, and were deployed in the Shilowa Poort area after I had given them a briefing. This first contact left me with some misgivings about how well the enterprise was going to work, and as an added complication I was due to go to Johannesburg for a few days. By way of reinforcement, therefore, I seconded the mapoisas at the Shilowa Picket to the artillerymen and departed for Johannesburg, hoping for the best and pleased that one of them would be Julius Mbombe, the supremely talented tracker who had run down the elephant that had nearly killed my old comrade-in-arms Amos Chongo (see 'Master of Life and Death'). Julius's local knowledge and vast experience, I reckoned, would be a great asset to the battery's commanding officer.

Alas, things didn't quite work out the way I had hoped. On my return Corporal Sandros Matsimbe told me of an incident at Shilowa involving shots fired at a buffalo by the troops. We had no radio contact with either the mapoisas or the troops, so early the next morning Sandros and I drove out to Shilowa, where we found that the gunner captain had confined Julius to barracks (in the form of the picket) for insubordination. Julius told me that he had been accompanying a patrol at the foot of Shilowa Hill – an area of dense scrub mopane and good grass – when he saw the very fresh spoor of a buffalo that was clearly injured because it was dragging its leg. Julius realised that this spelt possible trouble, informed the patrol commander that the area immediately ahead was unsafe because of the presence of the injured buffalo and suggested that they skirt it instead of going straight ahead. The patrol commander insisted that the patrol carry on straight through; Julius, in turn, refused to go with the troops and started heading back to the picket in spite of the patrol commander's objections. Sure enough, he had not gone far when he heard shots – 'itele', he said, which in the Tsonga language means 'many' – and knew that either the soldiers had run into the buffalo or the buffalo had run into the soldiers. Julius, although a naturally brave man, wanted nothing more to do with what was shaping up as a potentially disastrous situation and ran the rest of the way to the picket. There he and his partner climbed on their bicycles and hurried off to Mooiplaas, where they reported what had happened to Sandros and then cycled back to Shilowa to face the military music.

After leaving Julius I went to see the captain, who confirmed the story in its essentials and added that the buffalo had been severely wounded, although he could not tell me how many shots his troops had fired or how many hits they had scored. He then went on to make some pointed remarks about Julius's cowardice and lack of discipline, and how well-trained his own troops were. When I said I would have to find the buffalo and kill it if it hadn't died in the meantime, he scoffed that as far as he was concerned I would be wasting my time; the buffalo had been hit so many times that it couldn't have gone more than a few metres before going belly-up. This was good rousing motivational stuff, but it was obvious that the captain hadn't sent anyone to check on the buffalo's condition, or even thought about using vultures as tell-tales. Providing such tricks of the trade was precisely why I had seconded Julius and his partner to the army, except, of course, that their opinion had not been asked.

Julius and I soon locked on to the allegedly deceased buffalo's spoor. About an hour later we found him, more or less three kilometres from where the soldiers had shot at him, and put him down. He was certainly in poor condition – but not from the army's doing; there were deep gashes on his hindquarters, from which I deduced that he had been clawed by a lion or lions, injuries which would have accounted for the leg-dragging Julius had noticed. What we didn't find was any evidence of his having been pulverised by the soldiers' fire, as the captain so confidently believed. There was not one bullet-hole on his uppermost side, and when we turned him over we found one entry wound in his shoulder, about seven inches from the top of the back. Our feedback to the captain caused a certain amount of gloom and consternation, and I can only hope that our own amusement didn't show too clearly. Later, incidentally, we found 31 cartridge-cases at the scene of the shooting, and no doubt there were others that we didn't spot.

*

165

In Kruger we used to have staff Christmas parties, just like city firms all over South Africa. But a staff Christmas party in Kruger was not, needless to say, quite the same as it would be in a city like Johannesburg or Cape Town. The customary good cheer would suffuse everyone, of course, and the occasional couple would have a tumble in a makeshift love-nest, but we didn't go in much for funny paper hats and trays of snacks from some caterer. Also, it was much more difficult to turn away gate-crashers, these being party animals in more ways than one.

Kruger's Christmas parties for lower-band employees took place early in December, just before the technical service staffers went on leave. Such employees received monthly food rations of canned meat, dried vegetables, salt, maize meal and similar staples, and the Christmas parties – self-catered, naturally, living as we did at the epicentre of Nature's bountiful larder – were in the same gastronomic idiom. There was no fooling around with plastic cups of lukewarm sparkling wine and effete little shrink-wrapped snacks. Staffers who drank jabula – traditional sorghum beer – were given a suitable quantity on the house, while those who didn't received an equivalent issue of cold drinks, and each party-goer got a hefty chunk of fresh-killed buffalo meat, which would be braaied on the spot. How the buffalo meat was supplied depended on where the party was taking place. At the larger camps the processing plant at Skukuza provided the meat. Elsewhere the local ranger would go out and shoot a couple of buffalo just before the party (this might sound like an abuse of resources, but the number of Christmas buffalo shot would be subtracted from the annual quota to be culled). Going shopping for the main course on the day of the party, as it were, might sound a little hit-or-miss, but we had a good system in place. Buffalo, particularly daggaboys, are creatures of habit, so in late November the mapoisas would start afternoon patrols near the rest camps and ranger stations to keep tabs on the floating population, and then when the big day came the ranger would go out to a spot where the presence of buffalo was virtually guaranteed and pop a couple. If they stayed away, he would take a few impala rams instead.

It was a pretty foolproof system, although it sometimes developed a wheel-wobble in the actual execution. I remember one year – 1982, during my time at Shingwedzi – when it got considerably more than wobbly. We'd done our homework as usual, and on the afternoon of the Christmas party mapoisa Antonio Mandlaze and I went off to do our shopping at a certain spot along the Shingwedzi River where, according to our patrols, buffalo always gathered to drink at around four o'clock. Like a daggaboy, I tend to be a creature of habit, and my invariable custom on such occasions was to take two rifles with me, a light one in .222 Remington calibre for impala and my .375 Magnum for buffalo. But that day, for reasons I couldn't remember afterwards, I left them both at home and instead armed myself with my 7.62 mm R1 service rifle. We crossed the river in my truck and took the dirt road running parallel to the river, in the direction of the low-water bridge, with Antonio standing on the back as the spotter, as happily unaware as I was that we were about to be plunged into a strictly unscheduled drama.

I stopped when Antonio tapped on the roof of the cab, and he told me there was a buffalo off to the left, about 100 metres away. I climbed up next to him, saw the buffalo and shot for the heart, knowing it wouldn't go far. The buffalo took off and ran behind a mopane tree. When it emerged I gave it another heart shot for safety's sake, conscious of the fact that the R1 cartridge was perhaps a trifle light for the purpose. But this was one tough buffalo, and in spite of two heart shots it didn't drop but vanished among the mopanes again. I was pretty sure we would now find it dead, but, incredibly, it made another appearance. I gave it a third heart shot.

At that point Antonio asked me in a somewhat incredulous voice what I was doing. Since it was patently obvious, I replied rather abruptly: 'Shooting a buffalo for your Christmas party,' and was extremely disconcerted when he retorted: 'No, you've just shot three!' We went to have a closer look, and sure enough, found the spoor of three wounded buffalo. Well, no harm had been done. The staff members and their families didn't know it yet, but they were going to have a far bigger blow-out than they had bargained for, and to any good African, black or white, there's just no such thing as too much red meat to eat.

The only thing still left to do was fetch the tractor and trailer from Shingwedzi, round up a few willing hands and retrieve the buffalo, and this time I would bring my .375 Magnum along just in case one of them was not as dead as it should be – one of the early survival lessons you learn in the bushveld is that when it comes to buffalo it is wise to cultivate a belt-and-braces philosophy. Before I got in behind the wheel I unloaded my R1, one of the most important rules in this sort of hunting being never, ever, to climb into a vehicle with a loaded weapon. While doing this I noticed that for some reason the rearsight was set at 600 metres, rather than 200, as it should have been. How the hell had that happened? I had certainly not cranked the sight up to 600.

I didn't waste any time speculating about this mysterious development, because I now had a far more urgent concern, namely three wounded buffalo bulls. With the sight at the 600-metre present setting the R1 would have been shooting something like 40 cm high and inflicting flesh wounds that would make any old daggaboy about five times as irascible as he normally was. So now I would have to track down all three and finish them off, not only because of all those hungry party-goers but also because they were in pain and constituted a deadly menace to anyone they came across. Antonio agreed, adding just one word: 'Poison!' An old hand at the game, he knew what tracking and killing a wounded buffalo could entail, never mind three of them in one lump.

We came back from Shingwedzi with the .375, the tractor and trailer and some extra mapoisas who were to mark the locality of the buffalo carcasses and later lead the recovery team in. I anticipated the worst, given my run of luck so far, but everything turned out well. The buffalo had stuck together, and by the end of the afternoon we had caught up with them about four kilometres further on and killed all three.

With the last one safely down and the recovery team on its way, Antonio and I headed home for some hard-earned down time, feeling relieved that things had turned out as well as they did, considering the bad start. I'd scarcely opened my second beer, however, when Antonio turned up again. 'The tractor,' he said matter-of-factly, 'is broken.' It was not the sort of news I needed just then, but there was nothing I could do except fire up my truck and pick up the tractor driver to guide us to his stranded steed. It was broken, sure enough. I couldn't understand how it was possible for a tractor to break a stub axle at a speed of less than 10 km/h, but there it was. Kruger had won again! Maybe, I thought sourly, it was the same reverse miracle that had pushed my R1's sight up to the 600-metre notch.

To make things worse, the mechanics were going to leave next day and wouldn't be back until mid-January, so here I sat with not one but three dead buffalo and a trailer, but nothing to pull them with. More hassles! I managed to borrow a tractor from the rest camp and get the meat back, but the tractor would have to stay where it was until the mechanics finally got back, with a firebreak around it, just in case. The members of my working party were somewhat less than happy about being commandeered because they were already in a festive mood and looking forward to getting slightly drunk to mark the start of the holiday season, but unscheduled inconvenience is part of Kruger life, and we soon chopped and burnt a 100-metre-wide firebreak around the crippled tractor. Then we left the damned thing there to celebrate Christmas in well-deserved solitude and went home to get ourselves a little oiled.

*

As I've said elsewhere, one adage I always tried to imprint on the minds of new staff members was that the only predictable thing about wild animals was their total unpredictability. For a tyro this sort of apparent Irishism is sometimes hard to absorb, so that the lesson isn't really driven home until they see for themselves how true it is.

For Andrew Hofmeyr, one of the younger rangers during my stint as Chief Ranger, the lesson was cemented in place in very impressive – and, for Kruger, very expensive – fashion during a buffalo-culling operation. All the targeted buffalo had gone down as planned, the ground team had moved in to tackle its gory job of bleeding and gutting prior to loading the carcasses for transport to the processing plant in Skukuza, and the helicopter landed to drop Andrew off so that he could supervise the slaughtering.

Andrew had barely got his feet on the ground, however, before one of the allegedly dead buffalo jumped up, full of beans, and made straight for him with the obvious intention of adding him to the bodies lying all around. Andrew, no slouch when it came to quick reflexes, somehow managed to dodge the buffalo, but the chopper was less fortunate. The buffalo smashed into the tail-boom and thoroughly mangled it before tearing away into the bush, seemingly unscathed, to be seen no more. How all this could have happened was one of those great unsolved African mysteries, but there was no doubt about the damage to the helicopter, and it was grounded for several weeks.

Years later a possible explanation for the miraculously resurrected buffalo presented itself when Hugo van Niekerk and I were engaged in culling south of Shingwedzi. We were a slick team, and in just six minutes and 26 seconds there were 38 buffalo lying dead in close proximity to one another, the entire group that we had originally cut off from the herd. Hugo called in the recovery team while I packed my rifles and darts away, feeling justifiably proud about a job well done, even though it was an unpleasant one. But the euphoria evaporated pretty fast when I noticed that I had four darts out of 40 left in the box when there should have been just two! This could mean only one thing, that two of the buffalo were simply playing dead. My inner alarm bells went off immediately and I yelled over the intercom: 'Hugo! Stop the ground teams!'

Hugo and I had been culling for a long time and he didn't stop to ask questions, just passed on an urgent warning to the recovery team – whose vehicles were now less than 20 metres from the edge of the group of dead buffalo – to stay put and not get out. This done, he asked me what the problem was. I explained about the discrepancy, then hauled out my .375 Magnum again while Hugo turned and took the helicopter in very low, so that we could try to find the 'dead' buffalo. This didn't take long: we had barely started when they rose up from the ground right in front of the chopper's nose and headed for the bush at top speed . . . you can be sure I checked the other 36 very carefully, even though the mystery had solved itself.

Around the fire that evening we discussed the incident at

length, and I actually remembered something that had struck me as odd at the time but hadn't registered due to my preoccupation with the darting: two buffalo had gone down without exhibiting any of the usual signs of drug-induced collapse. The general consensus was that these two had become so confused by the fact that the rest of the group had apparently fallen asleep in spite of all the noise and dust that they followed suit, lying low until they were spooked into flight when the helicopter looked as if it would settle right on top of them. It might very well be that something similar happened on the day of Andrew Hofmeyr's near-miss and the helicopter's bull's-eye, given the nearly identical circumstances. Africa is full of surprises, isn't it? In any case, the record Hugo and I achieved that day still stands – even though it ended up being 36 instead of 38 buffalo downed in six minutes and 26 seconds.

*

On the other hand, long experience is no guarantee that you are going to walk away from an encounter with a buffalo, be it a daggaboy or not, and the proof of that statement is to be found in incidents like one in which my good friend and colleague Johan van Graan featured at a time when he was nearing retirement and had an almost unequalled depth of hard-won knowledge under his belt.

Johan spent the last couple of years before retirement as the resident ranger at Crocodile Bridge, and one day in September 2000, a year before he was to leave Kruger, his mapoisas told him that they had seen a buffalo cow along the eastern boundary with a snare around her left back foot. Her condition had already deteriorated to such an extent, they added, that she couldn't keep up with the members of her herd any more, although her calf of about 18 months old hadn't abandoned her. There was only one thing that could be done, and that was to put her out of her misery, so Johan took his .375 Magnum and set off with three of his mapoisas, August, Michael and Paul.

They found the cow and calf without much difficulty and stopped not more than 60 metres away from them; the calf was in full view, staring straight at them, while the cow was almost completely hidden by some round-leaf kiaat shrubs. Johan got out with his rifle, followed by the mapoisas. Moments later everything changed. First the calf exploded into motion, bearing down on them at full speed. The mapoisas jumped back into the truck, but Johan stood his ground, having made a quick decision not to shoot the calf but to sidestep it. This presented no great difficulty, but by now the cow had become alarmed at the threat to her offspring and launched a gammy-legged but still lethal charge.

All this happened in a breathtakingly short time, but like the veteran he was, Johan calmly fired two well-aimed bullets into the cow. To his dismay they seemed to have no effect on her, so Johan took aim again, but before he could fire the cow hit him. Johan started to fall, clinging to his rifle for all he was worth, but the rifle's sling got caught by the buffalo's horn, and she set about butting him on the chest and neck. Johan grabbed hold of her horns, knowing that if he didn't she could start throwing him around. Then she managed to get her horn hooked around his neck, and he could hear the bones inside it creaking as they started to cave in. Desperately he yelled at the mapoisas to shoot. They did, quickly and accurately, and the next moment the buffalo collapsed on top of him, her face only inches away from his, so close that later he could recall the smell of her breath; like freshly mown lucerne, he said.

The mapoisas dragged the buffalo off him, and like the veteran he was, Johan remembered to fire an 'insurance shot' into her spine in spite of his shaken condition. And shaken he was; by the time they had loaded the buffalo on to the back of the truck Johan was shivering so hard from shock that when he tried to light a cigarette he couldn't get the match-flame to its tip. Yet he suffered nothing worse than some bad bruising, although they kept him in the Barberton Hospital for a couple of days just to make sure.

*

My long-time sidekick Sergeant James Chauke had a few good daggaboy stories of his own, one of the best of which he told me in peculiar circumstances; not around a campfire, where most of the good stories are told, but near the end of a long, nerve-racking night walk through an area infested by – you guessed it – daggaboys . . .

The area concerned was Kruger's Crocodile Bridge section, which has always been known for the buffalo herds frequenting the plains between the Gomondwane welwitschia forest and the Lebombo Mountains. The time was midwinter, and James and I were returning from an inspection trip along the eastern boundary between Crocodile Bridge and Lower Sabie. One of the things we had to do was to deliver water to the mapoisas manning the Godleni picket, and on the way up the steep incline to Godleni I somehow managed to cut one of the rear tyres of the heavily loaded Land Cruiser. This wasn't an immediate problem, because we simply changed the tyre and carried on, stopping at Lower Sabie on the way back to see the mapoisas there and then heading home to Crocodile Bridge just as the sun was setting. Because it was getting late I opted for the shorter route back via the Mativuhlungu loop, which was a somewhat isolated dirt road. It turned out to be not such a good idea, as we soon discovered when we suffered another puncture about 15 kilometres away from Crocodile Bridge. So there we were, in the middle of the Park, in pitch darkness, with just two options: we could spend the night in the truck, which would be a pain in the neck but reasonably safe, or we could walk home, which would also be a pain in the neck and might turn out to be very unsafe.

Walking on roads at night in an area inhabited by big game is never a good proposition, especially in winter. It gets cold after dark, and lions and puff adders in particular like to lie on the roads and absorb some of the residual heat from the daylight hours. In addition, elephants are frequent nocturnal road-walkers, and, of course, in this case there were the buffalo to add some extra potential lethality to the mix. A final negative factor was that accurate shooting is difficult on a dark night because a rifle's sights become almost invisible. It will be clear, therefore, why I certainly wasn't keen to hit the road, and I don't believe James was either. But we were even less keen to admit that we were scared, so we took our rifles and started walking along what we hoped would be the least perilous route.

Normally we would have cut straight through the bush

towards Crocodile Bridge, but the Gomondwane welwitschia forest was almost impenetrable even during the day, and trying to cut through it at night would be equivalent to writing a suicide note; as it was, the night was so dark that from time to time we had to go down on our hands and knees to try to see if we could make out the skyline in the road ahead. About the only defence mechanism we had was our voices, so while we walked we talked as loudly as possible to advertise our presence, and thereby (we hoped) alarm anything we might meet. Believe me, two people can tell one another many stories in the time it takes to walk 15 kilometres in the black of night. Some were about things we had gone through together, while others were newly heard and sometimes made things known about the teller that the listener had never known or even guessed at.

James kicked off by reminding me of the lion, badly hurt in a fight but definitely not incapacitated, for which we had been looking near the Gomondwane windmill for the last two weeks. It wasn't actually a subject we relished discussing, though, because we really wouldn't have liked it to find us in our present situation. We swapped a few more lion stories with less immediate connotations, went on to elephants and, when these ran dry, got on to the subject of buffaloes. At this time James had been stationed at Crocodile Bridge for more than 20 years and had stacks of buffalo stories that lasted us almost to the end of our unscheduled stroll.

Sooner than seemed possible we crossed the Vurhami Spruit, only about two kilometres from home. From here on the the veld was wide open and infinitely less menacing than what we had passed through earlier in our perilous trek, so we cut away from the road and headed directly for my house. We were close enough to see lights when James stopped without warning. I thought he had seen something, but he hadn't, just said: 'I have one last story to tell you before we get home.' I waited. We had talked for almost 15 kilometres, but I knew that a compendium of untold tales still remained locked up in James's head. Africans of all races tend to be gregarious people, but James was the exception. He often went on solitary patrols and experienced things about which he didn't talk (his example later influenced my decision to

174

undertake so many single-handed wanderings after poachers). So whatever final story James had to tell would be worth listening to.

One day, he said reminiscently, he was walking alone in the area between the reeds and the false bank of the Crocodile River – not a safe area at the best of times, seeing that any animal you met there felt threatened because it was cut off on one side by the reeds and on the other by the bank, and many of them were genetically programmed to react violently in such a situation. That was precisely what happened in this case. A daggaboy emerged from the reeds just as James came past; they must have seen each other at very much the same moment. Both reacted almost instantaneously. The daggaboy charged, while James ran as fast as he could towards a large marula tree he had noticed growing in the space between the river's true and false banks.

It was a desperately close race for James, with his most valuable possession, his life, as the only stake. He poured every scrap of energy into his pumping legs, his ears filled with the sounds of the pursuing buffalo, and he knew that it was gaining on him with every step. He redoubled his efforts and reached the marula not more than a couple of jumps ahead of the daggaboy, running so fast by now that there was no question of being able to stop in time, so he caught the trunk in the hook of his arm and swung around it to temporary safety. Next moment the daggaboy smashed into the tree with such force that he knocked off a large disc of bark. That broke the pursuit; the daggaboy shook his head, probably dazed by the massive impact, and galloped off into the bush. Up to this point James had been speaking in Tsonga. Now he switched to Afrikaans: 'En daar hardloop die buffel weg, en agter die boom staan die kaffer en bewe,' which is to say: 'And while the buffalo ran away, the kaffir stood shaking behind the tree.'

We walked on towards the house, and I thought about the story and the way James had ended it. 'Kaffir' wasn't a polite term for a black man, and James knew it perfectly well. He had also had no need to switch languages because I would have understood the punch-line just as well if he had spoken in Tsonga. Knowing James as I did, I was sure that he had made both departures very deliberately: firstly to emphasise what a huge impression that very close

175

escape from almost certain death had made on him, and secondly, of course, as a cautionary tale, like so many I heard from the mapoisas over the years as they allowed their experiences and knowledge to trickle down to my ever-receptive ears. Is it any wonder that I remember them with such fondness and gratitude?

10

THE HIPPO –
KILLER AND COMEDIAN

The hippopotamus suffers from a bad press. In song, legend and movie cartoon it is usually portrayed as a big, fat, greedy and comical dolt – albeit a generally good-natured one – and it must be admitted that it is pretty comical-looking, while its name positively begs to be included in humorous rhymes. The fact that the hippo's nearest blood-relative is the pig, another favourite cartoon character, also does nothing for its image.

Hippos can be comical, all right. Once, when I was stationed at Crocodile Bridge early in my career, we decided to take some visiting friends to dinner at Lower Sabie. It was a pitch-dark winter's night and I had the men in the party ride in the back of my Land Cruiser with spotlights so that they would have an opportunity of seeing some interesting nocturnal animals. Sure enough, just east of Lower Sabie the lights picked up a hippo walking down the road. Our appearance on the scene clearly threw him into a panic. He ran down the road, heading away from us, then changed his mind, threw a tight turn and headed for the safety of the river. Unfortunately for him he didn't notice until it was too late that the road went over a culvert at that precise point, and after a quick teeter on the edge he went straight down, somersaulting in the process. For a few moments he lay on his back, kicking furiously and squealing like a pig while he gathered his scattered wits. Then, clearly none the worse for his impromptu flying lesson, he scrambled up and went for the river at a flat-out run, leaving us paralysed with hysterical mirth. One is tempted to misuse Neil Armstrong's famous phrase and say 'one small step for hippodom, one large laugh for mankind.' But don't be fooled by incidents like that. If ever there was an animal that fails to conform to its popular stereotype it is the hippo, as many people have found to their detriment.

In real life the hippo is an enormous animal – rivalled only by the elephant and rhinoceros as the largest living land mammal – and it is very dangerous indeed. Conservation literature often cites the hippo as being responsible for more human deaths than any other animal in Africa. This is not quite correct. The champion all-category murderers in the animal kingdom are the tiny blood parasites of the *Plasmodium* species that cause malaria (mosquitoes don't actually kill people, they only transmit the disease via the *Plasmodium* parasites when the females drink people's blood). But the hippo is certainly the deadliest of the large and not-so-large land animals, and it is easy to see why.

The average adult hippo weighs in at around two tons, with its balloon shape and stubby legs making it look definitely overweight, and at speed it resembles nothing so much as a kid's piggy-bank on wheels that is going down a play-park slide. But it can crank up an awesome turn of speed on land and is surprisingly agile in rough terrain (I have tracked them all the way into the Lebombo Mountains, where even a human has to watch his footing). Combine the hippo's weight and speed with a cavernous mouth heavily armed with several kinds of teeth, including canine tusks measuring anything from 10 to 70 centimetres, plus a built-in bad attitude, you have a killing machine which might not be lean but certainly is mean if you tangle with it at the wrong time or in the wrong place. Men, women, crocodiles or other hippos – all is grist to the mill of the animal that is known in Afrikaans by the quaint name of *seekoei*, or 'sea-cow', and even born bushvelders are vulnerable.

One such was Lizbet Maluleke, wife of one of our mapoisas, Corporal Makasane Maluleke, who was stationed at the Mahlangeni ranger section, where the Letaba River flows into the Kruger National Park through its western boundary. One day Lizbet – born and bred in Mozambique, like Makasane himself, and as familiar with veld ways as he was – went fishing with some of her friends, chattering happily as they headed for the river. But barely an hour later the friends ran shivering and wailing to the ranger, Kobus Kruger, to tell him that a hippo had attacked them and killed Lizbet. The women told Kobus that they had been crossing a patch of sand on the way to the river when a hippo, for no reason that they could think of, rose out of the water and charged them at full speed. Poor Lizbet, who was in her sixties and portly to boot, didn't have a chance. The hippo seized her and her friends fled precipitately, assuming that the scream she uttered was her last. Kobus hurried to the scene and came on a terrible sight: Lizbet had been bitten at least three times, but she was so mangled that he could not be sure. She was still alive, however, although only just, and he got her off to the hospital at Phalaborwa as fast as he could. But her wounds were too grave, and that same day she died.

A staff member who was killed by a hippo in the early 1970s while eradicating alien plants in the south of the Park was mangled even worse than poor Lizbet. The hippo literally bit him to pieces: when we went to the scene – a path in the reeds near the bed of the river – we found his head, one shoulder and one arm on one side of the path, his lower body and legs almost opposite on the other side, and the other arm and torso about 20 metres further along. We couldn't tell whether the hippo had dismembered him with one bite or chewed him up, and, frankly, we didn't spend too much time speculating about it: even to fairly hardened people like us it was an utterly sickening sight, and we were all thankful that the police rather than ourselves had to pick up the pieces, both figuratively and literally.

*

Deaths or injuries resulting from encounters with hippos are by no means always the result of aggressive behaviour, though. A hippo's first reaction when it gets a fright is usually to run headlong back to the safety of the water, and if anyone gets in the way the consequences are likely to be serious, even when the encounter is accidental. Colliding with a hippo while driving, especially at night, is another definite danger. At night a hippo becomes virtually invisible, even when the vehicle's headlights are on; about the only thing that gives it away at such a time is the pinkness of its belly and the lighter colour where the pink merges into the darker upper body. Especially to the unpractised eye – and often to the practised one as well – this is not all that easy to see, even at the best of times, and a stationary hippo on the road verge is a standing invitation to a fender-bender at the least and a disaster at worst. To the best of my knowledge there are more collisions between motor vehicles and hippos outside conservation areas than inside them. This might seem strange at first glance, but there are good reasons for the phenomenon. Firstly, the average motorist heading down a highway on his lawful occasions doesn't expect to find himself bearing down on a hippo, especially one that is all but invisible. Secondly, most conservation areas restrict anyone but experienced staff from driving at night, a very sensible rule for a number of reasons besides preventing motorists from side-swiping some itinerant sea-cow.

Generally speaking, it remains a good rule of thumb that no one – be he ranger or tourist – should muck about with hippos if he can possibly avoid it, and once again I speak from painful experience which dates back to 1969, before I even arrived in Kruger. At that time I was assisting a professional hunter named Mike Robinson in Botswana's great Okavango Delta in Botswana, and we were taking a group of people on a canoe trip from the northern to the southern parts of the swamp. It was a 'real thing' sort of trip – no tents or fancy equipment, outboard motors or anything like that. We paddled the canoes and lived off dehydrated and tinned food, plus what Mike and I were allowed to shoot for the pot and the fresh bread that the cook baked daily in a black pot in a hole in the ground.

It's strange to think that at the very time I was getting down and dirty with one of the few fairly pristine remaining parts of the old Africa, the cradle of mankind, Neil Armstrong and Buzz Aldrin were pushing back the frontiers of our species by setting foot on the moon! Many years later it was my pleasure to tell Aldrin about this marvellous juxtaposition when I spent a fortnight scuba-diving with him off Bonaire Island in the Netherlands Antilles.

One afternoon Mike was a little unsure of where we were and asked me to pitch camp on a small island while he went to have a look around in one of the canoes. Along with our two local staffers, Smash and Mohodi, I saw to the beaching of the other canoes on the island, which was about as large as a rugby field, and then I sent Smash off to look around for a good campsite.

While he was gone Mohodi and I stayed with the group, fighting off clouds of tsetse flies. Talk about aggressive animals! It felt as if those vicious little things wanted to devour us whole. We were all fairly chewed up by the time Smash returned, so I was not at all averse to his suggestion that we burn off the vegetation to get rid of the flies. We got our clients back into the canoes and told them to paddle off for 100 metres or so while we set the fires. This didn't take too long, and before long we began to set up camp.

This was not as grand a process as it sounds, given the no-frills nature of the trip, and amounted to no more than starting a cooking fire and laying out our sleeping-bags on relatively bump-free ground. We didn't know that a hippo lived in a small inlet near by and was not happy with this intrusion on his personal space. But we soon found out about it when the hippo heaved itself up out of the water and charged our clients with obvious malign intent. There could be only one outcome if he reached them, so I did the only thing possible in the circumstances, which was to shoot him without delay. The hippo went down as expected; what I did not expect was to see two Botswanan game guards in a 'makorro' – a traditional native canoe made from the hollowed-out trunk of a tree – appear as if by magic before the ash had even settled around its body. Thinking about it later, I concluded that they had been alerted in the first place by the smoke from our burning-off, after which my shot at the hippo really got them going.

Smash and Mahodi conferred with them in Setswana and then solemnly informed me that the game guards intended to arrest me for illegally shooting the hippo, which was considered 'royal game', and take me to Maun to be charged. It was a bleak prospect, but Smash and Mahodi were obviously old hands at the negotiation game and eloquently pleaded our case. This trip was a legally authorised operation, they said, adding that I was the only guide (a downright lie), that we still were about a week of gentle paddling away from Maun, that Maun was our only destination and that I had had no alternative but to shoot the hippo to prevent it from chewing up some hard-currency tourists. Much leisurely talk later a suitable deal was struck: the game guards would confiscate my passport and I would meet them at Maun in about a week's time to face the music. The game guards then went on their way with my passport, having eaten an amazing amount of the recently departed aggressor, not to mention a large quantity of maize-meal porridge and other items from our larder. My problem temporarily solved in this eminently civilised manner, we turned the rest of the hippo into biltong and continued our trip.

Five days later, having settled our clients into Afam's Safari Camp at Maun, I went along to put my case to the responsible Botswana Game Department official. He was clearly not very happy about the hippo, but after hearing my story and seeing my credentials he made a deal with me. I would report to him at 10 o'clock next morning and he would return my passport to me, which suited both of us because we knew that Mike and I were due to see off our canoeists two hours before that. Next morning I parcelled off the clients and reported to the official at 10 o'clock to retrieve my passport, after which we parted company on good terms, not knowing that just three years later our paths were to cross again when he ended up doing an honours degree with Helena at the University of Pretoria.

*

In 1973 – by which time I was stationed at Crocodile Bridge, having dug myself into the Kruger National Park like a tick on a buffalo's back – I had another little contretemps with a hippo which I shall have to come to by way of a tangent because it is tied up with an unrelated incident in which my colleague Ted Whitfield and I killed a troublesome buffalo that had nearly finished off one of our mapoisas, Ephraim Silinda. We followed our standard procedure, which required that if you did not kill the buffalo with your first shot you put as many more bullets into him as you could; if that didn't bring him down, you tracked him till you found him again, and if he had not died of his wounds you finished him off. This might sound like a messy way of doing the job, but anyone who has ever hunted buffalo will tell you that they are extremely tough customers in every way. Anyway, this particular buffalo had been brought down in the Crocodile River bed by a quick barrage of shots fired by Ted and myself.

To return to my hippo story, the farms along the Crocodile River rely on the river to irrigate their crops and often have to build structures in the river itself to facilitate water extraction by their pumps, especially when the level is low. One of these farms, Ten Bosch, owned by the Transvaal Sugar Board, extended from Crocodile Bridge almost to the border post at Komatipoort and had a weir near the Dzunwini Picket to channel water from the river to its pumps, and early one morning I was telephoned by one of the section managers, whom I shall call 'HT'. I lent a sympathetic ear because I knew HT would not waste my time. He was a keen hunter who often told me stories about his experiences, finding a ready audience because although I had accumulated quite a lot of experience for a young man of 25 I knew I still had a lot to learn and always enjoyed listening to the (comparatively speaking) 'old guys'. HT explained that he had a dead hippo floating alongside one of his water-extraction points. Since this particular point supplied water for domestic use at his house and at the labour quarters, could I please arrange for the removal of the carcass? Naturally I said yes, so we arranged to meet at his house, HT undertaking to make his bulldozer available because I lacked the mechanical means to move the enormous corpse.

I contacted the Veterinary Services stock inspector to supervise the disposal of the meat and then went to meet HT at his house, accompanied by Sergeant James Chauke. On the way to the pump station HT asked about the incident with Ephraim and the buffalo, because, it transpired, he had heard the five shots Ted and I had fired between us. I told him what had happened, but my little inner devil persuaded me to make one notable omission – that I had fired only two of the five shots. HT found this hard to believe, saying, quite correctly, that no one person could fire five shots that fast with a heavy-calibre rifle, but I had committed myself and stuck to the story. HT frankly didn't know what to think, and on this rather doubting note we reached the river.

HT went off to have a look at the northern bank of the river while James and I walked out on to the weir to inspect the dead hippo. It lay in crystal-clear water about two metres deep, and according to HT it had not moved for the past three days. But as I looked it over my little devil's decent brother whispered:

'There's something wrong here.' I was inclined to concur. Dead hippos tend to lie on their sides, whether on or in the water, but this one was right side up, its head buried in the reeds and its large backside facing us. I asked James to throw a stone at the hippo to see if we could get a reaction, but there was none to be found, as is usually the case when you need one, so I amended my request and told him to poke it in the bum with a length of reed. The first poke evoked no reaction, but when James poked a second time the dead hippo miraculously came to life and hurled itself at the bank to get at us. Fortunately for us it couldn't get enough traction and fell back with an almighty splash. Undeterred by this slight setback, it came for us again, at first swimming underwater and then surfacing no more than two metres away. Not a good idea because, albeit rather belatedly, I killed it with two quick shots. HT came hurrying back when he heard me firing, and rather grudgingly acknowledged that I had pulled off a good shot. My adrenalin was still pumping and I retorted: 'There were two shots, not one!'

HT didn't believe me, and he continued not to believe me until his bulldozer dragged the hippo out of the water and the two bullet-holes in its head became clearly visible. That's when the penny dropped. 'So it *was* you in the river bed the other day!' he cried, and then, of course, the full story of Ephraim's buffalo came out. I must be honest and admit that I felt no shame about being exposed as a yarner. Tall hunting stories are, after all, as much a tradition as anglers' terminological inexactitude about the size of 'the one that got away'.

*

Periodical hippo culling aimed at preserving a healthy ecological balance took place regularly in the Kruger National Park during most of my first two decades there. It first started during a severe drought in the early 1960s, when the Letaba River stopped flowing altogether for the first time during the winter months and the Olifants River reached its lowest level in living memory. This had an immediate knock-on effect as far as hippos were concerned, because during very dry periods there are not enough pools suitable for hippo habitation. The result was serious over-crowding, vicious fighting and the serious degradation of the surrounding area as a result of trampling and overgrazing.

In 1963 the hippo population of each of the two rivers had exceeded 1 000, and it was obvious that the critical level in the population curve had been reached, posing a very real threat of habitat destruction. The result was an experimental game-cropping project, the first in Kruger's history. Periodical culls were carried out at intervals for nearly three decades, until knowledge gained during the severe drought of 1992/3 showed for the first time that the hippo population, unlike elephants, can regulate itself naturally, increasing during wet years and decreasing during seriously dry ones. Since then no hippo culling has been carried out, and I do not think the cessation has been mourned by any real conservationist in Kruger. Culling is a traumatic operation for any conservation officer because it is so cold-blooded. It is one thing to kill a problem animal that poses a threat to people or property, or end the misery of one that has been wounded by poachers, but it is quite another to take the life of an animal whose only offence is that it belongs to a species group that has grown too numerous.

The Kruger management did what it could to alleviate the stress on both rangers and animals by evolving a procedure based on quick kills, selecting the best shots available and ensuring that they were practised and trained to maintain their concentration and focus. Quick kills and quick recovery meant minimum stress and minimum wastage – Kruger might not have been as efficient as the old Chicago stockyards, of which it was said that when a pig was processed, everything except its squeal was utilised, but it certainly had the same philosophy. In fact, 'culling' possibly creates the wrong impression; 'harvesting' might be a more accurate term. It was fast, smooth and cost-effective, and after discussions over the years with rangers from other organisations which culled hippos, I came to the conclusion that none of their methods came near to being as good as the one developed and used in Kruger since 1964.

The preferred time for a culling camp was in the winter, when the rivers were at their lowest and the hippos had concentrated at the last remaining pools. We would take the annual hippo census, select a suitable site and build a temporary but comfortable camp with as many facilities as we could organise, including a vegetable garden – it is so hot in the Lowveld in summer that winter is the only time you can really grow vegetables. I used to take adult lettuce, cabbage and carrot plants from our garden and replant them in the water run-off areas from the shower and kitchen, where they invariably thrived and could be harvested as required. Baboons and other garden-robbers were not a problem, because if we went home for a weekend we would always leave staff behind to caretake, and on our return we would bring back things like tomatoes and onions that could not be transplanted and kept alive so easily. All in all, we lived rather well in our culling camps, which made up somewhat for our absences from home and the gory nature of the task.

The best way to cull hippo, we had found, was to shoot them in the water around first light, when their stomachs were full of the previous night's food. The food soon fermented and generated gas that bloated the animals and brought them to the surface between 30 minutes and a couple of hours of being shot. The shooting team, usually two strong, would shoot the earmarked animals around first light and then wait for them to surface. Once they came up it was the turn of the recovery team – the boatman, a labourer whose task was to secure a rope to the hippo and an armed third person to take care of close-in emergencies; as an additional safety measure the shooting team would stand by on the bank. The recovery team would secure its rope to the hippo and tow it to the bank, where it would be pulled out and gutted, technicians collecting scientific data for Kruger's never-ending research programme. When all this had been done the carcass would be trucked to the meat-processing plant at Skukuza right away and the shooting team would head back to camp to clean up before embarking on the rest of the day's activities, the most important of which was to locate a spot for the next day's culling.

The first hippo cull during my time as a ranger along the Letaba and Olifants Rivers was in 1974. Rangers Dirk Ackerman and Jan de Kok, two masters of the profession, selected me to take part, a major honour for a newcomer. Dirk and Jan briefed me thoroughly on what had to be done, and early one morning we set up at a waterhole in the Letaba River, near where the Shimuweni Dam is today. The shooters were Dirk, assisted by Corporal July Makuvele and myself as the stand-in for Jan, who had opted to be a spectator. They were big boots I had to fill, and I knew it; at the end of the day, the only respect worth having is the respect of your peers, and these particular peers would not be easily satisfied.

The Letaba's profile at that spot was typical of a Lowveld river, with the bed much lower than the surrounding area, so that shooters had a clear field of fire and the inevitable spectators (of which there were a number that day, including a couple of wives) could sit on the true and false banks and enjoy a grandstand view without getting in the way. Dirk took up position on a sort of extended tussock, not more than 50 centimetres in diameter and a metre and a half high, with July in support below him, and the shooting started. Everything went according to plan, which was both a relief to me and a boost for my confidence, until very close to the end of the operation, when one of us wounded a hippo that then took cover in the reeds at the edge of the pool, and stayed there. Or that was what both Dirk and I thought, so we stood by to finish it off when it surfaced for air. Then Ian Whyte, a technician with the Department of Animal Health, saw it in another spot and crept down to the river to tell Dirk. Dirk looked a bit doubtful, but while he was turning over this information in his mind the hippo surfaced for air right where Ian had said it was.

Dirk immediately swung around and killed it with one .375 Magnum bullet, but now he was off-balance and his rifle's very substantial recoil sent him backwards off the tussock. Fortunately July was standing right behind him and saved him from a fall on to the stones below the tussock. An unseemly – and initially puzzling – tussle between the two then ensued. July was trying with all his might to push Dirk back up to the top of the tussock again; Dirk, on the other hand, was trying equally hard to get to the firmer ground below. It was only later that we discovered the reason. Dirk wasn't wearing underpants, so that his wedding tackle was in full view of the spectators directly above. A snap poll among the ladies after the end of the shooting, taken by a certain person who shall remain nameless, revealed that the womenfolk were certain that no injury had been done to Dirk's manly ego. But who knows? The bushveld has many mysteries, as they say.

*

That same year I had another hippo experience of a rather different kind when I went to build a temporary camp in the area west of the Letaba rest camp to serve as a base for the various teams involved in buffalo, hippo and elephant culling in the Phalaborwa and Letaba sections. I chose a site near where the tarmac road between Mopani and Phalaborwa now crosses the Letaba River – a lovely spot where seven very large Natal mahoganies, 'mkuhlu trees', as we called them, provided beautiful shade and a great atmosphere. I named the camp 'Lonely Bull' in honour of the lone buffalo and elephant bulls I found there on my first two reconnaissance trips. It was purely coincidental that our crowd at university had taken a solemn perpetual vow to do a strip-tease if two or more of us were ever together in one spot when the Herb Alpert classic of the same name was played.

Building the camp was quite an elaborate process because the culling would last for at least 10 weeks, and in that time the camp would have to accommodate nearly 40 people who would need proper toilets, showers and cooking facilities. We (including Helena, who took to the bush when she could, just like the other wives), frequently didn't even go home at weekends. For most of this time the hippos in the pools near by behaved themselves, but on the second night of our first stay in the uncompleted camp they decided to declare war on one another, starting soon after dark and carrying on well into the night. At first they concentrated on jaw-jaw, so to speak, raising an awesome level of sound as they growled, roared and did whatever else hippos do to express their feelings. But things got out of hand, and in no time it was war-war, with our camp as the battlefield. A hippo weighing several tons fleeing desperately from another hippo displacing the same weight tends to do grave injury to man-made artefacts, and so it was here as well. Chairs and tables were sent flying or transformed into instant matchwood, while tents caved in as their guy-ropes snapped like string under the impact of the massive bodies.

I think I lost a bit of manly standing that evening. Helena and I were (let me be honest) cowering wide-awake in our tent, although pretending to be fast asleep, while the battle raged around us, and at one stage in the evening she couldn't stand the suspense anymore and a very small voice asked out of the darkness: 'Are you awake?'

I said I was.

'I'm scared,' she said, obviously looking for just a touch of reassurance.

She didn't get it: 'So am I,' I said. I knew that this wouldn't make her feel any better, but it was the absolute truth.

By the time the combatants called it quits the camp was a shambles; our tent was one of the few still standing, more or less drunkenly. To my relief the support staff had all survived without a scratch. It turned out that they had been smarter than us and had taken to the trees for the duration of hostilities instead of lying waiting for some galloping hippo's steamroller impersonation.

*

There was another hippo cull in August 1975, and I remember it with particular acuity because I escaped death in not one but two of its many forms. A couple of weeks earlier I had been diagnosed with testicular cancer. I underwent an immediate orchidectomy, followed a fortnight later by my first chemotherapy treatment. I had been warned about the likely side-effects of the chemotherapy, but to my delight was not seriously affected, so I scrubbed thoughts of an extended stay in Johannesburg and made arrangements for the drugs for further treatments to be sent to Phalaborwa, where I could visit the hospital from the culling camp. Two weeks after my first treatment, with the culling camp already set up next to the Letaba River and about to start operating, my parents arrived in Phalaborwa with the next dose of 'muti'. On a Friday afternoon I drove in to the hospital, had the drugs administered and immediately went back to the camp with my parents for a quiet weekend before the culling started on the Monday morning.

I was confident that I would be able to shake off any after-effects as I had the first time, but I couldn't have been more wrong. This time the drugs hit me hard. By early evening I was feeling as sick as a dog, and, as if this was not bad enough, my stomach started running. I spent the entire night in a little spruit near the tent, armed with a spade and a roll of toilet paper, so weak that I couldn't muster the energy to walk to the long-drop toilet less than 50 metres from the tent, or even get higher off the ground than a crouch. Most of the time I just lay there on the sand, clutching the spade, which was not only part of my sanitation equipment but also my only weapon against the hyaenas that were expressing an interest in me. Any sick and helpless animal in the bush is hyaena prey, and that night I was as sick and help-less as any other animal; if truth be told, I eventually reached a stage of wretchedness where I didn't even care much about the hyaenas any more.

The next day, 8 August, was my father's birthday. I had in-tended to cook prawns for us as a celebratory supper; instead I spent all day lying on a stretcher under a shade-tree, so desper-ately ill that at one point, I heard later, I told my mother: 'Ma, if I get any sicker I'm going to die.' A fine birthday present for my old man! But next day I felt so much better that I could go out and identify the best hippo pool to work when the rest of my culling team arrived, which they did on schedule in the very early hours of Monday morning. As soon as they were ready I led the way to the pool, followed by Jan de Kok, a staff member's teenage son and Corporal Joe Rangani. Joe was carrying Jan's rifle, something that Jan was soon to regret, because we had barely reached the patch of sand where we planned to station ourselves when a hippo charged us for no reason that we could make out.

There is something a little sinister about a hippo charge like this, because at first you can't see the hippo itself, just the sort of bow wave it generates on the surface as it heads for you. But there is no doubt about what that bow wave means, and so we knew that at any moment the hippo was going to appear in the shallow water near the river's edge and climb up on to dry land to con-clude his business with us. Jan shouted a warning to Joe and ran back to get his rifle, but by the time Joe had handed it over the hippo had surfaced in the shallower water, and I shot it without further ado. In a somewhat thoughtful frame of mind Jan and I proceeded with the next step of the operation, which consisted of waiting for the hippos to surface again after the recent ruction – and this time both our rifles stayed within arm's length. What happened next, however, was not what we had expected. A very small hippo calf stuck its head out of the water and floated there, looking at us, and we realised that the animal we had just killed was probably its mother, which explained the unexpected charge. With regret we shot the calf; leaving it without her protection would have been a greater act of cruelty than killing it. This is the sort of unforeseen and unavoidable minor tragedy we often became involved in during culling.

The rest of the shooting and recovery took place as planned, and when I returned to the camp, somewhat shaky but still functioning, I saw something that was particularly beautiful to me: Helena standing in the shallow water of a side-stream, washing nappies in authentic African style while our little daughter Annie played in the sand near by. Yet because this was a bit of the old Africa the peaceful scene had ominous overtones that deeply concerned Oom Danie Yssel, my colleague Tom's father, because he knew that every year hundreds, if not thousands, of Africans are taken by crocodiles while busy with exactly the sort of task in which Helena was engaged. A crocodile attack is fantastically quick and almost invariably fatal. One moment the victim-to-be is peacefully washing clothes or pots at the water's edge, the next there is an explosion of water as the crocodile's jaws close on her. So Oom Danie's concern was a very real one – more real, in fact, than any of us knew, because only 15 months later a crocodile attacked his son Tom in the Sabie River.

In a strange way the attack on Tom Yssel had a connection with the three humorous 'basic laws' that govern sport fishing. Firstly, you won't catch anything if you don't have a baited line in the water. Secondly, the best fishing is always two days before you get to your preferred fishing spot or two days after you have left; and lastly, but equally important, there are always more fish on the other side of the river.

One Sunday morning, 21 November 1976, Tom and Louis

Olivier were both away from their sections and in Skukuza, where they were studying for their upcoming examinations, one of the way-stations to a national diploma in nature conservation, which had become a prerequisite for being a ranger. Sick and tired of being cooped up in a hut on a very hot summer's day, they decided to take time off and join some friends for a picnic along the Sabie River, about five kilometres from Skukuza. There they and one other member of the party heeded the third 'basic law' and decided to wade out through the clear knee-deep water to an island in the middle of the river. There they angled to their hearts' content and then set out on the return journey.

Now, there are many basic rules of survival in the bush – not humorous at all, but very real and often literally the difference between life and death. One of the most important is that you are seldom at threat from the big one that you can see; you need to look out for any buddies he might have. Another is that any piece of water in the Lowveld bigger than a cupful can and probably will have an unseen crocodile in it. Yet another is that if you have to cross a river and come back again, take a different route when you return, because the chances are good that a crocodile will notice you the first time and be lying in wait for you on your way back.

Perhaps their guard was down that day. Perhaps they were just dead out of luck. But when they were almost across and the front man, Tom, was barely a metre from the bank, a huge crocodile clamped its jaws around his lower right leg. When Tom screamed Louis looked up, somewhat irritated by what he immediately assumed to be a joke in poor taste about a subject that was too serious for humour. Then he saw the crocodile heading for deep water with his best friend in its mouth.

Louis was and is a fighter, and without hesitation he jumped into the water, seized the crocodile and tried to steer it away from the deep water. He found he couldn't get the crocodile to deviate from its course, so took out his folding pocket-knife and tried to stab it in the stomach. This didn't work either because the knife kept snapping shut. Now Louis was joined by Hans Kolver, one of the helicopter pilots, but even this added help achieved nothing. After about 20 minutes of fruitless struggle – by which time the crocodile had dropped Tom and seized Hans by the upper arms and shoulder – one of the women in the party passed Louis a kitchen knife. He slashed vainly at the crocodile's armoured chest, then chose a softer target and stabbed the croc in the eye. This persuaded the monster to let go of Hans as well and swim away, the knife still in its eye.

With the crocodile gone, Louis dragged Tom ashore, aghast at the severity of his wounds; his right femur was severed and his stomach torn open. By comparison Hans had got off lightly with shoulder injuries and a broken upper arm. The two injured men were hastily loaded into a truck and driven to Skukuza at top speed, Tom literally holding his intestines inside his body cavity. There they received emergency treatment before Tom was air-lifted to the Nelspruit hospital by helicopter. Two days later I shot the crocodile. It wasn't an act of revenge, which would have been a totally illogical reaction because it would have implied malice on the part of the crocodile; I was ordered to destroy it because it was wounded, probably blinded, and therefore helpless. All the same, although I have very seldom in my life enjoyed killing an animal, I came very close to it this time; but I think that in the circumstances I may be forgiven.

The entire episode received a lot of press coverage, and some of the reactions were totally unbelievable: the lunatic fringe of the ultra-greens actually complained about Louis stabbing the croco-dile in the eye, and sent hate mail to Tom as he lay fighting for his life. And that is not just a figure of speech. Tom was in the Nelspruit hospital for only three days before being flown to the Eugène Marais Hospital in Pretoria with a mysterious and life-threatening infection that kept him there for nine months, until the doctors finally discovered that the cause of it was not a bac-terium but a unicellular organism called *Amoeba proteus*. While he lay battling the mysterious infection Louis and Hans were de-servedly showered with honours: the Red Cross's highest award for lifesaving, the Parks Board's own Kruger Cross (Silver) for bravery and the country's highest civilian award for bravery, the Woltemade Decoration.

Tom lived with the consequences of the attack for a very long time. Although his body was healed on the outside, he spent the next 13 years walking around with a four-inch gap in his femur. Then his back began to give in under the strain, and a slice of bone from his hip was used to splice the ends of the femur together. This cost him many more months in leg-irons, but the operation was a success and eventually Tom could walk almost normally again. This is not a hippo story, true. But it shows how dangerous an African river can be, and points once again to the simplest yet greatest life-or-death maxim of all: stay alert, stay alive. It was a wakeup call for every one of us in Kruger.

*

I need hardly say that hippo culling could and did have its lighter moments. One time we were busy at the Sabie River, and among the usual crowd of spectators was a girl with the most magnificent blue eyes who had been invited along by Hessie, our bio-technician. We had a successful morning's shooting and recovery, and by mid-morning all the hippos we had shot had been recovered, gutted and laid out in a row on the bank, each one with its reproductive organs piled neatly next to it for examination and specimen-taking by Hessie. In the meantime Tom Yssel and I had got a cooking fire going near by and were tucking into a late breakfast furnished by one of the hippos and consisting solely of what I have heard called 'blue steak' – in other words, a chunk of meat so rare that it just about bellowed when you chewed it.

Now, Blue Eyes didn't look too happy about the well-ordered but indubitably sanguinary scene before her – in fact, she was positively green about the gills – and this inspired Tom Yssel, who had a little internal devil that must have been cloned from mine, to indulge in a bit of regrettable bushveld humour. Having noticed Blue Eyes' slightly verdant complexion, he immediately offered her a slice of our slightly singed steak. Blue Eyes took one look at the dripping mass and promptly tossed her cookies (rumour later had it that she didn't eat meat for months afterwards). I am ashamed to say – well, not very ashamed, in all honesty – that her reward for this performance was our unfeeling mirth; we tended to forget at times that visitors were accustomed to more delicate social mores than we were.

194

It was Hessie's turn next. She was a tougher proposition because she had been around the block a couple of times and knew us pretty well. But it was a case of cometh the hour, cometh the mischief-maker, and I knew that Providence had provided me with the necessary equipment when Eddy, the driver of one of the recovery trucks, called me over to show me a large barbel he had caught in the river during a spare moment. A plan sprang instantly to mind, and I asked Eddy to put the barbel into the visceral cavity of one of the hippos. A couple of minutes later Tom and I casually strolled over to look at the hippo, 'saw' the fish and called Hessie over to have a look. She was totally amazed and asked me how it could have got there. I adopted the serious expression I had been holding ready for just this moment and explained that after the hippo had been shot its nasal passages had probably filled up with blood, which had then leaked into its throat and from there into its mouth; the barbel, being a scavenger, must have picked up on the blood and then swum into the hippo's mouth, traversed the oesophagus and finally landed up in the visceral cavity. This was the sheerest nonsense, of course, but the success or failure of any scam depends on how you present it, and I must say I sounded pretty plausible, because Hessie accepted it without questioning any part of the preposterous explanation. At first, anyway. Then the penny dropped – either she suddenly remembered whom she was dealing with, or Tom or myself exhibited signs of glee – and she took after me with the butcher's knife she had been using on the hippos. That morning the female of the species was most definitely deadlier, or more murderous anyway, than the male!

*

The recovery phase of any cull was a testing time for the team involved, especially if there were still live (and obviously rather agitated) hippos sharing the water. I remember the time when the recovery team, consisting of Johnny Dragt, Eric Wood and a labourer, ventured out on to the very large Mahlanganzwane Dam south of Lower Sabie. At that time the dam had a population of about 40 hippos, eight of which we had shot, meaning that there were at least another 32 in circulation and probably in none too sweet a mood.

Johnny was riding shotgun, so to speak, and opted to take his military-issue R1 semi-automatic service rifle, which he tied to the boat for fear of losing it. I advised him to tie the rifle end of the rope either to the pistol grip or to one of the sling-swivels, but Johnny followed his own head and secured it to the trigger-guard, just in front of the trigger. The journey to the dead hippo started without incident, but then Johnny – naturally very conscious of the floater's alive-and-kicking friends – stood up with rifle at the ready to get a better view. The rope, which wasn't very long, promptly became taut enough to activate the trigger and the R1 let go a shot, fortunately straight up in the air. A totally flabbergasted Johnny jerked upright, thereby tightening the rope again, so the R1, which had reloaded itself in the meantime, fired again.

Eric, who was not aware of Johnny's little contretemps with the R1, immediately jumped to the conclusion that Tom and I had pulled another practical joke, flew into a rage and cursed us roundly for (as he put it) shooting at the recovery team when they were already in danger. By now Tom and I were rolling around laughing, which made Eric even angrier. There is no telling what might have happened if Johnny had not done the manly thing and confessed. That was that, but whether Johnny will ever live it down while there is any breath left in any of the other participants is another matter.

*

We still have a lot to learn about hippos. For example, we know how they eat. Unlike nearly all grazing animals, the hippo does not use its tongue to draw the grass over its incisors (the other exceptions are zebra, elephant and white rhino). A hippo clamps the horny horizontal ridges of its lips around a food-plant, plucks the plant with an upward sweep of its head and then opens its mouth again to allow a certain amount of food to drop down for swallowing. So the 'how' is no mystery. But very little is known about their actual feeding habits because they are nocturnal grazers. Stomach analyses of hippos made in the Kruger National Park indicate that they eat virtually only grass, plus a negligible amount of leaves and twigs of other plants, and these findings have been confirmed by studies made elsewhere. But I am not so sure that this is the whole story, and I have witnessed a few incidents that indicated to me that hippos are not averse to eating meat now and again.

I started thinking about this when I saw the well-publicised film, taken by Dick Reucassel at the Vervoer Dam in the late 1960s, which was said to show a hippo 'saving' an impala from a crocodile. This didn't make sense to me because it implied a sort of inter-species altruism that simply doesn't exist in the bush, and I had also seen a hippo spend hours worrying at a dead impala in the Sabie River, like a terrier working over a rat. Why? For fun? I doubt it. And there was no doubt about what the hippo was doing, because the Sabie's water was as clear as crystal at that spot. I picked up a little more evidence – although it was tantalisingly inconclusive – in August 1999, when I took a group of honorary rangers and their guests on a game drive at the Mahlanganzwane Dam near Crocodile Bridge. The previous day we had spotted a dead impala floating in the dam, and this time we all saw how a hippo and at least one crocodile literally tore the carcass to pieces. As luck would have it, this was very late in the day and the light was fading so fast that not even good binoculars could help us to see what the hippo did with the pieces, if there were any, that it tore off the impala's body.

Something that happened to my son Robert and me on the Letaba River is the clincher, as far as I am concerned. We were engaged in some catch-and-release fun fishing at a pool east of the Letaba rest camp that was known for its big barbel, our bait being golfball-sized dollops of chicken liver. Our lines hadn't been in the water for long before Robert shouted to me that he had hooked a very big one, and he wasn't fooling. His rod was bent into a bow, the reel was screaming and his bright yellow line, as taut as a bow-string, was slicing through the water as though there was a nuclear submarine at the other end. Then the 'submarine' broke surface at the far side of the pool, revealing itself as a hippo, and proceeded to 'tail-walk' like a marlin – a truly incredible sight – with the yellow fishing line clearly visible in its mouth.

I was completely nonplussed. Since when did hippos bother with minor things like lumps of chicken liver? Alternatively, if this hippo had not actively swallowed the bait, how did it get the line into its mouth? And if the hook had not embedded itself painfully somewhere inside its mouth or throat, how could the hippo possibly have been induced to tail-walk at the end of a 12-pound line? The only logical conclusion was that the hippo had grabbed the chicken liver. The inevitable happened, of course, and the line snapped while I was still gaping at the spectacle, thus depriving Robert of what would doubtless have been a world-record catch (of course, he did score a good second prize, since he acquired a one-that-got-away story whose equal will not easily be found).

As a serious-minded man I did not worry about such trifles at the time, of course, being too full of intellectual satisfaction at this further proof that hippos will turn carnivore if they feel like it. My suspicions were finally confirmed when tourists came to report to Helena, who wrote daily contributions for a local radio station, that they had seen a hippo chewing at pieces of an impala carcass in the Sunset Dam near Lower Sabie. Other sightings in the same vein (pardon the unintentional pun) merely provide additional evidence that hippos, like baboons, are not true-blue vegetarians.

Having said all of which, there is something wonderful about watching a herd of hippos of all sizes going about their business in a pool or river. Just remember not to get in their way or leave your car to try for a really close-up photo. That pic you click might be your last.

11

THE KING'S HUNTER

If there was one thing the years 1985 and 1986 did not lack it was action of one kind or another, both at home and abroad, ranging from a variety of wars (including South Africa's in what is now Namibia), the usual crop of either natural or man-made disasters, and all sorts of political upheavals. What helps me to remember them best, however, is two unusual and frequently bizarre personal experiences which were both far removed from my normal habitat at the time, the Kruger National Park, yet intimately connected with it. This might sound a trifle parochial, since neither involved events of earth-shattering international importance, but hear what I have to say and judge for yourself.

The 1985 episode involved a foray into Malawi, organised by Dr Anthony Hall-Martin, by then the chief research officer of National Parks. Its colours, sights and sounds remain bright in my memory because everything about it was so far out of the ordinary run of things, and also because it represented a rare opportunity to become involved with our opposite numbers in another country in our region. It must be remembered that in those days South Africa was still politically isolated from the rest of the continent – officially anyway, although there was a great deal more clandestine government-to-government contact than any of our neighbours was willing to admit to, and trade with the rest of Africa boomed. The fact was that South Africa was simply too advanced and too important in economic terms to be left out of the African equation, but all concerned had good reason to maintain the polite fiction.

Malawi was one of the few countries in the region to have formal links with South Africa, but it was so far away from our borders that contact in the conservation field was tenuous. But then Anthony Hall-Martin negotiated an unusual but very practical deal with the Malawian government which was intended to remedy the consequences of certain disturbances to the natural scheme of things in the Kruger National Park during the past century or so, dating back even further than its original proclamation as the Sabie Game Reserve. In the mid-1980s certain animal species that were formerly native to the Kruger area had long been locally extinct for reasons ranging from excessive hunting at the close of the nineteenth century, disease outbreaks like the 1896 rinderpest epidemic and the effect on movement patterns of the Park's boundaries, which in some cases included only small portions of certain Lowveld habitats.

The Parks Board's policy at the time was to redress this ancient and not-so-ancient damage by re-introducing these species, and this was the reason for the deal with the Malawians. In brief, they would let us come and help ourselves to 26 of their Lichtenstein's hartebeest, and in return we would capture and translocate some of their protected game animals from one reserve to another, a task for which they were not geared as regards personnel, equipment or expertise. It was a good deal that suited all parties – ourselves, the Malawians and, not least, the Kruger National Park itself, and we looked forward to getting cracking, blissfully ignorant of the fact that before the project ended we would have some strange adventures and misadventures, most of them completely unforeseen and unforeseeable.

As an opening gambit Anthony visited Malawi with a group of us who would be intimately involved in the project – head of wildlife management Johan Kloppers, veterinarian Dr Vossie de Vos, my ranger colleague Louis Olivier, myself and Pat Wolff, the pilot – to carry out an initial reconnaissance and finalise the necessary arrangements. The flight's first stages – from Skukuza to Messina, where we cleared customs, and then on to Harare in Zimbabwe to refuel our Cessna – were uneventful and indeed made memorable by the magnificent cumulonimbus clouds over the Zambezi Valley. Landing at Harare, however, brought us back to earth with a bump in more ways than one while we waited for the Cessna to be refuelled. Airport officials harassed

Pat about his flight plan, even though it had been submitted and approved before our departure, and Louis and I nearly got arrested in the pub for the heinous sin of taking our beers away from the bar counter to go and sit at a nearby table. Why this unfriendly reception? It struck me that our khaki uniforms and green epaulettes might have prickled someone's patriotic vigilance, relations between Zimbabwe and South Africa being, shall we say, none too warm at that time. Be that as it may, we took off for Lilongwe without any regrets about shaking Harare's dust off our boots. Now we were dodging in between those great clouds we had seen earlier, and it was an amazing sensation to be in a small aircraft like the Cessna as it threaded its way through veritable herds (or should one say flocks?) of these insubstantial but imposing monsters.

At Kamuzu Airport outside Lilongwe we were met by various protocol officers who escorted us to the VIP lounge – except for poor Louis, who was wearing shorts and was therefore a shade under-dressed for the privilege. It just shows that timing is everything. We Kruger people wore shorts 99 per cent of the time, but by sheer coincidence were all in longs that day except for Louis. So he ended up standing in a queue with the hoi polloi while we enjoyed the fleshpots of the VIP facilities. But at least he was allowed to travel with us to our hotel in Lilongwe. Anthony went to the embassy to confirm the arrangements for the next couple of days, and, since there is not really much to do in Malawi, the rest of us decided to go down to the hotel bar and field-test the local beer. It turned out that there was no such thing as home-grown beer, but a very nice imported tipple called Carlsberg Green made an excellent substitute. We immediately renamed it 'salad', and that is what it stayed throughout subsequent field-tests. The scientific rigour of the field-testing on that and subsequent occasions obviously left an indelible impression on the local drinking culture, because when we returned months later to the hotel pub and asked for 'salad' the barman immediately mobilised the Carlsberg Green.

Field-testing completed, we set about preparing for our first stop next day – Lilongwe Game Park, where our host/convener was to be a lady with a very British-sounding name. Louis, Pat and I had never met her, but we had had frequent dealings with the type, and so we composed an identikit which predicted that she would be between 20 and 30, with a darkish complexion, short hair, noticeable moustache, stout legs (probably unshaved) and a weight problem, and would probably be wearing khaki clothes, short socks and boots. Next morning the three of us could scarcely contain our mirth when she met us at the entrance to the park's reception area and fitted our home-made identikit like a glove. I hasten to add that by no means all ladies in conservation fit into that mould, but our hotel-room profile was based on long experience of female conservationists operating in Africa, particularly those from the foreign sector. Which just goes to show that conservation in this part of the world is sometimes as much about gut feeling as pure science. She was accompanied by Henry Insanjana, the deputy director of conservation and our host and guide for the trip – a real gentleman with whom we became great friends, so much so that Helena ended up buying clothes, shoes and perfume for his wife in South Africa. For starters Henry took us to Kasungu National Park, where the Lichtenstein's hartebeest were located, and then to Liwonde, where we were to catch game for the Malawians as our part of the deal.

On the way we suffered a minor misadventure (well, not so minor in the case of one of us) when we stopped at a fishing village on Lake Malawi so that Henry could buy some fish. These were packed into a plastic bag with ice and dumped into the back of the Nissan Safari alongside all our luggage. Needless to say, at some point the renowned Murphy's African branch office intervened: the ice melted, the bag started leaking and the distinctly aromatic water got at our kit. Vossie was the first to observe this, hastily examined his worldly goods and lamented aloud about the fact that his wife, Tokkie, would not be amused about the strongly piscine smell his moon-bag and passport had acquired. We expressed our sympathy with bursts of heartless laughter, Johan leading the chorus. Then, when we stopped for petrol at Liwonde village a couple of minutes later, Johan discovered that his green 'best' jacket had gone the same way as Vossie's moon-bag and passport; it goes without saying that this time around he did not join in the mirth . . . But this was merely the light entertainment. Liwonde was a marvellous place to visit. I'll never forget the sight of the cloud of fish eagles – there must have been between 300 and 400 of them – circling the harbour. Another thing that I won't forget is the enormous Lowveld chestnut trees (*Sterculia rogersi*) growing along the shoreline of the lake, so colossal that they actually looked like baobabs. Apart from their sheer beauty, they also provided me with clear proof that elephants had been absent from the southern shores of Lake Malawi for a long time, since Lowveld chestnuts are a favourite part of the Kruger elephants' diet.

We made all the arrangements we deemed necessary and then flew back to South Africa to work on our side of the project's logistics, satisfied that at the Malawian end everything was in hand. Or so we thought, anyway. But we still had a bit to learn. Our planning envisaged a project lasting nine weeks, from the time we left Skukuza until we had the Lichtenstein's hartebeests safely in the breeding enclosure in the northern part of Kruger. Into the calculations based on this time-frame we had to factor a large number of variables and possible contingencies, not least of which was how to handle the dozens of photographers and reporters we expected to accompany us on what was the biggest long-distance game capture and translocation ever undertaken by the Parks Board. We provided for all these contingencies by delegating tasks to specific members of our Malawian party. I was the operational head, while Vossie de Vos and a technical assistant named Ben de Klerk would be responsible for the chemical capture aspect and all animal health issues. Louis Olivier, assisted by Tom Yssel, would be in charge of the mass capture operations and the equipment. Ted Whitfield and Johan van Graan, both mechanical geniuses, were tasked to look after the equipment and fix anything that needed to be fixed. Piet Otto would fly the chopper, of course, backed up by his flight engineer, Mike Rochat, while Ben Pretorius would supervise the quarantine. Ted, Johan, Tom and Ben would also serve as drivers in between their other duties.

A host of rules and regulations, emanating from the animal health and agriculture departments of both countries, snapped continually at our heels to complicate things as we sweated through our planning. For example, we would have to keep the captured animals in quarantine for six weeks after their capture, the enclosure would have to be proof against both ticks and flies, and the feed would have to be weed-free and sterile. Before they could be moved the animals would have to undergo three separate tests to ensure that they were free of disease. A tall order, this requirement, and, as I say, it was not the only one. An additional complication (logistical, this time) was that Malawi did not have much in the way of specialised infrastructure, so that about all we could be sure of finding locally was the timber needed for building the quarantine and capture bomas. Everything else we would have to bring with us, or do without.

On the other hand, we also had invaluable offers of help from various organisations, without which our task would have been a great deal more difficult. We were happy to accept an offer from the South African Air Force to fly our animals from Kamuzu Airport at Lilongwe to Punda Maria inside Kruger, which would make things infinitely easier for us because we couldn't have transported the hartebeest overland. This required special crates that would fit into a Hercules C130 'flossie' on urine-proof pallets (for some or other strange reason, pilots don't like to have piddle running over the control wiring of their aircraft). Ted and Johan designed two sizes of crates, a large one and a smaller version that would fit inside it, as well as an ingenious lifting device that came to be known as the 'Pick-it-up-and-come-along', and built all three in the Transvaal Sugar Board workshops at Malelane.

Finally everything was ready. We spent about a week packing everything into a small convoy of three trucks – two large, one small – and then left Skukuza around midday on 30 May. We camped for the night in the caravan park at Potgietersrust and next day carried on to the South Africa–Botswana border post at Martin's Drift, where it was Harare airport all over again, except that this time it was Botswana's customs officials cutting up rough. Experience with border-crossing had taught us, however, that Africa is not a place where merely having the right paperwork guarantees a smooth passage, and we had catered for just such an occurrence by making sure that some bags of oranges were placed conveniently near the edges of each truck's load-space. This did the trick; suddenly our papers were found to be in order and we trundled over the border without having lost anything except the oranges and a certain amount of time.

By now Ted, one of the old school who abhorred this sort of minor skulduggery, was near the end of his patience, which was strictly limited anyway (before leaving Skukuza his son Steven had begged me: 'Uncle Bruce, please see that my dad doesn't *moer* anybody.' For those who don't speak South African English, 'moer' is an Afrikaans noun meaning a nut, of the kind that you screw on to a bolt, but it is also widely used as a verb, in any of several languages, to describe the act of hitting someone). Well, Ted manfully restrained himself from indulging in any moering on that occasion, but it was a close thing. As we left the border post behind us – he and I were riding in the chase bakkie – he pulled out two beers and opened them, gave one to me and gulped the other like a fireman dousing a blaze. I didn't realise just how tenuous his hold on his temper was until he threatened to chuck his empty beer can out of the window right there and then (in Botswana, and, in fact, in most of Africa, you don't need road signs to tell you how far you are from the next bottle store or town – just look for the cans next to the road; the greater the density, the closer you are). Then, bless him, the conservationist in him took over and he just couldn't bring himself to do it.

Around 4 pm we reached the Botswana–Zambia border post at Kasane, near where the Kasangula ferry crosses the Zambezi River, and promptly ran into a fresh set of problems. Clearing customs should have been a doddle, since we had gone to great pains to organise all the paperwork through a clearing agent and had arranged for our visas to be waiting for us at the Zambian border post. But Murphy's African branch had been busy again, and they weren't there; the best we could get out of the Zambians was that they would be there the next day. Since we were obviously not going to get any further that day, I went back to the Botswanan border police post and asked the commanding officer – a captain, to judge by his unfamiliar rank-badges – if we could camp at the river. 'No problem,' he said, so we pulled the trucks off the road, right next to the loading ramp of the Kasangula ferry, put up the tarpaulin between the two big trucks and made ready for the night.

This done, I started spinning for tiger fish, while the other chaps went about their camp routine. At this stage the police captain reappeared, insisted that the only way to catch tigers was by baiting a bare hook with a piece of Kariba weed (this was nonsense, but I humoured him, with the expected result) and then finally got to the point, namely that he wanted us to find another campsite. This might have been related to the fact that the ferry's loading ramp was a busy place, with frequent comings and goings by local inhabitants, but the captain claimed to be worried about the dangers we faced from wild animals, particularly crocodiles and hippos. It was clear that he didn't realise that we spent all our working hours among wild animals – we were not wearing uniforms, and the logo of the National Parks Board on our vehicles apparently wasn't known in Botswana – so we soon put him right. He then left, only to return yet again with a posse of Land Rovers carrying what looked like half of the soldiers in Botswana's small defence force. The soldiers promptly surrounded us, and, flushed with triumph, the captain told us to leave and go to the town of Kasane, where we could stay until our visas arrived.

I was in no mood to argue with the captain and told the guys to pack up, but I told him that I wasn't going to stay in Kasane; we'd go south and camp out on the escarpment above the river. He wasn't too happy about this, but I persisted and eventually he caved in. We were ready to leave with our military escort when Johan announced that he wasn't going anywhere until he had had a bath. In full view of the military contingent, he stripped and then strolled, towel over shoulder and soap and shampoo in hand, down the approach to the ferry ramp. We all knew Johnny and had no doubts that this would be a two-beer pause, so we relaxed in suitable fashion while he enjoyed a leisurely bath before allowing the military to escort us to a suitable spot next to the road on the escarpment. Here, vigilantly eyeballed by the soldiery, we spent a pleasant enough evening playing poker for matches which was notable for only one thing, that sly old fox Ben Pretorius trouncing Ted, a veteran bushveld poker hand, by some audacious cheating which was inevitably discovered. What the troops thought about the ensuing hilarity I can't say, but they must have been puzzled – this, surely, was not the way people under grave suspicion were supposed to act!

Next day, a Monday, I was allowed to go through the border post and cross the river on the ferry to see if our papers had arrived yet. Tom's and Johnny's were there, but none of the rest; the peculiar thing was that they had asked for and received multiple-entry visas, while the rest of us had applied for single-entry visas only, which one would think would have caused less of a bureaucratic problem than theirs. In any case, we got another promise that the missing visas would arrive 'tomorrow'. Which they did not, nor the day after. In desperation I sent Johnny and Tom to Livingstone to find out from the clearing agent what had happened. They arrived back in the late afternoon with everybody's visas except Ben's. By now time was getting short, so I decided to take the heavy trucks inland and leave Tom and Ben behind with the chase bakkie to wait a while longer for Ben's visa and return home if it didn't arrive within a reasonable time.

Early on the Thursday morning the rest of us crossed into Zambia for the 30-minute drive to the customs post, leaving a frustrated Tom and Ben behind (they waited for two more fruitless days, then turned around and drove all the way back to Skukuza). It was an ill-omened start to the project, and things didn't get better right away. We wrestled the heavily laden trucks over the nightmarishly bad road to the customs post – although we were soon to discover that it was actually just a gentle introduction to the *really* bad ones that lay ahead – only to find that the clearing agent was not there to meet us as he had promised. I told my group to stay put and walked to the border post. Finding it wasn't difficult, but unearthing someone to deal with was considerably harder. It took hours of wandering around the building, which looked more like a cobweb-infested coal bin than anything else, before I managed to get permission to carry on.

All this had left us hungry and frustrated, so I suggested that we have lunch at a restaurant before carrying on. The only eating establishment I could find this side of the Victoria Falls was a bakery that had no bread, although it did offer some hard-boiled eggs of unknown provenance. We passed on the eggs but managed to buy 48 beers, carefully preserving the bottles, not only for the sake of conservation but also because we had been warned that to buy beer in Zambia it was not enough merely to have money: you also had to have empty bottles to swap for the full ones.

By now we also needed diesel fuel – we hadn't run out, but our trucks were running low and we were reluctant to start using the extra fuel we had on board at this early stage, since we had no knowledge of what lay ahead – so we stopped at a garage in Pembe to refill. Even this expedient, so simple and obvious in South Africa, proved to be a problem: the owner, a South African, told us his tanks were dry. However, he assured us, another garage down the road still had a small amount of diesel for sale. His information was accurate and we managed to fill up, and to our delight the owner also ran a bottle store and butchery, so he exchanged our empties for fresh beers and sent us on our way with the gift of a massive beef fillet. Cool-boxes and tanks filled, we left Pembe in a decidedly better frame of mind, drove until nightfall, slept in the trucks that night (we had been advised never to sleep by the roadside anywhere in Zambia) and finally arrived at Chipata on the Friday afternoon after further hassles with roadblocks and the awful roads.

A friendly petrol-station owner allowed us to camp out in his forecourt and gave directions to a nearby hotel where we would be able to replace our stock of beer, which had been exhausted during our odyssey from Pembe. Johnny and I went to the hotel in the smaller of the two trucks, and while he stood guard over our belongings I went inside with my empties. I can't say I was exactly warmly welcomed. For some reason the receptionist took exception to my inquiries about getting refills and so did a group of men hanging around the reception area, so I decided to make myself scarce before we ran into yet another unwanted hassle. I found Johnny in conversation with some locals who greeted me like an old friend, and when they heard of my abortive conversation with the receptionist one of them, a young woman called Grace, offered to show us where we could buy beer if we would give her a lift home afterwards. We accepted Grace's offer, cleared a place for her in the front of the truck and headed for the Sunset Fiesta Bar in Chipata's back streets. This time our luck was in, and while Grace and Johnny stayed with the truck I exchanged our empties for full bottles.

It was a slightly nervy business, though. The only lights were candles, and empties were swapped one by one by passing the bottles back and forth through a set of steel bars. On top of that I seemed to be the only white person – and a foreigner at that – in the room, and I had the uncomfortable feeling that I stuck out like a sore thumb. The beer-buying went off without incident, however, and soon we were fulfilling our side of the bargain by taking Grace home. On the way she told us that she had been a student at a teachers' training college in Lusaka, but had been expelled for organising a strike about bad food. I sympathised with her, having had various brushes with uneatable viands while attending a very up-market private school in Johannesburg. It turned out that Grace lived quite near the filling station, and when she heard that we would be sleeping on or under the trucks she came very close to insisting that I spend the night at her house. I turned her down on the grounds that I couldn't possibly leave the other guys alone, and Johnny supported my stand in the best collegial style. But I knew that I was in for some heavy ribbing about Grace's offer, and that is exactly what happened when we arrived back at the garage, where Ted and Louis had got a fire going on the pavement in real African style and were preparing some *pap* (stiff porridge, to non-South Africans) to eat with the fillet.

Early Saturday morning we finally arrived at the Malawian border after a solid seven days on the road. I entered into this fresh confrontation with the Zambian bureaucracy in some trepidation, which was soon justified by events. All the clearance work went smoothly, but as we left the building an official who claimed to be the 'health officer' called me aside and told me to accompany him to his office. It was a veritable cave of filth: I noticed that on the window-sill, among a collection of other grubby objects, stood a kidney dish containing a dirty swab and a used disposable hypodermic syringe, all of it covered in flies and filth. This was enough to make me decide that there was no way on earth that this character, 'health officer' or no, was going to touch any of us in the line of business.

It turned out that he had business with us all right, but not of the medical kind, although he started by demanding proof that we had been vaccinated against yellow fever. I replied that our embassy had given us the vaccination requirements for every country we would have to traverse to reach Malawi, and yellow fever wasn't on the list. Moreover, we were leaving Zambia, not entering it, so what was the point of his inquiry? The 'health officer' scratched around in his desk's drawers to find the necessary substantiating documents and eventually came up with a yellowed piece of paper dating from some time in the 1950s, when Zambia was still called Northern Rhodesia and was part of the short-lived Central African Federation. I pointed out that these were hardly adequate grounds on which to detain us, at which he got to the real matter at hand, namely an attempt to extort 100 US dollars from me as his price for letting us through.

I told him to buzz off and went back to the trucks with the would-be extortionist hard on my heels. By this time all our documentation had been stamped and the trucks had passed through the border checkpoint, so that technically they were not in Zambia any longer, but this didn't deter the dollar-lover. He converted himself back into a customs officer, pointed to the 44-gallon drums on the vehicles and demanded to know what was in them.

'Diesel,' I replied.

'You can't export diesel out of Zambia,' he said, and would not be budged from this position. The drums were not integral parts of the trucks, he pointed out, and on top of that they contained fuel, so they would have to be left at the border post. I was in no mood to be swindled by this corrupt fool and tipped the wink to Ted, who

Above: My bachelor's party, in December 1972, with July Makuvele at my left.

Right: Helena, me, and Annie: even game reserve babies got christened.

Big game is not the only kind that bites: ranger 'Snorre' Dirk Swart looking for ticks on Bruce's bellybutton.

Above and left: The Watsons and Brydens at their favourite picnic spot on the Sabie River, between Skukuza and the Sabie highwater bridge. A nice fire under a sycamore fig, steaks sizzling over the coals ... and a visiting elephant bull. Who could ask for more!

Robert at the age of three, seated on the carcass of an elephant that had been suffering from a paralysed trunk; and much later, learning bush skills from two of the masters of the veld, Simeon Mulhovu and Salmao Mongwe, who was later killed by a leopard.

A permanent long drop with style – and a view.

Left: Ranger Sam Fourie doing a fire dance with a mamba. He was later killed by an elephant.

Below: Wouter and Sonja Jordaan with an immobilised leopard in their back yard at Skukuza.

Top: Yours truly – celebrating something or other at Tom Yssel's bar.

Bottom: A bar lunch bush-style for conservation staff.

Malawi, 1985: in return for 26 of their Lichtenstein's hartebeest we captured and translocated some of their protected game animals from one reserve to another.

Top: Rangers Ted Whitfield and Louis Olivier strategising.

Bottom: Loading Liechtenstein's hartebeest with Dr Anthony Hall-Martin. *(Photos by David Paynter)*

Top: Rangers Tom Yssel and Johan van Graan loading sable in Liwonde National Park.

Middle: Rigging capture nets with Ranger Louis Olivier.

Bottom: Setting up nets with Henry Nsinyana (Deputy Director of Malawi National Parks).
(Photos by David Paynter)

Top: At the request of Mswati III, the 'Official Hunter for the King of Swaziland' delivers an elephant, a hippo, a lion and a hyaena to the Royal household.

(Top photo by Jan van der Merwe)

Bottom: Doing a tiger fish survey in the Letaba River with July Makuvele and Piet Ackerman.

Shout at the Devil – I was Roger Moore's stunt double, complete with white linen suit and Panama hat. I can't say that I was required to show any great dramatic talent – mainly I had to kill elephants on some occasions and run away from them on others.

Top: Lee Marvin as Sean Patrick O'Flynn, 'hunting elephants' under my guidance.

Above: Standing in for Roger Moore as Sebastian Oldsmith.

My personal passion: teaching children the basics.

climbed up and began siphoning fuel into the trucks' tanks. Unfortunately they were almost full – we had got into the habit of filling up from the drums the night before each day's journey, and the border post was only a few kilometres from where we had camped – but Ted had been around for a long time and had a plan. So with each drum he did the customary suck-and-spit, allowed a little diesel to come through and then lifted the pipe. This would interrupt the flow and Tom would then declare the drum empty and move on to the next one to repeat the process.

Tom's performance didn't satisfy the health-cum-customs officer, who had obviously been around the block a few times himself, and he announced that he would check the drums in person. Then help came from a most unexpected source. The officer had obviously waxed fat in his job, because his trousers were at least two sizes smaller than they should have been, so that when he flexed his muscles before climbing up to the drums the stitching just couldn't take the strain and to our delight his pants split from waistband to fly. That was the end of him. He gave up on inspecting the drums and beat a hasty retreat, trying vainly to shield his seriously exposed buttocks from our gleeful eyes. With equal haste we hit the road in the direction of Malawi, fuel drums and all.

We got to the Malawian capital of Lilongwe without further incident and reported in at the South African Embassy, which passed the message on to our head office – where, no doubt, it was received with some relief, since they had not heard from us for a whole week. This done, we set off for Kasungu National Park, where we would be based for the first leg of our stay. It was a good place to start. Hugging the border with Zambia and covering an area of just over 2 000 square kilometres, Kasungu was and is one of the two largest national parks in Malawi, its main vegetation form being what is known as 'Miombo Woodland', or tree savannah.

That Sunday Henry Insanjana met us at Kasungu and we laid our final plans for the first step, the construction of a quarantine boma, which was to start next morning at seven o'clock. Being used to the South African approach, we didn't check up to make sure that the essentials were in place, and they weren't. Firstly, when our six-man team (now augmented by Tom and Ben, who had just flown in) reported for work we found no sign of the Malawian labour force that was supposed to meet us. This left me in an unhappy frame of mind, to put it mildly, because we had a great deal to do and our tight schedule had become even tighter as a result of all the delays in getting there. Henry arrived at 7.30 and explained the non-appearance of the workforce with 'we work on African time'. I remarked that I was unaware of the fact that Malawi was in a different time-zone. Henry assured me that we were in the same time-zone, but time wasn't important in Africa. I pointed to my watch and said that from this point on we would work on my time, otherwise we would pack up and go home. Henry got the message and made sure it was passed on.

My unhappiness increased when we discovered that there were no poles for building the boma, and no stock of fuel for the helicopter. This was resolved by the simple expedient of going out and buying both, losing yet more valuable time in the process. But at least we could get going at last, and we set a very stiff pace. Henry's crowd responded nobly to the pressure, which was an eye-opener to people accustomed to the more leisurely Malawian lifestyle. As Henry said to Louis one sweaty afternoon, 'you guys work like tractors,' which wasn't an understatement at all; we were under the gun and we did not dare to slacken off. We managed to complete the quarantine boma on schedule and the rest of the team arrived along with the helicopter, bringing us welcome letters and news from home, as well as some badly needed short-wave radios that would allow us to communicate directly with Skukuza. Now we could get down to capturing the 26 hartebeest and leave them in the boma while we carried out the rest of the operation.

The chopper also brought us some unexpected camp followers in the form of vultures. This was nothing new to us, because the culling programmes in Kruger had taught the vultures that our blue-and-white Jet Ranger usually meant a free lunch, but it posed an intriguing question: how had the Malawian vultures caught on so fast? I assumed that some of the vultures the chopper had passed on its way to Kasungu had been aware of the helicopter-food link and followed it in. I wouldn't go so far as to claim that the vultures had flown behind it all the way from Skukuza, but their Malawian colleagues had certainly got the message at the speed of light.

We captured the selected hartebeest by the simple expedient of chasing them into the boma with the helicopter, then closing it with nets; everything went smoothly, and after just two days of hard work all 26 were safely in quarantine. This was an excellent reason to celebrate, and so we did, although not without some intervention from Murphy's local branch, of which we first became aware well into the evening, when the Malawian game guard on night duty brought the news that one of the hartebeest bulls had broken out of his pen and was busy killing a calf in another pen. After some effort Louis and I managed to separate the two animals by using a crate door as a temporary barrier between them and then rejoined our colleagues in dishevelled condition, Louis sporting a three-inch gash on his forehead. Vossie the veterinarian administered a local anaesthetic in the form of a beer-glassful of Famous Grouse whisky donated by David Paynter, a member of the press contingent, and stitched up the wound. For some reason (or no reason) Louis refused to let Vossie bandage him, so after several failed attempts Vossie applied a strip of Elastoplast to the stitches and Louis applied himself to the rest of the Famous Grouse, suffering no adverse effects except a slight hangover.

Next day we set off for Liwonde National Park on the second phase of the project, namely catching and translocating sable antelope and impala for the Malawians. Liwonde was another beautiful piece of Malawi. About 580 square kilometres in size, it extended almost as far as the eastern wall of the Rift Valley, and from Lake Malombe to the town of Liwonde. Its herds of sable almost defied counting, so that it was nothing unusual to see 50 or more in one group. It also had the biggest, highest, most impressive mopane trees I had ever seen, although my delight was somewhat tempered by the fact that they made flying so difficult that we could only work on the airfield. Even then Piet's flying skills were tested to the limit, and I had more trouble darting the selected specimens than at any other time in my career.

We stayed on top of the job, however, and in due course Ben and Johnny took off for the Sacoma Sugar Estate on the Lower Shire River with a load of the sable we had caught. Their departure was a good excuse to take the day off and lounge around in what we referred to as the 'staff village' – in reality a house which had no fence around it, so that there was only a hedge between us and the similarly fenceless house next door, with the helicopter roosting on the front lawn in the absence of a hangar. Ben and Johnny were expected back for lunch, and on an outside fire I had an enormous piece of rump steak roasting in a black pot.

At this stage the resident bull elephant, an individual we had nicknamed 'Charlie', paid us an unscheduled and distinctly unwelcome visit. Like the other Malawian elephants Charlie was nothing much to look at, being small in both body and tusks. When it comes to elephants all things are relative, of course; it would be more accurate to say that all elephants are big – some are just bigger than others. All the same, when we compared Charlie with the hefty fellows we grew in Kruger, he looked as if he had grown on poorhouse gruel like Oliver Twist's pals. One could take the analogy further and say that like any poorhouse kid Charlie was filled with brazen cheek and didn't care a damn about the social proprieties or the rules that govern game capture operations. The first and most important rule was that no one messed about with either the helicopter or its pilot, and it was clear that Charlie had plans to tackle the chopper.

I was in the kitchen when I saw him headed for the gap between our house and the hedge and looked for something to hurl at him, but the only missiles I could spot were some torch batteries. Well, needs must when the devil drives, so I grabbed a couple, ran out of the kitchen and swore at him. Charlie ignored my profane cries and kept on going, so I went over to Plan B and let him have it with a torch battery, which hit him on the head with a hollow bang that sounded like a bass drum being thumped. Charlie obviously felt bitterly wronged by this, because he forgot about the helicopter and made a beeline for me. I waited not on the order of my going, but only just made it into the kitchen in time. Fortunately for all concerned, not to mention both house and helicopter, Charlie lost interest in us after I disappeared into the kitchen and went on his way, and after this never again paid us a close-in visit. I suppose the contact between my high-speed Duracell and his skull could be described as assault with battery.

Charlie's raid was actually that day's minor problem, although we didn't know it yet; the major one was in progress elsewhere. The delivery of the sables to the Sacoma Sugar Estate should have been a simple process, but once again local officialdom stepped in with the usual disastrous results. We had been assured that no permits would be needed to transport the animals, but Ben and Johnny found themselves virtually under arrest, from which they were only released after two days of intensive wrangling and the under-the-counter payment of some US dollars. Our greatest worry was the consignment of sable, which had to spend the entire time in the vehicle. All of them survived the trauma and arrived safely at their destination, but it was a minor miracle that we didn't lose any. This was too much, however, and I stopped all further operations until the Malawians assigned us an official from their veterinary services on a full-time basis to take care of such problems.

The stoppage prompted the Director of Wildlife, one Moses (I forget his surname, and it deserves to be forgotten), to pay a personal visit to our camp at Mvuu on the lower Shire River, accompanied by a party of friends and family. Long experience at Kruger had inured us to visits by bigwigs, of course, but not the Malawian version. Moses's first action after greeting us was to ask for petrol. In the interests of international amity we filled his tank, as well as two large jerrycans he produced when his car was full. That done, he and his entourage moved over to one side and ignored us, although from the timing of his visit he clearly intended staying for lunch. This created a certain capacity problem. Since it was a Sunday and we were all in the camp because of the permit problem, we had prepared a big lunch whose main ingredient was tinned buffalo that we had brought from Skukuza, a staple item of our daily diet because obtaining fresh meat in Malawi was a dicey subject. Obviously this would not stretch far enough to feed Moses's numerous entourage as well, so I delayed serving the meal as long as possible. Eventually, however, I saw that this was not one I was going to win, so I augmented our meal by adding more buffalo meat and cooking an extra pot of rice and then I invited Moses and his party over to join us. It turned out that they had brought their own food and eaten it already, but were not averse to having some of ours as well. They queued up for large plates of buffalo stew and rice, after which they went off and ignored us again while they consumed it . . . and then came back for seconds, equipped not with plates this time but with paper bags that they filled up to take home with them.

When Moses and his party of freeloaders finally left my state of mind wasn't too good as I contemplated the inroads that had been made into our food and petrol stocks, but I consoled myself with the fact that Moses had disengaged himself from the trough long enough to promise that he would arrange for an official from the Animal Health Department to join us. This was good, as far as it went, but, having learnt some painful lessons by now about how things were done north of Kruger, I told him that I would be at his office in Lilongwe at eight o'clock next morning to collect the newcomer. I made sure to be there on time, although I had a strong suspicion, which proved correct, that Moses wouldn't be. Since I was now acquainted with the concept of 'Malawian time', though, I didn't get my water hot but waited patiently until he drove into the parking area half an hour later, gave him a few minutes to hang his hat up and then followed him into his office. There I ran into an unexpected brick wall in the shape of his secretary, who insisted that he hadn't arrived yet and I must wait. So I sat down and for an hour or so listened to the allegedly absent director making telephone calls behind the closed door of his office.

After this my newly acquired Malawian-model patience had evaporated and I left to seek out the Director of the Animal Health Department, whom I had met at the Liwonde Game Park on our first trip there. He was totally unaware of our predicament and said he had no staff to help us, but added that if I could find anybody in the building who was qualified we could have him for a few days. This was better than nothing, so I scouted down the corridor until I came to a door marked 'Dr Soviet Kamvimbo'. I went inside and there was the man himself behind his desk, underneath a degree certificate in veterinary medicine from Manchester University with the warning 'Not valid in the UK or USA' printed across it in large red letters. Validity or not, this was a gap to be taken without further ado, so I introduced myself and said that the director of the Animal Health Department needed to see him right away. Then I escorted him to the director, who was as good as his word and told Soviet to pack his bags and get down to Liwonde with me.

Soviet and his permit book stayed with us for the rest of our time in Malawi, due at least partly to the fact that he had no transport of his own and therefore was at my mercy as far as movement was concerned. I have no hesitation in saying that the relationship was mutually beneficial. Our permit problems eased, and Soviet probably learnt more about veterinary science from us in three weeks than he had during his entire study period at Manchester University. And he had a lot to learn, particularly about the practical aspects. I remember him asking me one day, while we were darting buffalo, whether the knock-out drops were administered intravenously or intramuscularly. Now, I had always regarded Piet Otto and myself as a pretty hot darting team, but we weren't that hot, since merely hitting a running buffalo from a bush-bashing helicopter is difficult enough at the best of times, never mind shooting the dart into a vein except by sheer chance. On reflection I realise that I had missed a wonderful opportunity to start a new African legend about the Kruger National Park. Still, Soviet's presence ensured that things went well with the transportation of the captured animals, although we never managed to catch any of Liwonde's impalas because there was just no way we could get them to go into the nets. My own belief is that they had a bit of help from the over-inquisitive nature of the Malawian game guards who were responsible for running the nets and curtains used for a large-scale capture.

Before finishing up at Mvuu we had another culinary venture that came close, as the Bible would say, to sowing discord among brethren. The basic cause of the discord was a Malawian speciality called Nali sauce – a deceptively innocent-looking concoction that would probably be able to melt an armoured car's plating, and is strictly an acquired taste. Our hitherto cohesive little group divided into two camps, the Nali lovers and Nali haters. What sparked the discord was when Louis ran over a guinea fowl one day while he and I were on a trip to Liwonde village. By great good chance only the head of the guinea was crushed, so I plucked, gutted and skinned it while we were in transit and on our return placed it in a pot with the necessary spices to let it boil itself off the bone. That was where the trouble began. It would take a miracle of the loaves-and-fishes variety to turn one guinea into a meal for six hungry rangers, all of them intent on getting more than just a taste. Louis solved the problem by means of an underhand but effective stratagem, namely seasoning the guinea with a generous shot of Nali before serving it up. This reduced the number of consumers immediately because Johnny and Ted were out of the running right away, which led to a period of rather strained relations with Louis.

With our work done in Liwonde, we headed back for Kasungu. The lucky ones flew there in the helicopter but Ben, Louis, Tom and I got behind the wheels of our trucks for the inevitable kidney-punishing battle with the Malawian road system. Since we were going to suffer anyway, we decided to take a new route to Kasungu so that we would be able to see as much of the surrounding countryside as possible while we had the opportunity. We really enjoyed what we saw, the only mishap occurring while we were crawling up a very narrow, very steep tarmacked road out of the Rift Valley, when Louis ate most of a loaf of bread we had bought at dusk at a place called Salinas, then discovered it was literally green with mould and promptly donated everything he had eaten to the roadside biosphere.

Something a little better in the culinary line awaited us at Kasungu. Piet Otto's father, Oom Herbert, and his brother Guido had flown up from Harare to join us, bringing with them two enormous pieces of beef topside. After weeks of tinned buffalo stew, tinned buffalo curry and tinned buffalo whatever-else-you-can-produce, that topside had no chance of survival. Before the engine of Guido's aircraft had even had a chance to cool the first piece was in the black pot and the black pot was on a suitable fire. As an aside I would like to make it clear that we didn't eat too badly while in Malawi, all things considered. We were not short of meat, albeit of the tinned buffalo variety, no one drank water, only beer – a considerable hardship, of course – and we had lots of the delicious Tambala redskin peanuts to eat, not to mention a plentiful supply of cabbage, the only available vegetable, and for seasoning our meals we did not lack for onions, garlic and curry powder. I must admit that when these ingredients came together to make music, which happened on just about a daily basis, the night-time atmosphere in our dwellings tended to be interesting. Mosquitoes certainly didn't stand a chance.

In any case, being men of moderation, we stored the other piece of topside in a freezer at the laboratory to wait for the next great occasion. This presented itself the very next weekend, when Ben and Louis took a load of game southwards. I volunteered to have it roasted and ready for them when they returned that Sunday evening, seeing that our work was almost done and we could afford to splash out a little, and so on the Saturday evening I duly went to the laboratory to fetch the topside for thawing. When I opened the freezer, however, I found to my horror that the topside had disappeared. I made enquiries of the local inhabitant we had hired to do our washing and cleaning (he also ate with us, which was a definite perk for him), and he replied: 'Yes, I know where the meat is. Director Moses took it.'

When Louis and Ben arrived back late that night, having spent their journey obsessing about sinking their teeth into the topside, they were first struck dumb with shock and then accused me of having them on. When they had made sure that just for once I was innocent, they sat down to their tinned buffalo stew in a somewhat sullen frame of mind. If Moses had walked into the house that night he would likely have been spared the later embarrassment of being fired for having had a sable and a warthog shot for a barbecue function that he hosted at the Lilongwe Club.

Being a game ranger in Kruger teaches you to be wily, and we didn't often find ourselves bested in a battle of wits with the locals. One evening, for example, Piet the pilot and the resident scientist crossed swords about the numbers of zebra in Kasungu. The scientist, who had a pilot's licence and had done the aerial census of Kasungu, maintained that there were several hundred; Piet, who had naturally done quite a bit of flying in the area during the capture operations, said there couldn't be more than about 50. Both, of course, were adamant about their estimates, and finally agreed that when the buffalo capture operations were done next they would settle the matter once and for all by carrying out a quick zebra search. Next day the scientist accompanied us on the capture operation and on our way back to camp I told them that I could see seven zebra standing under a sausage tree about two kilometres away. Piet confirmed the number and place and we showed them to the scientist as well, who immediately remembered another appointment that afternoon which unfortunately clashed with the zebra search, and departed with the remark: 'Hell, you guys really can see.' What we didn't tell him was that those seven zebra spent every day under that same tree. Moral of the story: if you can't baffle them with brilliance, you have to blind them with bullshit.

Our numbers were now dwindling as each phase of the project was completed, with the chaps not needed for the next one heading for home. Soon Ted, Louis and I were packing up to go, leaving only Ben Pretorius and Ben de Klerk, who were scheduled to stay until the end of the quarantine period. We were at a loose end on our last weekend in Malawi, so we were happy to take up Tom Ullyat of the Sacoma estate on his kind offer to spend it at the company's beach house at Monkey Bay on Lake Malawi. The lake was worth seeing in its own right, and en route we would be able to see a little more of the beauty of the countryside.

Lake Malawi was known for more than a century as Lake Nyasa, which sounded fine to outsiders but was actually a nonsense name that resulted from a misunderstanding. The man responsible was none other than the explorer David Livingstone, who reached the lake in 1859 and, as explorers will, asked the locals what it was called. Their reply was 'nyasa', meaning 'mass of waters'. Knowing no better, Livingstone marked it on his maps as Lake Nyasa, which actually meant 'Lake Lake', and eventually the whole area became known as Nyasaland. When Nyasaland became independent in the 1960s its name changed to Malawi, a name commemorating a kingdom called Maravi which is said to have extended from the Zambezi River to the eastern part of Mombasa in the sixteenth and seventeenth centuries, and the new government promptly corrected the historical communications blip by replacing 'Lake Nyasa' with 'Lake Malawi'.

But I digress. The house at Monkey Bay was magnificent, the housekeeper was expecting us and the pantry was fully stocked and waiting for us to help ourselves. I had been playing cook since leaving Skukuza, however, and by now I was pretty tired of it, so we asked the housekeeper if there was a restaurant near by. There was, and we sent him off to get hold of a menu and find out if we could order take-aways. He came back empty-handed but said that he had booked a table for us, so we climbed into our hired car and set off. We arrived hot and thirsty, having bogged down twice on the beach, and were somewhat less than impressed. It was a ramshackle place, filthy – to put it mildly – and lit only by hurricane lamps whose purpose was definitely not simply to create a cosy atmosphere. The maitre d' showed us to our table, courteously chasing away a couple of chickens that were roosting on it so that we could take our seats (which were actually plastic packing crates, but let that be as it may), and handed us our menus, which informed us that we had a choice between fillets of chambo – a great Malawian eating fish – and rice, with or without sauce. We decided to take things as they came and all ordered a full house, plus a few 'salads'. Definitely not the best meal of the trip, but it was the first one I hadn't had to cook, and there was plenty of Nali sauce for Louis to pour on our viands so as to make them vaguely palatable. Poor old Ted, of course, had a bad time because the benefits of the Nali were denied him.

After a fine weekend we left for Lilongwe on the Sunday morning and arrived at the Capital Hotel in time for lunch on the terrace. It was the first decent meal (and, in my case, as I have explained, almost the first non-self-cooked meal) we had had since leaving Kruger, and we gorged ourselves on steaks and all the trimmings and extras. It cost us a fortune, but we had a lot of leeway to make up. Then it was off to our rooms for a good Sunday afternoon sleep, followed by a few other bits of informal research which proved firstly that the hotel bar's 'salads' were as cold as they had been on our first trip, and secondly that the Capital was justified in boasting that it provided the fastest room service in Africa, with two coffee deliveries clocking in at one minute 15 seconds and one minute 14 seconds respectively. The evening was enlivened by the sight of Ted and Louis, two of the most fearless people I have ever met, in full flight from a pair of prostitutes who had marked them down as potential customers while we were having pre-supper drinks in the hotel lounge. I have to admit that I precipitated this shameful retreat by seating Ted and Louis at our table so that they were facing the daughters of joy and could not avoid looking at them.

Next morning we had a final taste of the ways of senior Malawian officialdom when we went to pay the obligatory farewell courtesy call on Director Moses. Once again the Director wasn't in his office, according to his secretary, although as before I could distinctly hear his voice through the door. So I cooled my heels in the reception area for an hour until he finally 'arrived' and I was ushered into his office, only to find him with his telephone stuck to his ear. I sat down to wait him out, acutely conscious that we had a plane to catch, not to mention the fact that Ted and Louis were waiting outside in the parking area with their tempers quite likely edging into the red. After another three imaginary calls he was able to spare time to greet me. I was not in a mood for pleasantries, however, so I simply bade him farewell and headed for the door. Then my little devil spoke to me, and I paused in mid-stride to ask whether he had enjoyed our purloined topside. The average big (and not so big) shot would have cringed at this reminder of things ill done – certainly in South Africa – and quite possibly offered a feeble denial, but this worthy, with an effrontery so colossal that I still marvel at it, actually replied: 'Yes, I thought it was very tasty.' Savouring this last official experience, we drove to the airport and cleared ourselves through customs, although not by way of the VIP lounge this time, since we had served our purpose. Then Murphy's Lilongwe branch struck its farewell blow by seeing to it that our flight was delayed. Well past caring, we made for the bar and stayed there till it was eventually called.

But Murphy was not yet done with us. Both Louis and I needed to pump ship before boarding, but discovered that there was no toilet in the 'cleared area', so we left this holy of holies and used one we found elsewhere. For this sin we were intercepted on the way back, escorted into separate rooms and told that we would have to undergo a full bare-body search by (in my case) a female official. I offered strenuous objections and in the end Louis and I were free to head for home. There was another little contretemps when we landed at Johannesburg's Jan Smuts Airport, involving myself, an inquisitive customs official and a cool-box filled with dirty clothing that he wanted to inspect, but at last we were free to walk out through the airport doors and enjoy our first breath of good old South African petrol fumes. The Malawian saga was over. It had been an unforgettable experience in more ways than one, but now the siren song of my old stamping grounds was sounding in my ears.

And our hartebeest? A few weeks later they arrived safely, courtesy of the South African Air Force. So all was well that ended well. We had done some good work, we had seen some beautiful country, we had gained some valuable experience and we had had some good laughs in between. A man really can't ask for more than that.

*

The year 1986 brought another experience that was equally unusual, but with added flavour because it involved direct participation in a traditional African ritual that has become rare on this continent, where decades of upheavals have destroyed so many of the ancient societal structures and customs without replacing them with anything better or even just as good. One of the last African countries that really clings to its traditional way of life is South Africa's small neighbour, Swaziland, and this adherence to the old ways was the reason why I ended up with a meaningless but very grand title – and a new fund of stories to add to my collection.

The story of how I became the 'Official Hunter of the King of

Swaziland' actually began in 1982, four years before my involvement, when the aged King Sobhuza II died after a very long reign. In strictly traditional fashion, his death gave rise to a long and intense struggle about which of his wives would rule as queen regent and which of his numerous sons would ascend the throne. The squabble was finally resolved in 1986 when Crown Prince Makhosetive was designated to succeed Sobhuza as King Mswati III. This is where I entered the picture. By long tradition, the coronation of a Swazi king involves a hunt for an elephant bull that has visible tusks, with the king taking part and being in at the kill. A boma is then built around the dead elephant and various rituals and ceremonies take place, with the elephant as one of the main features.

Here the Swazis had a real problem. Things had changed mightily during Sobhuza II's protracted occupation of the throne, and there was not a single elephant to hunt anywhere in the little kingdom. Obviously another solution had to be found, and the diplomatic and political wires started humming. The end-result of all the humming was an instruction to me from the Director of the National Parks Board, Mr Brynard, to kill a suitable elephant on a certain day and then deliver it to the ceremonial boma in Swaziland where the king-making rituals were to take place. The Department of Foreign Affairs and I waded through the preparations – designating and organising exit and entry at border posts, obtaining the necessary permits, recruiting an escort team and pin-pointing the destination, that sort of thing – and we were ready on schedule. As assistant for the trip I picked Ludwig Wagener, the ranger in Skukuza, because he had served on the game-capture team previously and knew how to operate the hydraulic crane on the truck that we would use to load and unload the elephant.

Early on the designated day I shot the elephant out of a helicopter along the Mlambane River in the south of the Park. Ludwig loaded it on to the truck and wrapped it up in a large green tarpaulin, and we set off for Swaziland via the Jeppe's Reef border post. News of our highly unusual mission had spread like lightning, and hordes of people were at the border post to see us arrive, crowding around the truck the instant we stopped. We breezed through the South African customs and on the Swazi side were met by the Commissioner of Police in person, who took our passports for the duration of our stay and told us to follow him and not let him out of sight. This done, he got into his black Mercedes and sped away with three Land Rovers full of policemen following him and Ludwig and I struggling to keep up with our cargo of deceased elephant.

Following Mswati's chief cop proved to be easier said than done, given the relative vehicle speeds involved, and in his efforts to keep up Ludwig ignored a stop sign along the way. A vigilant policeman spotted this violation and pulled us over, only to suffer a rude shock when his colleagues in one of the chase Land Rovers grabbed him before he was able to say a single word to us and bundled him into their vehicle. We were still goggling at this when one of the cops apologised to us for the inconvenience and asked us to follow the Land Rovers, an arrangement with which we were quite content because the commissioner and his long black Merc had long since vanished into the distance. Talk about VIP treatment!

At the ceremonial boma we were met by another crowd, several hundred strong, whose members probably had never seen an elephant before, live or dead. Well, now they had one – not very fresh any more, regrettably. He had spent almost four hours on the road in an open truck, and as a result was very bloated from the fermentation in his guts. Still, what they saw was what we had, and so we uncovered the elephant under the rapt gaze of the spectators and prepared to unload. This should have been a simple affair – all Ludwig had to do was engage the truck's power take-off, which in turn would drive the crane's hydraulic pumps, and lower the elephant to the ground – but, inevitably, Murphy's African branch intervened: when Ludwig tried to engage the power take-off it refused to work.

The only alternative now was to push the elephant off the truck by hand. Getting help from the crowd was easy, and in no time dozens of volunteers were applying themselves to the elephant under Ludwig's guidance. The pushers really got into the spirit of things, all except one, clad in a green suit and blue tie, who presumably didn't want to soil his natty outfit. Ludwig had no strong feelings about preserving the fellow's sartorial splendour – this wasn't just any old dead elephant, it was the *King's*, damn it! – so he switched to fanakalo, the lingua franca in those parts, and summoned Green Suit to labour with a peremptory shout of 'shova lapa spugupuk!' which means, more or less, 'push here, you bloody fool!' Green Suit wasted no time in getting hands-on with the enormous corpse, and he and his colleagues soon had the elephant on the ground. Our mission completed, Ludwig and I made ready to leave, and we were just about to start up when the police commissioner came along and said that the Prime Minister would like to thank us bringing for the elephant. We thought this was rather nice, and a minute later we had assembled in front of a podium, from which the minister made a little speech of thanks, still natty in his green suit and blue tie in spite of having done some close-in work with the elephant. Like a true gentleman he made no mention of being called a bloody fool by Ludwig, whose embarrassed face looked something like a bowl of beetroot salad.

Ludwig and I had already agreed that we would go home via Swaziland's casino because casinos were illegal in South Africa at that time and the commissioner had instructed the various police border posts to stay open for us, which meant that we were free to waste all our money. The casino security men were a little doubtful about admitting two frankly dirty men in khaki who had arrived in a large truck, but they did not actually stop us, and in no time we were having our little flutter. Perhaps the Swazi ancestral spirits were smiling on us because of the favour we had just done the king, because I walked out with enough money to buy Helena diamond stud earrings and a pendant for her birthday. That was the beginning and end of my gambling career. The formula for being a happy gambler is to quit while you're ahead, and I did just that. These days casinos are legal in South Africa, but if I happen to visit one with someone who wants to gamble I'm quite happy just to sit and watch. The spirits, after all, repaid their debt to me very handsomely and have doubtless gone on to assist other deserving people.

This episode was not the end of my involvement with Swaziland and its king. A few years later the Parks Board received another request from Mswati, this time for an elephant, a hippo, a lion and a hyaena, the request and delivery being facilitated by the famous Ted Reilly, who is without doubt the father of nature conservation in Swaziland. The purpose of the request was unspecified but obviously involved some ceremonial occasion or other. What tickled me was that Mswati asked for me by name when it came to killing the animals and delivering them: all of a sudden I was the 'Official Hunter for the King of Swaziland'.

Fancy title or no, the affair was plagued by the usual pitfalls. A few days before the delivery date we got the lion and a hyaena which had become a problem animal due to man-induced actions, and the hippo and elephant I shot early on the morning of the day we had to do the delivery. This time I had three companions – Manie Coetzee, manager of Kruger's meat-processing plant, who was to operate the hydraulic crane, Ian Milne from our information department, because I had also been tasked to facilitate a press conference, and Ian's wife, Stefanie.

We made good time with our cargo of four dead animals and at 10 am arrived at one of the royal palaces, where Mswati was supposed to accept the animals in person. Ted Reilly was there, wearing his legendary outfit of tackies, shorts and shirt, but the King wasn't. After a long wait, during which we grew more and more worried because the day was hot and our cargo was beginning to show definite signs of bloating, we received a message that we were to link up with the King at another palace about 10 kilometres away. We set off again and were subjected to another long wait, after which another royal spokesman informed us that the King's mother wished to see the animals before the King accepted them. Where? At the palace from which we had just arrived! There was nothing for it but to send Manie back with the animals, which had now passed the bloating stage and were well on the way to putrefying, while I stayed behind to participate in the press conference.

Manie didn't take kindly to this change of plans because he wasn't a believer in the elasticity of 'African time', and Ted's efforts to calm him down were to no avail. Still, the job came first, and Manie set off in a highly disgruntled mood. Four hours passed before he returned, even more disgruntled than before. When I asked him why it had taken so long, he answered me in colourful terms that don't bear repeating. Later, when I finally got the story out of him, I could only sympathise with his frame of mind. When he arrived at his destination he had to cool his heels for a considerable time while the King's mother prepared herself spiritually for the occasion. When she had completed her lengthy preparations he was told to unload the carcasses – which by now were fairly ripe – for her inspection. The King's mother then appeared, walked around them once and disappeared into the palace again. Another wait ensued before a messenger came to tell him that he could load them up again and take them to yet another palace. There he was told to unload the animals on the front lawn, which he did, but only after a large percentage of the trees in the palace garden had bitten the dust. It was a thoroughly unpleasant task, since it was now fairly late in the afternoon and the carcasses positively reeked.

That, however, was not our problem. We had done our job and the King's Hunter was free to take his entourage back to Skukuza, except that all the waiting and trundling around had made nonsense of our scheduled return that night. On top of that, we hadn't had anything to eat or drink all day and were in a fair state of dehydration and hunger. I might add that if ever two people were extreme reverse anorexics it was Manie and myself, and on this occasion he beat me easily in the frustrated consumer department. In any case, we had no option except to take up Ted and Liz Reilly on their kind offer to spend the night on their farm, Mlilwane, although this caused further problems. I was the only one in our group who had foreseen the possibility that we might not be able to get back to Skukuza that night, so I was well-prepared with clean clothes, toothbrush and toiletries, as were the South African Broadcasting Corporation journalists and the rest of the press contingent, who were old Africa hands and had come prepared for everything. Manie got mad all over again, and Ian and Stefanie weren't too happy either. What made it even worse was that after a lovely dinner, during which a classic Lowveld thunderstorm broke, I joined the journalists in a visit to the casino, leaving my dishevelled colleagues behind at the Reilly farm. It was hardly surprising, therefore, that next morning Manie had us in the truck and heading for Skukuza long before sunup.

That wasn't the end of the story. In the next few days all hell broke lose in the press about what many people saw as the unnecessary slaughter of innocent animals for ritual purposes, although I suffered no personal qualms – I had been following orders, and in any case I felt strongly about maintaining traditional medicine-making and the associated rituals. Still, some of the hate mail was fairly nasty, although I was amused by an anonymous letter from somewhere in England that read: 'You murderer bastard. May you get cancer all over your body and die very very slowly. May you never stop suffering. Wicked wicked monster.' What this poor fool didn't know, of course, was that I'd done the cancer thing long ago.

Another person wrote: 'I am horrified at you and all those involved in the killing of animals to give to a head of state as a sign of goodwill. If it's goodwill to kill, you have gone wrong somewhere. When people see you, the conservationist, killing for a ceremony, they must then believe it is okay for everyone to do it – you do. Then why not kill for skins, horns, trophies, etc? This destructive violent act of killing only reinforces my general view of conservationists. Conserve for now so we can later kill at will. I believe this was a very image-damaging exercise for you.' This was a rather more thoughtful letter than the rantings of the cancer merchant, of course, but it was still out of context. None of the animals concerned was even remotely endangered, locally or otherwise – just the contrary – and the hyaena would have been destroyed in any case because it had become a problem; and game conservation in Africa must harmonise with the greater needs of the society around it. In that context, shooting four non-endangered animals for a ceremonial occasion that helped to keep the Swazi people close to their traditions was obviously worthwhile.

So I fielded all these letters with reasonable equanimity, but I got a bit of a shock a few days later when I received a telephone call from Swaziland's Minister of Internal Affairs, one Mr Dlamini. At first I thought that he wanted to thank me for my part in delivering the gift to the Swazi people, but instead he was quite abusive, telling me that the animals I had unloaded on the palace lawns were now rotten and that I had to remove them. This was not my business at all, and I told him so in the most diplomatic tone that I could motivate myself to muster. Mr Dlamini was having none of this, however, and the dialogue became quite heated before Mr Dlamini's thick Swazi accent suddenly vanished and he admitted that he was actually Jan van der Merwe from the South African Broadcasting Corporation's office at Nelspruit, who had been with me for the entire trip.

Thus ended my tenure as the official hunter to King Mswati III, not with a bang but with a leg-pull. Seeing that I was usually the chief leg-puller, I could hardly complain.

12

LESSONS IN SHOOTING STRAIGHT

It goes without saying that Kruger National Park rangers have to be good at handling firearms. I am sure that some people think those rifles they see Kruger rangers carrying in TV documentaries are more or less stage props, but nothing could be further from the truth. A game park is a fascinating environment, but it can turn lethal at any time and with startling suddenness. So the ranger's rifle, like an elephant's trunk, is both a tool and a weapon. It can be used for anything from destroying wounded or dangerous animals to protecting scientists on field trips. In my time in Kruger this meant some fairly rigorous training and periodical re-testing for a variety of park staff, not just the rangers themselves but also nature conservation-orientated field staff, such as day- and night-drive students, day-walk guides, interpretive staff, trails rangers and the guides who accompany the scientists on field trips.

We did quite a lot of basic and advanced training at Kruger, because a large proportion of new staff had had little or no experience of firearms. Strange as it might sound, the worst off were those unfortunates who had been taught by a father or older brother to fire the family pellet gun. It is true that mostly one uses the same muscles to fire any sort of shoulder weapon, but there is a vast difference in the basic techniques used to fire a pellet gun and a rifle chambered for the .458 Winchester Magnum round, one of our standard calibres. The .458, like any rifle in that general class, is a powerful brute. It makes a tremendous noise, fires a heavy bullet as thick as a large man's forefinger, kicks you brutally if you do not hold it the right way and positively demands that you develop a degree of tolerance for it (which some people never do), and there is no way around it. The same remarks apply to all the other rifles of the same general class, including my long-standing personal favourite, the .375 Magnum; only the details differ.

We provided three levels of training. Level 1 was the theoretical course that covered firearms handling at grassroots level, with the emphasis on safety, and included a basic accuracy test, starting with rifles in the .308 Winchester calibre, which was milder than the .458 Winchester and was used in a Mauser-action rifle whose 'feel' and operation were very similar to the .458's. Then the students moved on to the .458 itself.

The Level 1 course was designed to be both a complete instruction module for the day- or night-drive guides – who obviously didn't need the same level of skill as somebody taking people into the veld on foot, when all the advantages are with the animals – and a basic phase for advanced training. We laid great emphasis on the correct techniques, which are critical, especially with large-calibre rifles. A particularly important one was the right way to hold the rifle. Rifles might differ in design, but they are all held the same way, and the principles involved are universal. A simple point-and-pull stunt won't cut the mustard, and I have often seen this point illustrated in TV news footage of the fighting between the Israelis and Palestinians. The Israelis hold their rifles correctly and hit, while the Palestinians hold their rifles incorrectly and mostly only succeed in making a noise. And, by the way, any trained rifleman will tell you that you don't pull the trigger, no matter what might be said in action novels. You squeeze it, or your shot will go anywhere except where you're aiming. The correct holding technique comes naturally to some but not to others, but over the years I always managed, except in one case, to inculcate the right hold in firearms trainees. That exception simply couldn't learn to hold a rifle correctly, no matter how hard we tried to teach him, and every shot left him with a bloody nose. He eventually left conservation altogether and became an insurance broker.

Providing firearms training taught me a valuable personal lesson: eternal vigilance. When you live with firearms and people who know how to handle them, you tend to be fairly casual because you know that everybody will do the right thing, either consciously or unconsciously from sheer habit. But working with novices requires you to keep a sharp lookout all the time.

The worse case I ever came across during Level 1 training involved a trainee whom I shall call Suzi. Suzi was one of those people who are simply incompatible with firearms; she was so nervous about them she would whimper and hyperventilate the moment you handed her a rifle, a sure sign of mega-stress. She went through the basic course four times and was still not up to scratch; twice, in fact, she opted not even to attempt the final evaluations. Then she presented herself a fifth time, as terrified as ever of anything that kicked and went 'bang'; I can only think that her superiors had subjected her to heavy pressure. I had to write a full report on the trainees' performance after every training session, and in all conscience I simply could not give her anything but bad marks each time. But there was some 'connection' at a higher level than mine, because invariably I would be told to give her another chance. I did so with reluctance. I had trained literally hundreds of people to shoot and managed to bring them to reasonable competence at the very least, but this woman frankly scared me, at basic level and also particularly with the heavy-calibre weapons that are any ranger's stock in trade.

During her last evaluation she was on the range with a .458 Winchester Magnum in her hands, while I was standing about half a metre from her. I didn't dare stand any further back because I had to be ready to take control of her and the rifle at a moment's notice. When the time came to fire Suzi went straightaway into her usual whimpering, hyperventilating mode, but managed to squeeze off a shot. Not surprisingly, it was nowhere near the target. Somehow she managed to pull the bolt back and shove it forward again to load another cartridge into the chamber. So far, so good – one thing you learn in the bush is to reload as soon as you've fired, so as to be ready for any eventuality. But then she took her left hand away from the stock's fore-end. Except in the case of a southpaw the left hand is very much the control hand, and when she did this the rifle tilted down in her right hand, whose index finger was already inside the trigger guard and on the trigger. The weight of the rifle – a .458 has to be quite heavy, or it would kick you to pieces and slow down your second shot – hung on her finger for a moment, and that was enough. The second round went off with an ear-splitting bang and the big bullet tore into the ground not more than 50 centimetres from my left foot and even closer to hers; either would have been smashed beyond repair if that bullet had scored a hit.

Under the circumstances I was, I think, remarkably restrained: when I had recovered the power of speech and movement I took the rifle away from her, went for a quick walk to calm myself down and then told her to go home. I wish I could say that this narrow escape resulted in an outcome that proved satisfactory to all parties. But the fact is that Suzi never got over her crippling fear and never learnt to shoot properly, although she carries the obligatory rifle slung over her shoulder when she takes people out into the veld; this is one case where the cynics would be correct in regarding it as a mere stage prop. Unless a miracle has taken place she would be more lethal if she were armed with a can of pepper spray.

*

The other thing we did our best to hammer into the trainees was gun safety. A rifle is not a toy. It is an extremely lethal piece of machinery, and the mark of a really well-trained gun-handler is that he or she always treats the weapon as if it is loaded, whether that is so or not. That includes not fooling around with the action, not carrying it loaded into a vehicle unless you are going to need it at a moment's notice, and always making sure that the muzzle is pointing in a safe direction. Ignore the basic rules and sooner or later there is going to be an accident. We had one night-drive student who decided to disregard all his training and do things his way while riding through a rest camp in a minibus. As a result he accidentally fired his .458; the bullet tore the guts out of a book on birds, demolished a packet of dried fruit lying on the seat and punched through the floor, heading for destinations unknown. Since no casualties were reported, the consequences of this foolishness amounted to no more than a slightly ventilated combi and a shaken and embarrassed student, but it could so easily have resulted in a tragedy.

Ham-handed trainees weren't the only things we had to be vigilant about. One time, I remember, we had four Level 1 trainees out on the range with .308-calibre rifles, firing with ammunition from a batch of several thousand rounds we had just received. Each had four rounds that had to be fired in a set pattern, and I took up my position behind the most nervous one. I watched her load, squeeze the trigger and flinch, but nothing happened. She ejected the round and reloaded, and at this moment I heard a discreet popping sound to my right, looked around and saw the next student eject and reload as well. Alarm-bells went off immediately in my head. I told the right-hand trainee not to fire, grabbed the rifle and ordered an immediate cease-fire. Having checked that all the rifles had been made safe, I started hunting around on the firing point. First I found the dud round fired by the nervous one; the primer was properly dented by the firing-pin, but the bullet was still in place. Then I found the case of the cartridge that had gone 'pop', and when I checked the right-hand student's rifle, there the bullet was, about 50 centimetres up the barrel. It made me sweat a bit when I realised how close we had come to blowing up the rifle.

The mechanics of cartridge ignition are quite simple. The firing-pin hits the primer, sending a flash into the body of the cartridge case. The flash ignites the propellant powder, turning it from a mass of solid grains or flakes into a cloud of unimaginably hot gas. The only thing that can give way is the bullet, which is pushed up and out of the barrel by the expanding gas. If, for some reason, the bullet can't exit the barrel and the gas is trapped, there is no rifle action made by man that would not blow apart, certainly killing the firer (whose face is only a couple of centimetres away from the action) and probably whoever is standing near by as well.

It was obvious to me what had happened here. The first cartridge had been a partial misfire, generating just enough power to drive the bullet some of the way up the barrel, effectively plugging it. If a second bullet had run up against it there would have been an explosion. By way of experiment I took a round out of the magazine and tried it in a third trainee's rifle (but only after checking that the barrel was clear, you can rest assured about that!). All I heard was the click of the firing-pin hitting the primer. That meant two total misfires and one squib out of three cartridges fired! I aborted the exercise on the spot and made a less than friendly telephone call to the suppliers, who were horrified and replaced the entire batch, including all cartridges we had already fired, and weighed every cartridge of the new batch individually to make sure that it contained a full charge. That's how the game works. Something had gone wrong in the munitions factory – perhaps a momentary malfunction of some inconsequential piece of machinery – and many months and kilometres later two students nearly got their heads blown off on the rifle range.

*

Trainees who had passed Level 1 satisfactorily and were destined to become day-walk guides or trails rangers would then go on Level 2, the so-called 'bush lane' we had built north of Skukuza. This was basically a speed and accuracy test which required trainees to move through a predetermined course in a limited time period. During their movement through the bush lane they were expected to locate targets that had been put out beforehand, 'kill' them and go through all the drills needed to stay alive in the veld in the presence of dangerous, aggressive animals. The targets were made of drab-coloured masonite, cut into suitable shapes to represent two buffalo, two rhino, two lion and an elephant, each spray-painted according to a fixed pattern by using a template. There were no visible aiming points or scoring rings on the front aspect of the target, but the kill zones were marked on the reverse side and used for counting up points.

The rules were tough. Only killing shots counted, and the trainee failed automatically if he or she failed to spot one of the targets. The passing mark was 75 per cent, and there was a built-in penalty system, so that it was not unusual for a trainee actually to score a minus (the worst score I ever recorded was minus 274 per cent, which is right down there with the shark manure). The bush lane exercise was so difficult that during my years in Kruger only one person ever passed the first time, and he was definitely not your average trainee. He had grown up among the elephants and buffalo around Shingwedzi, could track and shoot before he could speak properly and was still at school when he won the annual rangers' shooting competition as a member of the Scientific Services team.

Difficult? Stressful? Absolutely. But we weren't engaged in playing funny buggers. A ranger who couldn't shoot well was a menace, both to himself and to the people in his care . . . except in the case of Suzi, apparently.

We used two evaluators. One – myself, usually – accompanied the trainee as he or she located targets, fired and reloaded. The other evaluator followed us, armed with the score-sheet, the stop-watch and a can of spray-paint for carrying out running repairs on the holes in the targets. Which is not to say that I did not see it as my bounden duty to lighten the tension from time to time.

One of my regular assistant instructors was Don English, son of the legendary ranger Mike English. As Don had often been the assistant instructor, I felt one day that it was time for him to walk up front with the trainee. We had a large group of more than 10 trainees that day, which is far too big, but force of circumstances did not allow otherwise. The two of them duly set off down the bush lane, and every time they came to a certain target I saw Don flinch, expecting to be hit by a ricochet – to be caught by a .458 bullet in normal flight is bad enough, but one that is tumbling head over heels after bouncing off something is too awful even to contemplate.

The last target in the bush lane was a buffalo, with the trainee being required to score two killing hits and then reload before running out of time, all this at less than two metres' range. The target was propped up against a clay bank that looked remarkably like rock, and I knew that the great moment had arrived. As the trainee let off his second shot I tumbled down like a bag of beans, the clipboard and stopwatch falling from my hands, being careful to fall with my back to Don because I knew I wouldn't be able to keep a straight face when I saw his reaction.

A few seconds' deathly silence followed the shot, then Don screamed, 'No!' and came running over to me. He wasn't very impressed when he found a dead man lying there and grinning up at him, but fortunately he has a good sense of humour and managed to see the funny side of it eventually. In retrospect, it was a terrible thing to have done, and in utterly bad taste. But I suppose the explanation is that I am a terrible man with utterly bad taste.

*

I'd like to add that I am not prejudiced against women shottists. In fact, with the exception of Suzi I always found women easier to teach to shoot properly because the men had often been exposed to incorrect methods and had built up a repertoire of bad habits. It is true that some of them found it a trial to handle the large-calibre rifles, where the shooter's body size and weight are definitely a factor, but correct handling techniques and an appropriate state of mind can compensate for many things. Some of them (and I suppose this remark will infuriate any militant feminist) were also very easy on the eye. One such, whom I shall call Kathleen, was a lovely blonde lass who had none of the hang-ups about looking feminine that you frequently find in women working in the admittedly rather macho field of conservation. She was a looker and proud of it, and I make no bones about saying that whereas khaki does absolutely nothing to enhance the looks of any lady, Kathleen really did something for khaki. At the same time she wasn't just a pretty face. She was as smart as a whip and had bounded up the training ladder two steps at a time.

My colleague Sony was the evaluator accompanying Kathleen on the day of her big test in the bush lane. Sony was a staid person, not given to flights of passion or fancy, but I noticed right away that his mind was not concentrated on the right things, and as we proceeded along the course, which took about 40 minutes to complete, he became progressively less focused. After scoring the second last target, I simply couldn't resist increasing Sony's agony, and when Kathleen was out of earshot I muttered: 'If that gluteus maximus (buttock in plain English) is going all the way to Tshokwane, I'll follow it.'

'Hell, 'I'd follow it to Shingwedzi!' was his fervent reply. Now, Shingwedzi was about 300 kilometres from the bush lane, so

Sony's remark pretty much said it all. And Kathleen? Oh, she passed, blissfully unaware of the mental melt-down she had inflicted on Sony. Well, maybe.

*

Level 3, the elephant-shooting exercise, was the ultimate test, and in my opinion was the best of its class anywhere in the world in the wildlife exposure field. The primary aim was not simply to kill the elephant but to use his preordained death to make sure that in future confrontations the student would know what he and his rifle could do, and would have the confidence to handle himself under pressure; it would be sheer folly to allow a ranger to take tourists for hikes in the bush without knowing how he or she would react when charged by a dangerous animal.

A selected elephant (Level 3 tests were usually timed to coincide with culling operations) would be herded by helicopter towards where the trainee was waiting, one instructor close by – I normally stood off just to one side and slightly in front of the student – and another riding in the helicopter. The aim was to be able to see exactly what happened and what the trainee's reactions were; the instructor was there to tell the trainee when to shoot and what to do if things went wrong, also to act as a backup if the trainee failed to kill the elephant, while the ranger in the helicopter could sort out any real mess the groundlings could not handle. This might sound like a belt-and-braces situation, but plenty of caution is only sensible when large animals get to close quarters with human beings under extreme circumstances.

There is an old military saying that the first 10 minutes of combat teach the soldier everything he needs to know about fighting. The same applies here, and in our case we were able to give a trainee those first 10 minutes under controlled conditions. One of my priorities was to note how the trainees handled real pressure. We could train and instruct a novice to within an inch of his or her life, but the acid test was the '10 minutes of combat'. There we could see not only how deeply our training had taken root but also what sort of inner resources the trainee could muster – and control – when the chips were down.

In later years we had to shelve the Level 3 exercise in its original form because of the culling restrictions forced on us by countries where you have to visit a zoo if you want to see an elephant, and this infinitely valuable training procedure went into the proverbial File 13. We tried to compensate by simulating the exercise in the bush lane, but naturally this had its limitations, because even the best simulation could not come anywhere near duplicating the real thing. I can't help feeling with some foreboding that the odds are beginning to pile up.

Human nature is a strange thing, and the longer I did this sort of training the better I learnt to predict the trainees' reactions. Almost invariably the first shot would be high, resulting in immediate panic and forgetting to reload. Next would be a pleading glance saying: 'Help me! What now?' to which the reply would be: 'Shoot again.' Sometimes that would be enough and everything would click into place, but at other times the little routine would be repeated until one of the evaluators stepped in. Then the trainee's quivering hand would be given a congratulatory shake, even if one of the old hands had had to finish the job. The point of the exercise would have been achieved, namely to allow the trainee to know where he stood and what he could or could not do. If you know your limits and can control them and yourself, you are safe.

In my mind, elephants are the bosses of the bushveld, and if you have hunted an elephant and won, then you have earned your spurs. But it must not be forgotten that a game ranger's version of elephant hunting is not the same as a hunter's. The hunter seeks the elephant that suits his aims; the game ranger is much more focused because of his greater conservation task, so he culls members of a herd (when this could still be done) or kills specific individuals that have become a problem, particularly along the boundaries, where the fences and our neighbours' crops had to be protected. This is why all the rhinos taken out of the park came from the boundary areas (poachable animals would also be moved to safer areas, but that is something else, of course).

Some armchair conservationists might find it abhorrent that elephants were shot simply to train novice rangers, and feel that it might have had a 'brutalising' effect on people who were supposed to be learning to conserve game animals, not wipe them out, but an argument of this type holds no water in the context of the Kruger National Park. Firstly, Kruger's problem was (and still is) not a scarcity but an oversupply of elephants, so there was no question of wiping out anything – in fact, the gene pool could actually be improved by culling undesirable animals. Secondly, the Park belonged to the animals, and we had to take all the precautions we could to protect the humans who came visiting. The figures speak for themselves. In 25 years of running trails while I was there we had about 452 000 visitors – an average of 56 people a day – on foot in the veld during any 11-month annual period, and we didn't suffer one fatality.

*

It goes without saying that some trainees fared better than others when they faced a simulated charge, which to a novice is every bit as terrifying as the real thing, and I cannot resist describing a couple of incidents. I won't mention any names or even nicknames, because some of these people are still around, while others are dead or have left, and it would be better to let these sleeping dogs lie.

I remember with particular clarity the coolest, calmest and most collected trainee I ever had the pleasure to evaluate. The exercise took place just north of Mooiplaas; the veld had been burnt and there was no cover to speak of, so all we could hide behind while the chopper herded the elephant towards us was a charred mopane bush – just the two of us, because the trainee had such a good track record that I opted to go in without back-up.

The chopper pilot did the necessary and in no time the elephant was not more than 20 metres away and coming straight at us. This was the signal for the trainee to stand up and take his shot. Well, he stood up all right, but nothing else happened. In a flash the elephant covered another five metres or so. Still no reaction from the trainee. Next thing the elephant was barely 10 metres away, and I'd had enough. I prepared to fire, fairly nervous by now – this was close-in stuff, and no mistake! Then I decided to hold off, because my trainee was very obviously not frozen with panic. The elephant took another couple of strides, and this time he drew a bead. Then his .458 roared and the elephant went straight down, so close that that to fire the insurance shot into the top of the neck the trainee had only to take two paces forward and one to the side.

To say I was relieved would be understating the case. In my time in Kruger I came close to making an intimate acquaintance with a mortuary slab on more occasions than I like to think about, and this was one of the occasions when the only way I would have got there would have been with the aid of a spatula and some blotting paper. I am sure that no one would have blamed me if I had blown my top, but I did not. There is a difference between foolhardy recklessness and icy, rock-solid control; and who could know the difference better than my trainee, who in a previous life had worn the maroon beret that identifies the special forces regiments?

I remember with equal vividness the worst trainee I ever had to deal with, not only because this individual was so well-nigh terminally lacking in the requirements but also because he had some pull somewhere along the line, so that every time I reported on his deficiencies I was told in no uncertain terms that he had all the qualities and potential required, regardless of what I might say. We had him out not once but twice, and on each occasion the only thing he got right was to refrain from running away – probably only because my hand was clamped firmly on his left shoulder. Yet after the second fiasco his supervisor called me in and told me to give the trainee a 'clean bill of health', as he put it. I refused point-blank. Our standards were high for a reason, and I would not compromise if it meant that people's lives might be put at risk – it was like allowing the driver of a minibus taxi to fly a Boeing 747.

Rank hath its privileges, however, and I was forced to schedule another outing. But I invited the supervisor to come along so that he could personally observe the candidate's performance. He agreed, and in due course we were in position on a koppie on the fairly hilly northern bank of the Crocodile River. The arrangement was that the chopper pilot, with whom I was in constant communication, would bring the elephants up to where we were in such a way that they would make their first appearance about 25 metres from us. I told the supervisor to stay within arm's length of my left shoulder, no matter what happened; I had the feeling that he was not comfortable with this arrangement, but that was his problem, not mine.

The first elephant arrived on cue, and the trainee fired and scored a clean miss. I deliberately let the elephant get uncomfortably close before shooting him, so that he fell about four metres from us. About 40 seconds later the second elephant arrived; the student, who was still in a near-catatonic state, missed again. This time I let the elephant get even closer before dropping him, after which the supervisor, a strictly occasional smoker, bummed a cigarette from one of the ground crew and demolished it in just two pulls.

Despite his obvious incompetence, this fellow became a section ranger after I had left the Park. How he copes is anybody's guess.

In a couple of other cases I have no hesitation in naming names because the people involved acquitted themselves so well. One was a trainee named Peter Davies. Peter wore glasses, which is nothing to be ashamed of, but they can make things difficult if you have to shoot in the rain, which is a natural part of working in the veld, and something you have to live with. So it happened that on the day of his practical we were crouching behind a mopane with the rain coming down like curtain-rods as we listened to the helicopter herding the elephant bull in our direction. Peter was as busy as a one-legged man at an arse-kicking contest, simultaneously wiping the persistent raindrops off his glasses, watching the elephant bearing down on us at a pace considerably faster than a leisurely stroll and cursing his goggles in memorably lurid terms, but he didn't get his priorities wrong, and when the moment came he laid out our visitor in textbook fashion. It's at times like these that an instructor gets that truly satisfied glow in his heart.

The other incident took place when my colleague Louis Olivier and I were testing mapoisa Joe Nkuna on elephants just north of the Crocodile River. I mention this affair because it was so truly strange. As was often the case, I was out in front, with Joe and Louis together a short distance behind. With the helicopter on their heels the two targeted elephants headed straight for where I was hiding behind a raisin bush. Now was the time for Joe to fire at the leader, but nothing happened, and naturally the elephant just kept getting closer and closer. Still Joe didn't fire: I could see that he was aiming and pulling the trigger, but without any result. Louis and I were old hands and knew our limits; by now I had reached mine, and I aimed quickly and fired at the same time as he did. The elephant went down, but the second one was only about 10 metres behind, making it a strictly shoot-first-and-ask-questions-later situation. To my horror the same thing happened. Joe aimed and squeezed off a non-existent shot, and Louis and I dropped the elephant at point-blank range.

Louis did not hesitate to tell Joe exactly what he thought about his ability. Joe, however, stoutly maintained that his rifle wouldn't fire. I took it from him and pulled back the bolt, ejecting the round in the chamber, then cycled the action a few times but couldn't find any mechanical problem: all the cartridges fed and extracted smoothly. I told Joe to take his rifle to Fritz, the gunsmith, who confirmed that it was working perfectly, so next day we tried again, only to have the same thing happen.

Something was clearly not right, because Joe Nkuna was no novice and was very familiar with both the bush and the elephants in it, so Louis undertook to get things straightened out. Two days later he came beaming into my office to announce that he had discovered the problem, and proceeded to tell me a story so unlikely that I would never have thought of it myself. Joe was a big man, with hands to match; when he closed the bolt while chambering a cartridge the base of one meaty palm would touch the safety-catch and move it slightly forward – not enough to lock the bolt, just far enough to lock the trigger-sear. Pulling back the bolt pushed the safety into the disengaged position again, so that the rifle was perfectly functional once more. And on that tiny thing had hung a field ranger's entire career!

The remedy was simple. We removed the safety-catch from Joe's rifle and scheduled another test, at which all went well. I derived some sideways satisfaction from this incident, because I have never been enthusiastic about safety-catches. I felt then, and feel now, that safe firearms handling should result primarily from good training that inculcates the right habits, not mechanical devices that are ultimately only as effective as the man who uses them. The computer boffins' acronym GIGO – 'garbage in, garbage out', meaning that if you input rubbish you will get a rubbishy result, no matter how many gigabytes you have at your disposal – applies with equal force to firearms and the people who use them.

*

One other lesson about hunting dangerous animals that I liked to hammer into my trainees was that speed was fine, but accuracy was final; put another way, what counts is not shots per minute but hits per shot. The bottom line is that if you don't hit a vital organ you will achieve nothing worthwhile, even if you work a miracle and fire four shots in four seconds.

On one occasion I was putting a trainee named Jaco Ackerman, a proven good shot, through his practical, and it turned out to be a pretty severe test for a youngster facing his first elephant shoot. Normally the chopper pilot would cut out two target elephants and herd them to us, but on this occasion he had to deal with a group of five, all between 10 and 12 years old, that positively refused to split up, no matter what he did. The pilot informed me of this and I told him to let them all come; it was late in the afternoon, and the elephants had to be gutted and transported back before nightfall. Jaco did not know about the number of elephants involved, of course, and the expression on his face when all five bulls appeared over a ridge not 50 metres away and headed directly at us had to be seen to be believed. Hastily I instructed him to start with the one on the left and work towards the right, while I would start from the right if they stayed together and kept on coming in our direction. In such a situation the helicopter would move off immediately the pilot saw the first rifle raised, and the elephants often changed direction when this happened, but not this time. For a trainee on his first elephant shoot this was an extreme test indeed, and perhaps a bit unfair on Jaco, but I had decided to take a chance because of his known marksmanship.

Jaco wasted no time and fired all five shots in his magazine, but only put down one of the elephants, a perfect example of the truth of the 'speed is fine but accuracy is final' principle. He now found himself in the classic hunter's nightmare: an empty magazine and four elephants bearing down at close range. I retrieved the situation by killing all four while he frantically shoved fresh cartridges into his magazine, then sent him to fire the insurance shots and test the eye reflexes while I reloaded. It was a win-win situation for Jaco: he had passed an extremely acid test and also learnt a very valuable survival lesson . . . and, moreover, walked away unscathed.

*

Safety and consistency are the watchwords of firearms handling. If you're doing everything right then things will work the way they are supposed to, but one little slip can be disastrous. Just as important is to know the anatomy of the animals you are dealing with to make sure you hit them where they should be hit. Experience has taught me that you can't go far wrong with the general philosophy of 'low down and far back'. You will see the truth of this if you study the placement of the vital organs of all dangerous animals except the hippo, whose brain sits at the very top of his head, but even then the 'far back' part still holds true.

All this is very logical. If you look at the size of all the dangerous animals' heads and the mass of muscles that are needed to move those heads in their various functions, then there can be no doubt about the enormous amounts of power needed to do so. This requires plenty of muscle and, of course, places to attach the muscles to the skull and spine. To facilitate this muscular system the spine generally is attached to the lower part of the skull, from where it drops down and back to make space for the neck and shoulder muscles. In the case of lions and leopards, the heart sits very far back in the body, much further back than in the case of an ungulate, for example.

Many people believe, erroneously, that you can give an elephant a brain shot by directing your bullet to a certain spot on its head. Not so! A bull elephant's head is enormous. It can exceed a metre in width and depth, and, if you take the base of the trunk into account, it can easily measure almost two metres in height. The brain is roughly the size of a rugby ball or a largish pawpaw, and to pinpoint its location in that massive skull takes a keen eye, a cool head and a clear understanding of the elephant's anatomy. We were at some pains to bring this point home to the trainees. We would give them detailed classroom instruction, using slides and overhead projections, and then a practical demonstration once they had actually shot an elephant in the final phase of Level 3. When the elephant was down and safely dead the trainee would be given a stick or rod about a metre long and told to point out the brain from various angles; the idea was to use the rod to illustrate the bullet's flight-path from the rifle's muzzle to the point of impact and then to the brain.

This system worked well, but it was far from perfect, and we used other methods as well. One was a red-dot scope mounted on a tripod (these sights have a built-in red dot that superimposes itself over the sight picture), which was a long way down the road from using a slide with a hole pricked into it to illustrate the position of a vital organ. But nothing stands still, and if some better technology comes along you must simply incorporate it. To a conservationist there is more than one meaning to the old phrase 'the game's the thing'. The best method I could find for pinpointing the brain's location, though, depended not on technological teaching aids but simply on the person's imagination. You would imagine that you could see a steel rod passing horizontally through the head from one ear-hole to the other, and a second rod passing vertically down through the head until it touched the first. If you then further imagined that there was an apple skewered on the two rods at the point where they intersected, you would be spot-on every time, regardless of the angle at which you were shooting. Hit the apple and the elephant would go down, stone dead.

This was where that all-important insurance shot came into play. If the back legs of an elephant collapse first the animal is invariably dead before it even hits the ground. Another sure sign of death is a quivering leg, usually a hind leg, raised after it is down, and often the tail also straightens out. Yet another sign of a good brain shot that is often seen is a strong flow of dark blood from the bullet-hole. On the other hand, it is not unknown for apparently dead elephants to come back to life, and when this happens the best thing that can happen is that the elephant disappears into the bush; the worst is that it will rise up in righteous wrath and grind the shooter into the ground like a splatter of spit. Thus the insurance shot. We taught trainees a specific way of doing it: kneel in the right position and fire a bullet into a top of the head–neck junction. The kneeling position was mandatory because the rifle would be almost horizontal and only minor sighting adjustments would be necessary to send the bullet into the hypothetical apple. We also taught the trainees a final precaution to take after firing the insurance shot, which was to check the elephant's eye reflexes; as with so many other things, survival in the bush requires an infinite capacity for taking pains. Incidentally, Jaco Ackerman (he of the five-for-the-price-of-one field test) later gave the Park a full head-mount of an elephant bull that now hangs in the Elephant Hall in Letaba and was an invaluable teaching aid.

Elephants are wondrous creatures, but they don't have the toughness and sheer bloody-mindedness of old buffalo bulls, so we got nowhere when we tried to use the helicopter-herding method on the latter to position them for trainees. The 'daggaboys' just weren't having any, and they went their own way in spite of the chopper pilot's best efforts. Helicopter-herding for buffalo might not have worked, but at least one attempt provided me with what I regard as a classic saying about the tenacity of these tough, irascible bush-folk, the man who coined it being none other than Jaco Ackerman. The chopper had actually managed to bring a buffalo to us, but it swerved away when the pilot sheered off. Jaco gave it a bullet at about 25 metres, but the buffalo kept going and vanished into the mopane. I decided to follow up on foot rather than by helicopter in order to provide Jaco with maximum value from the exercise. We caught up with the buffalo, but he was in no mood to give up and it took several more shots before he was dead.

When the buffalo finally expired we walked up to it and Jaco remarked, with great wisdom for one so young: 'Jy kan nooit seker wees dat 'n buffel dood is voordat sy biltong nie breekdroog is nie,' namely: you can't be certain that a buffalo is dead until its biltong is so dry that you're able to snap off a piece.

Too true. Which just goes to show that learning can be a two-way affair.

13

THE LEOPARD –
KILLER OF CONSUMMATE GRACE

I don't think anyone will argue with me when I say that the leopard is one of the most beautiful of all the animals of the bushveld. But there is more to the leopard than mere beauty, as I discovered when I began to know the species: grace, adaptability, ferocity – all these form parts of the whole animal. How dangerous are leopards? Well, let me put it this way: the leopard is the last animal in whose case familiarity tends to breed contempt. Many hunters of several eras have stated their belief that in real terms the leopard is the most dangerous of the Big Five animals, given his small size, his speed, his agility, his ability to conceal himself and his ferocity when attacking.

Among the various feline species, the leopard is second only to the ordinary domestic cat when it comes to versatility and the ability to adapt to new circumstances. One can't make a straight comparison – the domestic cat is, after all, much smaller than the leopard – but both are survivors par excellence. A well-fed domestic cat will turn into a hunter in the wink of an eye if the opportunity arises, simply because the prey animal is there. In addition, it can breed with various of the smaller wild cats and produce viable fertile offspring because there is no real genetic differences between them. So your placid old moggy sleeping on the windowsill is, to coin a phrase, a leopard in cat's clothing.

Many people are still under the impression that leopards live in mountains, feed on baboons and dassies (the rock hyrax, to be more formal) and occasionally venture into the river systems' riparian forests to search for other prey. This may be true for the majority of leopards, but I have also seen them on the open plains in the Kruger National Park and the Kalahari Desert. The fact is that leopards are extremely adaptable and are still found in most of their traditional haunts, which include places as far apart as mountains of the Western Cape Province and the Magaliesberg near Pretoria. Obviously they maintain a low profile in inhabited areas, but they're there, all right, and in fact few living mammals, apart from man and artificially introduced rodent species, have anything like the demographic 'spread' of the leopard.

A leopard's range of food sources is also very varied. I have seen them kill very small game like francolin and rodents at one end of the scale, and, on at least one occasion, large prey like waterbuck at the other end – the waterbuck kill took place in the Sabie River's bed on Christmas day 1971, right in front of the Skukuza rest camp's restaurant, under the fascinated gaze of hundreds of tourists. In the early days in Kruger Stevenson-Hamilton also recorded an incident in which a leopard caught a young giraffe that weighed 200 pounds, or over 90 kilos. Like their larger feline colleagues, the lions, leopards will also scavenge if there is the need or opportunity. Paul Zway, who was the ranger at Shangoni in the 1980s, once found a baby elephant's skeleton in a tree. There is some doubt as to who or what led to the little elephant's death, but only a leopard could or would have deposited the carcass in the tree. They will also turn man-eater on occasion. All the old rangers I have ever spoken to were sure that if humans exposed themselves to a leopard on a regular basis they were tempting the leopard to include them on his meal list as another potential prey animal, and nothing I saw in my time in Kruger made me think differently – on the contrary, in fact.

*

Leopards are very much the 'invisible men' of the bushveld, being solitary by nature and nocturnal by habit, so that it is usually only when they are mating that you are likely to see two or more of them in company. One of my most memorable game sightings ever was when Koos Kloppers, one of the Skukuza children, my son Robert and I saw five adults together all in one group near the Sand River Bridge. When I reported this unusual sighting, I was asked what I had been smoking that morning! Fortunately I had Koos and Robert to attest to the fact that this was not a Brydenian leg-pull.

They may like to keep themselves to themselves, but leopards are not entirely intolerant of high-population areas, as is generally believed. A study done in the Kruger National Park in the 1970s revealed that during one year no fewer than 25 leopards roamed an area within a five-kilometre radius of Skukuza, a village which then had a population of about 1 000 people. This was a lot of leopards in anyone's book, even though it is likely that they weren't all there at the same time, and therefore it is not surprising that over the years there were various interactions, ranging from funny to downright terrifying and sometimes tragic, between the leopard population and the inhabitants of Skukuza. In retrospect it is surprising that so few really bad things happened, although there were certainly some narrow squeaks.

I had several personal leopard experiences at Skukuza at various times during my career. The first was in 1971, soon after I had started working in the Park, when I was engaged in a parallel learning curve. Officially my job was to experiment with the chemical immobilisation of carnivores, and unofficially it was to soak up the sort of basic bushveld knowledge that cannot be taught out of books or on courses but has to be learnt by actual experience and from listening to wiser heads.

One morning early, Oom Obies Oberholzer, a Post Office employee who presided over the manual telephone switchboard and lived in what was later to become the resident ranger's house, discovered a leopard in his garden. Being the switchboard operator, he made sure that this news was transmitted with the speed of sound to the conservation offices. The reaction was nearly as fast, since the conservation office was a mere 50 metres away, and in any case, who wanted to get on the wrong side of the uncrowned king of Kruger's switchboard? Within minutes we had assembled a task team, armed with dart-firing crossbows and anything else that could propel a dose of drugs into the leopard. At its summit was the head of research and his assistant, Oom Chris Lombard, who carried the large muti box (actually more the size of a small cabin trunk) with the darts and drugs. The loyal troops consisted of myself.

Piling into a short-wheel-base Land Rover, which later was to play a pivotal role in the saga, we sped over to Oom Obies's house and found the leopard holed up in a coal-bin attached to the outbuildings. The leopard made it clear that he was not at all keen to leave, and I was promptly sent off to get an immobilising dart into him. This was the hairiest bit of the operation, of course, seeing that leopards tend to become extremely aggressive if they feel trapped. But then, I reckoned, I was the youngest and the fastest member of the team, so I was obviously the best man for the job. Crossbow in hand, I advanced cautiously on the coal-bin, not realising that my little enterprise was going pear-shaped before it had even begun: Oom Obies's mother, who must have been close to 70, was desperate to get a piece of the action, and so she was following right behind me as I headed for the coal-bin, sublimely oblivious to anything besides making the acquaintance of the leopard and then walking away in one piece. It must have been a comical sight, although I don't think my colleagues were laughing.

I reached the bin and slowly lifted the lid. There he was! And none too happy about his predicament, I might add. So I shot a dart full of Sernylan into the leopard as quickly as possible, then moved aside and crouched down next to the bin. The leopard's reaction to the dart was not much slower than mine in shooting it in the first place. It bolted through the hole in the bottom of the bin and took off like a spotted rocket without worrying much about where it was going. Which was, unfortunately, straight at Oom Obies's mother. Her reactions were as good as the leopard's, and she took off in one direction and the leopard in the opposite one. The leopard had the legs on her, however, and before she had got very far it had torn right around the outbuildings and was face to face with her again.

The two of them simultaneously slammed in their anchors, did a swift simultaneous about-turn and set off again; unbelievable as it might sound, the same thing happened – the leopard legged it around the building at top speed and ended up face-to-face with the old lady once more. If there weren't more than enough surviving witnesses to this farcical business I would not have the guts to tell the story and expect anyone to take me seriously. Heaven knows how this would have ended if they had kept at it, but at this stage the leopard had had enough of playing ring-a-roses and scorched down the driveway towards the open veld, the dart still firmly lodged in his shoulder. His approach spurred my colleagues on to the same sort of athleticism displayed by the old lady. The head of research got to the Land Rover first and slid inside like a hyper-active Houdini in reverse. Moments later Oom Chris arrived, his turn of speed apparently unhindered by the muti box, but found to his vocal dismay that all the doors were closed and locked. This caused something of an altercation, although in the heat of the moment it took a little time before all concerned realised that the leopard was long gone and in any case would soon be out cold from the effect of the dart. So all was well that ended well, but it certainly taught me a lot about hidden athletic talents. And no, the old lady suffered no after-effects, which goes to show that she was as tough as any Kruger veteran.

It was also a striking reaffirmation of everything I had learnt so far about the merits and demerits of chemical immobilisation. Many people think that any problem animal can be dealt with by darting and relocating it, but they are wrong. The dart was not a magic bullet in the early days, and isn't one now. It can't be too powerful or it will kill the animal. At the same time, a less-than-fatal dose takes a while to work, as Oom Obies's mother had discovered. I don't know whether she realised how lucky she was, because a leopard, like a lion, needs only a few moments to kill or inflict incredible injury on anything it encounters. That is why there can be no false sentimentality about shooting a problem animal, be it a leopard or anything else. In some case there is simply no alternative: the animal has to be put out of circulation as quickly as possible. Years after the coal-bin incident the game capture team darted a leopard that had got right inside the rest camp. It ran away, dart and all, took refuge in a nearby flat occupied by Beat Young – many people will remember her as the friendly and extremely efficient lady in the reservation office – and attacked her when she unwittingly walked into it. Beat might very easily have been killed, but the immobilising dart had obviously started taking effect, and she got away with light injuries.

After Helena and I were transferred to Skukuza at the end of 1975 for our first stint there, we moved into the very house where I had met the coal-bin leopard, and which had been taken over from the Post Office in the interim. In 1983, when we moved to Skukuza again, we moved into the house right next door. Here we had a number of close encounters with lions in and around its spacious and well-grown garden (see 'Lions on My Lawn and Elephants in My Lettuce Bed'), but our most frequent visiting predators were leopards, who naturally had no difficulty in getting over the perimeter fence. I found their spoor in my garden on many occasions, but, leopards being ultra-silent nocturnal prowlers by choice, actual sightings were rare. I actually laid eyes on them on not more than four occasions, and had only a couple of personal encounters, which I would say were a couple too many.

Probably the most frightening personal encounter took place, as most frightening things do, as a result of a small omission. During the day some impala had wandered in for a free meal and were inadvertently trapped inside when our domestic worker, Martha, closed the garden gate late one afternoon as per regulation without realising that they were still inside, in a spot where she couldn't see them. That night we were peacefully watching television − not even Kruger is outside the long reach of the idiot box − when Helena looked through a window and casually remarked that she could see impala outside. I decided to let sleeping dogs lie. An overnight stay in the garden wouldn't harm them, and in any case it would do no good to try and chase them out in the dark, because they might panic and kill or hurt themselves running into the fence. So we went back to watching TV and enjoying some peace and quiet.

But not for long. A little while later I heard a crash that I recognised as the small pedestrian gate at the front of the garden being thrown violently open. I switched on the outside lights, one of which was situated next to the gate. Sure enough, it was wide open. My guess was that one of the impala had run at it and hit it hard enough to force the catch, allowing it and its fellows to escape. This being the case, something must have given them a powerful fright, seeing that they are timid animals except when the rams get into rutting mode. Then I noticed a dead impala ewe lying between myself and the gate, and she couldn't have broken her neck by running into the gate or fence or she would have been lying at the point of impact. That could only mean one thing: a predator was or had been in the garden and had killed the ewe, setting the other impala off: a lion, perhaps, but more likely a leopard.

To be honest, I was not at all keen to enter the garden at that stage, but I had to close the gate to ensure that no other predators were drawn by the dead impala's scent. Whatever had killed it could leave the garden the way it came in, presumably over the fence. So I set off, more than a trifle nervously because I would have to pass three patches of dense vegetation, each capable of hiding a leopard or even a lion, and to reach the gate I would have to go within two metres of the dead impala. The predator involved would be quite likely to interpret this as an attempt on my part to steal its uneaten prey, and decide to attack. Oh, well . . . I gritted my teeth and set out, all my senses on high alert. I got safely to the gate, bent the catch back into operational shape and headed for the house again. The total distance was only about 50 metres, but believe me when I say that it felt as if I were completing a full-length marathon distance in slow motion. I didn't feel any better when I went out again at first light and found that the impala had been partly eaten in typical leopard fashion. So it *had* been a leopard, and it had been watching me on my journey to and from the gate . . .

*

During my years in the Park, three people whom I knew very well were killed by leopards, and possibly a fourth as well, although we could never prove it. The first was Thomas Rihlamfu, whom I appointed as a gate guard at Shingwedzi in 1981 or 1982. He manned the gate from nightfall to early morning for so long that eventually he became part of Shingwedzi's furniture. Then one particular Monday morning in February 1992 the bus that ferried the camp's children to school at Phalaborwa each week pulled up at the main gate, only to find it closed and Thomas nowhere to be seen. Freddie the bus-driver decided that Thomas must have overslept for once, and he and one of the older children went to Thomas's room next to the gate to wake him up. To their horror, they found Thomas's partly eaten body lying on the bed, where he had been killed by a leopard that had entered and left through an open window.

Freddie immediately reported to Louis Olivier, the regional ranger, who found and shot the leopard not more than 10 metres from the gate. It was a male, covered in bite wounds that he had suffered in a fight with another male (as Louis succinctly put it, 'it was a really bad sample of a leopard'). It's possible that the leopard's weakened condition had led it to attack Thomas instead of hunting down a game animal, but I always believed that Thomas's regular habits were a major contributing factor, and that the leopard had probably had an eye on him for some time before killing him. After all, the leopard could just as easily have visited the campers' area near the gate and pulled one of them out of a tent, but the campers' irregular comings and goings were probably their salvation.

I remember, too, the death of Charles Swart, a night-drive guide stationed at Berg-en-Dal, at the very time that he had a revelation about his future life. Call it coincidence, call it the intervention of forces over which we have no control but which rule our lives; to me it's the latter. I had often had dealings with Charles, but the first time I really got to know him was when he accompanied Interpretive Officer Vanessa Strydom and a group of others on a tour of the Park's historical sites. I agreed to lead the trip, since I believe that the more people who know where some of the lesser-known sites are, the better for all concerned.

We spent the first night at Louis se Gat (Louis's Hole), a camping spot near Shingwedzi. The next morning, as we were preparing to leave after a light breakfast, a male baboon rushed into the camp, grabbed a bun out of Charles' hand and vanished into the bush with it. Charles's hand was badly scratched by the baboon's long nails and he was visibly shaken, as well he might be, because a full-grown baboon is not the amiable buffoon of most popular portrayals. Whether this encounter with the baboon had anything to do with it I can't say, but at the Nyalaland trails camp the following night Charles confided something to me that had obviously sprung from his innermost feelings. The others in the group were sleeping in the camp's huts, but Charles and I had decided to bed down in the lapa, or braai-shelter. There is nothing like such a situation for inspiring some deep-down talk as the night grows old, and so it was on this occasion as well. Charles had had a couple of ups and downs in his life and was just then recovering from a bad down, but that night he told me with quiet joy: 'Bruce, I've found direction in my life; now I know where I'm going.'

Sadly, Charles never had the opportunity to explore that new direction. Just a few weeks later he took a group of tourists out on a night drive, and in accordance with a long-standing habit among the trails guides, he stopped on the Matsulwane Bridge part of the way through the tour to indulge in a smoke-break. While the tourists stretched their legs Charles strolled to the southern end of the bridge and perched on the railing with his rifle in his lap. He was still sitting there, listening to the night-sounds and pulling at his cigarette, when a leopard crept up behind him and crushed his neck, killing him instantly.

A group of mapoisas arrived on the scene just afterwards. Among them was Corporal Albert Maluleke, one of the pluckiest people I ever met, and he did something very few other bush-velders would have cared to do: he followed the leopard's spoor in the dark until he caught up with it, then shot it dead with his R1 service rifle. An autopsy revealed that it was suffering from bovine tuberculosis. This was probably a contributing factor, but I believe that the main cause of Charles's death, as it had been with Thomas's, was the night-drive guides' habit of stopping at the same place every night. It could have happened to any of the guides; it just happened to be Charles who was unfortunate enough to be the one in the wrong place at the wrong time.

We were devastated by Charles's death, as is usually in the case when a small, tight-knit community loses one of its members, but veld people tend to have the same sort of fatalism as soldiers, which is summed up in the phrase that if a bullet has your name on it, it will find you. That leopard had Charles's name on it, because his time had come.

Almost exactly two years after Charles's death a Skukuza mapoisa, Salamao Mongwe, disappeared from his quarters one Friday night. We feared the worst, because Salomao was a steady man, a veteran of 30 years' service who was due to go on pension in a few months. He was never seen again, in spite of searches by a mapoisa team and the police dog unit, but there was no ambiguity about the evidence we found in the bush – Salamao's park identity card, an official letter concerning his impending retirement, blood-smeared bits of clothing with bite punctures in a tree whose bark showed recent claw-damage, and a few pathetic scraps of bone. As with Charles Swart, there was a terrible irony about the fact that Salamao had been killed on the very threshold of a new stage in his journey through life.

I remember the circumstances of the third killing particularly vividly. It happened at a bad time for all of us. The country was at the dawn of the new millennium, but in Kruger the future seemed filled with darkness rather than light. The Park's financial situation was dire and the very air thrummed with political uncertainty, while the threat of large-scale retrenchments loomed over everything – a frightening prospect for our colleagues and ourselves, whose lives were so inextricably bound up with Kruger that in some ways the outside world had a strange air of unreality when we visited it.

Helena and I had talked about all this, of course, but somehow we had always skirted away from the logical end of the discussion: that it looked as if the time had come for us to leave Kruger behind us, with everything that that implied. By good fortune my annual leave had made it possible to get away from the poisonous atmosphere for a bit, and Helena and I spent the last week of it fly-fishing at the Castle Burn resort near Underberg in the southern Drakensberg. It was a wonderful place and we really enjoyed it, although it goes without saying that the thought of what we were going back to was always lurking in the background like an uninvited and unwanted guest. And then in one day two things happened – one very good, one very bad.

The good thing started off quite inauspiciously. I spent almost the entire day, starting early in the morning, plying my rod with such a conspicuous lack of success that I had not had even one strike. I'm not a quitter by nature, so I kept it up till late afternoon before throwing in the towel and falling into conversation with a couple who had also abandoned their angling and gone for a long walk instead. In the course of our conversation the couple pointed out a black eagle nest on the cliffs above us that had clearly been there for a long time but was still in use. I watched the eagles flying to and from the nest, and without warning my whole mental machinery changed gear. All of a sudden our personal troubles didn't seem to matter all that much any more. The eagles were totally unaffected by any of the vast changes sweeping the country; no matter what happened on the ground below, their lives would continue to follow the ancient pattern. Would it be any different for us?

A small tidal wave of relief surged through me as I realised that I was ready to face the facts. There was a time to stay and a time to go, and the moment had arrived for me to make the break with that vast stretch of bushland that I loved so much! Nothing lasted forever. I had had 30 good years that I could only believe made me the envy of other men, and now it was time to walk away from it and throw myself into the rest of my life. A little later I said goodbye and parted company with my chance acquaintance. They walked off happily, totally unaware of the watershed to which they had led me. I walked away just as happily, my soul at peace for the first time in a long while.

Helena told me a strange story when I got back to the chalet – just how strange I was only to realise later on. She had been out walking by the Castle Burn dam, she said, near a copse of trees, and just as she came up to the copse she was seized by a sudden and inexplicable fear that there might be somebody or something hiding among the trees, waiting to attack the first unsuspecting person to walk past them. The feeling was so strong – and remember that Helena is not a fanciful or fearful person, or she would not have lasted in Kruger – that she turned right around and headed back to the chalet. As the fear ebbed she started thinking about a very close and dear friend of ours, Kotie de Beer. At that time many Skukuza residents liked to go for a stroll in the village after work every afternoon, usually in couples or small groups, and Helena decided that when we got back she would join Kotie for afternoon walks, although she would drive to Kotie's house to meet her because it would be too dangerous to walk to Kotie's home from our house.

In the meantime something terrible had happened at Skukuza,

but we were blissfully unaware of it and spent a restful night, followed by an early start at the new day's angling for me. This time my luck was considerably better, and by nine o'clock I was back at the chalet, cheerfully sorting through my angling gear prior to another foray a little later in the morning. I was still thus occupied when I caught the tail-end of a radio news report which stated that a woman in Skukuza had been killed by a leopard. I told Helena and we decided to listen to the next hourly news broadcast, which would be more detailed. But again we only managed to catch the tail-end of the Skukuza item, so we were none the wiser. Around 11 o'clock we couldn't stand it any longer and decided to telephone Robert, who was at home in Skukuza, to find out if he knew any details. Helena spoke to him first, and knew straight away that the news was bad when Robert told her that both he and Annie had been trying to get hold of us since the previous afternoon, not knowing that there wasn't any cellphone reception at the chalet. Then he told her the news: the dead woman was none other than Kotie de Beer.

As Robert described it, Kotie had gone for a solitary walk in the village around 5 pm the previous day when the leopard attacked her. No one actually saw the attack but reconstruction of the event led us to believe that it was over quickly. As in Charles's case, her neck vertebrae were crushed. A staff member who was reversing out of his driveway into the street saw the leopard dragging Kotie and chased it away with his car, but by then it was too late. The fact that the leopard was destroyed soon after was small consolation. Now we recalled Helena's strange feeling of fear at the copse next to the dam, and realised that it had taken place about 15 minutes before the leopard killed Kotie. And why had she then started thinking about Kotie and planning afternoon walks with her? Once again I put the question: mere coincidence – or proof of another force?

We returned to Skukuza to find that Kotie's death had traumatised the entire village and plunged it into an even more morbid mood about the future, which turned out to be perfectly justified by the abrupt retrenchments of both white and black staff that started soon after. The autopsy on the leopard revealed a blockage about the size of a two-litre bottle in its intestine. Was this the factor that had spelt death for Kotie, or was it because the leopard had noted that the streets presented a choice of potential food sources every afternoon? I think that the routine factor was mainly to blame, and that something like this was bound to happen sooner or later. I don't believe that the attack would necessarily have been prevented if Kotie had had company, but on the other hand it's not impossible that the leopard chose her as his victim because she was by herself.

But let me finish with a happier leopard story that took place at Mokohlolo, the very place where Jan Oelofse's Zulus were scared out of 10 years' growth and my friend Rudi Sippel showed how a true-blue German can down a mugful of throat-burning schnapps without blowing a gasket (see 'Close-up Conversations with Lions'). Mokohlolo is my long-time favourite campsite in Kruger. The camp itself is about 300 metres from the Mokohlolo Dam, which always has water in the winter, even in very dry years, and it was invariably my first choice as a place to take the family or special friends for a weekend or so to recharge our batteries.

Mokohlolo Dam's special attraction for me is the fact that except in very wet times it draws an endless stream of game of all sizes, ranging from elephants right down to Kori Bustards, believe it or not; I've never seen these birds drink anywhere else. It is also a favourite watering place for rhino, especially at sunset and early in the morning. One early evening we saw no fewer than 13 of them, all drinking at the same time, and it was not unusual to see an entire herd of buffalo pour into the water, often spending hours in and near the dam – 'it looks as if someone kicked a tin of black paint into the dam,' as a friend of mine once aptly remarked.

With this sort of traffic it was also hardly surprising that Mokohlolo had its fair share of predators and scavengers, and hardly a night went by when you didn't hear a leopard's coughing call somewhere in the dark. It is a very distinctive sound, and the leopard expert Peter Turnbull-Kemp describes it very eloquently as 'a harsh rasping, frequently described as the uneven sawing sound produced by inexpert handling of a two-handed crosscut saw'. A leopard puts its all into making itself heard, dropping its head and visibly concentrating its body on the task. Possibly this is the origin of Mokohlolo's name, which means 'to cough' in Tsonga – it certainly seems likely to me.

On one visit with friends of ours something strange happened that was a 'first' in my book at the time and has remained so ever since. Each of the children had an electric torch, and this meant that beams of light were constantly being directed at everything and anything, whether the subject or the occasion was appropriate or not. I have yet to meet a child who is not fascinated by a torch. The main culprit, I should add, was neither Robert nor Annie, who had grown up in the veld and in houses where the only illumination was provided by a diesel generator that ran for strictly limited periods. As a result they used their torches only when necessary, and had long since learnt that if there was one thing that irritated me intensely it was the juvenile passion for switching them on during day-time.

Our friends' teenage son, Eric, was another story. From dusk onwards the beam of his torch was stabbing out all over the place, looking for leopards or lions. It was a vain quest, especially as far as leopards were concerned, but I wasn't going to spoil his fun, half of which consisted of shining the torch, whether he caught anything in its beam or not. So Eric scared the hell out of various hyaenas lurking on the other side of the campsite's fence, but that was all. This was probably just as well, because the fence wasn't anything to write home about, being made of stacked thorn-tree branches, and was about half a metre high where it hadn't collapsed, which was in most places. It was absolutely useless as far as keeping anything out went, of course, although it helped to provide our city-slicker friends with a totally illusory sense of security.

Around eight o'clock that evening my daughter Annie ventured into the dark to fetch some water from the water-drum a few metres from the fire, but returned very quickly to say that she had heard something move close by. This was Eric's big moment, and he was off like a shot to investigate, torch and all. Moments later we heard his voice, calling us excitedly but softly to come and have a look. We found that this time Eric had hit the jackpot. On the other side of the alleged fence, not more than five metres from him, a female leopard sat staring at us. Why she exhibited such un-leopardlike behaviour I cannot say. Perhaps she was totally puzzled by our presence, or perhaps she was hypnotised by the torch-beams (there were now four or five directed at her, although not in her face, or she would have taken to her heels at once). She watched us and we watched her until we got tired of the game and went back to the fire. Something about us obviously attracted her, though, because she came back at least once for another staring session before we left.

Once again, I can't say why she acted in such an atypical way, but encounters where the leopard is so casual are very rare, because they would rather seek cover as soon as they are noticed, or even before you spot them. As far as I was concerned the visits merely confirmed a long-held theory of mine, namely that if a predator approaches you out of curiosity, not hunger, then you have no need to fear it if you don't do something that makes you look like a threat. The problem with this theory, of course, is that you have no way of knowing whether the animal is hungry or not.

Mokohlolo was also the scene of the annual 'honorary ranger' fundraiser camps that were to become so famous. These camps were the brainchild of Rob Fisher, who used to head the counter-poaching unit of the Johannesburg region, and resulted from some brainstorming to come up with a concept that would raise money to buy equipment for the field staff. Whether it was the serenity of the camp, or the fact that with a bit of luck you would be able to see each species of the Big Five in less than 24 hours, the scheme worked very well and inspired some of our guests to make substantial donations, in cash or in kind. The state-of-the-art computers that were installed at Kruger's ranger offices were a direct spin-off from one Mokohlolo camp. Another camp resulted in a swap deal in terms of which a major cement manufacturer received an elephant logo and in return donated thousands of bags of cement, with which we built river causeways that made it much easier for the rangers to move around in wet weather.

Inevitably there were staff members who didn't like the idea and went out of their way to pull the rug out from under the HR camps, but nothing succeeds like success, and we managed to beat them back. Not only that, but on at least one occasion we actually improved on nature's ability to create ambience. The author of this trick was Johan (aka Johnny) van Graan, resident ranger of the Crocodile Bridge section in which Mokohlolo was located. Johnny was responsible for the day-to-day running of the HR camps, while Helena and his wife Kotie oversaw the cleaning and also did the catering until these tasks were taken over by the Park's restaurant staff. I suppose it was inevitable that sooner or later he would dream up a novel idea – which those who were aware of Johnny's reputation as a notorious prankster immediately identified as a masterpiece of Kruger leg-pull art.

To cut a long story short, Johnny had discovered that he could produce an extremely realistic leopard growl with nothing more than a cardboard box, a long piece of string and some candle-wax. The two most important ingredients of any great crime – means and motive – were therefore in place; all he still needed were the other ingredients, namely time, place and victim. That weekend's HR camp provided the place, and Johnny soon identified the victim, a guest who was particularly nervous about sleeping in a tent in the bush. He enlisted me to his banner (being a serious-minded person, I only agreed to help because I was loyal to my colleagues) and we set about creating the right time and circumstances. For the first day and night we told bloodcurdling stories about the dangers of the bush whenever the victim was within earshot. This soon started having the desired effect, and on the second night we really laid it on, concentrating on 'true' stories of lion and leopard atrocities at Mokohlolo, each one wilder than its predecessor.

I must say Johnny and I did a good job – if I hadn't been so busy making them up as I went along I might almost have believed them myself. We were still at it when the victim's nerve snapped. By now we had peopled the darkness with such an array of man-eating monsters that in his mind's eye he could see one of them come roaring out of the murk and snatching him right out of his camp chair by the fire, so he said a hurried goodnight to all and took to the safety of his bed. Our plan had been to let the leopard do his thing when the victim was in bed, but our timing was a little out, so that he was still undressing when

Johnny's candle-wax-and-cardboard leopard emitted a horrific growl outside the tent while I vigorously scratched at the canvas. The victim was instantly convinced that his last hour had come, and his panic infected all the other occupants of the tent. Within moments they were stampeding towards the fire in various states of undress and sleeping dress, to the vast amusement of their friends, who ragged them unmercifully. The runners vociferously defended their flight and waxed eloquent about the danger they had just escaped. Johnny, the womenfolk and I played down the incident, and eventually the dust settled, along with the drinks.

Act Two came when everyone had bedded down for the night. Then the cardboard leopard growled and scratched at the tent again. Another half-dressed exodus took place, and this time the occupants stayed put by the fire, where we found them huddled at daybreak, very much the worse for wear; one way and another, they had certainly had a night to remember. When I think back to this incident I can't help wondering whether the story of the Mokohlolo man-eater is still being told with appropriate embellishments around dinner tables in Johannesburg and elsewhere. I admit that the true story is slightly reprehensible, but on other hand you can't say that we didn't try to satisfy the customers.

So there we have the leopard, one of the jewels in the bushveld's crown, and despite all the personal grief that some of them have caused me, I can't help but agree with what Peter Turnbull-Kemp once wrote about them:

'Man-eater or mole-hunter, he is a creature of consummate grace who still lives among some of us. Small, more light than the average man who hunts him: handsome in the sun and ethereal by moonlight, the leopard is an animal for whom at least a grudging admiration should be found.

'Let us try to keep him as a neighbour – except where the sublimely unconscious individual becomes insupportable to man. Let us recall that the man-eater or stock-killer knows none of our laws, and should be pitied for the ill-understood retribution which man may inflict upon him . . .

'Let us recall, when we hear horrific stories of the leopard and his kin, that it is pity and understanding of the so-called lower animal which are required – not hatred. For pity, while a thing of which to be aware, is perhaps the mother of understanding.'

14

STRANGE BUSHVELD STORIES

It cannot be doubted that a game ranger's life is a pretty hands-on affair in every sense –sometimes, in fact, a little too hands-on for comfort – but one can't spend decades in the bush without experiencing incidents that defy rational explanation, and, certainly in my case, continue to defy explanation no matter how much I might think about them. I have certainly been aware from an early age of another sense that affects our lives and frequently allows us to perceive or experience things that are not readily explained. Studies suggest that we have ways of gaining information that bypass the ordinary senses. Long-used terms like 'sixth sense', 'second sight' and 'extrasensory perception' are gaining legitimacy among scientists as descriptions for perceptual experiences that transcend the usual boundaries of space and time.

My first experience of clairvoyance occurred long before I went to work at the Kruger National Park, when I was still in primary school. My grandparents had taken my brother Mark and myself on holiday to Ramsgate in Natal, and on the way home I told them that my father had just bought a new car to go and visit my uncle – who lived in the then Basutoland – because he had fallen ill. Naturally this was seen as a flight of fancy at the time of telling, but when we got home I turned out to be absolutely correct, right down to the timings. How did I know? I can't say. It just popped up in my mind without any warning.

Years later I had a similar experience when my parents took me to the Rand Easter Show in Johannesburg. As we came in through the north gate via Empire Road I told my dad that someone very important was going to be shot near us that day. Needless to say, not much notion was taken of this outlandish prediction, but not 10 minutes later, a slightly demented farmer named David Pratt shot and seriously wounded Dr Hendrik Verwoerd, the then Prime Minister, while he was opening the show.

These were isolated incidents, to be sure, but they were the start of a series of personal encounters and experiences that I still wonder about. One such experience took place in the early 1970s, when I was involved in the last phase of the water-provision programme for migrating elephants (see 'Last Sight of the Old Africa'). On one of the frequent walks I took to while away the time between measuring borehole water-flow I was climbing Shilowa Hill when I felt a strong compulsion to go to a certain spot about half-way up. I didn't know then what compelled me and I still don't, but the need was irresistible. Visually there was nothing remarkable about the place where I found myself. There was a large, almost sheer rock on the eastern side, partly covered at its base by a large creeping plant, and at the foot of this miniature cliff was a flat area covered with loose pieces of stone. But the mysterious something that had brought me there then urged me to look behind the creeper, where I found a dome-shaped hole, filled with closely packed smaller rocks.

I still had some time before the next water measurement, so I started removing the packed rocks. This revealed a hole about a metre wide and a metre and a half high. Still driven by that mysterious compulsion, I went inside, albeit very uneasily, if truth be told. The tunnel went downwards at an angle of about 30 degrees for about three metres, then split into two separate tunnels, one going north and the other south. It was obviously not a natural phenomenon, since rhyolite, the rock type of the Lebombo Mountains, does not produce cave formations. I was glad to leave the tunnel and return to fresh air, but the whole experience had set me to thinking, and in subsequent forays in the near vicinity I came across the ruins of what had obviously been an extensive settlement. I estimated it at five kilometres long north to south, and about 500 metres across at its widest, with areas of well-preserved walls up to 1.3 metres high.

My duties then took me away from the area, but later I went back there with a geologist friend, Dr Willo Stear, for another look at the cave. Willo had done his master's degree on ancient mining techniques at the Rooiberg Tin Mine, which is amongst the oldest mines in Africa, and immediately he noticed the tunnel's domed ceiling, exactly the same as Rooiberg's, and a clear indication that the so-called 'fire-setting' technique of breaking solid rock had been used. Rhyolite is very susceptible to rapid changes in temperature, and fire-setting involves building a fire on the rock which is to be broken, letting it burn a while and then dousing it with water, causing it to split. Properly done, it is a simple but effective way to work into a rock face, and in fact mapoisa James Chauke and I used this ancient technique when we built the eastern boundary firebreak at Crocodile Bridge in 1972 and 1973. The purpose of the tunnel? That has been obscured by the mists of time, but my personal belief is that it was a storage space for ivory and gold: why else would anyone go to such trouble? I base this assumption on the fact that in ancient times Shilowa Poort was a well-used pass through the Lebombo Mountains, and I have yet to find a more logical explanation.

I reported my findings to Professor Hannes Eloff, who was the head of the Department of Archaeology at Pretoria University. Professor Eloff carried out an on-site investigation that revealed that this area had a longer record of occupation than any other place in the old Transvaal Province. The area was never properly investigated, thanks to the turbulent political situation prevailing in next-door Mozambique at the time, but it later became apparent that the Shilowa ruins are linked to other architectural remains like those at Thula Mela further north, and might even have a historical connection with the legendary Zimbabwe Ruins.

Perhaps my mysterious compulsion was not all that mysterious. Shilowa has a serious mystical connotation for the Shangane tribespeople living in its vicinity; so much so that they will never point to it with a finger in the normal way, but use a chin or an elbow. Perhaps some part of this powerful mystic ambience drew me to the tunnel in the first place. But what impelled me to look behind the creeper?

*

Another experience with things unseen and inexplicable happened to me in 1973, when I stood in for the Crocodile Bridge ranger, Dirk Ackerman, who had gone to Pretoria to study for his honours degree. Since his absence was temporary he left most of his furniture and other belongings in my care, including a magnificent lion skin which he had put away on the beams of the stable's roof.

One Saturday morning, when most of the mapoisas were on field duty, I mobilised the storeman and the station's team of resident labourers for a general cleaning and stock-taking process. While we were thus engaged one of the mapoisas, Fickson Hlungwane, arrived from the Sabie Poort picket with his partner and a man they had caught illegally crossing over from Mozambique. According to his identity document the prisoner was actually a South African citizen who normally worked in Witbank as a traditional healer (in the old days they were called 'witch-doctors', but, like so much else, the term has been overtaken by political correctness). We weren't heavy on the odd illegal border-crosser or two at that time, and if they had a good story we would often let them go. Before we had decided whether or not to turn this one loose, however, the storeman reported to me that Dirk's lion skin was missing from the stable, together with another skin that belonged to me. We had absolutely no clue as to what had happened to the skins, so I decided to make use of what was on hand and see if the traditional healer's alleged sniffing-out skills amounted to anything. Sensing a good opportunity to talk himself out of his predicament, he was only too happy to oblige, and in short order we were gathered around him under a tree fuchsia near the office.

He set off in the standard sort of way by laying a reed mat in front of him and spreading out his bones on it to exhortations of 'savuma', meaning 'open up and talk'. When the bones were booted up, so to speak, he invited his expectant audience to present their problems. What happened then, however, was anything but standard. As the resident ranger I was given first crack as a matter of courtesy, but I declined in favour of one of my mapoisas, Corporal July Makuvele, because he had a truly pressing problem: his bicycle had been stolen the night before while he was visiting a friend on a farm near by. This, I reckoned, would be the acid test, because the diviner (for want of a better word) could not possibly know about the theft, seeing that July had arrived at Crocodile Bridge after him and had not told anybody but me about the loss of his bicycle. If I had been in the diviner's place at that moment I think I would have started up a light sweat, but he did not turn a hair. While his audience watched with breathless interest, he communed with his bones to further cries of 'savuma', and then told July that a woman had stolen the bicycle and that it was now tied with a piece of blue and white rope to the roof-rack of a bus which was about to leave the scene of the crime on its way to Bushbuckridge within a few minutes.

This was rich stuff! I sent July off in the truck to see if he could intercept the bus that the bones had so unerringly fingered, and the diviner turned to the rest of his band of 'clients'. I was the last in line, and when my turn came he told me I was upset because I had lost something, specifically, a skin, that I had been asked to look after for someone else. He also saw, he said, that I had lost something of my own. It was also a skin, he added, but what sort of skin he couldn't tell, because its former wearer had not left a spoor on the earth that he could identify. This was quite amazing, since the skin in question was that of a zebra foetus that I had rescued from a lion kill north of Satara while I was working on my master's degree. And the lion skin? Well, the diviner took a while to zero in on it, but eventually identified it correctly and pointed out the direction in which it had allegedly disappeared. At this stage July returned and the diviner was in the pound seats, because in the back of the truck was July's bicycle, and he reported that he had found it on the roof-rack of the Bushbuckridge bus, securely tied down with a piece of blue and white rope by the thief, a woman. A little later the man with the bones went on his way rejoicing; it would have been churlish to hang on to him after such a bravura performance.

At times like this it is hard to maintain one's scientific detachment. At the end of the day it came down to one simple fact: the diviner-cum-border crosser-cum-traditional healer-cum-whatever had been verifiably spot on in all three of his utterances in spite of the fact that he was not familiar with the Crocodile Bridge station and had been both chronologically and geographically distant from all the events concerned. This is not quite the end of the story, however. Years later we finally found out what had happened to the stolen lion skin, and it turned out that he had also been spot on about the direction taken by the thief.

*

Another incident that has given me much food for thought over the years involves two very different creatures but remarkably similar occurrences. The first part of the story started very early in the morning of 3 October 1974, when Helena went into labour with our first child, Annie, a fortnight before her time and just one day after we had temporarily moved from our house at Mooiplaas to Letaba Rest Camp where we would wait for the baby to arrive. This move was part of our contingency plan, because premature births were slightly more of a problem in Kruger than in most other places. There were no ambulances on call, and the hospital nearest to Mooiplaas was a long, bumpy 120 km ride away at Phalaborwa. This is not to mention several other potential problems such as being stranded by early rains or colliding with a large animal that had seen fit to materialise on the road at an unexpected time or place.

When the regular morning radio session started I told Dirk Ackerman, the district ranger at Letaba, that I was off to Phalaborwa with Helena and would call in on him on the way back. Then off we went, to the relief of the doctor, who had been having quiet nightmares about various dire possibilities, such as Helena reaching the crucial moment in mid-journey and having to give birth under a mopane tree. We managed to avoid this and all other catastrophes, and after a long and nerve-racking day I was back in Letaba that evening, having left Helena still in labour at Phalaborwa. Dirk and his wife Antoinette did what they could to alleviate my frazzled state by giving me supper and companionship, in the process of which Dirk said that if I had a spare moment next day he would be much obliged if I would shoot a buffalo bull which was harassing the mapoisas stationed near the Phalaborwa Gate. It might seem a little unfair of Dirk to lay such a hazardous task on a man who had quite enough on his plate already, but that was how we operated, and of course I said yes. Somehow it didn't seem strange that I should greet my first child and kill an ill-tempered animal on the same day.

Next morning I left Letaba, knowing only that Helena was in the delivery room but the baby had not yet been born (this vital information I received at the entrance gate as I left – there were no telephones at the station in those days, so the hospital had had to communicate the message to the official at the Phalaborwa Gate, who had then relayed it to Letaba by radio). At Phalaborwa Gate I told the waiting mapoisas to locate the buffalo so that I could deal with it later, and from there went straight to the hospital. I then spent what seemed like a year biting my fingernails in the waiting room; my state of mind was not improved by a nursing sister who came and gave me a swift bawling-out, her theme being that big men should marry big women and not small ones, and that I was murdering Helena. That wasn't particularly reassuring, of course, but only a few minutes later she made up for everything by returning to say that we had just acquired a daughter.

You could have cut my toes off right there and then and I wouldn't have felt it, I was that happy when I went to meet Ann and thank Helena. I stayed with them until both were fast asleep, then at 11 o'clock or so on that memorable Saturday morning I went off to attend to the rest of my business: first I would kill the antisocial buffalo, and then I would wet my daughter's head in the traditional way. Well, I did both, but in the opposite order. The priorities changed when the mapoisas reported to me that for once the buffalo was keeping a low profile and they hadn't been able to find him. At this crucial moment the resident park engineer, Brian Westcott, and his wife Dianne came driving by, stopped to say hello and, on hearing about the happy event, invited me over to their house for a beer. Just as we were getting down to it we were joined by my friend Tom Yssel, the ranger at Mahlangeni. This could have been a piece of impeccable timing by the finger of fate or as a result of having been primed by Dirk about what was happening at the hospital. Since the finger of fate's timing is usually a little off in my case, I suspected that the latter explanation was more likely. But I was past worrying about little things like that.

We were well into a serious head-wetting ceremony with the aid of the snacks and beer Dianne had set out when the mapoisas arrived to say that they had finally found the buffalo. That was the end of the head-wetting, and Tom and I immediately downed both drinking and eating tools to join the mapoisas at the Phalaborwa Gate. It turned out that the buffalo was only a few hundred metres from the gate, so that earlier the mapoisas must have walked past him several times while he kept his head down. Why he did this instead of acting like his normal aggressive self I can't say. Perhaps he realised that it was the right time to maintain a low profile, which is not a lapse into anthropomorphism on my part – it is widely accepted that animals, both wild and domestic, have senses far beyond those that we are aware of. Whatever the reason, the buffalo was still not acting in his accustomed way. Before Tom and I could get reasonably close to him he ran off south-eastwards. We set off after him, sweating out the celebratory beer we had so lately been imbibing. The bull let us approach and then made off again before we got close enough to do any good. A little later he pulled the same trick for the third time. This didn't look or feel good to me. He couldn't have scented us because he was upwind of us, so he must have been keeping an eye on us or he would not have run off; and I believed then, and still do, that if you flush a buffalo two or more times, and it only runs a short distance on each occasion, you're heading for trouble.

After the third flush the buffalo ran across a large bare area and through an adjacent donga before diving into some very thick mopane scrub growing around it. We thought we could see him in the bush at the edge of the donga, about 50 metres away, but we weren't sure, so we held a quick tactical planning session and decided that I would head for the donga by a roundabout route while Tom would stand by to drop the buffalo if he broke cover and I did not get a shot at him. I carefully worked my way to a spot at which, I calculated, I would be broadside on to the buffalo, then stood up with my rifle at the ready. But he wasn't there! He was about five metres to my left and heading towards me at full speed. I aimed quickly and fired, knowing that I couldn't expect any help from Tom because I was between him and the buffalo.

Fortunately the gods of the hunt were with me and the buffalo went down, but in the split-second before he ploughed into the ground some strangely piercing thoughts went through my mind, the focal point of which was that little hours-old bundle tucked up with her mother in the Phalaborwa Hospital, not three kilometres away. And so when the buffalo died, most of my recklessness and false sense of invincibility died with it. Which is not to say that all my Phalaborwa troubles were over. Just at that time John Denver's song in honour of his wife, Annie, was a world-wide smash hit, and when I went to register the birth of my daughter a few days later I was so overcome by the marvellous memory of how her tiny hand had held on to my finger at our very first acquaintance that I decided she deserved a tribute too, so I made a spur-of-the-moment decision – usually a bad idea – to put down her name as 'Annie' instead of 'Ann'. Helena, who, of course, had not been consulted about this impulsive act of homage, was less than impressed.

So much for the first part of the story. The second part took place 21 years later, when I found myself back at the very same spot where I had dropped the buffalo, teaching an aspirant trails ranger the finer points of shooting an elephant – the final part of marksmanship training (see 'Lessons in Shooting Straight'). Having passed the first and second phases of the course, the trainee now had the shooting skills to ensure that he would be able to walk away from most encounters with wild animals, but training was no substitute for the real thing because the bush has an infinite capacity for springing nasty surprises.

We were standing on the north-western side of the bare patch through which the buffalo had run 21 years earlier, the overhang of a *Capparis* bush masking our silhouettes from the elephant bull that was being driven towards us by a helicopter piloted by Piet Otto, with another ranger on board. Ideally the elephant would approach the trainee head-on, which would simulate a full charge and present the opportunity for a frontal brain shot like the one he would have to take in a real charge. I had instructed the trainee to fire his first shot as soon as the elephant came out of the donga on to level ground, when they would be about 20 metres apart. This would be far enough to allow a second shot if his first failed to kill, and if the second one also failed there would still be enough time for the elephant to be killed either by myself or by the ranger in the helicopter.

Piet Otto, being the best game-handling chopper pilot in Africa, brought in the elephant dead on course and heading straight for the trainee, exactly as planned. A few seconds later it was in sight, coming out of the donga . . . and nothing happened. No first shot from the student, and no second shot either. The elephant then changed course and headed straight for where I was crouched behind a mopane bush, presenting the student with a perfect and easy side-on brain shot. Still nothing happened. By now the elephant was getting very close to me, but I opted not to fire, hoping that either the trainee or the ranger in the helicopter would do so. Neither did, and suddenly time was up for everybody concerned. The elephant was now almost into the bush I was crouching behind and I didn't have a choice except to shoot, although I was virtually under his head and all the angles for a killing shot were wrong. Needs must when the devil drives, however, so I fired. The elephant half-turned away on taking the bullet, presenting a better target, and my second shot was fatal. He thudded to the ground literally a metre from me.

I was a bit shaken by this close call and had to take a quick turn in the veld to calm down before addressing the trainee about his lack of performance. Before I got back, however, Piet had whacked his chopper on to the ground and before the rotors had even stopped turning was giving the trainee a loud and expert bollocking on my behalf. I didn't even bother asking the student to explain his behaviour, given the good job Piet was doing – and besides I was feeling a trifle thoughtful. It's something else to come close to being killed by one dangerous animal and then have a second narrow escape from another dangerous animal in exactly the same place and to the day exactly 21 years later.

*

The north-eastern region of South Africa is traditional witchcraft country, but the only genuine, self-admitted witch I came across in my years at the Kruger National Park hailed from a good deal further afield. She was none other than my Scottish Aunt Molly, and I say 'genuine' because one night she forecast my immediate future with such accuracy that she deserves the benefit of the doubt, at least until someone can prove she shouldn't. More than 30 years later, that hasn't happened yet.

Aunt Molly, so her brother Willie Kinnear had told me, was the latest in a long line of witches who had lived in the Highlands since time immemorial. This particular witchhood (so to speak) was a hereditary calling that passed down the family line, with the eldest daughter of each second-eldest daughter becoming the witch in each generation. Because the witch wasn't allowed to marry, her sister had to give birth to her successor, and when the youngster was old enough her aunt would take charge of her and pass on all her powers and knowledge. This naturally pricked my interest, and on the evening of their arrival I decided to see if I could draw her out as we sat in the lounge after dinner. Aunt Molly was not at all reticent about her traditional witchly status, although she made it clear that she wasn't about to divulge any of her secrets. She was quite willing to demonstrate her occult skills, however. She asked me to shuffle and cut a pack of playing cards, then took them from me and assumed what I can only describe as a very strange attitude, from which it was clear that her eyes and mind were a long way from my lounge at Crocodile Bridge.

She took a couple of cards off the top of the deck, laid them on the coffee table and started talking. Her opening statement – that we were living in somebody else's house – was not all that memorable, seeing that it was a Parks Board house and I was relieving the resident ranger, Dirk Ackerman; a doubter could say that she had picked up that much from my mother, although the two of them had only arrived that afternoon. But then she got going on a string of predictions about what the future held for us that were to prove so accurate in the ensuing years that how she got to them remains inexplicable to me. We were going to be transferred before the end of the year, she said, but my new house wouldn't be complete and we would therefore have to stay in a place with very little or no infrastructure (this was news to me, since I didn't have a permanent position on the Kruger staff at that stage and had no idea where I would be going after the end of the year). The original plan, she said, would be to transfer us to live on 'the edge of the country', but this wouldn't work out, and so we would go and live on a mountain graveyard.

Having got off this opening salvo, she then proceeded to predict the events of the next two years, including the fact that we would become the parents of a daughter. Her final prediction was that we would be involved in a hippo census that would change my life, after which she stopped and refused to go any further. We didn't really believe any of this, especially Helena, who is not superstitious at all. But not long afterwards we found ourselves caught up in a train of events that chipped away at our disbelief. First of all I was summoned to the park headquarters at Skukuza. The ranger at Nwanetsi, a permanent staff member, had resigned. Would I be interested in his post? Well, you can guess what my answer to that question was. Helena and I were both delighted that not only would we be able to stay on in Kruger, we would be going to Nwanetsi, which was less than five kilometres away from the Mozambican border – as near to Aunt Molly's 'edge of the country' as made no difference.

Then Aunt Molly's second prediction came true. A couple of months later the plans changed and I was told that I would not be transferring to Nwanetsi after all, but to the Klipkoppies station. Now it so happened that the Klipkoppies house was falling to pieces and the water supply had failed, so a new spot had been selected, the section's name being changed to Mooiplaas at the same time. The new site was on top of a hill, near today's Mopane rest camp, and was located hard by the graves of various Lowveld pioneers (my predecessor had flatly refused to live cheek by jowl with the graves, but by that time the road up the hill had already been made, so the site had been confirmed). Helena and I first visited the site in the late winter of 1973, before my transfer had been confirmed, as part of a whole group of rangers who were on the transfer list. The party was led by the park head, Dr Tol Pienaar, and Chief Ranger Johan Kloppers. We drove from Skukuza in convoy, Helena and myself travelling with Dr Pienaar and his wife Annette in his Land Rover. Officially the idea was that after the visit it would be decided who should go to Mooiplaas, but I think Dr Pienaar had already made his choice.

The view from the hill at Mooiplaas was truly spectacular. The heaps of weathered stones marking the pioneers' graves that were scattered all over the place might have upset some sensitive souls, but not my companions. They were tough bushvelders, men and women alike, and the prospect of living cheek by jowl with an assortment of the long-departed did not give them any particular unease. Helena and I were the least bush-toughened of the group, but we had no qualms either, and when we were asked if we would mind living there once the house had been built we didn't waste any time in saying 'yes'. All that remained was where to locate the house. It was eventually placed so that it overlooked the eastern plains. This would not have been acceptable in today's age of environmental impact assessments, but that was then, and nowadays the house is screened by trees, so that it is almost invisible to tourists. The view remains as spectacular as always; this is one of the few places where you can lie in your bed with a view over hundreds of square kilometres of wild Africa and have the bonus of seeing elephants about 90 per cent of the time.

We left Crocodile Bridge at the end of November and moved to the Letaba camp while the Mooiplaas house was being built. Letaba was closed during the summer months, so we looked forward to storing our furniture and living in relative luxury for a bit, but after a couple of days the fences and restrictions of camp life started to grate on me, so I opted to settle in at Shipandani, a basic rangers' camp less than two kilometres away from the Mooiplaas house's site. So once again Aunt Molly had been right. She was also right about the daughter, because Annie was born in October 1974, and in July 1975 her final prediction came true – and I realised why she had stacked the cards and stopped at that point. I was busy with a hippo census in the Letaba River when I became aware of an uncomfortable feeling in my scrotum, which was the start of a three-year battle against cancer.

All of which proves – maybe – that witches don't have to be clothed in bones and feathers or kitted out with pointed hat, long black dress and broom. They can be perfectly respectable-looking Scots ladies of a certain age with a thick Highland accent, and distance from their home ground does not diminish their powers.

*

The bush can evoke dark fears in some people, and subsequent events prove them right frequently enough to give one pause for thought. Corporal July Makuvele, for instance, had a phobia about a certain spot on the road between the Nwanetsi ranger's post and Mpulangwene, his home in Mozambique, and he carried this aversion over to another place near Dzunwini Picket on the Crocodile River that reminded him of it. He went to great pains to avoid this spot whenever we were working in this area, and I respected his fears.

One evening we happened to be near Dzunwini Picket, returning on foot from an anti-poaching patrol with July in the lead. It was quite late when we reached the spot July dreaded so much, and because it was already as dark as the inside of a cow's guts we had to use the path instead of just crashing through the bush. Suddenly July let out a scream of fear and then took a sideways leap into the bush, simultaneously shouting a warning to me. I struck a match and saw a massive puff-adder lying right in the middle of the path. How July had seen it I don't know. Or perhaps he saw something else that warned him of things to come. That sounds a little portentous, but it is a fact that about a year later he went home on leave to Mozambique, reached his original place of fear and died of a heart attack.

Another experience that I still can't quite get my head around occurred when Sergeant John Mnisi and I were walking along the Nwaswitshaka Spruit one summer afternoon. While we were thus occupied I had an impulse to climb Milalene Hill right away, which was actually a pretty stupid idea on that very hot February day. But climb Milalene we did, up the north face and then across to the southern side, where there was a fairly steep cliff. Then, when we looked down from the top of the cliff, we saw a female leopard with her cubs below – a rare sighting, given the leopard's

281

nocturnal habits and disinclination for social intercourse, especially with humans. They were totally unaware of us, so that we had a wonderful opportunity to spend a long time watching them. So in the end we were richly rewarded for our strenuous exertions in the fierce heat, undertaken on impulse in response to an urging I could not have explained, either at the time or later.

When we had seen enough of the leopards we wasted no time heading for lower ground because an enormous thunderstorm was building to the west over Hazyview and Sabie, only to see it vanish before our astonished eyes. But this time the explanation was not mysterious at all – the Lowveld Tobacco Cooperation sent their Lear jet into the clouds, loaded with the appropriate rockets and chemicals, and within 15 minutes the clouds were gone; not knowing this until later, we watched goggle-eyed as the clouds disappeared, scarcely believing what we saw. But then John reintroduced the element of bushveld mystery by predicting, as we headed for our truck, that we would soon come across an 'mpangela' (the Tsonga name for a pangolin, or scaly ant-eater). I found this a bit hard to accept, since you rarely see a pangolin in broad daylight, but I had complete faith in John – and sure enough, we had walked less than 500 metres when we saw the mpangela, daylight or no daylight, just as he had predicted we would.

According to scientists – the boffins with the 'long hair and thick glasses', as we used to say – prosaic explanations can be found for many seemingly inexplicable hunches. One is that on a subconscious level we are always thinking and coming to conclusions, but these register only as hunches to our conscious minds. Another is that we pick up telling cues from body language, subliminal sounds or peripheral vision without being consciously aware of doing so. A third is that we remember successful hunches but conveniently forget those that don't pan out. A fourth theory is that in retrospect we modify our memories for our own convenience, creating a connection where it actually might not have existed.

All sound plausible enough, but the bottom line is that there are definitely cases where none of these theories are of any help in finding a rational explanation for some happening. I remember, for example, the time I took my mother, her sister, a cousin of mine and her family on a trail at Olifants. At some time during the weekend my mother lost one of her diamond stud earrings, which upset her very much because the earrings had been a wedding anniversary present from my father and therefore had great sentimental value. We looked everywhere but couldn't find the earring, which was hardly surprising. Nevertheless I went through the motions to console my mother, among other things asking Phanuel, the camp cook, to keep an eye open for it, and promising him a substantial reward if it was found. Phanuel promised to do so, but, needless to say, found nothing.

Then, almost exactly a year later, we held a trails staff meeting in a lapa at the same camp. At one stage I went to my hut to get my briefcase so that we could start with the formal agenda, and on my way back Arrie Schreiber, then head of trails, shouted: 'Hey Bruce, guess what I've just found?' 'My mother's diamond stud earring,' I answered immediately, and then came closer and made a positive identification. Arrie found this hard to swallow – we had come a long way together, and he knew that I was a bullshit artist of some skill when this was necessary. So I called Phanuel the cook and asked him to recall what I had said when I was last in the camp with my mother. Without any prompting on my part Phanuel told the story of how I had asked him to look out for an earring. That clinched the matter, and a rather disappointed Arrie handed over the earring, which he had already begun to visualise as the centrepiece of a ring for his wife.

Now, for almost an entire year the lapa had been swept and levelled at least three times a day and visited by at least 16 people every week. What could the odds have been against the chance that after all that the earring would make its appearance when Arrie idly dug the toe of his boot into the sand floor? Pretty near zero, I would have thought. Still, there it was. I can record that there was a fairly happy ending, because although Arrie's grand plan for adorning his wife's finger was thwarted, my mother was so grateful to regain her long-lost treasure that she rewarded him with considerably more whisky than would normally be consumed during the average weekend.

*

So there we have it: half a dozen tales that can't simply be written off as third-hand bushveld legends. I leave it to my readers to decide for themselves what they think about it all.

As a footnote: here's a strange bushveld story that doesn't fit into the tales I have just told, but provides a good starting-point for a talented spinner of yarns. I was on my way through Letaba one day when I was flagged down by a tourist with an urgent every-moment-is-vital tale to tell. He had been travelling along the tourist road between Letaba and Phalaborwa, he said, when he had stopped at Rhidonda Pan and heard someone in the veld calling for help. Being unarmed, he obviously could not go and investigate, and so he had come to get help. I knew that the Letaba section ranger was away, so I loaded the tourist into my vehicle and we sped off on our mission of mercy. On arriving at Rhidonda we stopped to listen. Sure enough, there it was, a piteous cry for help, apparently coming from somewhere near the pan's windmill. I told the tourist to stay in the truck, took my rifle and went to find the unfortunate person.

It was a strange business. Sometimes the calls were few and far between, but when the windmill's blades turned in the light breeze they became more frequent. What did the one have to do with the other? I had got quite close to the scene when the penny finally dropped. What I was hearing – and what the tourist had heard in the first place – was not some grievously injured person lying in the veld but the windmill telling us that there was no oil in its gearbox. Maybe windmills aren't totally inanimate objects after all, although as far as I know the only person who believed this was the late Don Quixote, who took them on with lance and sword.

15

THE LADIES –
GOD BLESS 'EM

When I arrived in the Park in 1971 there were 14 ranger stations, and as far as I was concerned, every section ranger was a hero. What I did not realise, in my youthful ignorance, was that if they were heroes, their wives were heroines. The wives enjoyed a much lower profile than their husbands because for the most part they stayed out of the limelight, but they all had two things in common: their love of the veld and the way of life there, and the great inner strength that enabled them to endure domestic hardships that would have driven most citified spouses up the wall or straight into the divorce court.

Life in Kruger is more comfortable today in terms of what are usually referred to as 'the civilised amenities', but in the earlier days of my career the wives had to cope with some severe 'challenges' (these are problems that nobody wants to admit are problems), and did so very successfully. That is why I am convinced that no story about the way we worked and lived would be complete without a part dedicated to the ladies who backed us up. What sort of challenges? Looking back, they are almost too numerous to count. The most obvious one is probably the fact that it was nothing unusual for a ranger's wife to be left alone for days or weeks at a time in a wilderness swarming with wild animals, frequently without even a telephone to keep her company, and only the barest of what would now be seen as absolute necessities.

At the start of my career the rangers' houses in the more remote sections depended for their electricity on tiny Lister generators which were so feeble that at night a ranger's wife could either switch on the lights or do her ironing, but not both. Since no one has yet worked out how to iron clothes and sheets in the dark, this choice wasn't actually a choice at all. The Listers had other drawbacks. For one thing, there was no way of switching them off in the house, so when a ranger was away on a field trip or some such occasion the lady of the house would either have to venture out into the dark – which always held the potential for unwanted excitement – to do the necessary, or arrange for one of the station staff to switch off at a given time. This was somewhat more of a choice, but not all that much. Then again, the Listers were well-worn and tended to die on one. Replacement parts sometimes took weeks to arrive, and in the interim you had to make do as best you could. This wasn't so bad for the men, who were busy and out of the house most of the time, but for their wives, who had to contend with all the many and varied daily household tasks, not to mention cooking large meals at short notice, it was a grind and no mistake.

The alternatives to electric power weren't all that much better. Our fridges and freezers all ran on paraffin, a messy and trouble-some way of keeping things cold. Note that I have not used the word 'frozen'; in summer, when things get distinctly torrid in the Lowveld, these smelly monsters could hardly keep the food fresh, let alone deep-frozen. Most of these machines had the trade-name 'Zero', and more than once I concluded that they had probably been named after the Japanese aircraft that caused so much mess and destruction at Pearl Harbour. It was nothing unusual for a ranger's wife to get up in the morning, go into the kitchen to make breakfast and find that during the night the monster had gone on strike and now sat inert and emitting acrid smoke, its contents ruined. Women didn't swear as much in those days as they do now, but I am pretty sure that some solid unprintables were uttered on many such an occasion.

Then again, imagine standing outside your house, watching it burn down with everything you own inside it, knowing that there is no fire engine within about 200 kilometres, and that when the ashes cooled you would simply have to pick up the pieces of your life and start all over again. That also happened more than once. Or imagine not just the terror felt by a mother on finding an 'mfezi', a Mozambican spitting cobra, in the cot where her baby was lying asleep, but also the steely strength that enabled her to fetch a handgun and kill the snake with one well-aimed shot that would have to pass within scant centimetres of the infant. This is not an apocryphal story: it happened at least once that I know of.

Most people have an inherent fear of snakes which is conditioned into us at an early age, but snakes have had a bad press. Given the choice, most of them will try to avoid both humans and their dwellings. But there are some notable exceptions, like the brown house snake and the mfezi, which will enter a house if they have an opportunity, probably in search of rats or mice. The mfezi is a particularly nasty customer that can spit venom with great accuracy for anything up to two and a half metres, often into the other party's eyes.

A pretty frightening incident in which we were involved near the end of 1974 illustrates the sort of thing that rangers' wives had to put up with. At the time my colleague Dirk Ackerman and his wife Antoinette were in Johannesburg, where Antoinette was exhibiting some of her artwork, and their elder children, Henk and Antoinette, were staying over with us at Letaba. Henk and Antoinette were playing in the back garden one very hot Sunday afternoon when they spotted a hefty-sized snake entering the house through the open kitchen door. The kids, already bush-wise backvelders, promptly called me, and I responded at top speed. The last thing anybody in Kruger needs in his house is a large snake of unknown type; most of the very poisonous snakes are big ones, the most notable exceptions being the non-venomous python and mole snake, and even they need to be approached with caution, because they might not have venom but can inflict deep wounds when they bite. I put on safety glasses, grabbed a hippo-hide sjambok and started searching (the sjambok was always my weapon of choice for killing a snake; you can inflict a devastating blow with it, and unlike a shotgun it doesn't end up damaging everything in the near vicinity). But the snake had vanished. We couldn't believe that a large snake could hide itself with such success in a house with a finite number of places to crawl into, but that's the way it was.

In the meantime Antoinette had grown bored with our fossicking around and decided to give Henk and myself a good scare with a rubber snake she had in her toy-box. Highly pleased with herself for thinking of this first-class prank, she went to the kids' room on the verandah, got out the toy-box and grabbed the rubber snake's tail to pull it out from under the box's other contents. When the rubber snake starting pulling in the opposite direction, however, Antoinette realised that something was badly wrong and she sounded the alarm. I made sure everyone was at a safe distance, then got hold of it and killed it. Sure enough, it was a full-sized mfezi. We were a bit rubbery in the legs afterwards, because Antoinette had been very lucky to escape without being bitten or getting an eyeful of venom. What might have happened if the mfezi had stayed undetected in the toy-box did not bear thinking about.

As a matter of interest, the mfezi, although an extremely dangerous creature, is not the major cause of snake-bite incidents in Africa. That dubious honour probably belongs to the puff-adder. Puff-adders are deceptively lethargic characters, but when aroused they strike with astonishing rapidity and accuracy, and they tend to have encounters with human beings on a frequent basis. One reason is that they are common to so many parts of the continent, and another is probably that they're fond of lying in pathways at night to collect a bit of extra heat from the exposed ground, or hiding under logs which might be picked up for firewood.

*

Just moving house when a ranger was transferred to another section – and remember that when one ranger moves, so does another to make room for him – was a traumatic event that involved moving a seemingly limitless number of men, women, children, with furniture, linen, dogs, chickens and other birds and plants, so that at times it resembled a scaled-down cross between Noah's great adventure with his ark and the Israelites' hurried departure from Egypt. You grabbed what transport was available and somehow crammed everything into it, and the convoy that finally set out would always look more or less the same, regardless of who was going where.

Behind the removal vehicle would be the ranger in his four-by-four, accompanied by his personal assistant, and possibly one of his sons in a state of toothy, freckled excitement, dressed for the great occasion in a much-laundered khaki shirt with homemade epaulettes just like Dad's, equally much-laundered khaki shorts and 'mapashanes' (sandals made of rubber car tyres). Next in line would be the station truck, piled with the ranger's personal assistant's bicycle and household goods, his wife with a runny-nosed child or two, the furniture, assorted other household goods, the house-plants, the dogs, a cage full of chickens from which cock-crows would emanate from time to time, a few black pots and a tripod or two, as well as a fishing rod and folding camp-stool chair which had been among the ranger's treasured possessions for many a year. Concealed somewhere inside this more or less organised chaos would also be a cool-box containing sausage and other eatables for a road-side lunch, together with a spade for heaping up the cooking-coals from the main fire. Bringing up the rear would be the lady of the house, at the wheel of the family Volkswagen Beetle or Peugeot – the make usually depending on her husband's length of service – together with all the other kids and the maidservant, unless she also happened to be the personal assistant's wife and was riding in the truck.

That's why I always believed that if there was one activity in Kruger that was more fascinating to watch than the animals, it was the sight of a ranger transferring to another station. That it was also considerably harder work I can attest from frequent and painful experience. I have no doubt that the only people who thoroughly enjoyed a move – other than a wife going to a station that provided much better amenities than the present one – were the rangers' children. These kids were (and still are, I am sure) the salt of the earth, and blessed beyond compare, because they grew up in the veld with the animals, surrounded by people who could teach them what the real Africa was all about. Some followed in their fathers' footsteps, while others became surgeons, lawyers and members of just about any other profession you can think of. But even those who now live far from Kruger will remain enriched by their childhood to the last day of their lives.

The four sons of Oom Gert and Tant Sannie van Rooyen were

classic examples of those kids who were bred in the Park and just never lost its ethos when they grew up. Two of them became rangers and the other two became helicopter pilots. It's strange how many families with multiple sons in our community had this sort of combination. In his novels about the escapades of the Sackett brothers, the Western writer Louis L'Amour always said that they were a breed that had been born, not made, and I tend to believe the same about rangers and chopper pilots. Rangers' daughters did not get the same degree of exposure to bushveld life in my early days at Kruger, when gender-stereotyping was much more rigid than it is today, but inevitably quite a lot of the general ethos rubbed off on to them, because in the more remote stations the front line is everywhere.

I have my own theory about why so many rangers' children went on to excel in their chosen fields. It was genetics, more than anything else: they were bred by phenomenally dedicated people who had cast aside the easy life to devote themselves to protecting the biodiversity (actually I hate that word as much as society conservationists love it); and so they tended to be determined, dedicated and hard-working people themselves. Selective breeding is selective breeding, whether the subjects are people or animals. One thing is sure – these bushveld kids never had any problems at school when it came to selecting a science or biology project, or finding an interesting subject for an essay . . . although they weren't always believed, as Dirk and Antoinette Ackerman discovered when they moved temporarily to Pretoria in 1973 so that Dirk could study for an honours degree in Wildlife Management at the University of Pretoria.

One of the first things they did was to enrol their elder children at the local school. This was a new adventure for Henk and Antoinette Junior, whose only acquaintance with educational institutions up to then had been with the school at Phalaborwa. Nevertheless, they settled in very well, which was hardly surprising, seeing that both Dirk and Antoinette were former teachers. Or so it seemed until half way through the first term, when Dirk was summoned to the school for a meeting with Henk's primary school class teacher. When he got there he was surprised to find not only the class teacher but the headmaster and the school psychologist as well. The reason soon became clear: Henk needed professional help, the psychologist said, to wean him away from the wild fantasies in which he constantly indulged in both his speeches and his essays. A particularly notable example of these fantasies, the psychologist said (ignoring or perhaps not detecting certain warning signs that Dirk was becoming agitated) was the story Henk had told about the night Dirk had gone camping at Tshokwane with his family and his resident mapoisas, Corporal July Makuvele and Elias Nzima. According to Henk, the incredulous head-shrinker went on, Elias was more accurate with a stone than Jonty Rhodes was with a cricket ball, and when a pride of lions paid a visit that night and made a nuisance of themselves, Elias let them have a couple of well-placed rocks with such salutary effect that the lions not only cleared off but didn't come back again! Dirk replied that the story was absolutely true, adding that in fact his children had often experienced this sort of thing. This was obviously not the reply the psychologist had expected, and he suggested that Dirk might also benefit from a little professional treatment. I don't know what happened next, but it must have been interesting, because Dirk isn't the sort of person who will take kindly to that sort of advice. Anyway, Dirk's children survived the onslaught on their psyches in good shape and went on to forge very successful careers in the 'real' world; but maybe that's because they were only in Pretoria for a year or so before the Ackermans all returned to Kruger – no doubt with a sigh of relief.

On this subject, probably the hardest aspect of the Kruger parents' lives was the first time they sent off their children off to boarding school. This was always a real tear-jerker, and once again I speak from experience, because I went through it not only with my own children, but with some of the other rangers' kids as well. Even later on, when both parents and children had fallen into the routine, there were sometimes hazards and hassles not normally encountered in more densely populated places. When we were stationed at Shingwedzi, getting Annie to school on a Monday morning involved leaving home at four o'clock to get them to Letaba in time for the six o'clock bus to Phalaborwa.

Helena did the driving on these occasions, my job being to load the sleeping Annie into the back seat of the car, which we used to park outside the back door on a Sunday night to make my journey shorter. Anyway, on one such Monday morning I stepped out of the back door with Annie in my arms, barefoot, as usual, and stood on something soft and squishy which I thought was an itinerant and now very deceased frog. I waved goodbye to Helena and the kids and promptly forgot about it – but only until I left the house later in the morning on my way to my office and found a 75 cm-long puff-adder lying outside the back door with a very thoroughly squashed head. Some frog! It had been a lucky escape. If I had stood on some other part of its body the result would have been a very nasty and painful bite, and because my foot had landed squarely on its head my not inconsiderable weight had prevented it from freeing itself with the sudden convulsive jerk characteristic of puff-adders.

Another thing just about all the rangers' wives were expert at was preparing a large and wonderful meal at a moment's notice, using only what was immediately to hand – a vitally important skill in a place like Kruger, where most of the sections were located hours away from the even barely adequate shopping facilities. A shopping trip in that part of the world was an expedition rather than a pleasant morning's excursion, and usually it was only part of all the things that had to be done when a ranger and his wife went to town. Typically a day in town started with a drive of a couple of hundred kilometres just to get there, after which both husband and wife would plunge into a round of essential activities such as renewing licences, handing in the car to be serviced and visiting either the doctor or the dentist or both. Then, and only then, could the lady of the house get down to doing her shopping. Eventually, frazzled and laden like a beast of burden, she would stagger back to the freshly serviced car (unless, of course, this was taking longer than it should have) and settle back to enjoy (?) the long road home. Furthermore, when you consider that such a shopping trip took place once a month for the fortunate but only every two or three months for the unfortunate, it will be understood that the average ranger's wife had very little room for error or omission when it came to buying the necessary supplies.

One such venture to the outside world proved to be not only tiring but very nearly fatal for our close friend Kotie de Beer (who was later killed by a leopard) when she went to Nelspruit in a double-cab bakkie one rainy day to pick up some new office furniture. It was a rainy day, and before leaving Skukuza Kotie took a large tarpaulin from the garage and stowed it on the bakkie's back seat so that the furniture could be covered on the trip home. Fetching the furniture was, of course, not the only thing Kotie wanted to do, so she decided to leave it until she had visited the shopping mall, where she bought groceries and couldn't resist acquiring a new suit for herself as well. On her return to the bakkie she dumped the plastic shopping-bags on the floor in front of the back seat, collected the furniture and set off with the tarpaulin stretched over the load area in case of rain.

Back at Skukuza, Kotie fished her parcels out of the cab and headed for her house. On the way to her front door she could not help taking another look at her new suit, and was surprised to see that somehow it had acquired a belt, although it had not had one when she bought it. Kotie was so surprised that without a second thought she reached into the bag to remove the 'belt', which turned out to be an mfezi that rose up and spat a cloud of venom at her. A veteran Skukuzite, Kotie instantly averted her face so that the venom missed her eyes and flung the bag across the lawn, and when it came to rest the snake escaped into the nearest flowerbed. As Kotie reconstructed it, the mfezi had been hidden in the folds of the tarpaulin when she had loaded it onto the back seat that morning, and at some time before she fetched the furniture had either crawled directly from the tarpaulin into the shopping-bag or into the space underneath the seat and from there into the bag. Whichever had been the case, Kotie had three times come very close to death or serious injury in just one day: first when she loaded the tarpaulin into the back seat, then on the homeward journey, when any movement of hers that the snake interpreted as a threat would have meant a strike, and yet again when she opened the bag on the way to her front door.

*

Naturally the wives were not as dependent on handy butcheries, groceries and supermarkets as their urban colleagues. During the winter months they could grow fine vegetables that would be shared with the station staff and the wild animals on a basis of roughly a third each (although I don't think we ever got our full third, but let that be as it may). Generally we ate very well, although, contrary to what some people might believe, we did not generally live off the land, since our job was to conserve the animals rather than eat them. On the other hand, we were all imbued with the park's 'waste not, want not' philosophy, and if a legitimate little eatable or two resulted from our activities we were not averse to taking the gap.

Hippo meat was always a welcome addition to our larders. Their flesh is very tasty, regardless of what they have been eating, and one of my personal favourites is a slice of hippo brisket that has been lightly salted and grilled on the coals. The fat literally melts away, leaving a lovely snack that tastes very much like beef, except that it is a bit tougher and the grain is much coarser. I never turned down the opportunity to eat a bit of hippo when we were on culling operations, and if some of my colleagues were temporary vegetarians because of all the blood and guts, that was strictly their problem. During culling operations it was obviously necessary for as little time as possible to elapse between the time an animal was killed and its arrival at the meat processing plant at Skukuza, and now and then a hippo would sink after being shot and for some reason only float back to the surface after the recovery trucks had left with the other animals. To us this was not a hassle; just the reverse, in fact. We would haul it out, skin it and feast on the meat, which was a treat for everyone. This was an acceptable practice – the only rule the management insisted on was that none of the raw meat be taken away from the camp, and especially not out of the Park itself.

In between culling camps or late-rising hippos we could also indulge our taste for *filet de sea-cow au naturel* by ordering fresh meat or delicious sausage from the meat-processing plant. I retain a memory, both painful and pleasant, of one very large and obdurate piece of hippo topside that caused some consternation during the cooking process. Helena put the meat, which she had carefully cured beforehand, into the pressure cooker and fired up the gas stove. At first all was well, but then things went wrong somewhere along the line and the safety valve blew, spewing hot fat, water, spices and shreds of meat all over the kitchen's ceiling and walls. Helena burst into tears, being pregnant at the time and consequently prone to mood changes. Then, having got it off her chest, she tackled the cleaning-up and had another go at the top-side. The same thing happened again, and then a third time, after which we abandoned the weak-kneed pressure cooker and stuffed the topside into that old stand-by, a three-legged black pot squatting on a bed of coals of suitable temperature. That did it, and the topside was despatched to its pre-ordained destinations. I'm tempted to make a real Luddite remark and say that this proved that sometimes the old ways are best.

The rangers' wives were far more than pillars of the domestic side of life. Although their days were full – among other things a wife would be fully involved in running the section in tandem with the station's sergeant or corporal when the ranger was away – they turned their ever-busy hands to many interesting pursuits in what spare time they had A few became well-known artists, authors and wood-carvers, while others cultivated sensationally good gardens, and most of them were also accomplished knitters and dressmakers.

Dressmakers? For sure. It is true that the average wife spent considerable time on carrying out running repairs, since ranger work is notoriously tough on clothes, but we were not slobs just because we lived in the backveld. There were always more or less dressy occasions, and once a year everybody would get together for the annual rangers' party that was then held at the Letaba rest camp. This was Kruger's prestige event: the men actually wore long trousers, and the ladies knocked 'em dead in outfits that had been weeks or months in the making.

*

Most wives also learnt to shoot, albeit out of sheer necessity, and some became so expert that they competed in the shooting competitions held by the local commando, to which virtually all the men belonged; some even went further and joined up themselves.

As was to be expected, given the nature of the job, the commando's shooting team was a pretty good one. This did not go unnoticed, and one weekend we were visited by a contingent of top Permanent Force shottists, consisting of one women's and two men's teams, whose aim was quite clearly to take us on and courteously put us in our place. Big mistake!

The Permanent Force ladies were a smart lot, snappy in their brown battledress – I remember this clearly because one of them, a Springbok shottist, fired in the detail just before mine. I was right behind her, and was amazed to see the recoil from each shot roll down her back, through her gluteus maximus (buttocks to the scientifically challenged) and then down into her legs. I recall thinking how strange it was that a shock-wave should change rhythm when it encountered tissues of different composition.

I am sure the women soldiers were slightly amused when they saw the Kruger ladies' team, whose members were definitely a very mixed bag. One was eight months pregnant and rocked back on her heels after every shot, another was well into her forties and a third was so petite that when she fired a shot it seemed likely that she would take off in the opposite direction to the bullet. So it was a great shock to all the visitors when our ladies, God bless 'em, not only knocked the stuffing out of the PF women's team but came very close to taking the men to the cleaners as well. I would have liked to hear the tall tales told at the visitors' debriefing when they got back to Pretoria.

*

The first real home Helena and I had in the Kruger National Park was at Shipandani, next to the Tsende River, on the Tsende Loop about five kilometres by road from today's Mopani rest camp. You will not find Shipandani on the map of the present-day Kruger National Park. Its buildings were more or less flattened in 1976, when the floods caused by Cyclone Emily broke the Pioneer Dam, and later on its remains were removed when the Mopani rest camp was built; recently people returned there, however, when the park management built a sleep-over hide, ideal for bird-watching, on the site of the old camp. The understanding was that we would be at Shipandani for about two months while the new

Mooiplaas house was being built, but very wet conditions prevented the builders from collecting sand and other building materials, and in the end we were there for a total of five.

To a lesser person than Helena, Shipandani would have been a nightmare. It was a fairly basic rangers' camp where park staff stayed when they were engaged in culling operations or other 'away' activities in the area. Our accommodation consisted of a thatched hut with doors that wouldn't close properly, windows in which mosquito gauze substituted for glass (for serious occasions each window had a hardboard cover, which hung from the roof on a wire hook), and roof with a generous leak. There was an electric light, it is true, but no generator to actually make it work. I wish I could say that the kitchen made up for deficiencies of the accommodation, but in truth it was even more primitive, being no more than a thatched roof on poles that exposed the interior to every breath of wind – as a result of which our paraffin-driven fridge and chest freezer flatly refused to work – and a stone floor so uneven that it would take you down without warning unless you watched constantly where you put your feet.

It goes without saying that there was no such thing as running water. What we needed had to be fetched in drums from the waterhole in front of the camp, and if we wanted it hot, we had to pour it into an old paraffin drum that had been fitted with a tap at the bottom, then build a fire underneath the drum. The ablution facilities adhered to the same low standard. The shower was an open-topped reed construction with a small tank on top that had to be filled with bucketsful of water, laboriously carried one by one up an attached ladder. From the bottom of the tank projected a pipe fitted with a tap and a showerhead. Showering was an all-or-nothing affair. If there was no hot water or you were in a hurry, you had a cold shower. If the water was too hot, you either endured or waited for it to cool. Or, of course, you could always go to the extra labour of climbing the ladder with a bucketful from the cold tank. The toilet consisted of another roofless reed enclosure around the not-so-long long drop, into which chemicals had to be poured at intervals to kill the flies and eliminate the smell (they didn't quite). The whole thing was totally disgusting.

Helena and I immediately pitched in to get the camp into some sort of operating shape. As a start we screened the side of the kitchen facing the prevailing wind and shifted the beds around in the hut to avoid the leak – this rearrangement was no problem because the rest of the furniture consisted only of a wardrobe, a chest of drawers and a small table – and established a routine of hooking the light up to the truck's battery every night. I also added on an office in which I attended the daily 7 am radio session. 'Office' is perhaps a bit too grand a description, since it consisted of a tent I pitched between the hut and the kitchen and equipped with a bed and a table on which the radio stood.

Every now and then we would have nocturnal visitors. One variety that we were worried about was lions; we remembered all too well an incident the previous year at Wankie, in what was then still Rhodesia, when a lion had got into a hut and seriously mauled the occupants. The northern part of the Park has never been real lion country, but the Tsende River had permanent pools that supported enough game throughout the year to feed a substantial population of the big cats. So they often walked past or around the hut at night, and now and then would seek a poultry snack at the field rangers' picket, which was about 50 metres away.

Elephants also came to investigate, especially after dark. One night I was woken by a sound I couldn't identify, although I could smell an elephant close by – when you live in the veld, your senses tend to be sharp and your sleep light, particularly if your accommodation doesn't have much in the way of doors and windows. I peered out through the doors and windows without seeing anything, noting that the unidentified noise stopped as soon as I started moving around. My dog Eggs watched all this in tense anticipation but remained quiet, as she had been taught. I thought about going outside, but only briefly, because it was pitch dark and raining lightly, and decided to get back into bed. Then I heard that mysterious noise again and realised at the same time that dust was falling on me from the roof. Suddenly it dawned on me what was happening: an elephant was busy pulling thatch out of the roof and brushing his body with it! I let him have a fortissimo burst of bad language and Eggs now broke her silence and followed suit. Our out-bursts evidently were too much for the elephant, and he took himself off.

Helena's parents came to visit about six weeks after we had moved in at Shipandani (this was to become a regular routine as we moved around Kruger, because her father, who was univer-sally known as Oupa Trappies, fell into the habit of checking up on each new set of domestic circumstances in which I landed his daughter). I don't think they were very impressed by Shipandani, and I don't blame them, because it was pretty grisly. Just to make it worse, it was time for a hippo culling, so that on the first night of their stay I was away shooting hippo.

The original pre-culling plan had been that we would give up the one and only bedroom to the old folks and sleep in my office tent, but Helena was disinclined to spend the night there on her own, so she and Oupa Trappies moved the tent's bed into the hut. At least they were all together when the middle of the night brought another of Shipandani's attractions, a typical Lowveld thunderstorm that subjected the three of them to a sort of bush-veld artillery bombardment which included an unprecedented number of lighting strikes in the near vicinity. Helena was put through yet another ordeal, because she and Oupa Trappies had contrived to place her bed directly under the roof's leaky spot, so that she got a thorough soaking when the rain came down. Helena was so embarrassed by her domestic circumstances that she spent the entire night lying awake in the damp and chilly bed rather than say anything to her parents (her self-sacrifice was for nothing, incidentally, because they found out about it anyway). The good news about all this was that Oupa Trappies did not abduct his dear daughter forthwith and take her away from this primitive squalor, and neither did Helena throw her-self at his feet and beg to be taken away. Like me, she actually *liked* the bushveld life, noisome long drop or not.

It was a very wet year in 1973, as I've said, with the Tsende coming down in flood almost every other day, and I got quite a lot of work done on my thesis because we couldn't move around much, at least not in our Volksie. We did make a foray, however, to visit the family in Johannesburg, and this turned into a classic

Kruger hair-raiser. I had to have my official Land Cruiser serviced, so on the day of our departure I went off ahead to Letaba, the plan being that Helena would follow a few hours later with the Volksie and meet me there; Amos would be with her to help if she got stuck somewhere along the 60 kilometres of very wet road to Letaba. I drove through the Tsende drift in a cheerful frame of mind, not knowing that soon afterwards the river would be swollen to several times its normal size as a result of flooding in two major tributaries upstream, the Shabarumbi and the Shabagadzi. As a result the Tsende drift was under several feet of water by the time Helena and Amos reached it.

Amos went to investigate and came back to say that in his opinion it would be too dangerous to try a crossing. Helena was having none of this, however, so she stepped on the accelerator and charged into the drift at full speed. Heaven only knows how they got through without being pushed off the drift's relatively hard standing, or at the very least being marooned in the river with a dead engine, but they did, and they arrived at Letaba in such a soaked state that I would not have been surprised to see fish swimming around in the engine compartment. The Volksie looked like hell, though, and I asked Blackie, the Rondalia Touring Company's man on the spot, to check it out. He did so and reported that no serious damage had resulted from Helena's argument with the Tsende, but that the tappet cover's gasket was out of place. This spelt certain disaster in an engine that only travelled on dirt roads and had recently been all but submerged, so it seemed an auspicious moment to think about buying another car. Datsun had just introduced its magic 1800 SSS, and on top of that Helena was pregnant with our first child, so as soon as we got to Phalaborwa I ordered a red Datsun, although it would cost me the equivalent of a year's salary.

At the end of April 1974 we finally said goodbye to our ramshackle home-from-home and moved to the new house on the top of the hill at Mooiplaas. Contrary to what might be expected, we could feel the place tugging at our hearts as we left, and to this day Helena and I remain agreed that our stay at Shipandani was probably our happiest time in the Kruger National Park. Why? Well, we were young and full of hope, we were in the bush where we wanted to be, we could foresee great adventures lying ahead of us and our first child was conceived there . . . and on the very day we left for Mooiplaas Helena felt our baby move inside her for the first time.

16

THE BUSHVELD LIFESTYLE

The personal lifestyles of the Kruger National Park ranger staff changed dramatically during my time there, most of the time for the better, although sometimes in ways that reduced the intimate hands-on nature of the old days. On the other hand, the fundamental features of the job – odd hours, long absences from home, disruption of down-time by unforeseen and unforeseeable emergencies, arduous tasks that had to be undertaken, moments of danger – did not change very much, and so certain things remained constant. Yet it was a good life in most of its permutations if you had the right temperament, enough energy and, most of all, the dedication to conserving the enormously varied community of animals that inhabited the park. It provided plenty of action because there was always something on the go, and plenty of job satisfaction because we knew that we were engaged in an immensely meaningful task. What a contrast to those hordes of poor bastards in other walks of life who spend their lives toiling away at something they aren't really interested in, counting the days remaining before they go on pension!

In the broader context the most dramatic change was in our relations with neighbouring Mozambique. My career at Kruger started in time for me to taste the old style of life that had prevailed for so many decades before Mozambique's descent into turmoil and warfare in the 1970s destroyed it. We rangers were on excellent terms with Mozambique's local government officials, farmers and general population. The best word to describe our relationship would probably be 'easy-going', the general rule being that you just weren't supposed to be found on the wrong side of the fence without the knowledge of the people on that side. It goes without saying that there were chancers on both sides, but mostly they did not disturb the even tenor of life, and we let them be unless they went too far. The result of this pleasant coexistence was that we used to move freely across the border to visit the 'Chef da Posto' or 'Administrador,' or sometimes just the local shopkeeper, to buy Laurentina – a very good beer, very reasonably priced – or that magical Portuguese 'long-life' bread that would last for weeks if you kept it in a reasonably cool, dry place. The local storekeepers frequently baked it themselves, but more often than not flour-bags full of the little round loaves would arrive from Lourenço Marques (later Maputo) on the back of a truck.

As a youngster working in Mozambique in the mid-1960s I had acquired a certain amount of basic Portuguese that often came in useful during our visits to our distinctly polyglot neighbour-state – it was not unusual to find ourselves sitting on the verandah of a shop somewhere in the bush, listening to four languages being spoken at once, every speaker or listener understanding the other, with a floor show consisting of the shopkeeper's wife and children raiding the baby chicken population to provide us with lunch. Lunch? Well, time was an elastic concept. Exactly when lunch was served just wasn't all that important. If your visitors were hungry you fed them, whether it was 11 o'clock in the morning or three in the afternoon. This exercise in relaxed internationalism vanished for good in the early 1970s when Mozambique became independent under the Frelimo government. The new rulers hated and feared South Africa because of apartheid and also because it was an active ally of Rhodesia, and things were to get a great deal worse in the next two decades or so before they started getting slightly better.

The last of what might be called the ancien régime passed through the Kruger National Park in January 1976, when Mozambique was fast falling to pieces. Numbers of Portuguese – both native-born and locally bred – left over from the former dispensation had decided to tough it out till better days arrived, but now they finally gave up hope and headed southwards by whatever means presented themselves. I remember one such group, whose flight was a typical mixture of drama, tragedy and farce. It consisted of about 12 vehicles, ranging from a few small motorcycles and Mercedes-Benz saloon cars to trucks loaded with an assortment of goods that included whisky and foodstuffs such as crates of instant coffee and condensed milk . . . plus a couple of other items of which I was only to become aware a little later.

The group reached the Kruger boundary one Saturday, gained entry by the simple expedient of cutting through the boundary fence near Pumbe Pan, and then calmly asked for directions from a mapoisa who had came to investigate. There might have been a linguistic mix-up at this stage, but I doubt it, seeing that most mapoisas at that stage were Mozambicans themselves; whatever the case, he directed them towards the roughest road along the eastern boundary, then hastened to the Maplanguene police station to pass the word about the soon-to-be-bogged-down convoy. The group managed to reach Eight Miles and then stuck. Next morning all hell broke loose when some Frelimo soldiers crossed over and attacked them. The people scattered into the dense bush, while one vehicle managed to escape. This vehicle headed south, eventually ending up at the Crocodile Bridge ranger station, where the driver told the ranger about the attack. The ranger then set the official wheels in motion by informing the security police, who in turn notified the park management. The local commando, of which I was a member, had prepared itself for just such an event, and as soon as possible a group of volunteers was mobilised, given a few policemen to represent the civil power and despatched to Eight Miles; we took with us a radio so that we could call in two South African Air Force Puma helicopters carrying a reaction force of paratroopers if they were needed.

So far, so good, but when we got to Eight Miles the Frelimo soldiers were still engaged in shooting and looting, and they started shooting at us as well. We tried to call in the reaction force but found that the radio had gone on the blink. The affair dragged on inconclusively for several hours, and late that afternoon, while we were taking stock of our situation, one of the refugees informed us that his wife and three-week-old baby were missing; another refugee reported that he had seen a Frelimo soldier manhandling the woman after throwing the baby over the boundary fence. We mounted a search but failed to find either mother or baby, and so we took the refugees back to Skukuza; we didn't bother to leave a guard element at the vehicles because the Frelimo soldiers had decamped. By the following morning the paratroopers we had been promised still hadn't arrived, and they were still absent the day after, so we had to go out again to salvage the vehicles. On arrival we ran into a small party of Frelimo soldiers who had returned to look for whisky, but their heart wasn't in the enterprise, and they left without firing a shot.

Now we could finally get around to taking the vehicles and what remained of their cargo back to Skukuza. We hadn't given them much thought so far because our main priority had been to rescue the refugees themselves, but now we began to get certain intimations of mortality. The vehicles had been standing in the veld for days, and it was not impossible that some or all had been booby-trapped, although as far as we could tell the Frelimo men had been interested in freelance looting rather than securing their country's borders (and in any case the convoy had reached our side of the fence before they attacked it). The truck I was assigned to recover was the second one in the convoy. It had clearly been abandoned in a great hurry, because it was jammed up at an absurd angle against the elephant-proof fence, like a drunkard propping up a bar counter, so close to the wire on the driver's side that the only way of getting into it was by the cab's passenger door. I eyed it with some distaste for what I had to do. My tasks were not exactly brain-straining – all I had to do was slither in from the passenger side like a baboon ducking into a rock-crevice and then see that the brake was released and the gears in neutral so that the culling recovery truck we had brought along could pull it free. But I couldn't stop myself from considering the possibility that some Frelimo eager beaver had taken time off from his looting to install a little surprise for us.

I carried out a thorough external inspection, found nothing and climbed into the cab. There I spotted a red rhyolite rock wedged against the dashboard with a branch cut from a shrub. I went cold: here was a classic improvised booby trap. All the rangers had been trained to deactivate such devices, but this was the first one I had actually encountered. I felt an urgent need for outside consultation, so I summoned the head of Kruger's mechanical workshops and told him what I had found. He inspected the apparent booby trap and concluded that trying to disarm it was more trouble than the truck was worth, so we decided to try to set it off by remote control and let the truck take its chance. I tied a cord to the stick, ducked behind a boulder a long way off and gave it an energetic tug. Nothing happened, so I counted to 100 to allow for a delayed-action explosion. This didn't take place either, so I returned to my alleged booby trap, the purpose of which remained a mystery to me.

With this source of concern out of the way I checked for other possible major and minor threats, but found nothing more lethal than a plastic envelope measuring about 45 by 12 centimetres, very similar in size to the rifle-cleaning kits we had recently been issued with (it turned out to be a folding hazard triangle) and then summoned the culling truck in a vastly easier frame of mind. At Skukuza we parked all the vehicles under guard outside the police station and went gratefully home after what had been a rough and somewhat frightening day. Next morning I discovered that I had been sitting on a fortune when I drove the jammed-up truck back to Skukuza. The owner of the truck opened his hang-down toolboxes to reveal green bags full of US dollars – a lot of them. I goggled, then asked the logical question: 'What if Frelimo had asked you where your money was?' By way of an answer he pulled out a plastic envelope like the one I had found in the cab, except that it contained hundreds of dollars.

There was one final twist to this story that did not emerge until the very end. Just about everything the refugees had brought with them – whisky, cars, condensed milk, motorcycles, coffee, you name it – had been stolen from suppliers in Mozambique and pre-sold in South Africa. So, while most refugees find sanctuary with little more than what they can carry on their backs – and there were lots of those reaching South Africa from both Mozambique and Angola in the next few years – this bunch would be doing pretty well, thank you very much. Except, of course, for the mother and baby Frelimo had abducted and carried away into the ironwood forests. Our search parties could not find a trace of them, or even any clue as to their fate.

By the grace of God the Kruger National Park was not sucked into the turmoil and tragedy in Mozambique, although we had to deal with the side-effects, such as intensified poaching and the unscheduled arrival of refugees like the Pumbe Pans group. In later years, as conditions continued to deteriorate in Mozambique, we had to contend with a steady influx of illegal immigrants. Some met their deaths at the hands of predators or simply died of their privations, others were caught by us or the security forces and thrown out at the Komatipoort border post, which they seemed often to regard as a mere technical hitch (the commander of the locally recruited army battalion we had stationed in Kruger once told me, half-amused and half-despairingly, of one inveterate border crosser who had waved goodbye to him at Komatipoort with the words: 'I'll be seeing you again, Commandant'). An unknown number (few or many – who knows?) evaded both the predators and the border patrols and made it to Johannesburg, where they worked happily and illegally for sweatshop wages that were enough to give any trade unionist a heart attack but represented wealth to them. There must have been a lot of them, though, because South Africa now has a floating population of political or economic refugees from all parts of Africa that supposedly numbers at least a couple of million and quite likely far more.

*

But that is by the way. This is about aspects of the Kruger lifestyle that have vanished beyond recall, and the only place to begin is with the prefabricated asbestos structure erected at Skukuza in 1963 as male single quarters for park staff. Almost inevitably this building soon became known as the 'Ramkamp', or 'ram camp', which is actually the traditional sheep-farming term for the enclosure where rams are penned, but has long been applied by humorists to any all-male place of residence or recreation. Admittedly the Ramkamp was not out in the bush but part of what passed for a population centre in that part of the world, but in Kruger it is not always easy to separate one from the other, either geographically or by style.

307

My first abode when I arrived at Skukuza was naturally a room in the Ramkamp, and it was not exactly palatial: a typical Rampkamp room measured four metres by three, with a small window and a built-out wardrobe that effectively cut almost a metre out of the available space. Add to that an army-type fold-able bedstead and (if you were lucky) a small table and chair, and you had just enough space in which to swing the proverbial cat, providing it was a very small one. Just to add to its attractions the Ramkamp's rooms were very hot because there was no ventila-tion or air-conditioning, which led to some very interesting sleep-ing arrangements during the customary blistering Lowveld sum-mers.

The fact that their accommodation wasn't exactly five-star didn't dampen anyone's spirits, because there was plenty of good company and plenty of home-made entertainment to occupy your spare time. The Ramkamp's inmates came from all walks of life, so that at any time you might expect to find people like builders, carpenters, students, surveyors, veterinary technicians or others in residence. Most of us were in our zestful early twen-ties and worked elsewhere than at Skukuza, so things were hec-tic at the Ramkamp when its residents returned at weekends to get their washing done, indulge in one or other type of sport and do a little serious partying. In fact I don't recall any great demar-cation between the sport time and party time, since one would inevitably lead to the other – the usual weekend consisted of ferocious rugby or some such on the Saturday afternoon, a de-dicated slaking of thirst in the evening, some 'ceiling inspection' during the later hours of darkness and then a lunch-time Sun-day braai, followed by a beer or 12 on the verandah of Skukuza's restaurant. It might not have been very intellectually stimulat-ing, but it certainly was a lot of fun. I was exposed a little less to the bushveld high life than some of the others because my research programme required me to stay in the veld most week-ends, but I did my best to pay flying visits to hand in my washing, play some rugby and enjoy a little ice-cold liquid refreshment with my colleagues.

Like all Skukuza residents we were subject to the rules and regulations needed to run a village in a national park, but there was also one restriction that applied only to the inmates of the Ramkamp: no girls in the rooms under any circumstances! I don't know if such a rule would be possible today with the very liberal national constitution we have, but that was then. It was not, I regret to say, strictly adhered to. The drawer-up of this rule – we all knew who he was – had obviously forgotten about the frightening glandular energy and fiendish ingenuity of fit, lusty and happy young men when he put pen to paper, and I need hardly say that not only did we treat it with the contempt it deserved but never got caught either. As a result there were constant, if discreet, comings and goings by girls for the purpose of – ahem – providing a little stimulating conversation during the night hours.

Occasionally this led to some unsettling incidents for the handful of older residents of the Ramkamp, who were accorded honorary uncle status and addressed as 'Oom' in traditional style (when you're in your early twenties, a 40-year-old is like Methuselah). One Saturday night, I recall, two of the honorary uncles, Oom Godfrey and Oom Gert, went on a binge of such proportions that when they finally fell into their beds it was generally agreed that they would not be seen again until midmorning on Sunday, when they were due to get the braai fires going. Thus in the earlier part of Sunday morning it was considered safe to give free run of the bathroom block to the Ramkamp's temporary female residents, who numbered about 10 all told. The girls were shepherded into the ablution block and promptly took it over as only a group of women know how to.

I was lounging on the back verandah outside my room, which was only two doors from the bathroom block, when I beheld a fearsome sight: Oom Godfrey stumbling down the verandah towards the ablution block, completely unclothed except for his striped pyjama trousers. I doubt if he even saw me, since he was obviously still in the please-let-me-die stage of a hangover, and it was clear that the hammers in his head had drowned out the girlish screams and giggles coming from the showers. I should have warned him, but, swine that I was, I listened to the little devil in my head who whispered: 'Let him be,' so I kept my peace and allowed him to find his painful way into the ablution block.

What sights befell his eyes there I don't know, but after a very short time he came out of there in a great hurry and disappeared down the verandah. A couple of minutes later he was back, accompanied by Oom Gert, who was no better attired that he and definitely in no healthier physical condition either.

'Gert,' Oom Godfrey said, 'there are naked girls in the shower.'

'Godfrey,' Oom Gert mumbled, 'you're drunk,' and he was probably right, to judge by the way they clung to each other for mutual support.

In this fashion Oom Gert got to the ablution block's door, looked inside, recoiled in shock and said: 'Godfrey, you're right, there really are girls in the shower. Let's have a drink,' which they did, the overall result being that they got distracted and missed the Sunday braai altogether.

As I mentioned earlier, the Ramkamp's rooms were so hot that on most summer nights we slept on the front lawn to make the best of what little breeze might be blowing. Very few of us contracted malaria, probably due to the fact that all black staff members were required to take prophylactic drugs, which kept the parasitic loads low (this would probably be unconstitutional in post-1994 South Africa) – and, of course, drug-resistant malaria had not become the problem it is today. The mosquitoes weren't the only potential drawback to sleeping on the lawn. The yard's gates were never closed and animals of all sorts, from impala to lions, wandered in and out of the yard at times, yet no one was ever attacked. I would not like to try it today, however, in Skukuza or anywhere else, because for years now the lions and hyaenas have been preying on the steady stream of illegal immigrants crossing into Kruger from Mozambique on their way south, and the lesson they have learnt is that humans are literally easy meat.

The Ramkamp's double entrance doors were also seldom closed; in fact the only doors that were routinely closed were the gauze screens to our rooms, although that was only because they were spring-loaded to close automatically. This easy access led to a few out-of-the-ordinary occurrences. Very late one night I needed to pay a call to the toilet and was somewhat shaken to find a fully grown leopard lapping at the water in the urinal. I went straight into adrenalin-overload mode and plunged back the way I came with what can only be described as indecent haste, my need of a moment earlier temporarily forgotten. The leopard took it much more calmly; when he had imbibed as much of the slightly flavoured water as he wanted, he strolled unhurriedly out of the ablution block, traversed the lounge and departed via the front door, obviously very comfortable with his situation. It made a good story for later, but, the bushveld being the bushveld, the leopard's late-night visit could have had a very different ending. The door through which I had entered the bathroom was the way in or out of the block, and if a leopard feels trapped its first instinct is to attack, very swiftly and very violently. In any case, from that time on I never scoffed at the old stories about a leopard dropping in to use the Ramkamp's facilities. I had always thought there was a pink elephant involved, but now I knew different.

*

Practical jokes were a staple of Ramkamp entertainment, which was to be expected in any establishment where most of the residents were high-spirited young men whose feet (as the Bible would say) ran readily to mischief, and naturally there were also a few favourite victims who could be relied on to react strongly to any such jape. One of these was my friend Louis Olivier, then part of the game capture team, who tended to react so strongly that it was wise not to be within arm's length of him during the denouement. Take the case of the mysterious intruder, involving a lamp-stand belonging to one of the residents. It was made out of a leadwood log about 1.8 metres high, surprisingly humanoid in profile, and it positively cried out for something better than merely supporting a lamp. So one night we draped it in a great-coat, topped it off with a mapoisa's hat and positioned it in a strategic part of Louis's bedroom while he was out. This done, we all gathered by the window to see what would happen when Louis returned, and what happened was that when he saw the 'intruder' looming up in the dark he punched it hard – so hard that he hurt his hand. This hadn't been part of the plan, of course, and we all apologised fulsomely, and, being the good man that

311

he was, he smiled and forgave us, although the hand was actually very painful.

Sunday morning at the Ramkamp was revival time, although not in the evangelistic sense; in our lexicon it indicated how long you needed to start feeling normal again so that you could resume the high jinks. Each of us had his own revival method, Louis's being to sit on the throne and read in the toilet block, the doors of which, like the equivalents elsewhere around the Ramkamp, were never closed. This regularity of habit, and the fact that Louis's hearing had been below standard for a long time, were like a gold-engraved invitation to his so-called friends; and one Sunday morning, while Louis was engaged in reviving himself, his fellow inmate Ian Whyte quickly lay down in the next-door cubicle and commenced breathing heavily, like some large and presumably dangerous animal. It took a while for the penny to drop, but when it did Louis reacted in characteristically forceful fashion, throwing down his book and lunging up to destroy the threat, whatever it might be, although somewhat hindered by the shorts around his ankles. Ian was ready for this and headed south, pursued by Louis's only weapon, a cake of soap, which hit him squarely between the shoulder-blades. Ian did not mind this at all, knowing that if Louis had remembered to kick off his shorts the consequences would have been rather more serious.

Since all the inhabitants of the Ramkamp were involved in conservation in one way or another, it was inevitable that sooner or later we would adopt an orphan animal for a pet, and in our case it was a young baboon. He was named 'Kees', the traditional South African baboon name, and taken into our hearts. As a result Kees lived like a veritable bushveld king. He had his own flat (a box on top of a pole in the yard), lots to eat and lots of attention. Almost inevitably, given the generally vinous atmosphere at weekends and baboons' custom of snapping up any unconsidered or untended trifle, he also acquired a taste for booze, specifically vodka and sparkling lemon.

Baboons have a definite weakness for liquor, which probably supports Darwin's theory about the origin of species, and eventually Kees became a real soak who hated the arrival of early

Sunday mornings as much as people like Oom Gert and Oom Godfrey. He would hunch mournfully in his box, shielding his eyes from the light, until he heard the beer cans hiss open and the ice-cubes chinking in the glasses; then he would descend from his box, as ready for the next round of partying as any of the rest of us. Sad to say, liquor was the ruination of Kees, as it has been with many another party animal, and soon after I moved to Crocodile Bridge I heard that his liver had given in. I suppose one could make the point that this was a better end than becoming a leopard's lunch.

The Ramkamp is no more, which is probably a good thing, considering. A while after my departure it was turned into the headquarters of the Kruger National Park's commando and the party animals were accommodated elsewhere. So at last it achieved the respectability that it lacked so sorely during our tenure. Long live the Ramkamp! It certainly was fun while it lasted.

A quintessential form of bushveld lifestyle that vanished as completely as the Ramkamp during my time in Kruger was the culling camp. A culling camp was always a major event in our year. First a campsite would be selected and essential facilities (toilets and showers) would be constructed of corrugated iron sheets. Then a considerable number of temporary inhabitants would descend on it – a pilot, the rangers involved, the recovery team, scientists to collect data, state veterinarians and invariably a few camp-followers in the shape of staff members' family or friends. There, but for occasional trips back to Skukuza or elsewhere, they would stay for an extended period until that particular part of the culling programme had been completed.

All culling camps had something in common, specifically things like toilets and showers, no matter where they were located – Pafuri, Magamba, Shipandani, Lonely Bull and Mondzo, to name a few – but some were more special than others. For me, one such was the Pafuri camp, because Pafuri was always one of my favourite places. The camp was put up on the bank of the Luvuvhu River, under some gigantic sycamore fig trees, and was particularly good for bird-watching, so everyone was always on the lookout for some rare bird species.

There were several reasons why we would camp out while

culling. The main aim was to get close to where the culling would take place. Another was to maintain as low a profile as possible, seeing that the helicopter and the large recovery trucks and tractors were always prime crowd-pullers; an additional, if unstated, reason was that it gave all hands an extra opportunity to get into the veld. We frankly enjoyed ourselves at these camps. The work was hard, messy, sometimes depressing and occasionally dangerous, but we ate well, shared in the veld's inexhaustible cornucopia of sights and sounds, and at night swapped scores of good stories around the fires – sometimes until very late. We paid for such late nights the next day, but nobody minded the price. True, we had the odd mishap here and there – one year Eric Wood, who headed the recovery team, cut his leg badly on a tamboti log at Magamba, near Punda Maria – but that sort of thing came with the territory, and in fact injuries worth remembering were surprisingly few, especially when you consider what we were up to.

If necessary we manufactured our own amusement. One of the best, as I recall, starred our pilot, Piet Otto. Piet, I might add, was a strange combination of qualities. On the one hand he was a maestro when it came to piloting an aircraft, which demands nerves of steel and superhuman calmness of decision in tight spots, especially in the sort of flying we had to do. On the ground, however, he was highly strung and liable to go off at an unexpected tangent when subjected to a sudden onset of the 'fight or flight' syndrome, which is never too far under the surface of the average Kruger-dweller with ambitions of reaching a ripe old age. A man of regular habits, Piet liked to start off his day with a spot of contemplation while sitting on the thunder-box, and on this particular morning he set off for the long drop as usual, cigarettes and a magazine in hand, to commune with nature. Well, that was the idea; but of course Murphy is never very far away in Kruger, and things went badly wrong almost as soon as Piet sat down. Specifically, he opened his magazine and lit a cigarette, dropping the match into the pit without bothering to blow it out. Next moment an almighty explosion rocked the loo to its precarious foundations; milliseconds later a miraculously unscathed Piet emerged from the door, having managed to work up a considerable turn of speed in a very short distance.

When the hysteria died down I set about investigating the cause of the explosion. Long drops have their disadvantages, as any former user would be the first to admit, but in general they are not prone to spontaneous explosions, so obviously something was very wrong. It didn't take me long to get to the bottom of the matter (pardon the unintentional pun). During the preparation process somebody had obviously written down the wrong item number on the acquisition form, because instead of the slaked lime required to keep the long drop reasonably civilised we had been issued with a drum of HTH swimming-pool chlorine. Nobody had noticed this, least of all the cleaner whose task it was to sprinkle the slaked lime into the pit at regular intervals, and so the swimming-pool chlorine resided in its noisome new home and quietly built up enough gas to disrupt Piet's early-morning routine.

No real damage was done, and in no time the toilet was once again being heavily patronised . . . except by Piet. His soul still bore the scars of the HTH incident, and for the next couple of days he answered the call of nature in a very literal way by strolling off into the bush, armed with the essentials for this sort of foray, a spade and a roll of toilet paper. There came the morning, however, when Piet headed for the toilet, the psychological scars clearly having healed. I regret to say that it was as if a mist passed over my eyes, and when it cleared I found myself stalking the unsuspecting long drop and its equally unsuspecting occupant as carefully as if I were coming up to a bull elephant in musth, clutching an old torch battery that had somehow materialised in my hand. I gave Piet enough time to get comfortably settled with cigarette in mouth and magazine in hand, then hurled the battery at the loo's corrugated-iron side. It hit like the crack of doom; Piet very naturally came instantly to the conclusion that the HTH was up to its former tricks and flew out of the door at a rate of knots, to be confronted by an audience consisting of virtually every living soul in the camp, all killing themselves laughing. Piet did not laugh, however. In fact he was distinctly annoyed. Talk about a bad start to your day!

*

As I noted earlier, we ate well at the culling camps. We harboured not a few handy bushveld cooks in our ranks, and this invariably gave rise to a competitive spirit. Each camp was preceded by some careful planning, and everyone brought cabin trunks full of food, spices and other ingredients which stood in the cooking area and could be dipped into by whoever was tending the pots on a particular day. Allow me to go even further and say that we not only ate well but sometimes gorged our way through meals so memorable that I can just about taste the food today, even though it has been less than dust for many years. I remember in particular the spread laid on for us one year by Peet Rossouw, a wildlife photographer tasked to produce a film on culling, and his wife Marianne. Peet had to travel to Phalaborwa or Louis Trichardt every week (he and Marianne always brought back bananas, which, along with milk and ProNutro, made up the standard bushveld fare for my infant son Robert) and this made him even more formidable an opponent in the cuisine wars. He returned from one of these trips with an entire sheep, minus the hindquarters, a bag of garlic, two litres of cream and a monstrously large piece of beef rump steak, as well as a steel cross about one and a half metres high. We were all vastly intrigued, of course, but asked no questions: we would find out soon enough, because he was down as the next day's cook and he was obviously planning some tremendous coup.

Next morning Peet got off to an early start. First he built a special cooking fire a little way from the main one and fed it with small pieces of wood rather than dragging a log across to it. When the fire was going to his satisfaction he tied the sheep to the iron cross, planted the sharp end of the cross in the ground about a metre from the fire and turned his attention to mixing his later-to-be-famous 'Asador' sauce in a mixing-bowl on the kitchen table (the name is a corruption of the Spanish 'asado', meaning 'cross', incidentally). Once he had the sauce the way he wanted it, he poured it into an empty one-litre Coke bottle and set it aside to mature. Marianne had got stuck into peeling the garlic while all this was going on. I was at a loose end until we went out on a reconnaissance flight a little later, so I pitched in to help her, seeing that it is always a good thing in principle to stay in the catering staff's good books, and we had finished about half of the Italian penicillin by the time I had to leave. Peet left us strictly alone during this time because he was concentrating on the meat, changing the angle of the cross from time to time while taking pains to keep the inside of the sheep exposed to the flames.

When I returned to the camp the area had been transformed. It looked the same, but there was a magnificent aroma wafting out from Peet's cooking fire, where he was anointing the sheep with liberal amounts of Asador sauce. A little later the rest of the team arrived and took up station around Peet like a bunch of hungry hyaenas waiting for an ailing buck to die. The mutton was not quite ready, so Peet kept the wolf (or hyaena) from the door by clamping a large slice of rump steak into a grill, flip-flopping it in the flames a couple of times and then serving it to us in thin slices on a plank with a generous topping of sauce. This was only the hors d'oeuvre, he explained with the false humility common to all great chefs. Would we care to test it?

We would, and did. We tested it so eagerly, in fact, that Peet dispensed with the plank and simply dumped each of the following steaks on the table, where we dealt with it in traditional fashion. I won't say we growled and squabbled over it like the average bunch of lions, but the spirit was more or less the same. When we had done with the rump the main course was ready. Peet cleared away the debris from the table and served the sheep piping hot with freshly baked bread and a salad on the side. The truth is that we weren't good for much that afternoon, and to this day the Bryden family regularly salutes that great occasion by bringing to its table the rump steak hors d'oeuvre and *mouton à la Peet*. In fact we have extended our culinary horizons and use the Asador sauce on chicken and fish as well.

Through sheer necessity all of us could prepare a reasonable meal on an open fire, with the emphasis on 'reasonable'. Any fool could make drinkable tea or coffee (although I have known individuals to fail even this elementary test of skill), but after that there was a sliding scale of difficulty, starting with grilling sausages and moving upwards through chops, stews and the odd pudding. What really separated the men from the boys, however, was baking pot bread. Your classic pot bread is baked in a black, flat-bottomed pot of cast iron sitting on an open fire. The dough may be prepared in various ways – there are probably as many recipes as there are bakers, ranging from beer bread (the easiest option) to traditional 'boer bread' recipes that use a yeast plant and have been passed down from one generation of a family to another for decades or even centuries.

Baking pot bread is deceptively simple at first glance. The dough is placed in the pot. The pot is placed on top of a few coals, and embers are piled on the lid to supply the downward heat that will brown the crust of the loaf. But there is much more to it than that. Estimates of the baking time and temperature are critical, since a fire obviously does not have luxuries like a thermostat or timer. Then again, little details can be important, like oiling the inside of the lid to make sure that the bread doesn't stick to it. This is delicate stuff, of course, and it is hardly surprising that on the whole the rangers' wives of my time were better at this sort of thing than their husbands. Of course, they had the advantage that the range of witnesses to their flops was confined to immediate family members, whereas a ranger in the bush always had a hungry and thus very critical and vocally uninhibited audience to contend with.

A notable exception to this rule was Gert Otto, otherwise known as 'Otch', who commanded the infantry battalion stationed in Kruger. Somewhere in the pursuance of his military duties he had become a very good bushveld cook, his speciality being pot bread. When it came to baking pot bread Otch was as good as any wife, and he knew it. But pride goeth before a fall, as the Bible says, and Otch was no more immune to the workings of Providence (or Murphy, depending on your persuasion) than the rest of us. I remember one Saturday afternoon when a batch of us were over at Otch's house in Skukuza, watching a rugby test match on TV. The results of the match were disappointing, with the Springboks going down to ignominious defeat, but we remained in good spirits because we had taken some medicinal doses of beer and rum and Coke, and knew that Otch was going to treat us to a braai afterwards. Naturally this included his famous pot bread, which had been rising since before the rugby and was duly placed on a bed of red bush willow embers at the right moment.

Secure in his mastery, Otch went about the other preparations until he got a telepathic flash from that great kitchen in the sky to tell him that his bread was done. He scraped the coals off the pot's lid and with fine flamboyance lifted it high above his head to reveal his latest masterpiece. To his utter befuddlement the pot was empty. He goggled at the indubitably empty belly of his faithful utensil and wailed: 'Where did my bread go?' His audience's response was not a cry of superstitious horror but a shriek of laughter. The bread hadn't evaporated, fled or been stolen; clearly Otch had forgotten to oil the underside of the lid, and so there the bread was, firmly stuck to it and dangling in mid-air about 10 inches above his head. It's as they say: the devil is in the details. You can be sure that Otch didn't neglect lid-oiling again.

Open-air cooking has changed in Kruger, as it has everywhere else in South Africa, with gas and Weber braais making big advances. But purists like me still prefer to use decent coals, be they mopane, red bush willow (rooibos), leadwood, or, at a push, charcoal – and may real bushveld cooking always remain synonymous with open fires. The boffins might say that this is not ecologically sustainable, but bush braais are not the problem, because they only make use of what has already been discarded. The real problem is the fact that there are just too many people over-using the scanty natural resources we have left. The so-called experts have not come up with any answer – the recent circus-like international congress on sustainable development in Johannesburg certainly didn't – because the causes of the problem lie elsewhere. Until they do come up with something, keep away from my Saturday afternoon braai, stranger.

As much a part of camp life as the food was the radio session at seven o'clock every morning. All rangers were expected to be at their sets, no matter where they happened to find themselves or what they were doing, because this was when the news and plans for the day were relayed. The radio sessions were a bit like the old party-line telephones, with every word you uttered being heard by everyone else, and so you had to be a trifle guarded in what you said. Naturally we all had the occasional slip, but not many of them were as embarrassing as the one that my colleague Louis Olivier made during a culling operation north of the Letaba. On this occasion Louis was sharing a tent with Noel Borehill, a stock inspector from the Department of Animal Health. For the sake of convenience Louis had rigged up his radio so that he could sign in without stirring from his blankets, and when someone asked where Noel was, Louis – who was obviously not thinking clearly yet – answered: 'Lying next to me in bed.' As can be imagined the radio waves were more or less clogged up by yowls of hyaena-like laughter for the next several minutes, and then and later Louis experienced the futility of explaining that of course he had meant to say 'lying in his bed next to mine in the tent'. Sometimes a man just has to accept that he is on the losing side of a battle, and this was undoubtedly one of those times.

The old-style culling camps faded out long before the culling operations were banished to the back burner by international opinion, their demise being brought about by Kruger's increasingly sophisticated guest facilities and road infrastructure. Instead of congregating at selected spots, culling teams operated from Skukuza; when the culling locations were far away, shooting took place from mid-afternoon onwards, with carcasses being brought to the processing plant after sunset to ensure that they stayed as fresh as possible. One unfortunate result, at least to my mind, was that staff members tended to sit around drinking tea at the restaurant during the day instead of being out in the veld. In my opinion it looked bad to have hordes of staff sitting around in apparent idleness in the rest camps, but on the other hand it was also true that under the old system members of the permanent culling team had had to spend months away from home every year. I didn't resist it, though; the world has been in a constant state of change since time began, and its denizens, whether human or animal, have to adapt to those changes. The fundamental law of the bushveld applies to all of us and everything we do: adapt – or die. But I am glad I had a good taste of the old camp lifestyle, and I can only feel myself privileged above my successors.

*

Coping with natural disasters, a commodity of which Africa has never had a shortage, was also part of the bushveld lifestyle. During my time in Kruger we experienced not only the highest temperatures since James Stevenson-Hamilton started keeping meteorological notes in 1912, but also the two most serious droughts and the second largest flood ever recorded, and it is difficult to describe the effect of all of these on ourselves and, more important, the environment in our care. For the average city-dweller a drought usually means restrictions on filling swimming pools; high temperatures can be dealt with by switching on the air-conditioning; and floods are more of a distant inconvenience seen on TV than anything else. For Kruger denizens like myself the perspective was somewhat different because we were right there in the belly of the beast, and no handy switch existed that could soften the impact of the nastiness or make it go away.

The two droughts I have mentioned came within a decade of one another. The first was in 1983/84, when Pafuri had the lowest annual rainfall (98 mm) ever recorded by any of Kruger's rainfall stations. During the second, in 1991/92, the mean annual rainfall for the park was 235.6 mm, only 44.1 per cent of the long-term mean. Each had serious effects on the environment and the animals, because the lack of rain not only reduced drinking water but also affected the vegetation off which the animals lived. February 1992, at the height of the second drought, was when temperatures soared to the highest ever recorded in Kruger. On 26 February the temperature in Skukuza was 45.6° C, but it was worse at Shingwedzi, where the thermometer showed 48° C that same day, an all-time record for the Park.

We were not unduly deterred by the high temperatures and played tennis as usual, but such sang-froid has no place in the worst of the range of natural disasters, floods. A drought is a creeping disaster that takes months and sometimes years to do its malign work, and the slowness of its pace allows one a little elbow-room to take counter-measures or at least save oneself. A flood is something else altogether. It is Nature in full battle array, striking swiftly and inflicting instant devastation, often on a scale that makes attempts by humans to ameliorate its effects look like the feeble things they are. My first personal recollection of a flood dates from early 1953, when I was staying with my grandparents in Johannesburg so that I could attend an English school, as my parents were still living on the farm in the Free State. One Friday morning my grandmother casually told me that I would not be going home that weekend as promised because the rivers were all in flood. This was a bit much for a four-year old to comprehend, but I understood things better when I saw that the tar road to our farm stopped at Vereeniging, about halfway there.

It wasn't until I got to Kruger, however, that I found out what heavy rains really meant, and I found out pretty soon. The summer of 1971, when I was living in Satara and working on my master's degree, brought an extended period of high rainfall that turned the ground underfoot into such a porridge that my old blue Land Rover, Betsie, actually bogged down right inside the Satara rest camp without any help from me – I woke up one morning and found that the old thing had sunk up to her axles in mud during the night. During that same period I made what seemed like an epic journey (little did I know what awaited me in the years ahead!) when Jan de Kock, the Satara district ranger at the time, called on me for help. Jan needed to know how much water there was in the Ngotsa Dam, about 22 kilometres away, but was temporarily without a 4x4 vehicle. Could I take him there to have a look? Blithely I said yes, unaware of what I was letting myself in for.

I soon found out. The tarmac road between the Sabie and Olifants rivers was still under construction at that stage, so Jan decided on an alternative route. This condemned us to an unending battle with the basaltic black turf between Satara and Ngotsa; the mud was so bad that the packed clay and grass constantly built up on the wheels till it was rubbing against the chassis. When that happened the only thing to do was to stop, take off the wheels and scrape away the mud. Then we would be all right – but only for a while, after which we would have to repeat the process. In this stop-and-start fashion we crawled along to Ngotsa . . . and found the dam was empty! So we turned around started crawling painfully back to Satara. By the time we got back to the rest camp we had spent the entire day on the road, and what we and Betsie looked like beggars description.

At the time this seemed like pretty rough stuff, but the 1971 rains were small beer compared to later ones. Like 1974, when Helena and I were living in Shipandani while our house at Mooiplaas was under construction (well, it was supposed to be under construction). I've described the effects of the 1974 floods on our holiday travels elsewhere in this book (see 'The Ladies – God Bless 'em'), but there was a lot more to it than that. The first morning of the floods I woke to what sounded like a strong wind blowing, although, strangely, there wasn't a breath of air in the hut, in spite of the fact that our windows had no panes or curtains and the door was made of nothing more substantial than gauze. Rather puzzled, I went outside. There was no air moving outside either, but I could clearly hear the big blow coming from the west – it had obviously just not reached us yet. Then I noticed that the ground was crawling with insects, all heading inland from the riverbed; it was clear that they knew that the mango and the fan were about to make close acquaintance.

Then the penny dropped. The Tsende River was coming down in flood, and the 'wind' was the sound of a wall of water heading towards us at breakneck speed. We watched with some apprehension as the water engulfed the banks we had become accustomed to seeing. Surely it was only a matter of time before everything we had was under water? We still had some leeway in hand, however – the camp's location had been deliberately chosen years earlier because it was reckoned a safe spot – so we made tea and watched the river's remorseless advance. Before too long the water was on three sides of us and we began to feel definitely nervous, but it never quite reached us. Another bushveld lesson learnt: listen to the old guys!

The floods became an almost daily occurrence, and this temporarily put paid not only to the building of the house at Mooiplaas but also to movement along all our supply routes: with no tarred roads and high-water bridges we were properly stuck. This was not an immediate problem for ourselves and the support staff, though: we had meat on the hoof, powdered milk, fowls that produced eggs and plenty of fish . . . if we could catch them, of course. I also had part of a jug of sweet wine made by Helena's grandfather from which I could take a slug at night to fend off the mosquitoes, although it was not as full as it had been. After three weeks of isolation, however, the sweet wine was finished and the food situation began getting to the critical stage. Helena was particularly badly off, because she was in the initial morning-sickness stage of pregnancy and couldn't face eating venison (although her enthusiasm for chocolate had not been similarly dampened).

I was too damn proud or hard-arsed – or both – to ask for a helicopter to drop supplies, and in the end I decided to drive to Mahlangeni with Helena and Corporals Amos Chongo and Sandros Matsimbi, borrow a rowing boat and then cross the Letaba River to the Letaba rest camp to buy supplies. If I could get there, of course, which was easier said than done. Mahlangeni is only 40 kilometres from Shipandani, but it took us all day because every stream along the way was flowing strongly; time and again we had to dig open the approaches, which had been eaten away or eroded by the flowing water. We also got stuck at more or less regular intervals. Contrary to what some people might think, even a 4x4 can bog down if conditions are bad enough, and then there is no way of getting it out again that does not involve back-breaking work with spades as the main tools. For traction we cut tree-branches and packed them under either the front or rear wheels (we were in four-wheel-drive mode all the way). Momentum being the secret of going through mud, we would charge into the long slushy patches in the road at relatively high speeds, which worked most times, but on occasions led to yet another bogging-down when our hard-gained speed carried us too far.

The next morning I used the last two teabags as well as the remainder of the powdered milk to make tea, while Helena whipped up a few fritters from our last two cups of flour, the remaining two teaspoonsful of baking powder and four eggs that the chickens had produced. That was just about it. Apart from some meat, the only thing left in our portable larder was a bottle of Angostura bitters, which was not very nutritious or filling. Obviously there was no other option but to row across the Letaba, as I had planned originally, although I had very scanty information about what to expect. I knew that the low-water bridge across the Letaba at Mingerhout was under water and that the Tsende Drift was still fordable, but the condition or passability of the roads between Shipandani and Letaba was a mystery. Having swallowed our paltry breakfast, the mapoisas and I loaded the boat on to my Land Cruiser, together with our bicycles so that if we got badly stuck we could cycle home and ask for the helicopter to help us. My plan was to use the tourist road for as far as I could get, then travel along a firebreak just north of the river until we were as close to Letaba as possible. There I would launch the boat, row across to the opposite bank, pick up fresh supplies and then go back the way I had come.

This seemed to be a sound enough plan of action, but it did not survive a reality check. The firebreak road was so overgrown that it was all but invisible; it was also badly eroded where the various spruits crossed it, so that we sometimes had to hoick out the picks and shovels to cover the worst ditches. We made reasonable progress, though, until I drove over the edge of a donga that was completely concealed by tall grass. The Toyota went nose down on to its right side into the donga, tipping everything in the back – bicycles, boat and, not least of all, Amos – into an untidy heap to one side. Sandros, who was sitting inside, landed on top of me and promptly went into a state of catatonic shock that put him completely out of action, even though neither of us was hurt. With some difficulty I finally managed to get his inert body off me so that I could crawl out through the passenger side-window. By now Amos had disentangled himself from the boat and bicycles, and between us we dragged Sandros out of the cab. This done, we inspected the Land Cruiser and found to our surprise that the damage it had sustained was minimal, so we unearthed the picks and shovels to start digging a way out of the donga. A couple of sweaty hours later we were free and heading for Letaba again. There we took the Land Cruiser as close to the river's edge as we could get and I launched and set off in the boat, the agreement being that Sandros and Amos would wait for my return.

At that point the river was at least 400 metres wide and flowing very swiftly, but I tackled it with reasonable confidence: I was about 500 metres upstream of the rest camp, and as a former school and university oarsman I knew how to row. My confidence was not misplaced, and I crossed the river without any problems . . . until I ran into a small herd of hippos inhabiting a placid side-stream near the rest camp. For some reason, or no reason, the herd took exception to my presence, and every time I tried to land one of the hippos would make its appearance in front of me. After what I had been through that day this interference failed to tickle my sense of humour. On the other hand, there wasn't anything I could do about it, so I persevered – watched, so I was told later, with bated breath by the camp staff and resident tourists – and eventually managed to land on the eastern edge of the camp.

I tied the boat to a tree, explained to the tourists what I was trying to do, apart from getting myself drowned, and was then carried off by Oom Dries Botha, the man who was supposed to be building the house at the Mooiplaas station. Oom Dries, a kindly soul, took me to the restaurant and treated me to a T-bone steak and a few beers. Now, I might very possibly be totally subjective about this, but my memory insists that that was the tastiest steak and the coldest beer I have ever had in a long career of consuming both. After that there remained only the task of taking my replete and rather more cheerful self to stock up on what we needed (not forgetting hamburgers and beers for Amos and Sandros, and chocolates for Helena) before setting off on the return journey. I had no trouble crossing back to the other bank, where a famished Amos and Sandros cried hosannas and leapt on their take-away meal. Then it was time for the slog back. Even this went relatively easily, and there were happy campers at Shipandani that evening – not least among them being Helena, who hadn't had a chocolate for three weeks.

With typical fickleness the river then subsided a couple of days later and we could cross via the Mingerhout Bridge, but that didn't last long, and soon the waters rose and marooned us for another three weeks. Near the end of the flood Corporal July Makuvele, who was stationed at Letaba at the time, returned from home-leave at Masangiri in Mozambique and tried to cross the Letaba by way of a low-water bridge – actually a causeway about 100 metres long – which was normally about a metre above the river's surface. This was a risky enterprise: the Letaba was flowing strongly and was so high that the bridge was at least a metre below the surface. Just to make it even riskier, there was a dam about 50 metres upstream that formed an effective barrier to fish movement, the result being that there were many crocodiles in the water. None of this deterred July, who might have been no taller than the average Grade 7 schoolgirl but had hardly a fearful bone in his body, so he waded in and was promptly swept off. Having managed to swim to the bank without ending up as a crocodile's lunch, he reported the bridge's non-functional status to Dirk Ackerman, then the district ranger at Letaba. In turn Dirk ordered me to go and see whether it had, in fact, been washed away.

Looking back now, I realise that there was actually no point to this. If the bridge had been damaged or washed away it could only have been repaired once the water had subsided, and the reconstruction couldn't be planned until then because it would not have been possible to determine the extent of the damage while the water was so high. Still, orders were orders, so I set off next morning with Helena, Amos and Sandros. Along the way we stopped off at Hatlane on the Letaba's bank to drop off Helena with Oom Jim Meiring and his wife Ellie while we were busy at the bridge. Oom Jim was supposed to be sinking boreholes as part of the intensive water-provisioning programme, but like everything else this had been temporarily kiboshed by the floods. So he and Aunt Ellie, who were accustomed to and prepared for anything, like all veteran bushvelders, were contentedly sitting it out in their caravan until the river subsided. The rest of us headed for the bridge. Our plan of action was not complicated. Amos and Sandros each had a long pole with which they would probe for damage to the bridge, while I would walk in the middle with my rifle to deal with any crocodile problems.

On arrival we took up our various tools and waded out on to the invisible bridge, with Amos, who was by far the smaller of the mapoisas, on the upstream side. The flow was powerful, but we leaned into it and made progress for a bit. Then Sandros lost his footing – probably as a result of the turbulence along the sides of the bridge – and went straight into the water. Amos promptly offered him the end of his pole, but when Sandros grabbed it he too lost his footing and fell in. I knew that neither Amos nor Sandros could swim, so there was no option for me but to jump in, rifle and all, and help them. By now both were in a blind panic, and did what non-swimmers in fear of drowning usually do – they clung to me like leeches. I knew we were in big trouble, and no mistake. I was fighting a losing battle: unencumbered I could have just held my own against the strong flow, but I was laden beyond my capacity.

What frightened me most, however, wasn't fear of drowning but of being taken by a crocodile; in between my struggles with Amos and Sandros I had spotted several heading upstream in an ominously determined fashion. Crocodiles are normally stealthy and low-profile when stalking a potential kill, but these ones made no bone about their intentions – they were forging up against the current like canoes, heads held high and bodies showing above the water. Anyone who doesn't believe in the dramatic effect of a surge of adrenalin should have seen me that day. For a moment I must have been as strong as an Olympic weight-lifter, because I rose out of the river like a veritable bushveld Poseidon and flung myself back on to the bridge with the greatest of ease, rifle, sodden clothing, mapoisas and all. When the crocs saw this they changed their minds and pushed off. So did we. We'd had quite enough excitement for the day.

The Meirings and Helena were having tea and home-made biscuits when I joined them, a good deal earlier than expected and in considerably more bedraggled condition than should have been the case. I don't normally have much of a sweet tooth, but what I had just been doing certainly wasn't normal, and in any case I hadn't had one of Aunt Ellie's wonderful 'koekies' for ages, so I not only made some inroads on the plate of biscuits on the table but put a few in my pocket in the grand old South African tradition of taking padkos – food for the road – on any journey. On the way home I hauled out one of the biscuits and offered it to Helena, who was not grateful but furious. Now, she said, she understood why the plate of home-mades had emptied so fast! She gave me a quick bollocking about bad manners and then insisted that I take them back. I explained why this was not an option, so she bowed to the inevitable and helped me to eat everything I had filched. This just proves that ideally a bushveld wife should be a bit philosophical about life's twists and turns.

*

After the floods subsided the Mooiplaas house could finally be built for us, and the Pioneer Dam was later constructed in the Tsende River just upstream from Shipandani. But then in 1976 Cyclone Emily brought new floods which washed away both the dam and, for good measure, our rickety first home at Shipandani. As I've noted elsewhere, both the dam and the Shipandani camp have been rebuilt. But there's always a next time . . . and in the Kruger National Park 'never again' is the sort of phrase that tends to return and bite you in the backside.

In 1984 two other cyclones, Demoina and Imboia, got the rivers going. This time my family and I were not personally affected to any great extent, and afterwards life went back to its normal rhythm. But it was literally the calm before the storm, because the grandfather of all floods was still to come, although not until more than a decade had passed. Just before Christmas of 1999 the Hazyview and Sabie areas were plunged into chaos by two enormous thunderstorms, and on New Year's Eve the millennium celebrations at Skukuza were dampened, so to speak, by another thunderstorm of such magnitude that by a quarter to three that afternoon it was pitch black both outside and inside the houses. But worse was to come. A few days later a similar storm hit the Pretoriuskop area and the Mtshawu River came down in flood, taking out the bridge on the Doispane road and topping up the Sabie.

The heavy rains lasted into January 2000 and left Kruger's soil saturated and its rivers full, a recipe for future disaster. Then in the first fortnight or so of February many areas in the Northern Province, Mpumalanga and the Highveld catchments of the Limpopo and Olifants Rivers experienced heavy rainfalls and severe floods; 630 mm fell at Graskop, 612 mm at Levubu, and 593 mm at Tzaneen (Grenshoek). More heavy rain also fell at Hazyview and Pretoriuskop. The reason for such an extended period of heavy rain was the unusual southward extension of an equatorial trough and the passage of a tropical depression from Beira southwards to the Limpopo River and westwards in Botswana. That was the science of the matter. The hands-on effect for the likes of the Kruger rangers was much more dramatic and much more uncomfortable.

We soon felt the effect of the rains. On the morning of 7 February, a Monday, we all went to work as usual. The 'usual' part of the equation ended abruptly at 8 am, however, when we got word that that big water was on its way. Helena and some of the research staff immediately drove to the low-water bridge over the Sabie to see the not-so-common event. They were still there when they heard that the water was already over the high-water bridge at the Kruger Gate. I knew nothing of any of this because I had been entangled in a meeting since early morning, but when Helena got back she let me know, and of course it was something we (not to mention just about everybody else in Skukuza) simply had to see. On our way to the Kruger Gate we found that the Nwaswitshaka River, which had long since covered the low-water bridge between the rest camp and the personnel village, was already topping the decks of the high-water bridge on the Kruger Gate tourist road, the first time this had happened since its construction in the early 1970s. All this from a spruit with a catchment area of less than 500 square kilometres!

After watching this unusual spectacle for a while we moved on to the Kruger Gate to see the Sabie River rising, although there was a chance that we might not be able to get back to our offices and homes on the other side. Fascinated, we watched as the boiling, stinking brown water started to flow over the 70-metre-long bridge, while enormous trees on the banks toppled over and were immediately rolled away by the force of the river. Before long the water was lapping at the thatched eaves of a house across the river in Sabie Park. In our hearts we all knew that a tragedy was in the making, and we weren't wrong.

As always an amusing interlude appeared to light up the gloom, when a baboon came down the river, riding a log that somehow did not roll over. A solitary branch stuck out vertically, for all the world like a short mast on a ship, and the baboon clung to it with all his might, uttering a stream of baboon-talk – one assumes to a ghostly crew of other baboons which had been washed off the log during an earlier part of the journey. When the log hit the bridge – which was awash with water and debris by this time – the baboon made a flying leap for the guard-rail and headed west at top speed. When he noticed the crowd of sightseers in his path he did a rapid about turn and headed east. Here another crowd of sightseers awaited him, but by now the baboon had obviously abandoned the niceties of bush behaviour and went at them like an express train. The crowd parted like the Red Sea before Moses and the baboon ran straight through, cheered on by the more sporting types and with sighs of relief from everybody else that he had made it.

We couldn't stay at the Kruger Gate for long because we were worried about getting back over the Nwaswitshaka, so we headed back to the offices, only to find that the Nwaswitshaka Bridge was now so deeply under water that an ordinary road vehicle could not be risked. Then someone arrived with a Land Cruiser, which is higher on its wheels, and movement was resumed. I didn't go with the rest; I wanted to see how things were going in Skukuza village. This was the right decision, because all was definitely not well. The village was now totally cut off, and because most of us had gone to work that morning without any intimations of disaster, the helicopter had to be pressed into service for one ferry trip after another. The rain kept falling intermittently while all this was going on, and it was clear that things were very likely to get worse before they started improving. Staff members who lived along the Sabie and Nwaswitshaka had already started moving their furniture to higher ground, or at least out of harm's way – although not always very logically. One woman who lived right next to the river heard about the possibility of a major flood and immediately moved her very expensive bedroom suite to a bedroom on the other side of the house, which was about as useful as mammary glands on a bull, because both bedrooms were at exactly the same level.

It was soon clear that our worst expectations were going to come true. All able bodies started pitching in to help friends to rescue their possessions, while the water kept rising inexorably and sent before it all manner of unwelcome refugees to complicate matters even further. Literally millions of many-legged creepy-crawlies advanced on the rescuers, not to mention a small army of snakes. If a snake managed to find a dry spot, and the dry spot happened to be someone wading through stinking chest-deep black water with a TV set on his head, that was just his tough luck. Fortunately none of the snakes could spare the time to sink their fangs into anybody, but some of the insects were less inhibited about literally biting the hands that inadvertently rescued them.

One of the houses to vanish under the floodwater was the residence of the Park Director, David Mabunda. The gardener was so conscientious about trying to rescue his employer's possessions that he overstayed his welcome and ended up perched on the roof, shouting for help. Research Officer Danie Pienaar, JJ van Altena of the game capture team and my son Robert, who was doing day walks in Skukuza at the time, rescued him in a little boat whose only means of propulsion consisted of one oar and a keep net.

A major cause of Skukuza village's problems, then and later, derived from the fact that the strong flow of the Sabie blocked the Nwaswitshaka and dammed it up. When the pressure became too great the Nwaswitshaka burst its banks and exploded through another part of the town, flooding more homes and also the doctor's surgery, taking with it all the medical records and everything else that wasn't cemented or bolted down. The water kept rising until about five o'clock and then went down almost as quickly as it had come up in the first place. Now we could assess the damage, and it was staggering. No less than 65 living units were under water; so was the surgery, a large part of the rest camp, including the shop and restaurant, and the school. The school suffered particularly heavy damage. Some of the classrooms had been completely swept away, and one large tree on the bank of the Nwaswitshaka next to the low-water bridge was so plastered with papers washed out of the classrooms that for weeks afterwards it looked more like a Christmas tree than anything else. Many houses were submerged up to roof level, although luckier householders had to contend with only a few inches of water, but for practical purposes the depth of water didn't matter so much as the fact that habitation was impossible and precious possessions and documents had been damaged, totally ruined or lost. Sometimes the losses were devastatingly personal: family photographs, not only old ones but the pictorial record of the household's children growing up – the first baby smile, birthdays, holidays and weddings – all gone forever.

Everybody pitched in to help their colleagues and sometimes themselves. All empty accommodation was made available and emergency park homes were brought in. Some people shared their houses with friends and the community hall was pressed into service as a temporary school, while a soup kitchen was set up and for about three weeks fed the homeless. Slowly Skukuza started to get up off its knees, and after about a week many residents were able to start moving back to their devastated houses, often living in caravans in their own backyards while they restored some semblance of order. Now we could count the cost – and our blessings. In spite of everything there had been no loss of life, a small miracle in itself; it was agreed that the effects of the flood would have been much worse if it had happened during the night. But the general mood stayed sombre for weeks, with those personally unaffected by the flood sharing the anguish of close friends who had lost so many precious things.

Skukuza wasn't the only place to suffer that day. The Crocodile River, the southern boundary of the park, also burst its banks, flooding many houses on the riverbank and part of Crocodile Bridge rest camp as well. The damage here was negligible in comparison to Skukuza's, but there were some tense hours for the resident ranger, Johan van Graan, and his wife Kotie: they stayed awake the whole night in fearful anticipation of their house and everything in it being submerged, but to their great relief the water subsided before rising any higher than the front step.

The flooding went on throughout February, fed by the enormous amounts of rain that fell during most of the month. The villain of the piece was Cyclone Eline, which started as a tropical disturbance more than 2 500 kilometres east of Mauritius and then moved towards the coast and inland, so that by 23 February it was about 200 kilometres southeast of Harare. By now Eline was weakening, but heavy rainfalls were recorded all over the northern parts of South Africa, Zimbabwe and southern Botswana until 25 February, and were to continue in Botswana and Namibia up to the end of the month. Four rain stations in Mpumalanga and Limpopo provinces – at Graskop, Tzaneen, Levubu and Thohoyandou – received more than 1 000 millimetres of rain during February, and the several rivers that had begun to subside started rising back to flood level. This time the worst culprits were the ones in the north of the Kruger National Park – the Limpopo, Luvuvhu, Shingwedzi, Letaba and Olifants. The most serious damage was probably to the approaches to the bridge across the Letaba and Sirheni camp, which was under water, but at Pafuri, four kilometres from the Limpopo, the cells of the police station had to be evacuated to save various miscreants from the water, which eventually filled them up to the ceilings.

The effect of the floods was spectacular. The approaches of both of the two big bridges across the Sabie were washed away, the riverbeds were scoured out to bedrock and their vegetation vanished downstream, and thousands of trees growing on the banks fell victims to the roiling waters. Scientists regard this kind of phenomenon as beneficial because it is part of the natural rejuvenating process, but the people who have to suffer the consequences tend to take a less detached view. Yet we in Kruger were the lucky ones, although we didn't know it then and any such statement would likely have earned the maker of it a punch in the mouth. But that's how it was: the worst of the disaster was in Mozambique, where more than half a million people were left homeless. It was so bad that satellite photographs showed the almost unbelievable sight of the Limpopo and Komati river systems flowing into each other, although the Limpopo enters the Indian Ocean at Xai-Xai and the Komati just north of Maputo, about 100 kilometres away.

As we counted the cost there was a general belief that this had been the worst flood in Kruger's history, but we were wrong when we compared it with the flood of 1925 which James Stevenson-Hamilton described so graphically in his book *The*

334

Lowveld, Its Wild Life and Its People. Stevenson-Hamilton had given specific facts about the height of the water below the railway bridge during the 1925 flood, and there was no doubt about which had been the greater of the two. What made the difference, as far as damage is concerned, was that in Stevenson-Hamilton's time there had been no infrastructure near the river except for his garden. At least two retired Kruger employees remembered that when Stevenson-Hamilton heard that huts and houses were being built on the banks of the Sabie River he warned the then Director that he was looking for trouble because the area was prone to flooding.

Stevenson-Hamilton knew what he was talking about; after all, he had been Warden of Kruger for a staggering 46 years. Naturally no one listened to him, and so eventually a heavy price had to be paid.

I've said it before, I'll say it again: 'Listen to the old guys.'

17

ALL PEOPLE,
GREAT AND SMALL

It takes all types to make a world, all right – and sooner or later at least one of each surfaces in the Kruger National Park. That was how it was in my years there, and I don't expect it's going to change any time soon. Kruger's attractions draw people from all walks of life, whether to sightsee or work, and the bushveld is one of the last places where individuality is still tolerated (or perhaps 'ignored' is a better word). Add to that the fact that what is now the Kruger National Park has always had plenty of people passing through on the way to somewhere else, and it is inevitable that I encountered a rich mix of unusual personalities in my time there and can foresee the same thing happening to all my successors. Some were humans, others went on all fours, like Kees, the inebriate baboon of my Ramkamp days (see 'The Bushveld Lifestyle'). Whichever their mode of locomotion, each of them had a unique personal style that makes them stand out in my memories.

The type of rangers and other staff members has changed. These days most have been career conservationists since entering adulthood, but during my time, especially in the early stages, rangers in particular tended to be retreads, in the sense that they had had other careers, sometimes quite unusual ones, before they realised what they really wanted to do and managed to find the right place to do it in. This hard core of varied life experience and ingenuity bred of hardship was one of Kruger's greatest strengths in the hard days of war and want on its eastern boundary. And this didn't apply only to the rangers.

Claude Berteaux, the helicopter pilot who got me safely to the ground in the first of my bad landings (see 'Adventures with Wings and Wheels'), was a prime example of a Kruger retread of the 1970s. Belgian by birth, Claude had a colourful career behind him by the time he became Kruger's first in-house helicopter jockey, including a stint as personal pilot to Moishe Tshombe in the wild days when the former Belgian Congo fell into a state of civil war a month after independence in 1960. Tshombe, strongman of the Congo's copper-rich Katanga province, decided to secede, and to make it stick he recruited mercenaries for his air and ground forces. Claude was among the many South Africans, Belgians, Frenchmen and others who flocked to Tshombe's rebel banner out of a thirst for adventure or money or both, and his tales of the half-tragic, half-comic episode that followed before Tshombe was forced to yield made good telling around campfires. Nowadays mercenaries are frowned on, but Africa was different in those days, and its new leaders had no hesitation about using hired guns.

One of Claude's stories was about how he and his colleagues of Tshombe's tiny makeshift air force manufactured backyard aerial bombs. They would jam grenades with their pins pulled into beer glasses so that the arming levers stayed in place, then pack the glasses into boxes and drop them over the target. On impact the boxes would break and so would the glasses, thus releasing the arming levers and causing a good-sized explosion which, at the very least, had a paralysing psychological effect on the recipients. Claude also had a genuine appetite-killer that he liked to trot out at the worst possible time. Cannibalism was an old tradition in the Congo, he would point out, so much so that the locals did not make any secret of their liking, and apparently they assumed that everybody else enjoyed the same gourmet tastes. That was how he had once come to a succulent piece of meat, only to be told, when he asked what it was, that he had been eating a piece of somebody's cheek.

Despite experiences like this – or perhaps because of them – Claude was an expert and enthusiastic chef in his spare time. His speciality was using elephant meat to make the most magnificent steak tartare, which, having an evil sense of humour like the rest of us, he delighted in serving to unsuspecting diners without telling them where it came from. Claude was particularly happy if the diners, having consumed everything on offer (and preferably having enjoyed seconds as well), asked him what sort of meat he had used. Then would come the denouement; quite often the diners would turn slightly green and, if we were particularly lucky, immediately heave it all up again, I know this makes us sound pretty awful, but there was no malice in our rough games, and usually no offence was taken once the victims had recovered.

This is not to say that sometimes the food didn't bite back. One day he was travelling to his home in Skukuza in his enormous black and white Dodge Monaco when he ran over a francolin. Ever conscious of the value of good food, he put the deceased bird in his boot with his dirty washing and carried on. He must have been in an abstracted frame of mind, however, because by the time he arrived he had totally forgotten about both the francolin and the washing. Next morning his wife asked him to bring in his dirty clothes, and when Claude opened the boot, the alleged corpse shot out with a typical ear-splitting francolin scream that so startled the hero of the Katanga secession that he tripped over his own feet and ended up on his backside. It took him a while to live that one down.

One of the home-grown characters I worked with was Johan Steyn, and I mustn't omit to add a sub-character – the pipe that never seemed to leave his mouth. We spent a lot of time together, and over a period of years shared many almost magical experiences. I was still pretty green when we first met, and he taught me a lot, being a very experienced ranger who had even worked at the Etosha reserve in what was then South West Africa under the legendary Peter Starke.

Like many other rangers, Johan was very possessive about his section, and nobody, but *nobody*, was allowed to do anything on his patch without his being present. Once, I remember, we were culling lions in his section and needed a buffalo for bait. Any one of us could have collected the buffalo, but Johan insisted on doing it himself. His reasoning was that if a buffalo ended up wounded in his section he would have to bear the responsibility. The real reason, of course, was that Johan didn't like anyone else shooting his game, large or small. Johan eventually returned with the buffalo, and to our delight we saw that one of its hind feet had been shot off – as perfect an opportunity to pull his leg as ever presented itself. But Johan insisted that he hadn't; when he had taken his first shot, he said, the buffalo had turned so fast that its foot had fallen off by itself. That was his unlikely story, and he stuck to it. We finally stopped ragging him. This, after all, was the respected veteran Johan Steyn of Etosha. Strange things happened in the bush; perhaps the buffalo really *had* shed one entire foot on a tight turn. But, with all due love and respect, I have to admit that it is a dodgy story. Still, it shows what sort of a man he was, since just about anybody else would have been laughed out of countenance.

Johan was also a stickler for good bush manners. The same day that he came back with the footless buffalo he spotted one of the members of the culling team relieving himself within the general boundaries of the camp. What exactly the camp boundaries were was somewhat vague, given the circumstances, but Johan was deeply offended. He immediately declared the person a 'werf-kakker' ('yard-shitter' in Afrikaans) and went on and on about his lack of camp etiquette. The person concerned, who shall remain nameless, maintained a respectful silence while Johan ranted on, mistakenly interpreting the newly christened defiler's suppliant attitude as remorse and acquiescence; in fact the defiler, who had more little devils in him than there are sparks in hell, was already plotting a suitable response which was not long in coming. As soon as Johan left the defiler mixed up a ghastly-looking paste out of instant coffee-powder and water, smeared it on to a length of toilet paper and semi-buried it in the earth next to Johan's stretcher in such a way that it remained very visible. Johan's reaction when he returned was, to put it mildly, volcanic, and he was so incensed, particularly when no one would own up to turning his tent into a toilet, as he put it, that he upped sticks and moved his personal camp a good five kilometres away from the lion-cullers.

The dawn of the aerial survey era was painful for Johan, who was prone to motion sickness but naturally did not use this as an excuse to shirk his duties. I remember once when, as the section ranger of Nwanetsi, he was required to be part of a fixed-wing aerial survey being carried out there. This was tougher than it might sound. The team would spend anything from two to five hours a day flying in parallel legs 800 metres apart at an altitude of 65 metres, and the thermals from the ground made things so bumpy that it felt (as one memorable phrase had it) as if the light aircraft had square wheels. The surveys were normally split into two sessions with a refuelling break in between, and during one such pause Johan clambered to earth in a distinctly dodgy state. His antidote for the trouble behind his belt buckle was to eat a toasted ham, cheese and tomato sandwich, washed down with a container of grape juice (being Johan, he also complained about the price, but that was par for the course). It was not, frankly, a very good essay at self-medication, and after the first leg of the second session an internal revolt put everything he had eaten back into the bag. Filled with the false relief that one feels after a first puking session (we always seem to forget that there is more where that came from, just waiting for an excuse to make a dash for freedom) Johan prepared to dump the bag out of the window. Research Officer Butch Smuts, who had been watching Johan's dolorous progress, spotted an opportunity that (so he thought) was too good to miss and called: 'Hey, Johan, you can't do that. At least give me the big pieces of ham first!' This was more than the veteran of the Namib could bear; and he painted his immediate surroundings with everything else he'd eaten in the past 24 hours with such dreadful thoroughness that we had to land and clean up the cabin. So it is possible that, thanks to Johan's stomach and Butch's ill-timed humour, the day's count was slightly off.

When the motorcycle era arrived in Kruger (see 'Adventures with Wings and Wheels) Johan was allocated one, which presented a certain problem stemming from the fact that he was a bakkie man, first and foremost, and had never bestridden a motorbike in his life. I was delegated to teach him the art, and in due course had him sitting on his iron horse, pipe in mouth as usual. As my opening move I suggested that, just for the moment, the pipe might be better off in his pocket. Not a damn, Johan said. Wherever he went, so did the pipe. The average instructor might well have balked at this, but I knew better than even to try, and so Johan and his smoking apparatus qualified simultaneously. And he was no Luddite, mind you: in no time he was tooling around in front of the conservation offices, smoke trailing behind him as if he were a two-wheeled locomotive. I had a mental image of a weathered Hell's Angel who had swapped his leather lummie for a khaki shirt, but I said nothing: Johan wouldn't have seen the likeness, even if he had known what I was talking about.

Poor Johan . . . one of the worst experiences in my life was having break the news to him that his son had died – and, less than 48 hours later, his uncle as well, his greatest friend. Johan never fully recovered from this tragic double blow; his life fell to pieces and he died a broken man, long before his time.

Then there was Nick de Beer, the white Shangane. In addition to possessing a sparkling infectious laugh that could bring a smile to even the most sour face, Nick had an encyclopaedic knowledge of the Shangane tribe's customs and folklore, in addition to being a truly fluent speaker of its language, Tsonga, a rare thing among non-Shanganes, white or black.

One morning Dirk Ackerman and I were interviewing an applicant for a ranger's post, at the very time when a protracted conversation in Tsonga was in progress in Nick's office next door. Nick's fellow conversationalists were engaged in spinning a convoluted tale of grievance, a not unusual occurrence because Nick was in charge of the Skukuza village staff living quarters and was also responsible for the well-being of the support staff. Dirk obviously also overheard this conversation, because he nudged the interview towards the subject of knowledge of tribal languages. I could see the way things were going and tried to change the direction of the conversation, but Dirk wasn't having any, and his next question to the interviewee was, 'Can you tell which person in the discussion next door is white?' At this point the spinners of the long yarn came to the end of their tale, and I knew what was going to happen: Nick would put his hands behind his head, rock back in his chair and have the last word in the discussion. Which would be a dead giveaway, seeing that Shanganes do not normally terminate long conversations in their own language with an emphatic 'bullshit!' And that's exactly the way it happened.

Nick had a most unfortunate personality quirk for one whose chosen place of work was the Kruger National Park, namely a deep phobia about spiders. Flesh and blood would have found it unbearable not to trade on this, and so Nick tended to be subjected to the appropriate practical jokes. In a sense it was his own fault because he always responded so well to them. Anyway, one day somebody gave me a magnificent hairy black plastic spider which I knew would freak Nick out completely, and from there everything went straight downhill. Dirk and I waited till Nick was away from his office and then rigged up a little surprise for him. His telephone was on a table to the right of his office chair and slightly behind it, so we tied my spider to the receiver with nearly invisible fishing line and left it to hang next to the telephone table: the idea was that when Nick next answered the telephone the spider would swing around and land in his face.

Dirk and I waited for Nick in the parking lot and then followed him at a distance, and the gods of misrule were smiling on us that day, because as he entered his office the telephone rang. Hurriedly Nick sat down behind his desk and grabbed the telephone's receiver, and sure enough, as he was about to utter a greeting the spider landed on his face. Nick reacted so violently that he overturned his desk, spilling everything on it to the various corners of the office, then departed in a cloud of non-biblical vocalisation. I went into the office to see if any real damage had been done. There hadn't, although it looked as if a bomb had gone off, but from the receiver dangling on the end of its cord I could hear a voice asking: 'Nick! Nick! Are you all right?' I assured the lady at the other end that he was, explaining that we had just helped him to make the acquaintance of a spider. She was distinctly unamused and said so, so that Dirk and I were filled with remorse that must have lasted at least two seconds. When Nick finally returned he wasn't amused either, but, as Dirk always said, if you want to run with the big dogs, you have to learn to pee high. There is a bit of a tear behind this laugh, though: it was Nick's wife Kotie who was later killed by a leopard in Skukuza village.

*

Kruger's baboons definitely qualify as characters. For most people, ranger staff not excluded, there is something peculiarly beguiling about a baboon, and vice versa; in former times there was hardly a farmhouse in South Africa that did not have a baboon perching on a pole. Perhaps it's simply that baboons are human-like enough to strike a certain chord, or it might be no more than the fact that almost everyone knows someone else who looks or acts like a baboon, give or take small differences like a sickle tail and terrible table manners; not to mention their dreadful habit of fouling themselves and their surroundings if they become agitated. Whatever the case, interactions between Kruger's baboons and tourists – usually to the detriment of the latter and the amusement of the staff – were a regular feature during my career there, no matter how much visitors were warned not to get to close quarters with the animals.

On one occasion a family of tourists in a big white Cadillac 'invited' a baboon into their car with the aid of some tasty morsels. This was bad enough – feeding the animals is strictly a no-no – but then they made the mistake of closing all the windows. The baboon didn't like this, tried to get out and couldn't, and so did what a baboon in such a situation normally does: it anointed everyone and everything inside the car with the contents of its bowels. This was more than enough reason for the doors to be flung open, allowing the baboon to make its escape. The tourists didn't realise how lucky they were; a baboon is not very large, but it's disproportionately strong and can inflict fatal injuries with its large fangs and long nails. In any case, the family headed for the ranger's house at Tshokwane in their luxurious but now very smelly car to have it washed, only to encounter another hostile local inhabitant in the shape of the resident ranger, who was famous for his irritability with tourists who insisted on illegally feeding the animals. The ranger wasted no time in telling them to get the hell out of his garden and have their car washed somewhere else, which happened to be Skukuza, a good 40 kilometres away. It must have been a fast and unpleasant journey.

Tourists of a slightly different kind were Roger Moore and Lee Marvin, who found themselves in Kruger for the filming of 'Shout at the Devil', one of the best of Wilbur Smith's many engrossing novels. No doubt most people see the novels only as a good read, but in my opinion they're actually chronicles of episodes in Africa's later history that the textbooks don't seem to bring to light in an interesting way, if at all. Many of them are set in the bushveld and are quite accurate in their details, which is hardly surprising if one remembers that Smith is a keen hunter/conservationist. 'Shout at the Devil' was set in East Africa and concerned the adventures of a disreputable elephant hunter/poacher, Flynn Patrick O'Flynn (a role tailor-made for Marvin, needless to say) and his disgraced but rather gormless partner, Sebastian Oldsmith (tailor-made, in turn, for Moore). East Africa or no, the film had some elephant scenes and Kruger was engaged in culling elephant, so the necessary wangling took place at higher level (so I assume), because next thing the entire film crew invaded my life at Letaba.

Willy-nilly I found myself knee-deep in the world of show business, especially when, to the great enjoyment of Helena and my colleagues, I was made Roger's stunt double, complete with white linen suit and Panama hat. I can't say that I was required to show any great dramatic talent – mainly I had to kill elephants on some occasions and run away from them on others, as required by the director and his cameraman – but Roger certainly was grateful that it was Bruce-Sebastian handling the close-up conversations with the big ones and not Roger-Sebastian.

There was nothing plum-in-the-mouth about Lee, a battle-hardened former US Marine of World War II vintage who was a wild man all the time and didn't act so much as play a slightly exaggerated version of himself before the cameras. He was sloshed to a great or lesser degree most of the time, whether in front of the cameras or not. Lee was suffering from flu or some similar ailment that generated large amounts of phlegm. So whenever he felt the need he would hoick up a wad which, judging by the sound effects, had had to be retrieved from somewhere near his ankles, and deposit it on the nearest mopane tree; an impressive, if stomach-turning, performance about which his fans never heard. He too had a stunt double, a fellow named Larry whom I saw later in a whisky advertisement, although I don't think he particularly needed one – merely breathing on the average elephant would probably have been enough to bring it to its knees. But on that sort of multi-million-dollar production you didn't take chances.

Like all film shoots, this one was a strange mixture of make-believe and reality. One scene, for example, required Sebastian to shoot an elephant, after which he and O'Flynn had to walk up to it. Because of the close-ups of the two at the elephant, Larry and I were stood down while Roger and Lee did it themselves, and there was a certain amount of nervousness in the ranks of the production team about the chances of one or both of their stars ending up as flat as a Bushman painting. No sweat! Near Mooiplaas I darted an elephant, which went down nicely on cue when Roger fired his blank, and then the entire crew followed Roger and Lee as they approached the 'kill'. Out of the frame, of course, was Bryden-Bryden (as opposed to Bryden-Moore), rifle in hand, in case the elephant got inspired by the fuss and woke up too soon. It didn't, and a couple of 'takes' later we were happily on the way back to the Letaba, while the elephant, having got a shot of wake-up juice, was somewhat less happily on the way to heaven-knows-where.

As an ex-marine Lee was familiar with real firearms, but like most Americans of that era he had never fired a rifle built for the sort of dangerous big game found in Africa. His prop rifle was a very good .450/400, which in today's terms would be more or less the equivalent of a double-barrelled .416 Remington, and he wanted to know what sort of recoil it would have in real life so that he could simulate it during filming. I was only too happy to show him and produced my back-up rifle, a .458 Magnum. The inside of the barrel was well-oiled, and I wanted to run a couple of patches through it before we fired, because there is nothing like an oily barrel to turn a stiff kick – which the .458 has – into something ferocious. Lee couldn't be bothered, and when he fired the .458 it rattled the fillings in his teeth. He lowered the rifle, wiped the tears from his eyes, fingered his bruised cheekbone and delivered his verdict: 'My Gawd,' he said, 'that's *something*!' That .458 was a real spoiler for Lee; when he took up his prop .450/400, which obviously was loaded with blanks and scarcely squeaked when he pulled the trigger, he said disgustedly: 'What sort of pissin' thing have you given me here?'

Watching those two consummate professionals in action was a real education; one thing I discovered was that if they had to do a retake of a scene the dialogue was never exactly the same words. Nobody worried about it. They knew the story and wouldn't say anything that didn't fit in, so if they ad-libbed some of it to fit their mood of the moment, why complain? What really impressed me, though, was the fact that between shooting the two stars and some other members of the crew would play poker at R10 a chip, wetting their whistles with top-grade Grand Mousseaux and smoking genuine Cuban Hoyo de Monterrey cigars at R50 apiece. In these times of a sadly devalued rand that might not sound a lot, but at the time it was worth most of one pound sterling – and I was earning less than 300 smackers a month!

Of course everybody wanted to meet these two, such totally contrasting characters in every way, and one day, while Helena was pushing our little daughter Annie (then just a few months old) through the camp in a pram she bumped into Roger, Lee and myself. I did the necessary introductions, and Roger, always appreciative of female pulchritude, simply had to pick Annie up. Annie was normally a friendly child, but took one look at Roger and screamed blue murder. Lee took this in with sardonic amusement and then rasped in the celebrated Marvin style: 'Hey, Roger, my boy, you must be losing your touch with the ladies.' Or at least with one young lady who didn't like to speak to strangers, even a handsome and friendly one with a world-famous name.

Over the years we became quite blasé about the dignitaries of various kinds who came calling at Kruger. Most of them turned out to be fairly ordinary people in close-up, but some were just the reverse. One of the most amazing and unforgettable of the latter was Sir Laurens van der Post, whom I met for the first time in 1974 when I took him to Pafuri. Sir Laurens became many things – soldier, writer, novelist, philosopher, bushveld sage – during the incredible journey through life that took him from Eastern Cape farmer's lad to confidant of the heir to the British throne. He touched the hearts of most people who knew of him through his stories about Bushmen and Africa, but his greatest ability was to predict the future. At the end of the Pafuri trip he gave me a signed copy of his book *A Far-Off Place*, a prophecy about southern Africa at the dawn of the millennium, which is still one of my most treasured possessions. Our paths crossed again a number of times in the ensuing years, because he never forgot us, and would call or drop in whenever he made one of his frequent trips to Kruger. A one-of-a-kind man, sure enough, and you don't meet many of that breed.

All Kruger rangers, past and present, would surely count their dogs as major personalities in their lives. The bushveld is a hard and very dangerous place for a ranger's dog, and few of them live to their natural span – crocodiles and leopards are their principal enemies – but they are as much a part of a ranger's life as the rifle he carries . . . and, like the rifle, might well save his life at one time or another. Then again, they provide the uncritical companionship that we all crave, especially if a ranger, as was the case with so many of the early ones, lived a solitary and isolated life. These days each ranger is allowed to keep only two dogs, but in former times there was no restriction, and some rangers maintained whole working packs. Harry Wolhuter once admitted to keeping 25, but the record probably belongs to Major Affleck Fraser, whose pack reached a high of 26 and who was obviously an extreme believer in the 'man's best friend' philosophy, to judge by one of Wolhuter's reminiscences.

Wolhuter once slept over with Fraser at Sabie Bridge, and, this being in winter, the temperature dropped off so rapidly in the small hours that he was driven to go to his host's room to ask for another blanket. The light of a solitary candle burning in the room revealed an empty bed, although in one corner was a big, dark heap from which an unearthly snoring emanated. Closer examination revealed that the heap consisted of Fraser lying on his back on the floor, fully clothed, with his entire motley pack of mongrels heaped over him. Next morning an understandably curious Wolhuter tentatively raised the subject of this unique sleeping arrangement with Fraser, who explained that he had given all his blankets to his guest and added that in any case he often slept like that because dogs kept one warmer than blankets.

The kind of affection that rangers have always felt for their dogs is probably best illustrated by the story of Mary, the favourite dog of an Irish-born ranger of the earlier days named Healy. Mary was accompanying Healy on horseback patrol west of Sabie Bridge one hot summer's day, and near a nameless spruit suddenly collapsed with heat exhaustion. Desperately Healy tried to revive her, failed, and carried her back to Skukuza, 10 kilometres away, to try and nurse her back to health. Despite all his efforts she died later that day. Healy was devastated and, like a good Irishman, summoned his entire staff to join him in a traditional wake. Then he buried her in the original dog cemetery near the blockhouse at Sabi Bridge and later chopped out a suitable sandstone headstone for her. The dog cemetery was later moved to a large tree next to the nature conservation offices and then again to a spot near today's Stevenson-Hamilton Library inside the rest camp. Healy's beloved Mary and her equally beloved colleagues lie there to this day, gone but not forgotten . . . and, 10 kilometres away, the spruit where Mary collapsed now has a name: 'Inja-ka-Mtephe' (Dog of Healy).

Some dogs, like some people, discovered that they just couldn't take the strain of bushveld life. One such was a bumptious Dobermann named Boetietjie ('little brother' in Afrikaans), belonging to the then Chief Ranger, Dirk Ackerman. Boetietjie's epiphany came one day when Dirk decided to take him along on a visit to a hippo cull that was in progress at the Letaba River. The normal arrangement during a cull was to have no more than two people at the water's edge – the actual shooters – while the shooting was in progress, the mapoisas staying under cover until they were needed. In this particular case, however, it was the school holidays and the world and his wife were staying in the camp. The children and various adults were keen to see some of the action, so we decided to let some of them accompany us, but under strict control and only after a briefing about what to do and what not to do, with emphasis being laid on the need for absolute silence.

This done, the shooters – Tom Yssel and I – set off, followed by our entourage; the plan was that we would park them in a safe spot and then go about our business. My blood-pressure began fluctuating between lows and highs at an early stage as people forgot about the noise made by a 4x4's door being slammed, but worse was to come when Boetietjie suddenly headed off into the reeds and ignored all our efforts to call him back. So we had to wait for him, steaming gently at the edges – he was the Chief Ranger's dog, after all – until he had completed his leisurely investigation of who-knows-what. When he condescended to come back we finally were able to head for the water's edge, Boetietjie out in front in a serious state of excitement, although he didn't yet know what he was excited about.

Boetietjie's keenness was short-lived, however. One of the hippos let out an enormous thundering grunt that obviously threw the fear of God into him, because he streaked back to Dirk's truck, trailing a drawn-out yelp of fear and an equally drawn-out stream of urine. He covered the 200 metres or so in what must have been record time, found an open back door and flung himself inside. An eye-witness, Manie Coetzee, the manager of the Skukuza meat-processing plant, later claimed Boetjietjie not only took refuge in Dirk's truck but slammed the door behind him, which might have been a bit of hyperbole but certainly sketched Boetietjie's frame of mind quite accurately. That was more or less the end of Boetietjie's wildlife adventures, and he spent the rest of his life in useless safety in Dirk's garden. It was not a long life, unfortunately, because Boetietjie, like so many other Kruger dogs, came to a premature end when he was killed by a leopard in his own sleeping pen.

My own once-in-a-lifetime special dog was Eggs, otherwise known as Eggeritius Darling, whose acquaintance I first made in a tobacco-drying shed near Rustenburg. Eggs's geneaology was, to put it mildly, shrouded in mystery. She was mostly black, with a bit of white here and there, like her fox terrier mother, but her father seemed to have been a travelling gentleman whose identity was totally unknown. But if Eggs lacked a formal pedigree, she had everything else that counted, and for years we were the closest of boon companions. Eggs was at my side in many pursuits after wounded buffalo, lion and assorted other animals, an invaluable extra pair of eyes and ears that helped me but very cleverly never got in the way or got me or herself into trouble. She even went with me in the helicopter on culling operations, which was not something other dogs got to do.

In spite of the fact that she was definitely in the pint-size category Eggs was also, believe it or not, very good at intimidating elephants. It's not uncommon in Kruger to find an elephant blocking the road with the sort of lordly unconcern that comes from being bigger and stronger than any other creature in the vicinity, and if Eggs happened to be with me at such a time I'd let her out and tell her to go for it. That was all the encouragement she needed – pint-size or not, if there was something she really enjoyed, it was chasing an elephant . . . and for sheer slapstick comedy, there's not much to beat the sight of several tons of panic-stricken tusker scrambling to escape from a yapping terrier whose entire inconsiderable body could fit under one of his great flat feet with nothing left sticking out. Now and again an elephant would realise that it was being made a fool of and turn on Eggs – at which I would apply some heavier intimidation by revving the truck's engine, hooting, banging on the door and uttering words related to blood, thunder and fornication – but this was the rare exception to the rule. Mostly they were just happy to be rid of this tiny but fearsome demon snapping at their heels.

But there was more to Eggs than ratting on a grand scale. I will always remember how her intelligence and devotion saved me from nasty injury one day when I was stationed at Mooiplaas. I had just had lunch at our house and was about to go back to my office when Eggs bit me as I was about to go through the outside door. I was astounded, because this was not like her at all, and I turned around to give her a smack. Then I saw that she was staring intently at a huge puff-adder lying just under the doorstep. I don't believe in anthropomorphism, but can there be any doubt that Eggs had bitten me to prevent me from going through the door?

Eggs and I had a lot of good years together. Eventually she began to feel the onset of age and became quite deaf as a result of a snakebite, but her devotion and fierce little terrier spirit never flagged. And then the bushveld claimed her life, as it had done to so many rangers' dogs. Even now I can't help feeling a little guilty, because she and I were creatures of habit and had fallen into a regular routine, always a dangerous thing in Kruger. If we happened to be home of an evening Eggs would wait until I had watched the weather forecast on television and then scratch at the door to indicate that she wanted to take a pre-bed walk; when she was finished she would scratch again and I'd let her in for the night.

One night at Shingwedzi we went through the evening ritual as usual, but then suddenly I heard her yelp. My heart sank: I knew immediately what had happened to her. I ran to the kitchen door and flung it open, and saw my worst fears realised. About five metres away stood a leopard with Eggs dangling limply from its mouth. I shouted, and it dropped Eggs and fled. She was badly bitten but still alive, so I brought her inside, and for the next half-hour or so Helena and I did everything we could to doctor her. But then we realised that she was bleeding internally and was beyond any help that we could provide, so I gave her a fatal injection, and my old friend slipped quietly out of my life forever.

Helena and I didn't sleep a wink that night. Next morning we buried her in the station-house's garden and then walked around like zombies for a couple of days, acutely conscious of the huge gap Eggs's death had left in our lives. Inevitably I reproached myself. Of all people, I knew how dangerous it was to fall into a set routine, and I should have remembered how deaf Eggs was – quite likely she had been unaware of the leopard till its teeth closed on her neck. It was yet another lesson, a very hard one, in the need for eternal vigilance. I wasn't angry at the leopard, which would have been the automatic reaction of most people. Rangers don't think that way. The leopard had committed no crime; he had been on his home ground, hunting at his time of choice, and to him Eggs had been just another prey animal. So if any blame were to be laid, it would have to be at my own door.

Eggs's successor was a contrast to her in almost every way, especially looks. He was a truly enormous red Dobermann. Like many of the Kruger rangers of those days he was on his second career; he had failed to graduate from the police attack dog school and would have been put down if I hadn't approached a police general and offered to take him over. The general was only too glad, and so we acquired a new member of the family, whom we named 'Knersus', after a dinosaur in a cartoon strip that was popular at the time. Knersus and I got on like a house on fire, and he wouldn't leave my side unless circumstances absolutely required it. When I wasn't around Knersus transferred his devotion to the rest of my family, which suited me fine, because this was the early 1980s and I was spending a lot of time away from home struggling against the Mozambican poachers on Kruger's eastern boundary. But Knersus's possessiveness turned inward and went bad. At the start of one of the counter-poaching trips Helena dropped me off at a spot where our teams were to get together and then collected a Staffordshire bull terrier puppy for my son Robert, who was still far too small to play with the towering Knersus.

Knowing Knersus, it probably wasn't a smart move to introduce another dog into the household, especially at a time when I was away, but neither of us had encountered such a degree of possessiveness before and didn't give it a thought. The result was a minor tragedy. When Helena arrived home with the puppy Knersus literally went out of his mind. He wouldn't allow anyone to leave the house, and even his old acquaintance Corporal Antonio Mandlase, who locked him in his sleeping quarters every night, couldn't enter the yard for fear of his life. Helena took the only correct decision in the circumstances and shot him. I knew nothing about this, of course, being off hunting poachers, but the moment I got home I realised that something was wrong. Knersus wasn't waiting for me at the gate, as he invariably did (how he knew when I was coming home remains a mystery), and the kids didn't come out to greet me as usual. Fearing the worst, I bounded up the steps and met Helena at the kitchen door, and she burst into tears and told me what had happened. I was heartbroken, but I knew she had done the right thing; in a very real sense Knersus had been killed by his devotion to us. Later I went to say my personal goodbyes to him where he lay buried next to my beloved Eggs in the garden.

In due time they were to be joined by another Dobermann, Knersus's replacement. We called her Debbie and she was a wonderfully brave and faithful dog, just like her predecessors, but the bushveld claimed her, too, when she was bitten by a huge Mozambican spitting cobra from which she was trying to defend us.

Eggs, Knersus, Debbie . . . the story of the Kruger rangers is also the story of their dogs in all their infinite variety, and it is one part of the great park's ever-changing chronicle that will never change.

*

The place of honour is not always at the head of the line; he who commands the rearguard protects everyone. That is why I have saved the story of Sergeant Helfas Nkuna, the greatest of all the mapoisas in the history of the Kruger National Park, to the very end. In an astonishing 46 years of truly dedicated active service as a ranger he saw Kruger's wheel turn full circle, from horse patrols to aerial surveys, and helped to make it what it is today, one of the finest national parks in the world. What better man could there be to command the spirits of all the departed rangers in defence of our heritage's rearguard? Helfas personified the thousands of old-style mapoisas – mainly unsung, always underpaid, largely invisible to visitors – who served Kruger with dedication over the years, often at the risk of their lives. In all humility and gratitude I say that without people like Helfas there would have been no Kruger National Park as we know it today.

Helfas Nkuna started his career in Kruger as a youthful 'voorloper' – literally 'the one who walks in front', who leads a span of draught oxen – in the days before Kruger had such things as motor vehicles and anything heavy was transported by wagon; reputedly he was also responsible for scraping out Colonel James Stevenson-Hamilton's pipe! From those very humble beginnings Helfas went on to become a mapoisa and the right-hand man of the pioneering rangers Harry and Henry Wolhuter, and later their successors at Pretoriuskop, people like Gus Adendorff and Thys Mostert. Helfas was one of those people who commanded immediate respect and attention. Personally fearless and a born conservationist, he worked tirelessly for a cause he passionately believed in, although never losing sight of reality, and in his time apprehended an enormous number of armed poachers. How many of the powers-that-be in conservation today can honestly say the same about themselves?

I came to Kruger at the tail-end of Helfas's long career and had little to do with him, but by that time he had become a living legend and was the subject of so many stories that, in a sense, he belonged to all of us and, of course, to the park he had served so long and so faithfully. So if I talk about him as if he were an old comrade of mine . . . well, that's what he was. I well remember the first time our paths crossed, when I was still a young assistant on the lion research project. Some time before my arrival in Kruger, in October 1961, there was a historic moment when four white rhinos, two cows and two bulls, arrived from the Umfolozi park in Natal to re-establish the species in its old stamping-grounds after many years of absence.

The breeding pairs were released into a special 300-morgen enclosure at Faai, near Pretoriuskop, which was to be a protected breeding area and also a facility at which to study them. The enclosure was something of a personal triumph for the man who had built it, Thys Mostert of Pretoriuskop. There had been a school of thought energetically pushing the Crocodile Bridge area as the best place for the enclosure, but Thys had dug in his heels, his argument – a telling one – being: 'No, you're already killing buffalo there to protect the grass.' The original four rhino settled down very well and another two were released into the enclosure in 1962, followed by two more bulls in 1962 and a further two bulls in 1963. The original occupants of the camp accepted the female arrivals, but the two bulls were immediately set upon. The first one was so severely injured in the ensuing fighting that he had to be destroyed. The other bull would probably have suffered a similar fate had he not been released from the camp. But apart from these hiccoughs the project was up and running by the time I got to Kruger.

Thys was in charge of the rhino camp, with Helfas as his section sergeant, and they threw themselves into the welfare of their little kingdom with great enthusiasm, to the point where they not only knew each rhino by name but also where it was most likely to be at any given time of the day or night. There was also no doubt as to whose interests came first. The camp was patrolled daily to guard its occupants from intruders, be they on four legs or two, and Thys insisted that visits be by invitation only. That was how it worked, and Thys's and Helfas's 'subjects' enjoyed the good life in no uncertain terms. Then one day – ironically enough, while Thys was on leave – two male lions decided to climb over the fence. Their arrival was soon picked up by the daily patrol and the news sent through to Skukuza. Chief Ranger Don Lowe immediately told Dirk Swart, the resident ranger of Skukuza, to send me to remove the intruders because my research work on lions made me the obvious candidate for the job.

Armed with the necessary capture equipment, Dirk and I arrived at Pretoriuskop well after dark, by which time Helfas had gone to bed after placing the camp's patrol rangers in charge of the removal operation. One of the technical staff members at Pretoriuskop, Chris Smit, asked if he could come along, and I was glad to agree, because he had a truck with a wire cage on the back which we could use to take the camp patrol people along. This would make it easier and safer for all involved. I organised some bait by shooting an impala, which we dragged around the camp for a while before tying it to a tree and withdrawing to a hide about 20 metres away, the maximum accurate range for the enormous immobilising darts we used in those days. Then we settled down to wait. It wasn't long before the lions were drawn by the impala's scent, and I darted one of them. It staggered around and then passed out as scheduled. The second lion got an attack of the cautions and wouldn't let itself be drawn within my 20-metre effective range, so Dirk shot it: better that a lion should die than a precious baby rhino.

We loaded the two lions onto Dirk's truck, which we had left at the entrance to the camp, dropping the dead one at Thys's house to be skinned while leaving its unconscious chum in place with the camp patrol staff in Chris's truck to keep an eye on it till it woke up and left under its own steam. Dirk and I had a couple of beers and then went to bed, pretty pleased with the way the whole operation had gone. But Helfas wasn't pleased. The sun was barely over the mountains in the east the next morning when he marched into my bungalow and tore me off a strip for not killing both lions. On reflection, he was probably right, given what was at stake; my only excuse (which I did not raise) was that I was young and so wrapped up in studying lions that I had felt I had to protect them from the likes of myself. But, as I say, I didn't argue or protest. Who the hell was I, a mere snotnose with some book-learning, to contradict a bushveld sage like Helfas Nkuna? Again, a lesson learnt: keep your eye on the bigger picture at all times.

Helfas's life remained eventful almost to its very end; at 78 he had the last of his many narrow escapes from death when an injured leopard leapt on him, intent on killing him; but for the fact that his old friend Thys immediately shot it right off him, Helfas would surely have died horribly right there. A lesser man of that age would probably have had a heart attack on the spot, but Helfas was not a lesser man, and he lived on until 27 March 1978, when he died at the ripe age of 80. The following Saturday morning we buried Sergeant Helfas Nkuna west of Phabeni Spruit, about a kilometre from the Albasini Ruins. It was a day of weeping for all of us. When a man dies at the age of 80, there is sadness but also the realisation that he has had a long and fruitful life, and that all of us are living on bonus time after we have notched up the biblical threescore years and ten. But in Helfas's case it was as if one of the cornerstones of that mighty edifice called the Kruger National Park had been uprooted. I suppose that is as fine an epitaph as any man could want on his life.

18

THE KRUGER NATIONAL PARK:
QUO VADIS?

If there is one thing all South Africans surely know, it is that the Kruger National Park is one of their country's greatest treasures, but what they might not know is just how great that treasure actually is in both physical size and international importance. There can be no doubt that without Kruger not only South Africa but also the world would be immeasurably poorer. At the very beginning of this book I gave a few basic facts about the Kruger National Park, but only enough for immediate purposes; my aim in this final chapter is to tell my readers some more about Kruger, past and present, and to cast my eyes a little way into the future in an attempt to divine what might still lie in store.

Kruger is one of the 20 largest national parks in the world, and its vital statistics are awe-inspiring in their magnitude. It is of immense size, larger than many entire countries – just under two million hectares (or 20 000 square kilometres) – and takes up a substantial part of the north-eastern corner of the Republic of South Africa. Kruger's northern boundary is the Limpopo River, which is also the RSA's border with Zimbabwe. From there it sprawls over an elongated area stretching along the Mozambique border for about 320 kilometres between latitudes 22°25′ and 25°32′, with a mean width of about 65 kilometres, roughly between longitudes 30°25′ and 32°02′. The southern boundary is the Crocodile River, where the lush citrus plantations and sugar fields on the southern bank have proved so irresistible to generations of Kruger's four-footed marauders, while the western boundary is a meandering north–south line that does not follow any natural boundaries or accord with any planners' logic. Its neighbours to the west are mostly subsistence farmers living north of the Olifants River, but a number of private nature reserves lie along the western boundary south of the Olifants; these have now been added to Kruger and together they form the Greater Kruger National Park.

It is no coincidence that so many of its boundaries are rivers: Kruger is blessed with streams both great and small. It is drained from west to east by two major river systems, the Limpopo system in the north and the nKomati system in the south, and it has six perennial rivers, the Limpopo, Luvuvhu, Olifants, Sabie, Sand and Crocodile. Closely allied to the state of the rivers at any given time is the climate, whose workings determine how much water there is in them. Kruger has two distinct seasons. The wet season starts in September or October and lasts until March or April, with peaks in December and February, most of the rain being brought by truly awesome thunderstorms whose lightning displays have to be seen and heard to be believed. The overall mean annual rainfall is in the region of 500 mm to 550 mm, although in some years it is considerably more, at which times Kruger's inhabitants – both man and beast – have their hands full. Around April things dry out again until the next rainy season. During the summer the Park is as hot as the hinges of hell, and seems sometimes to be considerably hotter. In an average year the daily temperature in January usually hovers around 30° C, but that's in a good year – it's not uncommon for the thermometer to shoot up to 40° or more. During a winter month like July, on the other hand, the average temperature is mostly around a balmy 23° C or so, and at night it can get quite cold, although frost is not a common occurrence.

Topographically Kruger is fairly uniform, with typical Lowveld terrain for the most part. The greater part of it is flat or gently undulating, sloping gradually from the west, and studded with ridges and koppies which are either smooth grey granitic extrusions or hills topped with fractured stone. In general it is between 200 and 400 metres above sea-level, the lowest point (122 metres) being at the bottom of the Sabie River Gorge, and the highest (839 metres) on top of Khandizwe, near Malelane in the south. The south-western corner and the area north of Punda Maria are more mountainous, but the most outstanding feature – in every sense of the word – is the Lebombo range, which stretches along the border with Mozambique from the Shingwedzi River in the north right down to the Park's southernmost point.

Geologically, Kruger is divided into two almost exactly equal parts, with the western half consisting of predominantly granitic formations and the eastern half of basalts. A narrow belt of sandstone and shale, which runs the whole length of the Park from north to south, divides the two. Between them, these three areas with their distinctively different soil types are mainly responsible for Kruger's botanical diversity because they support different plant communities.

The Park falls within the Savannah Region (the largest biome in South Africa), which is characterised by a ground layer of grass in which scattered shrubs and trees occur. Its floral diversity is almost incredible: there are nearly 2 000 different plant species, made up of about 460 types of trees or shrubs, nearly 250 grasses, 27 ferns, 16 woody lianes, 20 aloes and over 1 000 herbaceous plants. The wildlife community is just as profligate in its variety. Apart from thousands upon thousands of invertebrates, many of which have yet to be described, Kruger has over 40 species of fish, more than 50 amphibian species, over 100 species of reptiles, about 500 bird species and 114 species of small mammals, although, of course, it is best known for its extensive variety of large mammals – five species of carnivores and 23 species of herbivores.

Most people don't know that in addition to all these animal and plant species Kruger is also particularly rich in archaeological sites, and in the 100-odd years of its existence a great deal of knowledge has been gathered about the area's former inhabitants. For instance, its first known vertebrate was a dinosaur called *Euskelosaurus*, which roamed there an estimated 65 million years before the great beasts became extinct. Artefacts unearthed from at least four localities indicate that the earliest humanoid to live in the area was *Homo erectus*, in the latter part of the early Stone Age, about 200 000 years ago. If there were earlier humanoids, their traces have yet to be found. Perhaps they will be: Kruger has yet to yield up all its secrets. Research at these spots has revealed that the environment then did not differ much from what it is at present, the trees in particular having stayed more or less the same. The animals differed markedly, though, and included many species that have long since become extinct. Among these were more than one type of elephant (as an aside, can you imagine the management implications if there were *two* elephant species in Kruger today?), as well as giant hartebeest, pig, baboon and buffalo, two types of horse and a giraffe with a short neck. The modern species occurring in the Park today were also present, except for the modern elephant, bushpig and warthog.

Refinements in spearheads, arrow points and various types of scrapers found by archaeologists indicate that noticeable technological improvements started appearing towards the end of the Early Stone Age, about 125 000 years ago. Exactly which type of humanoid was living in the Park area during these transitional times is not known, but the experts suspect that it was *Homo sapiens rhodesiensis*, whose members showed physical resemblances to the Neanderthals of North Africa and Europe. The humanoids now also started to acquire a much more 'modern' look. Certain anthropologists have identified a physical type known as *H. s. afer*, which is considered to be the primeval forefather of the Bushmen, or San, the first representatives of *Homo sapiens* ('thinking man') to occupy what is now South Africa, about 30 000 to 40 000 years ago. They were also the last people in southern Africa to possess a pristine Stone Age culture. They therefore represent, both culturally and historically, the end of the Stone Age and the pure hunter-gatherer way of life. Their former presence was detected early in Kruger's history in the form of rock paintings, and thus far more than 100 of these sites have been discovered inside the park.

The Stone Age era with its emphasis on hunting and gathering began to fade towards 400 AD, when the area around today's Letaba River was settled by newcomers who started to arrive from the north and brought with them domestic cattle, cultivation practices, metal-preparation skills and the art of pottery. Shortly afterwards more people arrived and settled in the vicinity of today's Sabie and Crocodile Rivers. Now the Iron Age had arrived, although the hunter-gatherers stayed on for about another 1 000 years before disappearing altogether. Between 700 and 800 AD there was another wave of immigration from the north and northwest. But the Lowveld was not overrun. Although large migratory developments took place elsewhere in southern Africa during the period 800–1000 AD, at least six centuries passed before they exerted much influence on its affairs. It is likely that something happened during that period that discouraged migration – disease, perhaps, or certain climatic phenomena, such as oscillating high and low rainfall – but so far no certain indications have been found.

Things started changing to some extent in the seventeenth century, with more arrivals bringing new iron-working skills from East and Central Africa. They settled near sources of iron ore, and by the end of the eighteenth century several tribes were established along the main rivers, particularly in the vicinity of today's Phalaborwa. These tribes ran domestic livestock, grew crops and hunted to augment their food stocks (Stevenson-Hamilton found rows of holes that they had dug on the plains west of Nwanetsi into which animals could be driven and speared to death). Even so, the population density remained relatively low. During the nineteenth century this might have resulted from the prevalence of a number of diseases, such as malaria, which is lethal to people, nagana (sleeping sickness), carried by the tsetse fly, which is fatal to cattle, and two tick-borne diseases that kill cattle and other livestock, East Coast Fever (malignant theileriosis) and buffalo or corridor disease.

It appears that the tribes enjoyed a fairly peaceful existence until the first quarter of the nineteenth century, when the area started feeling the shock-waves spreading out from the extremely bloody campaigns by which Shaka built a Zulu empire for himself, in the process destroying literally dozens of the tribes around his small original power-base. Shaka's campaigns completely destabilised all of the central part of what is now South Africa and launched a period of suffering and mass migration which is still known in the Nguni languages as the 'Mfecane' and in the Sotho languages as the 'Difaqane'. One of the results of Shaka's marauding was that the Tsonga tribes living over most of the Mozambican coastal plains moved westwards and settled in what is now the Kruger National Park, forcing some of the Sotho and Venda inhabitants, in turn, to move farther inland.

Until the latter part of the century there was no settlement by whites in the Kruger National Park area, only a few venture-some travellers and pioneers like Vaughan Kirby and Henry Glynn visiting the Lowveld. The last significant change in the cultural history of the area was the arrival of the Voortrekkers, transport traders plying the route to Delagoa Bay in Mozambique and a motley crowd of hunters, prospectors and other fortune-seekers. This led to increased hunting of elephant, rhino and other game, and in the middle of the nineteenth century the so-called sport hunters appeared on the scene as well. The result was inevitable: the known game herds shrank, and hunters moved farther and farther inland to seek out new ones. The process was not unique to South Africa: it was taking place in Europe, Australia, New Zealand and North America as well, although sometimes for different reasons. The main reason, though, seems to have been that Victorian Man did not realise that the game herds were finite, or perhaps it was simply the enormous self-confidence of an age in which it seemed that mankind could do anything, and enjoyed a sort of divine right derived from the Book of Genesis, which stated that God had given man dominion over all other living creatures. Whatever the reason, the result was the same, and in conservation circles all over the world the second half of the nineteenth century is known as the 'era of extermination'. But, fortunately for both man and animal, this was also to become the century of conservation, as far-sighted people began to realise that man's influence on his environment was so absolute that continued abuse of it would lead not only to the total extermination of wild animals but ultimately to mankind's demise as well.

This change of heart and attitude was expressed in the passing of laws containing restrictions and control measures designed to protect the remaining game stocks. The first law to control hunting in the old Transvaal or South African Republic was passed by the Volksraad (People's Assembly), sitting at Andries Ohrigstad in 1846. No restrictions were placed on the hunting of elephants, because this was the main source of income of the district, but hunters could shoot only enough of other species for their own use. At a public meeting in the

Soutpansberg district in March 1857 a second hunting law was passed, and this was followed by several others. None of them were very effective until a new measure came along in 1870 which contained three new principles: rangers would be appointed to enforce the law; there would be a closed season for certain species; and the use of traps or snares would be banned. This was an improvement, although still not a very effective one, because the frontiersmen, white and black, were used to going their own way, and the old Republic's style of government was minimalist to the point almost of anarchy. But things were about to change quite radically.

During the late 1870s and the beginning of the 1880s conservation was one of the issues that went on the back burner because Great Britain annexed the Transvaal Republic on rather doubtful grounds, leading to the First Anglo-Boer War. The conservation cause was not dead, however, merely biding its time, and once the short-lived war was over and the Republic was its own master again, more and more citizens began to petition the government to do something concrete. By 1884 a very considerable body of correspondence on the subject had piled up, and now the cause also gained a powerful advocate, none other than President Paul Kruger himself. A frontiersman almost from birth, he had been a fearless and mighty hunter in his day, and perhaps this was why he became interested in conservation (the anti-hunting lobby of today often does not realise, or perhaps want to realise, how many hunters are also passionate conservationists). Be that as it may, Kruger put his money where his mouth was, and at a meeting of the Volksraad in 1889 he stated that he would like all state-owned land in the Republic to be closed for hunting, adding that it was imperative that steps be taken to conserve the remaining wilderness areas for future generations. This was a move of some daring, given the fact that most of his constituents were also hunters of one kind or another who were not used to any sort of let or hindrance, and it is likely that only Paul Kruger, a national hero, had the standing to make such an announcement and carry it through.

One of the areas he mentioned was the territory between the Limpopo and the Olifants Rivers, although it was not until 1894 that his dream was realised in part with the proclamation of the Pongola Reserve. It was a start, however, and in 1895 the idea of proclaiming a reserve in the Lowveld was accepted in principle, although it did not happen right away because of the intervention of two disasters, one man-made and one natural. The first was the ill-conceived and ill-fated raid launched from the Bechuanaland Protectorate by Dr Leander Starr Jameson, one of the events that led to the outbreak of the Second Anglo-Boer War in 1899. The second was the great rinderpest epidemic that swept through the Republic between April 1896 and February 1897, killing hundreds of thousands of cattle and game animals, the eland and buffalo populations being especially hard hit.

Once again the Republic had more urgent things than game reserves to deal with, and another two years passed before RK Loveday was able to confront the Executive Committee of the Volksraad about the reason why the proposed game reserve in the Lowveld had not yet been proclaimed. This eventually led to the proclamation on 26 March 1898 of the 'Goewerment Wildtuin' (Government Game Reserve), comprising the area between the Sabie River in the north and the Crocodile River in the south, the boundary on the eastern side being the border with Mozambique and, in the west, the Nsikazi (Logies) River. Sadly, however, the outbreak of the Second Anglo-Boer War soon afterwards made nonsense of the proclamation, and during the period of hostilities there was an appalling slaughter of wild animals by members of the armed forces, so that for practical purposes the game reserve ceased to exist. But after the close of hostilities in May 1902, the British interim government in what had become the Transvaal Colony decided not just to re-proclaim the original reserve – now to be called the Sabie Game Reserve – but to expand it by adding on the area between the Sabie and Olifants Rivers. Soon after, in July 1902, Lieutenant-Colonel James Stevenson-Hamilton was appointed to run the new reserve, his main tasks being to introduce law and order and save the pitiful remnants of the game population from sliding into total extinction. One gathers that he was pretty much given a free hand, since his instructions included the exhortation to 'go down there and make yourself thoroughly disagreeable to everyone.'

Stevenson-Hamilton was not a professional conservationist (the government could not have found one in any case, since no such discipline existed then) but a career soldier. Born of a well-established Scottish family – he was later Laird of Fairholm in Lanarkshire – and educated at Rugby School, he had spent the formative years of his life in the British Army, passing through the Sandhurst Military College before being commissioned into the renowned 6th (Inniskilling) Dragoon Guards. He was also, of course, a passionate amateur conservationist, and the combination of tough cavalryman and equally tough nature-lover was exactly the right mixture of qualities required to turn his lawless bailiwick into a game sanctuary. Small in stature but great of heart, Stevenson-Hamilton threw himself into his task, and but for his unstinting efforts it seems unlikely that we would now have the unique national treasure called the Kruger National Park. When he took over as warden the area didn't have many established residents, mostly people who had gradually filtered in from the adjacent tribal territories, but even these were too many for Stevenson-Hamilton, who was convinced that wild animals and people could not live together. So, having set up his headquarters at what was then known as Sabie Bridge, he went to much effort to persuade such human inhabitants as there were to return to their traditional tribal domains. The park headquarters is still in the same place, although changed out of all recognition when compared to Stevenson-Hamilton's primitive little original establishment, but its name, Skukuza, is a direct link with the early days, because it means 'the man who sweeps clean'.

Stevenson-Hamilton tackled his daunting task on two fronts. His primary job was, of course, to protect the area under his jurisdiction, but he also spent much time petitioning for an extension of the reserve to both the north and west . . . and his efforts paid off. To his great delight the Shingwedzi Reserve – the area between the Letaba River in the south and the Luvuvhu/Limpopo Rivers in the north – was proclaimed in May 1903. Then in August 1903 he marked up another triumph when the area between the Sabie and Olifants Rivers was also added, linking the two reserves. Until 1916 the Sabie and

Shingwedzi game reserves remained separate entities, at least in name, but then they were consolidated and collectively renamed the Transvaal Game Reserve; although it was not until 1923 that the corridor between them was attained and incorporated into the reserve as well. Two years later, in 1925, the Transvaal Game Reserve was proclaimed a national park and renamed the Kruger National Park. It was an appropriate tribute to the crusty old president whose courage and foresight had sown its seeds almost a generation earlier.

History remembers Paul Kruger mainly as the symbol of the Boers' long, desperate and ultimately unsuccessful battle against British imperialism, but his greatest legacy to South Africa is the huge game sanctuary that rightly bears his name today. It will still be instructing, educating and entertaining both South Africans and visitors from elsewhere long after the military and political events in which he featured have become part of the faded tapestry of the nation's heritage. Just as much a member of the Kruger National Park's pantheon of heroes, however, is Stevenson-Hamilton himself. Kruger sowed the seeds, but Stevenson-Hamilton was the one who cultivated and harvested them, often against well-nigh insuperable odds; it is difficult today to grasp the challenges he faced when he took over responsibility for the Sabie Game Reserve.

With resources which were always scanty or nonexistent, he revived the almost-vanished game populations and nursed them back to viability, fought against poachers and institutionalised mind-sets, badgered his superiors for the tools to do the job and waged endless campaigns to protect the Park's integrity from land sharks and ore-hungry mining companies. And he beat the odds. Today Kruger's natural attributes are internationally famous, it has hundreds of kilometres of road, good visitor accommodation and an efficient administration. Small wonder that on average a million visitors from near and far go through its gates every year. And in spite of all this development, the Kruger National Park still belongs to the animals that make it what it is, and retains its famous bushveld ambience.

What makes it all even more intriguing is that Kruger has not nearly reached the final phase of its long journey, but is playing a key role in the latest development in southern African nature conservation, the creation of 'peace parks' – Trans-Frontier Conservation Areas, to use the more formal term – that transcend frequently arbitrary and usually illogical national borders. No doubt some sceptics would tend to write off the 'peace park' concept as essentially politically motivated, and to some extent it certainly is, but that should not be allowed to detract from its logic and feasibility. It is a fact that the removal of the man-made barriers that prevent natural game migration in search of water and veld food will do a great deal towards restoring a healthy natural balance. In many parts of the world it is no longer possible to restore the game highways, but here it is feasible and achievable. Africa does have serious overpopulation problems in some areas, but much of it is still comparatively empty.

In Kruger's case the 'peace park' concept has migrated from concept to reality. In December 2002, after long deliberations, a treaty was signed between South Africa, Mozambique and Zimbabwe to develop what was named the Limpopo Trans-Frontier Park. This park covers about 35 000 square kilometres and integrates the Kruger National Park with the adjoining Limpopo National Park that was created in 2001 when the former Mozambican concession-hunting area known as Coutada 16 was upgraded to national park status. The ultimate aim is to join the Kruger and Limpopo National Parks with Zimbabwe's Gonarezhou National Park by means of a corridor stretching between northern Kruger and Gonarezhou. The idea is to restore the area to what it was in the past – one of the most productive wildlife areas in the subcontinent – and to enhance cross-border co-operation. It is also aimed at benefiting local communities by creating job and business opportunities, and allowing sustainable utilisation of renewable resources.

All of this is quite 'do-able', but its success will depend on the way it is carried out. Establishing a game park of any kind is a time-consuming and complex process, and those who undertake such a project need to bear in mind the popular South African saying that there are some things you simply can't press into ripeness. I have an uneasy feeling that the process might be going too fast. For example, it is a well-known – although not widely published – fact that thousands of people live right in the centre of the Mozambican side of the new park, where its main water resources are located. What is going to happen to these people? They are already complaining bitterly about the fact that they had not been consulted in the process at all. The same problem is likely to arise in Zimbabwe. The corridor that is supposed to link Kruger with Gonarezhou will have to run right through the densely populated Sengwe communal lands in the south. The affected people in both Zimbabwe and Mozambique are mainly subsistence farmers. If their interests are not appropriately looked after, confrontation between man and animal, not to mention subsistence poaching or worse, is almost inevitable. I speak here from long and painful experience.

In past times the conservation areas in South Africa were established and maintained mainly by exclusion and enforcement. This resulted in a rift between park managements and those living in the vicinity, to the distinct detriment of both – particularly the parks. We shouldn't let this bit of history repeat itself, and there would be no excuse if it did; after all, we are supposed to learn from our mistakes, which is why we have long since developed a new approach of involving local people in conservation. A further problem – also an old one – is that animals sometimes have minds of their own. For instance, the first elephants that were released in the Limpopo National Park were all back in Kruger in just a few days. Subsequently, hundreds of animals have been released into a fenced area. But are these animals safe? I have said elsewhere that you can't preach conservation to hungry people. Having said all that, let me add right away that the 'peace park' idea remains a really great one, and we can only hope that this pioneering effort works properly. There certainly are serious obstacles to bringing it to fruition, but if people like Stevenson-Hamilton succeeded in achieving the seemingly impossible, there is hope yet.

Wildlife management in the new trans-frontier park is obviously going to be another critical success-or-failure factor. Today's wildlife management problems are basically the same as those Stevenson-Hamilton had to contend with a century ago – climatic cycles and water provision, animal populations, veld fires and poaching. Policies and practices regarding all these factors have been developed, changed, redeveloped and changed again in the light of general experience and lessons (sometimes painful ones) that have been learnt. That the cycle of change will continue is a certainty, because the value of parks and their management imperatives mutate along with the political, social, scientific and economic priorities of any society. One of the most recent changes in South African National Parks policy is a paradigm shift with regard to wildlife management. In the past, populations of animals like hippo, buffalo and elephant were actively managed to maintain a state of equilibrium. Now the ecosystem is allowed to fluctuate to a greater extent, with built-in 'thresholds for potential concern' (often abbreviated to 'TPCs') or 'worrying levels', to warn about serious effects of change due to the direct or indirect influence or actions of man. The elephant population explosion, for instance, is directly attributable to the actions of man, because it is man who erected fences around the area in which they occurred. The ultimate goal is still exactly the same, however, namely to conserve the full range of organisms that historically have been present in the ecosystem.

Unfortunately the very best efforts of Kruger's managers and scientists to 'conserve biodiversity in all its natural facets and fluxes and to provide human benefits in keeping with the mission of the South African National Parks in a manner which detracts as little as possible from the wilderness qualities of the Kruger National Park', to quote from its mandate, are backfiring because of the increasing elephant population. To my mind, as I have indicated earlier in this book, elephants are the glory of the Kruger National Park, and their resurgence from literally nothing when Stevenson-Hamilton arrived in 1902 is one of Kruger's great success stories. But when there are too many elephants for the area's carrying capacity the result is immense and quite possibly permanent damage to the environment. This is also an old problem. As long ago as the 1950s and early 1960s there was a growing feeling among some prominent biologists, including Beuchner, Buss of the Murchison Falls National Park and Glover from Tsavo (Kenya), that elephant numbers should be controlled to prevent habitat change. The Kruger National Park's biologists, who also felt that it might become necessary to limit elephant population growth in the Park, shared these sentiments.

The first culling operation took place in 1967, and between then and 1996 about 13 000 elephants were killed. Culling was and is an unpleasant business, and in 1990 an attempt was made to improve the culling method and make it more humane by darting the elephants with scoline to bring them down and then brain-shooting them before they started suffocating. In practice, however, it was sometimes impossible to shoot an elephant before suffocation began, so nowadays scoline is not used at all, and each animal is brain-shot from a helicopter. Culling operations as such, however, stopped in 1995 when South African National Parks undertook to review its policy for the management of elephant in the Kruger National Park after a public debate held in Midrand, Johannesburg. After that, scientific and management staff drew up a policy that focused on the extent and intensity of elephant impacts on biodiversity, rather than on the numbers of elephants *per se*.

The policy was based on four fundamental principles. Firstly, that ecosystems were not static; that fluctuations of conditions and population responses were an inherent and desirable attribute of the Lowveld ecosystem and thus contributed to biodiversity. A range of elephant impact, achieved through maintaining different densities of elephant in different areas at different times, would thus be natural and desirable. Secondly, that elephants were important agents of habitat modification and thus contributed to biodiversity. Thirdly, that elephants should not be viewed in isolation, but as one component of a broader, integrated system. Fourthly, and most importantly, that elephant populations that were confined – but whose growth was not limited through management – were very likely to ultimately increase in number to the point where there were negative impacts on the system's biodiversity. The thrust of this policy proposal was that the elephant population should not be managed purely for its own benefit; instead, elephant *impact* should be managed in conjunction with other ecosystem processes (such as veld fires) to promote biodiversity in general.

Apart from culling, there are two ways in which to limit the elephant population: translocation and contraception. Translocation is the more attractive option, but it is just not feasible any more, because almost all of the available habitats have already been utilised. To make matters worse, most areas to which elephants have been transferred have reached saturation point. As a result, translocating elephants to new areas is creating more problems, since these populations will all have to be controlled eventually. The other option is contraception. Some experiments in this field have failed, while others have succeeded. One specific method, immunocontraception, which uses porcine zona pellucida (pZP) vaccine, is safe, non-hormonal, non-lethal, reversible and effective in stabilising elephant populations, although its success in doing so depends on factors like numbers and the size of the habitat. The pZP basically prevents sperm from penetrating the egg (ovum) by forming an antibody layer around the egg. To date, there have been no behavioural or physical side effects noted; and all reproductive functions are maintained in the target animal, namely oestrus cycles, lactation and foetal development (should a cow be pregnant). Because the elephant has an oestrous cycle of 15 to 17 weeks, contracepted cows coming on heat do not create a significant disturbance factor to the family unit or any associated bulls such a unit might have. Contraception seems to be the answer as far as smaller game reserves are concerned, but there is still a huge question-mark about the feasibility of applying it in Kruger and ultimately in the Limpopo Trans-Frontier Park. This is one field in which I have the same kind of reservations about the process as the extreme 'greenies', although we make odd bedfellows, because they tend to anthropomorphise the elephant to such an extent that their emotions actually govern conservation and management principles about culling. But we both have the same question to put: is it really more ethical?

In the end one can eloquently criticise new management ideas, but Kruger, being as large and diverse as it is, has survived more than a century despite mistakes by managers and researchers. Obviously the correct decisions made up for the bad ones. Therefore one should remain confident about the future of Kruger and the Limpopo Trans-Frontier Conservation Area. Providing that they work out how to keep the elephant population under control, that is! People can be educated and convinced about certain basic necessities, but an elephant destroying a 100-year-old baobab tree to fill his guts is going to continue doing that and other far worse things to the environment if something is not done very soon. My gut feeling is still that culling is the quickest and easiest solution, apart from the fact that it could provide a sustainable income which could be used for so many good purposes. As I write this, the latest news on culling in Kruger is that everyone now believes that there are far too many elephants in the park except the ultra-greens, who are totally opposed in principle to the killing of any animals at all – although one can't fail to notice that their compassion doesn't seem to require that they should all be vegetarians or use shoes and bags made of something other than leather.

The official elephant population number in Kruger is somewhere between 12 000 and 13 000, although the Director of Conservation stated in a recent radio debate that there are 17 000, which would not surprise me at all. The decision to cull or not to cull apparently does not reside solely with South African National Parks, however; SANP would have to go through a lengthy process of discussing the matter with the public, after which a decision would have to be made by the Minister of Environmental Affairs – all of which would take at least a year. Before critics of the present government start pointing fingers, let me hasten to add that it has always been like this: before elephant culling started in the 1960s the then South African Parks Board had to go through a similar process. What most South Africans are not aware of is that – contrary to what some people like to say – there is significant scientific evidence of the negative impact of the current elephant population on the environment, especially on certain sensitive and rare plant species. Another factor, of which the general public also appears to be unaware, is that Kruger has been divided into a number of zones which include wilderness areas and botanical reserves. These reserves, one in the far north and one in the south, both contain some very rare plant species which are currently under threat.

SANParks have realised that contraception is not a proposition in an area the size of Kruger. Those who believe that the trans-frontier conservation area is the answer also live in a fool's paradise. The plan last year was to transfer at least a thousand elephants to this area, but logistical, financial and other problems have made it unachievable. Realistically, that leaves only one option: culling . . . and the longer a decision to resume it is postponed, the worse the problem becomes. Over the last 10 to 12 years the elephant population has increased by an average of about 2.81 per cent per year. To make it easier to grasp what this means in real terms, let me put it this way: one year from the time you read this there will be another 300 to 400 elephants in Kruger. Theoretically speaking, the game processing plant at Skukuza can handle about 600 elephant carcasses a year. This means that even if the plant were to operate at top level throughout the year (which it obviously does not), Kruger would only be able to keep the elephant population at its present undesirably high level, whereas what is needed is to substantially reduce it – unless the park management was willing to litter the veld with the rotting corpses of elephant that it could not process.

That is a frightening possibility. The unique world-within-a-world that is the Kruger National Park can only achieve its purpose if a proper population equilibrium exists. That basic fact is not going to change or go away. Emotionalism that refuses to confront the facts will not cut the mustard, any more than expressions of noble sentiments that are not followed by concrete action. The Kruger National Park almost literally rose from the dead because the government took decisive action by sending Stevenson-Hamilton into the wilderness to get on with the job, together with any tough choices this would entail, even if it meant making himself 'thoroughly disagreeable'. These days governments tend to take a slightly less cavalier attitude, but tough choices still have to be made, and this is one of them.

GLOSSARY

This glossary is a compendium of terms that, for one reason or another, might be unfamiliar to readers, especially non-South Africans. It is a veritable mixed bag. Some are purely technical and are included because not all readers will be familiar with, say, firearms; others derive from one or other of the languages spoken in South Africa, whether in pure or corrupted form, while yet others are local or regional slang.

I could have sanitised the non-technical terms into 'proper' English, but that would have taken the taste of dust, wood-smoke and remembered good times out of them, which would never have done for a book about the corner of the old Africa called the Kruger National Park.

Aardvark *Orycteropus afer*, a large nocturnal ant-eater. Originally a Dutch word meaning 'earth-pig', it is now not only universally used in South Africa but is known throughout the world.

Afrikaans One of South Africa's 11 official languages, spoken as a mother tongue by millions of people of all races. It developed out of seventeenth-century Dutch but is actually a separate language that incorporates words and grammatical forms from several other languages, both indigenous to Africa and originating as far afield as Indonesia.

AK-47 The 7.62-calibre Avtomat Kalashnikov assault rifle, designed in the Soviet Union but also made in several of the former Warsaw Pact countries. Huge numbers were pumped into Africa in the 1970s and 1980s and will be the bane of conservationists for generations to come because the AK-47's relatively low-intensity cartridge tends to inflict ultimately fatal wounds on the larger animals rather then kill them outright.

Askari   Originally KiSwahili for 'soldier', but in this context a young bull elephant who accompanies an old one that is not part of a herd or family group.

Assegai   A spear, as made and used by various tribes. The exact design of an assegai, such as the type of blade and the length of the blade and shaft, varied according to where it was made and the purpose for which it was made.

Backveld   Any remote area of the bushveld whose contact with the outside world is sporadic. A backveld inhabitant is known, naturally enough, as a 'backvelder'. Not often used in today's world, where distances have shrunk dramatically.

Bakkie   A light utility vehicle, usually with a load capacity up to one ton. Originally an Afrikaans word, which is now universally used in South Africa.

Boer   Originally 'farmer' in Dutch and Afrikaans, it is now mainly used as a qualifier, such as the generic name 'boerewors' for a type of beef sausage most South Africans love to eat, or 'boer bread', denoting bread baked in the veld.

Boma   An enclosure, classically of thornbushes but now mainly of other materials. It is thought to be of East African origin.

Braai   Originally an Afrikaans term, now in almost universal use as both a noun and verb, relating to outdoor cooking. A classic braai requires that a fire be made from certain types of wood, such as thornwood or old vine-stumps, with sausage, steaks, chops and even fish being grilled over the coals.

Bullet   A projectile, consisting of lead, a lead core with a harder metal jacket or even solid harder metal, fired by a rifle or handgun. Often used interchangeably (and incorrectly) with 'cartridge' by the ignorant.

Bush/bushveld   Two versions of a virtually universal term, denoting the far places where the animals are still citizens of their land and not mere livestock.

Cane spirit   A potent colourless liquor distilled from cane sugar and popular with South Africans in combination with a variety of mixers.

Cartridge   The object that puts the 'bang' in a rifle. It consists of a brass cartridge-case, containing a charge of propellant; a primer at its base for igniting the propellant; and a bullet at the front end. The ignition sequence is as follows: the shooter squeezes the trigger, thereby releasing the firing-pin, which hits the primer. A flash travels from the primer to the propellant, igniting it. The propellant turns into incandescent gas under high pressure and propels the bullet down the rifle's barrel.

Commando   An indigenous type of military unit, born at the Cape of Good Hope in the late seventeenth century from a blending of tribal Khoi tactics and classic European doctrines, resulting in a famously mobile and elusive mounted unit. In the rest of the world 'commando' denotes elite special forces (the name was first used in this context during World War II by Winston Churchill, who had been impressed by the Boer commandos during the Second Anglo-Boer War of 1899–1902). In South Africa, however, it still denotes an organised group of citizen-soldiers.

Condyle   Generally a projection of the skull. In this case it refers to the point where the lower jaw hinges into the skull. In the case of an elephant it is a massive piece of heavy bone.

Dassie   *Procavia capensis*. A small animal that lives in rocky habitats, sheltering in crevices and venturing out to eat the leaves of grasses, trees and shrubs. There is also an arboreal subspecies found in forested areas. 'Dassie' is its most widely used colloquial name, originally deriving from the Dutch 'das', or rabbit. It is also known as the hyrax or rock-rabbit.

Daggaboy   A solitary old buffalo bull, often smeared with mud from lying in a wallow. Daggaboys are notorious for their irascibility.

Donga   A small ravine, usually caused by water erosion. Originally a Zulu word, it is in universal use in South Africa.

Draai   Literally 'corner', 'twist', 'bend', or 'turn' in Afrikaans and Dutch. It is occasionally used to describe a curving terrain feature.

Drakensberg   Literally 'Dragon Mountain' in Dutch, this enormous mountain range runs for almost 2 000 kilometres from the Eastern Cape Province, through KwaZulu-Natal (forming the boundary between this province and Lesotho) and into Mpumalanga.

Drift   A ford through a river, of varying construction. A drift may be a natural shallow, a hard standing constructed by laying rocks on the riverbed or a visible or submerged concrete causeway. Originally a Dutch word that is now in universal use.

Duwweltjies (also dubbeltjies)   Afrikaans for 'devil's thorn'. A plant normally found on disturbed soil, with a spiked seed that plays havoc with bare feet and bicycle tyres – the main mode of transport of the mapoisas.

Flossie   Soldiers' slang for a military transport aircraft, particularly but not exclusively the Lockheed C130.

Gate (of Kruger National Park)   There are nine gates by which to enter the Kruger National Park from South Africa:
Pafuri: the northernmost gate, east of Musina
Punda Maria: east of Louis Trichardt
Phalaborwa: at the town of Phalaborwa
Orpen: named after Eileen Orpen, who donated large tracts of land to Kruger
Kruger Gate: 13 kilometres from the park's headquarters at Skukuza
Phabeni: the newest gate, situated between Hazyview and Kruger Gate
Numbi: for years the main entrance to the Park until the construction of Kruger Gate in 1975
Malelane: now one of the busiest gates, just off the N4 to Mozambique
Crocodile Bridge: just 12 kilometres from Ressano Garcia, which is the border post between South Africa and Mozambique.

Hartebeest   A rather awkward looking antelope, weighing

around 140 kg when full-grown. The red hartebeest (*Alcelaphus buselaphus*) was once found in great numbers in most of southern Africa but is now restricted to a few areas, although it is not endangered. Lichtenstein's hartebeest, named after a German explorer in the early nineteenth century, is larger than the red hartebeest and can be recognised by its reddish-golden colour and what appear to be white boxer shorts. It previously occurred in the northern part of the Soutpansberg region, but is now restricted to Mozambique and Malawi.

Highveld The high plains of South Africa, averaging about 1 500 metres above sea level and extending mainly west and north of the Drakensberg.

Inspan From the Afrikaans 'span' ('team'); put to work as part of a team.

Jabula Indigenous beer brewed from sorghum. Milder and healthier than hard liquor, its kick is not to be despised, however.

Joysak A slang term for the haversacks carried by rangers and mapoisas.

Kees A favourite Dutch diminutive of 'Cornelius', it is a virtually universal South African personal name for a baboon, like 'Towser' for a dog. Why 'Kees'? It's one of those great African mysteries.

Koekie An Afrikaans word, but widely used by speakers of other languages, indicating any of a variety of hard or soft biscuits or similar snack items that are customarily served with tea or coffee.

Kop/kopje/koppie A hill, usually but not always small. Originally Afrikaans, the term has been widely used in South Africa for generations.

Lapa A shelter for a braai. In its classic form it consists of a thatched roof with open sides, but takes many forms. Originally an indigenous word, it is now used by all South Africans.

Long drop A toilet consisting basically of a deep hole in the ground with a suitably apertured wooden seat on top. Although they tend to be aromatic and provide handy shelters for snakes and other creatures, long drops are still in wide use in the bushveld, for obvious reasons: they're easy to build and never need a plumber.

Lowveld The area between the Indian Ocean in the east and the Drakensberg in the west. It is generally less than 300 metres above sea level and is characterised by hot summers and mild winters.

Magaliesberg A mountain range that starts near Rustenburg in the North West Province and runs east through Pretoria, the administrative capital of South Africa.

Mapoisa A locally recruited field ranger, picked for endurance, local knowledge and tracking and bush survival skills. For decades mapoisas were a vital part of the Kruger National Park operation, acting as right-hand men to the game rangers.

Mapashane A cheap and very durable sandal made from a section of old car tyre.

Marula *Sclerocarya birrea*. A commonly found tree in the Lowveld, which bears edible fruit and nuts. The fruit is often used for brewing alcoholic beverages and making jelly. The generic name *Sclerocarya* is derived from the Greek words for 'hard nut' or 'kernel'.

Morgen A traditional unit of land measurement, obsolete since the adoption of the metric system. It is approximately the same size as a hectare.

Mpahla A Tsonga word for 'goods' or 'possessions'.

Musth A phenomenon that occurs in both male and female elephants during raised hormonal levels, the outward sign being secretion from the temporal gland on the side of the head and in males a constant dribbling of fluid from the penis with frequent small urinations with the penis sheathed. Periods of temporal gland secretion in males are accompanied by increased aggression, longer and more continuous movements and more time spent with breeding herds.

Muti A vernacular name, now in universal use in South Africa, relating to remedies of both the medicinal and magical varieties prepared by traditional healers, formerly called 'witch-doctors'. Some types of muti actually work, while others are life-threatening. One of the dark undersides of South African life is the occasional murder of a child and removal of certain of its body parts for making certain kinds of muti.

Oom Literally 'uncle'. Originally a Dutch/Afrikaans word of respect not only for a blood relative but any older man, it is still widely used in South Africa by both Afrikaans-speakers and non-Afrikaans-speakers.

Oros A popular orange drink, used as a thirst-quencher by children and teetotallers and as a mixer by drinkers of stronger waters.

Oupa Literally 'old father', it is the Afrikaans word for 'grandfather' but is sometimes used by other groups, as term of respect or even as a baby name.

Pap Stiff porridge of several varieties that many South Africans of all races eat with different additions both at breakfast and later in the day. Originally Dutch/Afrikaans in origin, the term has now become virtually universal.

Picket An isolated, strategically placed outpost in the form of a hut, normally manned by two mapoisas, often with their families.

Poort Literally 'gateway' in Dutch/Afrikaans, it has become virtually a universal word also used (as in the Kruger National Park context) for gaps in mountains through which pedestrian – both human and animal – and sometimes wheeled traffic can pass.

R1 rifle The locally manufactured version of the Belgian FAL 7.62 mm-calibre service rifle, the standard personal defence weapon issue in the South African Defence Force from the early 1960s until the middle 1980s, when it began to be phased out in favour of the R4, a locally manufactured version of the 5.56 mm Israeli Galil. R1s were issued to all rangers and mapoisas. Since its cartridge was identical to the well-regarded .308 Winchester sporting round except for bullet type, it was sometimes also used by rangers for culling and other duties.

Rand The South African unit of currency after decimalisation in 1961. At that time it was worth 10 shillings sterling, but has since gradually depreciated from two to the pound sterling to about 12 at the time of writing.

Renosterkoppies Literally 'Rhinoceros Hills': 'Renoster' is the Afrikaans word for 'rhinoceros'.

Rest camps A fenced area where guests stay overnight, in either luxury huts or camping areas. Most of these rest camps feature petrol pumps, shops and restaurants, while a few 'bush camps' are self-catering.

Revolver A handgun carrying its cartridges, usually six, in a cylinder which revolves every time the trigger is squeezed or the hammer is thumb-cocked.

Rifle A shoulder-held weapon, firing a cartridge of greater or lesser intensity, which can be either bolt-operated or self-loading. Some self-loading weapons fire a single shot every time the trigger is pulled, while others have a regulator switch that also allows bursts of automatic fire. The heavy rifles used by rangers, which fire high-powered cartridges, are all bolt-action weapons.

Rinderpest A highly contagious and usually fatal viral disease of livestock and wildlife. Its symptoms include fever and bloody diarrhoea. The greatest of all rinderpest epidemics, that of 1896, was so devastating that to this day South Africans will jokingly say 'oh, that was before the rinderpest' to indicate something that happened long ago.

Rondawel Originally a Dutch/Afrikaans word, now in universal use, describing a small round cottage, typically of one room. The classic rondawel had a thatched roof, but modern ones often use more durable low-maintenance material.

Seekoei Literally 'sea cow', the Afrikaans term for a hippopotamus.

Shangane A large tribe whose traditional home area is in and around the Kruger National Park.

Shotgun A fairly short-range shoulder weapon whose cartridge contains not one bullet but a quantity of 'shot', or pellets of varying size. Shot guns are used for anything from shooting birds or snakes to dealing with lions; in the latter case they are loaded with very large pellets.

Sisal The tropical American agave plant, which has a large rosette of spiny leaves with strong, durable fibres used for making ropes and grain-bags.

Sjambok A short whip, used by South Africans of all races; the best ones are made from rhino or hippo hide. Reputedly the ultimate sjambok was made from a rhino's penis by attaching a weight to it while it was still fresh, but this is something like the legendary American 'swoose' – half-swan and half-goose. At least one South African firm has made sjamboks of plastic, to the horror of purists.

South African Republic (ZAR) The independent Boer republic, centred on Pretoria, which was founded in 1855 by Boer trekkers and vanished when it was invaded and conquered by the British during the Second Anglo-Boer War (1899– 1902).

Spoor The trail left by humans or animals, meaning anything from foot- or hoofprints to disturbances in the vegetation. Originally a Dutch word, it is now in universal use.

Spruit A creek. Originally an Afrikaans word that is now in universal use.

Tackies A universal South African slang term of unknown origin for tennis shoes and similar footwear.

Tamboti *Spirostachys africana*. A tree characterised by its pungent smell when burnt, also for its ability to cause diarrhoea when used as a wood in a cooking fire, as well as the lovely dark, oily wood it produces.

Tannie Literally 'auntie'. Originally a Dutch/Afrikaans term of respect not only for a blood relative but any older woman, it is still widely used in South Africa by both Afrikaans-speakers and non-Afrikaans-speakers.

Tickey pocket The small money pocket on a pair of trousers. 'Tickey' was the universal slang term for the threepenny coin which was a feature of South African life for generations until it was swept away when the currency was decimalised.

Trek Originally a Dutch word meaning 'pull', it has become universally used to indicate a long or arduous journey, not only in southern Africa but internationally, as in the title of the long-running television and movie science-fiction series 'Star Trek'.

Tshombe, Moise Moise Tshombe led the copper-rich province of Katanga into a secession from the newly independent Congo republic in mid-1960 that lasted for more than two and a half years. In 1964, after Katanga had returned to the fold, Tshombe became Prime Minister of the Congo, but later died in mysterious circumstances.

Tsonga The language spoken by the Shangane nation, the main ethnic group in the Kruger National Park area.

Veld Originally a Dutch word denoting 'field', now a universal South African term used interchangeably with 'bushveld'.

Velskoen/vellie Literally 'skin shoe'. Originally an almost heelless home-made shoe worn by frontiersmen of all races; 'gentrified' modern versions are still very popular in southern Africa. Probably the most famous 'vellies' (a fairly modern diminutive) are made from kudu-skin in Swakopmund, Namibia.

Voorloper A Dutch/Afrikaans term literally meaning 'one who walks in front': a term deriving from the ox-wagon days, when a 'voorloper' would lead a 'span' of 16 oxen drawing a wagon. Although this was a responsible task, it was almost always performed by a youngster.

Weber braai A patented braai system, using charcoal, which has gained considerable popularity in South Africa but offends purists.

White rhino *Ceratotherium simum*. The species is not white, any more than the 'black' rhino (*Diceros bicornis*) is black – both are grey in colour. The name derives from a corruption by nineteenth-century English-speakers of the Dutch word 'wijd', meaning 'wide' or 'broad', a reference to its broad, flat mouth.

The 'black' rhino is characterised by its pointed upper lip. Once nearly extinct, the white rhino has been brought back to a safe population level after a decades-long struggle that ranks as one of the most successful conservation projects in history.

BIBLIOGRAPHY

AIKEN, B, 1988. *The Kruger: A Supreme African Wilderness.* Durban: Butterworths.

BAILEY, TN, 1993. *The African Leopard. Ecology and Behavior of a Solitary Felid.* New York: Columbia University Press.

BENGIS, RG, 1992. Wildlife diseases of animals and public health significance in the Kruger National Park. *Proceedings of the Symposium on Wildlife Utilisation in Southern Africa, 28 June– 6 July.*

BRAACK, L, 1990. War refugees and malaria epidemiology: The Moçambique-South Africa situation. *Proceedings of the 7th International Congress of Parasitology, Paris, France, 665–665.*

BRAACK, L (ed), 1997. *A Revision of Part of the Management Plan for the Kruger National Park.* Volumes VII & VIII.

BRYDEN, BR, 1976. The biology of the African lion (*Panthera leo,* Linn. 1758*)* in the Kruger National Park. MSc thesis, University of Pretoria, Pretoria.

DORST, J & P DANDELOT, 1970. *A Field Guide to the Larger Mammals of Africa.* London: Collins.

HALL-MARTIN, A, 1986. *Elephants of Africa.* Cape Town: Struik.

HALL-MARTIN, AJ, 1987. Role of musth in the reproduction strategy of the African elephant (*Loxodonta africana). South African Journal of Science* 83(10), 116–120.

HALL-MARTIN, AJ, 1994. *The Magnificent Seven.* Cape Town: Human & Rousseau.

HALL-MARTIN, A & J CARRUTHERS (eds.), 2003. *South African National Parks. A Celebration. Commemorating the 5th World Parks Congress 2003.* Auckland Park: Horst Klemm Publications.

JOUBERT, SCJ, 1986. The Kruger National Park – an introduction. *Koedoe* 29, 1–12.

PAYNTER, D & W NUSSEY, 1986. *Kruger – Portrait of a National Park*. Johannesburg: Macmillan.

PIENAAR, UDV, P VAN WYK & N FAIRAL, 1966. An experimental cropping scheme of hippopotami in the Letaba River of the Kruger National Park. *Koedoe* 9, 1–33.

PIENAAR, UDV (ed), 1990. *Neem uit die Verlede*. Pretoria: National Parks Board.

PLUG, I, 1982. Man and animals in the prehistory of the Kruger National Park. *Transvaal Museum Bulletin* 18, 9–10.

SCHUTTE, IC, 1986. The general geology of the Kruger National Park. *Koedoe* 29: 13–38.

STEVENSON-HAMILTON, J, 1949. *The Lowveld: Its Wildlife and its People*. London: Cassel & Company.

STEVENSON-HAMILTON, J, 1956. *South African Eden*. London: Panther Books.

TURNBULL-KEMP, P, 1967. *The Leopard*. Cape Town: Howard Timmins.

WOLHUTER, H, 1950. *Memories of a Game Ranger*. Johannesburg: CNA.

ZAMBATIS, N, & HC BIGGS, 1995. Rainfall and temperatures during 1991/92 drought in the Kruger National Park. *Koedoe* 38(1): 1–16.